ARMING
IRAQ

The Northeastern Series in Transnational Crime
Edited by Nikos Passas

ARMING IRAQ

How the U.S. and Britain
Secretly Built Saddam's War Machine

MARK PHYTHIAN

NORTHEASTERN UNIVERSITY PRESS
Boston

NORTHEASTERN UNIVERSITY PRESS

Library of Congress Cataloging-in-Publication Data
Phythian, Mark.
Arming Iraq : how the U.S. and Britain secretly built Saddam's war
machine / Mark Phythian.
p. cm.
Includes bibliographical references and index.
ISBN 1–55553–285–3 (cloth : alk. paper)
1. Illegal arms transfers—Iraq.   2. Illegal arms transfers—
United States.   3. Illegal arms transfers—Great Britain.
4. Military–industrial complex—United States.   5. Military
–industrial complex—Great Britain.   I. Title.
HV6321.I693P48   1997
382′.456234′09567—dc20   96–18166

Designed by Janis Owens

Printed and bound by Maple Press in York, Pennsylvania. The paper is
Sebago Antique, an acid-free sheet.

MANUFACTURED IN THE UNITED STATES OF AMERICA
00   99   98   97   4   3   2   1

To Anne-Marie and Jamie

". . . there are two things necessary to Salvation . . .
Money and gunpowder."

Andrew Undershaft in
George Bernard Shaw's
Major Barbara, 1905

CONTENTS

Selected List of Acronyms   ix

Dramatis Personae   xi

Acknowledgments   xvii

Foreword   xix

Introduction   xxiii

CHAPTER ONE
Western Relations with Iraq and Iran Prior to 1980   3

CHAPTER TWO
The United States, the West, and the Geopolitics of the Iran-Iraq War   19

CHAPTER THREE
Arming Iraq   59

CHAPTER FOUR
The Supergun   94

CHAPTER FIVE
The Strange Case of Astra Holdings plc   125

CHAPTER SIX
Intelligence Monitoring of the Western Arms Trade with Iraq   189

CHAPTER SEVEN
Matrix Churchill, Dual-Use Exports, and Government Knowledge   226

CHAPTER EIGHT
The Scott Inquiry   257

CHAPTER NINE

Why Did the West Arm Iraq?   287

Epilogue: The Scott Report   303

Selected Bibliography   311

Index   317

SELECTED LIST OF ACRONYMS

BAe	British Aerospace
BMARC	British Manufacture and Research Company
BNL	Banca Nazionale del Lavoro
CARDE	Canadian Armament and Research Development Establishment
CCC	Commodity Credit Corporation
COCOM	Co-Ordinating Committee for Multilateral Export Control
DESO	Defence Export Services Organisation, previously DSO (Defence Sales Organisation)
DIA	Defence Intelligence Agency
DIS	Defence Intelligence Staff
DOD	Department of Defense
DTI	Department of Trade and Industry
EASSP	European Association for the Study of Safety Problems in the Production and Use of Propellant Powders
ECGD	Export Credit Guarantee Department
ELU	Export Licensing Unit (of the DTI)
EPREP	Explosives, Propellants and Related End Products
FAC	Foreign Affairs Committee
FCO	Foreign and Commonwealth Office
GCHQ	Government Communications Headquarters
HARP	High Altitude Research Project
HUMINT	Human Intelligence
IDC	Inter-Departmental Committee
IMM	Industrial, Mineral and Metals division of the DTI
IMS	International Military Services
ISC	International Signal and Control
JIC	Joint Intelligence Committee
LISI	Licensed for Singapore
MBB	Messerschmitt-Bolkow-Blohm

MOD	Ministry of Defence
NSA	National Security Agency
NSC	National Security Council
NSD-26	National Security Directive 26 (October 1989)
PII	Public Interest Immunity
PRB	Poudreries Réunies de Belgique
RNEE	Royal Naval Equipment Exhibition
RO	Royal Ordnance
SAS	Special Air Service
SGB	Société Générale de Belgique
SIGINT	Signals Intelligence
SRC	Space Research Corporation
TISC	Trade and Industry Select Committee

DRAMATIS PERSONAE

JONATHAN AITKEN

Former Defence Procurement Division minister and chief secretary to the Treasury. Former nonexecutive director of BMARC. Resigned from the Cabinet in 1995 to pursue a number of libel actions.

JOHN ANDERSON

Former secretary of Astra Holdings.

ROY BARBER

Installed as chairman of Astra Holdings in 1990 following the removal of Gerald James.

PRESILEY BAXENDALE

Counsel to the Scott Inquiry.

FARZAD BAZOFT

Observer newspaper freelancer detained by the Iraqis on espionage charges. Executed in March 1990.

GERALD BULL

Ballistics expert and founder of SRC. Designer of the supergun. Also involved in various military projects for Iraq prior to his murder in Brussels in March 1990.

SIR ROBIN BUTLER

Cabinet secretary and head of the civil service from 1988.

ALAN CLARK

Minister of trade from 1986 to 1989 and then minister of state at the MOD from 1989 to 1992. A leading advocate of easing restrictions on all British trade with Iraq. Star witness for the prosecution in the 1992 Matrix Churchill trial. After his testimony the prosecution collapsed. Publicly blamed by government ministers for its failure.

JIM COUSINS

Labour MP on the House of Commons TISC investigating the supergun and exports to Iraq.

CHRIS COWLEY

Project manager for Project Babylon from 1988 to 1989.

CHRISTOPHER DROGOUL

Manager of the Atlanta branch of BNL from 1984 to 1989.

REGINALD DUNK

Former director of Atlantic Commercial. In 1994 his conviction for illegally exporting submachine guns to Iraq via Jordan was overturned.

TRISTAN GAREL-JONES

Former Foreign Office minister and outspoken critic of the Scott Inquiry.

LT. COL. RICHARD GLAZEBROOK

MOD official who argued against sales of arms and related equipment to Iraq, and one of the few civil servants to emerge from the Scott Inquiry with his credibility enhanced.

HENRY GONZALEZ

Democratic member of Congress from Texas; chair of the House Committee on Banking, Finance, and Urban Affairs. A leading figure in official U.S. investigations into "Iraqgate."

SIR DAVID GORE-BOOTH

Head of the Foreign Office's Middle East Department from 1989 to 1993, and since then British ambassador to Saudi Arabia.

PAUL GRECIAN

Former director of Ordtec; Special Branch and intelligence informant.

JAMES GUERIN

Intelligence-connected founder of ISC and convicted fraudster.

CHRIS GUMBLEY

Former managing director of Astra Holdings.

MARK GUTTERIDGE

Former Matrix Churchill export sales manager and MI5 informant.

SAFA AL-HABOBI

Director of Nassr and a senior Iraqi arms procurement official. Later chairman of TMG, the Iraqi holding company for Matrix Churchill.

DAVID HASTIE

Former BAE director. Attended 1989 Baghdad International Military Exhibition while seconded to the MOD.

PAUL HENDERSON

Former managing director of Matrix Churchill and MI6 informant. Acquitted in November 1992 of illegally exporting arms-making equipment to Iraq.

MARK HIGSON

Former official at the Iraq Desk of the Foreign Office. Spoke out after leaving the Foreign Office against what he claimed were government efforts to mislead Parliament and the public over the sale of arms to Iraq.

GEOFFREY HOWE

Foreign secretary from 1983 to 1989, in whose name U.K. government guidelines on arms sales to Iraq and Iran were issued in 1985, although they had been drafted almost a year before. Chief critic of the Scott Inquiry.

DOUGLAS HURD

Foreign secretary from 1989.

GERALD JAMES

Former chairman of Astra Holdings.

HUSSEIN KAMEL

Saddam Hussein's son-in-law and head of Iraqi Ministry of Industry and Military Industrialization. Fled with his family to Jordan in 1995. Murdered almost immediately after returning to Iraq in February 1996.

STEPHAN KOCK

Intelligence-linked former nonexecutive director of Astra Holdings and BMARC.

SIR RICHARD LUCE

Former Foreign Office minister. The first public witness at the Scott Inquiry and subsequently a critic of it.

FRANK MACHON
Glasgow-based haulier; owner of Polmadie Storage and Packing Ltd.

DAVID MELLOR
Former Foreign Office minister. Witness at the Scott Inquiry.

SIR HAL MILLER
Former Conservative MP for Bromsgrove who in April 1990 revealed that he had informed various government departments of the existence of the Walter Somers supergun contract in 1988.

PETER MITCHELL
Former managing director of Walter Somers. Initially charged, along with Chris Cowley, in connection with the export of the supergun to Iraq.

CHRISTOPHER MUTTUKUMARU
Secretary to the Scott Inquiry.

SIR NICHOLAS RIDLEY
Former trade and industry secretary who, upon the seizure of the final sections of the supergun barrel in April 1990, made the misleading statement that the government had only then recently become aware in general terms of the existence of the project.

GEOFFREY ROBERTSON
Paul Henderson's defense counsel at his trial in 1992.

ROBIN ROBISON
Former JIC official.

SIR RICHARD SCOTT
Judge selected to conduct inquiry into the Matrix Churchill affair and the sale of arms to Iraq. Appointed a chancery judge in 1983. Later promoted to the Court of Appeal. Became a vice chancellor in 1994.

TONY SLACK
Project manager for Project Babylon from mid-1989 following Chris Cowley's departure.

HOWARD TEICHER
Former NSC official during the Carter and Reagan administrations.

MARK THATCHER

Son of former Prime Minister Margaret Thatcher; alleged middleman in Middle Eastern arms deals concluded in the 1980s.

LORD TREFGARNE

Minister of state at the MOD from 1985 to 1989. Swapped roles with Alan Clark to become minister for trade from 1989 to 1990.

PETER VEREKER

Former head of the Foreign Office's Arms Control and Disarmament Department.

WILLIAM WALDEGRAVE

Junior Foreign Office minister from 1988 to 1990.

KENNETH WARREN

Conservative MP and chairman of the House of Commons TISC investigating the supergun and exports to Iraq.

GEORGE WONG

Former N. M. Rothschild bank director. Accompanied Gerald Bull during his work in China and remained in contact throughout Bull's involvement with Iraq.

ACKNOWLEDGMENTS

I would like to thank all those who have helped in the preparation of this book, without whose cooperation it could not have been written. I owe them a huge debt of gratitude. In particular, Chris Cowley and Gerald James were more generous than I could have hoped, both in terms of the time they were willing to spend discussing various points and details and in allowing me access to documents in their possession of which I have made extensive use. I am very grateful to both of them.

A number of people were kind enough to agree to be interviewed, to discuss various points, and to send me or allow me access to important material. In this respect I would particularly like to thank John Anderson; Kevin Cahill; Tam Dalyell, MP; Paul Henderson; and Robin Robison. In addition, at various points in the course of writing this book, as well as in the past, I have been fortunate enough to have the use of CAAT's (Campaign Against Arms Trade) resources, and I would like to thank Ann Feltham and everyone at CAAT for their hospitality. The School of Humanities and Social Sciences at the University of Wolverhampton provided the funds without which the research for the present work could not have been carried out.

I would also like to thank Bill Frohlich of Northeastern University Press, both for his interest in the subject and patience with the project; Emily McKeigue and Deborah Fogel; Nikos Passas, whose editorial comments were both incisive and welcome; and an anonymous reviewer for further comments on the manuscript.

Finally, I would like to thank Anne-Marie and Jamie, who had to live with me while I wrote this, and to whom it is dedicated.

FOREWORD

Is it not ironic that the permanent members of the U.N. Security Council are the world's main arms producers and traders? Is it not possible that the embedded conflict of interest resulting from the simultaneous promotion of peace and arms sales can lead to serious problems? How can Western proponents of nonproliferation retain their credibility when they are the ones fueling conflicts and flooding markets with their weapons and military-useful technology? That these are no idle academic questions is clearly demonstrated by recent devastating experiences, such as the Iran-Iraq and Persian Gulf wars.

The official policy of the West, including NATO allies and European Union member states, toward the deadly Iran-Iraq war was to remain neutral and avoid arms or other sales that would prolong the conflict. Hidden from the public were the actual practices of supplying arms to both sides, of ensuring that the war went on without a clear victor, and of ultimately favoring Iraq. As Mark Phythian points out, U.S. and British officials have openly admitted that, as long as the balance of power in the Gulf was not altered, the continuing carnage was in the interest of the West. No single country would then dominate the oil reserves of the region, while the oil-rich and anti-Communist regimes in the lower Gulf would be threatened neither by fundamentalist Iran nor militaristic Iraq.

After the cease-fire, despite reports that Saddam Hussein was gassing Kurd civilians, the West secretly relaxed even further its policy of supplying sensitive equipment to Iraq, which was making significant progress toward the development of a domestic nonconventional weapons capability. Not all transactions were directly with Iraq. The range of sophisticated modi operandi included the use of friendly countries (e.g., Jordan, Egypt, Saudi Arabia) as conduits, the systematic use of false end-user certificates, the breakup of the production and transfer process by the involvement of numerous companies, the deliberate false description of shipments in official documents, and the use of trusted companies that kept "black books" on "joker contracts" to deceive even their own employees, managers, and shareholders.

All those and other signals led Saddam Hussein to believe that he could invade Kuwait without serious opposition. The ensuing Gulf War proved his calculations wrong. More important, it exposed Western hypocrisy and duplicity, gross incompetence of policymakers to consider the potential costs of their decisions, and a network of symbiotic relations among arms traders, bankers, politicians, government officials, and military personnel. It also revealed how endemic corruption is in this network—one is tempted to think that previously known corrupt practices by Lockheed, Exxon, or even BCCI are no more than the publicized part of routine activities in international trade and commerce.

Mark Phythian's careful analysis shows that behind the arming of Iraq lay a combination of economic and strategic considerations—such as a widespread "culture of exports" and concerns about access to oil, the reduction of the perceived Communist threat, and intelligence needs (e.g., to know what Iraq was up to and to be able to frustrate its efforts to develop nonconventional weapons). Government officials had no difficulty justifying sensitive sales to Iraq, even after the Gulf War, by referring to the needs of domestic industries and preservation of jobs, which might be jeopardized if Britain did not do what other, "less inhibited" Western nations were doing.

Yet such arguments are weak. The commercial benefit is doubtful at best, given that the defense (or, as others may call it, "death") industry is heavily subsidized and protected by governments. American, British, and French taxpayers have lost billions of dollars in unpaid export credits extended to Iraq. As the *Financial Times* pointed out, ". . . the losses that arose from sales of weapons to Iraq or Argentine generals could have been avoided by giving every worker in the relevant industries £5,000 and 10 weeks' extra holiday" (2 March 1996: p. xx). A British government official noted the absurdity of the intelligence need argument once it was known what the sensitive machines would be used for, "but the machines had to be provided in order to protect the source that was telling the purpose for which they were going to be used." Strategic advantages are also unclear; revelations of cynical policies, like the encouragement of the carnage between Iran and Iraq, reinforce Middle Eastern suspicion of Western powers and intentions and in turn fuel Islamic fundamentalism and terror.

After the revelation that Western allies in the Gulf War were fighting against their own technologies and military equipment, which they had partly financed, the companies and those who managed them became expendable.

To cover up their own role, governments appeared prepared to let business-people who had been instrumental in the realization of their hidden political agendas go to jail. British Cabinet ministers signed the so-called Public Interest Immunity (PII) certificates, effectively denying the defendants access to documents showing the government's knowledge and support for the very activities for which these people faced imprisonment. The scandal that followed led to the Scott Inquiry into the government's real policy regarding trade with Iraq, the [in]accuracy of information provided to Parliament and public, and the [in]appropriate use of PIIs.

Drawing on a wealth of letters, other documents, and the evidence presented to Sir Richard Scott, Phythian shows how this aspect of British foreign policy was deliberately kept secret from Parliament and carried out through private companies, which could then be held to blame if something went wrong. He documents the cover-up efforts and abuses of power that resulted in company bankruptcies and travesties of justice that would have continued, but for the decision of trial judges not to withhold information vital to the defendants' case.

This sort of privatization of foreign policy and externalization of blame, quite reminiscent of the Iran-Contra affair, suggests that private business and government are connected in ways that impede accountability and undermine the democratic process.

The Scott Report, not deviating too much from the tradition of ambiguous and narrowly focused official reports, is an 1,800-page document out of which all political parties can cite something to claim vindication, even though overall it is extremely damaging to the credibility and integrity of the Conservative government. The role played by major companies, City figures, and banks that financed the trade fell outside the scope of the report. Nevertheless, some have indulged in theories of omniscient agencies and well-coordinated conspiracies.

By contrast, Phythian's thorough research analyzes networks of influence and corruption in a structural rather than conspiratorial fashion, looking, for example, at the shared interests of businesses, farmers, industry, and intelligence or other government agencies in such a way that no conspiracy is necessary for the same results to be produced. Thus, he can attribute responsibilities to various individual and organizational actors without clouding the systemic problems that generate such international misconduct and scandals.

The mistakes made in foreign policy in the case of Iraq beg the question of whether arms sales themselves are a legitimate, ethical enterprise at all in democratic societies. Beyond the abstract ethical issues, this case highlights the enormous human costs of the "defense" industries and the "goods" they deliver, costs that are sanitized through terminology like "collateral damage" or remain hidden from the public because they happen in Third World countries to which the media and politicians pay little or no attention. These "goods" contributed to the making of a monster that Western soldiers were called upon to destroy with Western taxpayers' money. And it is not even certain to what extent soldiers have been exposed to chemical weapons there, because governments still refuse to take serious action or even recognize the visible problems these victims of the Gulf War face. The conclusion is inescapable: What is good for the "defense" industries is not necessarily good for the West or anyone else.

Unscrupulous Third World states usually have to bear all the blame for indulging in weapons proliferation, feeding terrorism, and manipulating the arms trade. This book shows that the blame is far more widely shared. There is, however, an optimistic message from all this. Since the West plays an active role in encouraging proliferation, it has the means to do something about it. The problem is not beyond the control of Western governments. If they are indeed eager to prevent such disasters from happening again, decision makers must learn from history. Unless something is done to open up the policy-making processes in a democratic fashion, building in more accountability and fewer rationalizations of questionable practices, unless the cozy relationships among the "military-industrial" complex, the intelligence community, and the political leadership are undone, little change is to be expected.

Phythian provides plenty of history in this informed and contextual analysis of the social organization of the arms trade. This engrossing book is indispensable reading for policymakers, historians, political scientists, sociologists, criminologists, and the wider public alike.

Nikos Passas

INTRODUCTION

September 1987. Motherwell, Scotland. It is a typically fresh day, and Dr. Richard Fuisz, a businessman from Chantilly, Virginia, is being given a guided tour of a heavy truck plant owned by the U.S.-based Terex Corporation. As the tour is coming to an end, Fuisz notices two trucks that are vastly different from the standard vehicles under construction elsewhere at the plant. For one thing, these trucks are much bigger, and the chassis have been modified. For another, they are painted in desert camouflage. He points them out to the plant manager and asks him what they are. They are missile launchers for the Iraqi military, the manager tells Fuisz. But surely Terex can't legally sell these things to Iraq, Fuisz ventures. No problem, he is told, it is easy if you know how. You simply modify a portion of the serial number to make it look like a civilian mining vehicle.

Still, Fuisz couldn't bring himself to believe this story, and so he brought the subject up with the president of Terex, Randolph Lenz, when they met a few days later. Rather than dismiss the idea that a U.S. company was illicitly shipping mobile missile launchers to Iraq, Lenz told him that he was doing work for the U.S. government, and that in reality he was a hero, but he wasn't allowed to discuss it. Later still in his search for answers, Fuisz claims he brought the matter up with the vice president of Terex, David Langevin, who explained: "You have it all wrong about Terex and the Iraqi military. These shipments were all requested by the CIA with the cooperation of the British intelligence people." Fuisz said he was surprised that the British were involved in this along with the CIA. "You're naive," Langevin told him.[1]

During the 1980s, Iraq converted over two hundred trucks into mobile missile launchers. They were used extensively during the Iran-Iraq War, and when Operation Desert Storm was launched in 1991, they became the basis of the most indiscriminate terror weapon deployed by the Iraqis. Is it possible that the modified trucks Fuisz claims to have seen could have been a part of this fleet?

25 January 1991. Dhahran, Saudi Arabia. A typically cool desert evening. Billeted in a warehouse are 127 U.S. soldiers. Over half of them come from the same army reserve unit, the 14th Quartermaster Detachment from Greensburg, Pennsylvania, and they are charged with the job of purifying water for the troops gathered for Operation Desert Storm. It is 8:42 P.M., and a group of nine soldiers is idling away the evening under the metal roof playing a game of Trivial Pursuit. As one of the group gets up to leave the warehouse, a siren begins to wail in the background. Just thirty seconds later, an Iraqi SCUD missile thunders through the flimsy roof above the board game, caving the roof in around it as it careers on down, its explosion leaving a twelve-foot crater in the floor, sending metal and concrete flying in all directions, and setting the warehouse ablaze. Of the eight remaining soldiers playing Trivial Pursuit when the SCUD hits, six are killed instantly. The two who survive are among the many writhing around the floor in the midst of the flames, screaming in pain, some of them dying, one left fumbling at the bloody mess around his thighs where his legs used to be.[2]

It was the largest single loss of life suffered by U.S. forces during Operation Desert Storm. Twenty-eight Americans were killed in the attack, including thirteen members of the 14th Quartermaster Detachment, and another ninety-eight were wounded. Yet the media did not dwell on the attack, preferring to report on the progress being made elsewhere in the campaign. If they had dwelt on it longer, perhaps they would have reflected that the attack that left these Americans dead or crippled had been launched by a state that the Bush administration had gone out of its way to embrace and bring within what Bush himself had termed the "family of nations." They might have gone further and noted how, together with other Western states—notably Britain—the U.S. government had facilitated the arming of Iraq, and that without this assistance, Iraq might not have been in a position to invade Kuwait, let alone launch this particular attack. Subsequently, they might have observed how vigorously the U.S. and U.K. governments denied this to be the case.

There was good reason for this. U.S., U.K., and Western policy toward Iraq in the 1980s turned out to be the biggest foreign policy blunder of the post-1945 era next to the Vietnam War. It fortified the grip on power of a ruthless autocrat; facilitated the genocide of elements of his own population; fueled his war with Iran; cost U.S., U.K., French, and other taxpayers millions of dollars required to meet the government-guaranteed loans that Iraq failed to repay; brought Iraq to the brink of nuclear-power status; led to the invasion of Kuwait; and required the mobilization of a multinational force to expel Iraq from Kuwait, at considerable financial and some human cost, in order to restore something of the regional status quo that the arming of Iraq had been intended to guarantee in the first place.

This book is about that policy. It looks at the global nature of the operation launched during the 1980s to ensure that Iraq did not lose the Iran-Iraq War and the leading U.S. role in this tilt toward Iraq; in particular, it examines the British contribution and involvement that led up to the trial of three executives of the Matrix Churchill machine tool company and the lengthy official investigation that arose from the debris of that trial. One of those executives, Paul Henderson, had been spying for Britain's MI6 while conducting business in Iraq; yet when he came to trial, the government claimed public interest immunity (PII)—the right to suppress certain information in the public interest—rather than release official documents that would have confirmed Henderson's role and revealed the government's duplicity. Henderson's personal liberty was deemed less important than the need to keep quiet about the fact that the British and U.S. governments knew all about the arming of Iraq. They knew because they themselves had encouraged it during the 1980s, even though at the time both maintained an official stance of neutrality in the Iran-Iraq War.

The public and parliamentary outcry when the PII claim over the Matrix Churchill trial was rejected, and the British government's role was forced into the open, required the government to move fast to limit the damage. However, so great was the protest that its response had to be substantive if it was to be credible. It therefore set up an official inquiry under Lord Justice Scott. The Scott Inquiry deliberated for over three years, finally delivering its verdict on the British government's actions in the case and its policy toward Iraq in February 1996. The government had been able to defer the verdict, but not to alter it.

In effect, during the 1980s both the U.S. and U.K. governments operated an "under the counter" foreign policy toward Iraq whereby actions and official policy positions were very different. It was a complex policy web involving a wide range of characters. It included people like ballistics expert Dr. Gerald Bull, who attempted to build a supergun in Iraq, an enterprise for which he always maintained he had U.S., U.K., and Israeli support. It also embraced the board of the emerging armaments company Astra Holdings, which in its rapid expansion bought companies dealing illicitly with Iraq. In addition, it encompassed Matrix Churchill and the dual-use machine tool industry. And the web further included a range of conduit countries willing to channel arms to Iraq—most notably neighboring states like Jordan, Kuwait, and Saudi Arabia—whose relationship with Iraq was based largely on fear of Iran and the old adage, "My enemy's enemy is my friend." Clearly, the arming of Iraq raises a number of central questions that have been considered under the generic banner "Iraqgate." But we need to be clear precisely what is meant by this term, which first entered the British political vocabulary after the collapse of the Matrix Churchill trial. By this time it was already being widely used in the United States as the 1992 presidential election campaign reached its climax, as congressional committees began to poke around the realities of the Bush administration's "family of nations" initiative, and as other candidates sought to use the issue to neutralize the electoral benefits that Bush sought to reap from the successfully prosecuted Gulf War. Independent candidate Ross Perot advised: "If you don't like guys like Saddam Hussein, don't spend 10 years and billions of dollars of American taxpayers' money creating him, which . . . George Bush did. There's a long clear record . . . President Bush made Saddam what he is."[3] For his part, vice-presidential candidate Al Gore thought that the Bush administration's policy toward Iraq "not only struck the match" that ignited the war but also "poured gasoline on the flames."[4]

Is Iraqgate, then, as the application of the -*gate* suffix suggests, concerned primarily with the governmental cover-ups of illegality and willingness to see individuals jailed rather than have government actions exposed? Is it primarily about the covert arming of Iraq? Is it about the way in which companies involved in Iraqgate perished in its wake, causing attendant unemployment and hardship? It is about all of these things, but on a deeper level, it is about who makes foreign policy and, in democracies, on whose behalf foreign policy is conducted. Above all, the arming of Iraq is a case study of how foreign policy is developed in relation to sensitive countries and regions, especially in cases where neither the public nor the legislature can interfere with elite definitions of national interest or national security.

NOTES

1 This account is taken from Seymour Hersh's story in the *New York Times*, 1.26.92. and Peter Mantius: *Shell Game: A True Story of Banking, Spies, Lies, Politics—And the Arming of Saddam Hussein*, New York, St. Martin's Press, 1995, pp. 80–82. Terex was a subsidiary of KCS Industries, Inc. of Westport, Connecticut. Mantius cites telexes and Customs documents showing

that Terex trucks were sold to a Buckinghamshire company, Gatewood Engineers Ltd., for onward shipment to Iraq.

2 This account is drawn largely from Rick Atkinson's *Crusade: The Untold Story of the Gulf War*, London, HarperCollins, 1994, ch. 15. See also P. Mantius: *Shell Game*, pp. 1–5.

3 Quoted in the *Independent on Sunday*, 5.24.92.

4 J. F. O. McAllister: The Lessons of Iraq, *Time*, 11.2.92, p. 49. During the final presidential debate, Perot leveled the same charge against Bush. Stung into a response, Bush claimed, quite erroneously, that "there hasn't been one single scintilla of evidence that there's any U.S. technology involved" in the Iraqi nuclear weapons program. Ibid., p. 50. In a speech in Utah in February 1991, former President Reagan admitted: "We committed a boner with regard to Iraq and our close relation with Iraq." *Guardian*, 3.12.91.

ARMING
IRAQ

Western Relations with Iraq and Iran Prior to 1980

The centuries-old rivalry between Iraq and Iran spilled over into war on 22 September 1980, when Iraq invaded Iran on several fronts and simultaneously began bombing various military and economic targets, seeking what it thought would be a rapid victory over what it considered to be a weakened adversary.[1] In the event, the Iraqi offensive did not produce any such victory. Instead, it marked the beginning of a bloody eight-year war—the longest conventional war of the twentieth century—which resulted in an estimated 400,000 Iranian and 300,000 Iraqi dead and a further one million Iranian and 800,000 Iraqi wounded.[2] It also provided the backdrop to a number of arms sales scandals in the West that led to resignations, prosecutions, and even deaths. At worst these scandals partially immobilized governments, at best they caused severe embarrassment. In the United States and Britain in particular, they also produced high-level postmortems on the policies that had ultimately necessitated fighting the 1991 Gulf War. The U.S. House and Senate conducted investigations into Banca Nazionale del Lavoro (BNL) and U.S. policy toward Iraq, while in Britain the Scott Inquiry carried out an investigation of the British role in what came to be termed Iraqgate.

In response to the outbreak of the war, leading states in the international community had moved to introduce restrictions on the sale of arms to Iran and Iraq so as not to exacerbate the conflict and facilitate further killing. At the same time, both belligerents had to secure the means to fuel their conduct of the war. This need became more important as the war dragged on in a bloody stalemate. However, open access to the war materiel that Iran and Iraq needed was being denied, in many cases by the imposition of restrictions on the sale of arms and related equipment. This became the case particularly for Iran as the Reagan administration's Operation Staunch—designed to deny arms to Iran—took hold. Iraq and Iran both responded to this situation by resorting to importing arms and related materials in roundabout ways aimed at beating the restrictions placed on them. They drew the lesson that reliance on any one arms supplier was dangerous, whereas reliance on a range of suppliers could still create difficulties. The only way of fully overcoming these difficulties would be ultimately to end the need to import arms by developing indigenous arms industries. It was a vision that Iraq, with its more open access to Western technology, was to come closest to fulfilling.

Because of the geostrategic sensitivity of the Gulf region, a number of states felt they had an interest in the outcome of the conflict—Saudi Arabia and the lower Gulf states, the United States and the Soviet Union, Israel, Egypt, Britain, France, and so on. In this context, national restrictions on the sale of arms to the belligerents, and the policing of apparently illegal arms deals with these states or their agents, were not always what they seemed at first glance to be, or could have been. In particular, the West had an interest in the outcome of the conflict based on the region's mineral wealth, and as the Gulf's principal arms supplier the West also had the capacity to influence that outcome. This is what the evidence suggests occurred—both directly, as Western governments encouraged and facilitated arms deliveries, and indirectly, as they turned a blind eye to the largely clandestine commercial activities of various Western companies. What follows is an account of that process.

◆ The Politics of Middle Eastern Oil

Underpinning the region's geostrategic importance is its vast oil wealth. As Yahya Sadowski wryly observed: "If the region's major export was cotton, it is doubtful that the big powers would have the same interest in selling arms to local allies, much less in deploying hundreds of thousands of troops to defend them."[3] Stephen Gill and David Law have characterized the importance of oil as lying

> in the fact that it has been, and still is, the major form of energy consumed in the post-war world. Oil, because of cheapness, availability, flexibility and relative ease of transportation, became the primary energy source for most industrial nations. . . . Because so much rests upon energy supply, it would be plausible to claim that energy industries, and oil in particular, are strategic industries, *par excellence.*[4]

The question of access to and control of Middle Eastern oil has been defined since the 1950s in terms of superpower competition, and its implications have been behind superpower responses to all of the postwar conflicts in the region, whether Suez, the 1967 and 1973 Arab-Israeli wars, the Iran-Iraq War, or the Iraqi invasion of Kuwait, which precipitated the 1991 Gulf War. Oil politics has also been behind various Western interventions in the domestic politics of Middle Eastern states, including the buttressing of dynastic power structures in the name of preventing the spread of subversion—in other words, keeping oil in friendly hands.

The reliance of the West on importing oil from the region arises because its consumption outstrips production and because most of the world's known reserves are concentrated in the Middle East. The West has traditionally feared losing its influence over and access to oil, either as a result of foreign (in classic cold war terms, Soviet) intervention, or internal revolution. Therefore, the three most important issues in oil politics have been access, reliability of flow, and stability of price.[5] Western interests have therefore revolved around maintaining the regional status quo and, should this break down, minimizing the impact of any dislocation. It has even been argued that "[m]any of the political arrangements that characterize the region—borders, ruling families, economic structures and more—exist and persist because of the stake that oil has represented for Western industrialized countries."[6] Hence, the centrality of oil has bestowed a greater geostrategic importance on the Middle East than it would otherwise have enjoyed. As it is, arming friendly states is seen as a way of preserving the status quo and access to oil. As then U.K. Defence Procurement Minister Jonathan Aitken pointed out at the 1993 Dubai arms show: "It is only right that our moderate friends and allies [in the region] should be able to defend themselves . . . We only export responsibly and cautiously to countries *which are themselves forces for regional stability.*"[7]

The arms trade also represents a means by which the industrialized West has sought to recoup some of the money paid to Middle Eastern states for oil. By selling them arms that without their oil wealth they could not afford, they recycle a proportion of the petrodollars earned in the region and at the same time tie those Middle Eastern states closer to their military suppliers. In this way they also encourage the stability of oil flow. This makes dependence a two-way street. Hence the observation: "Without petrodollars there might still be conflict in the Middle East, but it would be fought with hand grenades and machine guns rather than with advanced tactical bombers and ballistic missiles."[8] Although an exaggeration, it contains an important germ of truth.

Western interests in the region, then, rest on several oil-based considerations, as illustrated in the accompanying tables and figures: that advanced

| Table 1.1 |

Principal Producers and Exporters of Crude Oil, 1988

Producers		Exporters	
Country	Thousand b/d*	Country	Thousand b/d
Soviet Union	11,679	Saudi Arabia	2,325
United States	8,140	United Kingdom	1,734
Saudi Arabia	5,288	Mexico	1,204
China	2,728	Nigeria	1,073
Iraq	2,646	Iraq	988
Mexico	2,512	Soviet Union	951
Iran	2,259	Norway	944
United Kingdom	2,232	Iran	911
Venezuela	1,903	Libya	867
Canada	1,610	United Arab Emirates	836
United Arab Emirates	1,606	Venezuela	639
Kuwait	1,492	Indonesia	636
Nigeria	1,450	Algeria	502
Indonesia	1,328	Kuwait	454
Norway	1,158	China	357
Libya	1,055	Angola	322
Algeria	1,040	Oman	284
Egypt	848	Egypt	247
India	635	Qatar	181
Oman	617	Malaysia	115

Source: The Economist Book of Vital World Statistics, London, Hutchinson, 1990.[9]
*Thousand b/d = thousand barrels per day

Western states are heavy consumers of oil; that they are net importers and import a significant amount of this imported oil from the Middle East; that this is where the vast majority of the world's known oil reserves lie; and that global consumption is on the increase (from 2,807.4 million metric tons in 1984 to 3,034.5 in 1988 to 3,136.9 in 1990 to 3,172.4 in 1994).

The United States, for example, imported 8,929,000 b/d in 1994 (a quarter of all oil imports, and up from 8,026,000 in 1990, 7,240,000 in 1988, and 5,380,000 in 1984), 1,817,000 b/d of which came from the Middle East. At the same time it consumed 16,915,000 b/d (up only fractionally from 15,170,000 in 1984), that is, it imported almost 53 percent of its total consumption.[10] However, although clearly reliant on oil imports (especially considering reserves versus consumption) the United States is not, as table 1.4 shows, the most dependent amongst Western states.

Table 1.2

Main Oil-Consuming Countries, 1994

	Thousand b/d	% of Total
United States	16,915	25.5
Japan	5,770	8.5
Russian Federation	3,265	5.1
China	3,030	4.5
Germany	2,880	4.3
France	1,930	2.9
Italy	1,915	2.9
South Korea	1,805	2.7
United Kingdom	1,775	2.6
Canada	1,735	2.5
TOTAL of 10 leading consumers	41,020	61.5
TOTAL world	66,700	100.0

Source: BP Statistical Review of World Energy, June 1995.

Figure 1.1

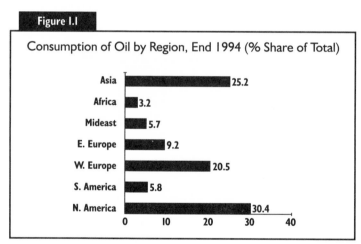

Consumption of Oil by Region, End 1994 (% Share of Total)

Asia 25.2
Africa 3.2
Mideast 5.7
E. Europe 9.2
W. Europe 20.5
S. America 5.8
N. America 30.4

Source: BP Statistical Review of World Energy, June 1995, pp. 7–8.

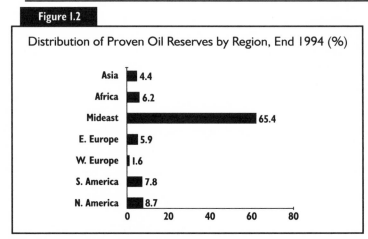

Figure 1.2

Distribution of Proven Oil Reserves by Region, End 1994 (%)

Asia 4.4
Africa 6.2
Mideast 65.4
E. Europe 5.9
W. Europe 1.6
S. America 7.8
N. America 8.7

Source: BP Statistical Review of World Energy, June 1995, p. 2.
Note: In figures 1.1 and 1.2, North America includes the United States, Canada, and Mexico; South America includes Central America; Asia includes Australasia.

Table 1.3

Distribution of Proven Oil Reserves by State (Top 5) End 1994

	Thousand Million Barrels	% of Total
Saudi Arabia	261.2	25.9
Iraq	100.0	9.9
Kuwait	96.5	9.6
Abu Dhabi	92.2	9.1
Iran	89.3	8.8

Source: BP Statistical Review of World Energy, June 1995, p. 2.

◆ Pre-1979 Western Relations with Iran and Iraq

Sir Richard Luce, a minister of state at the Foreign and Commonwealth Office (FCO) during the mid-1980s, opened the very first public session of the Scott Inquiry, established in the wake of the Matrix Churchill trial revelations, in May 1993 by outlining the background to British and Western interests in the Gulf region:

> Britain had a very long connection with the Gulf states going back to the last century. In the 1970s, of course, we had pulled out of our responsibilities in the

Table 1.4

Reliance on Oil Importation, Selected Areas, End 1994

	Thousand b/d		
	Imports	Consumption	% Reliance
United States	8,929	16,915	53
Canada	761	1,735	44
Mexico	178	1,660	11
S. and C. America	1,424	3,980	36
W. Europe	9,840	13,795	71
Africa	866	2,100	41
China	548	3,030	18
Japan	5,612	5,770	97

Source: BP Statistical Review of World Energy, June 1995[11]

Gulf in 1971, and throughout the 1970s there was a fairly stable relationship on both sides of the Gulf with Iran, between Iran, Iraq, and the various Gulf states.

This was very much in Britain's interests. The British interest as we saw it in the Gulf at that time . . . was to see stability in the Gulf region. We were, of course, as the western world as a whole, very dependent on the free flow of oil from the Gulf states.[12]

The shah of Iran had been placed on the Iranian throne during World War II. However, his grip on power was tenuous, and he owed his continuation in power to a coup orchestrated by the CIA and its British equivalent MI6 in 1953, which overthrew Prime Minister Mohammed Mossadegh. Subsequently, fearful that the fall of the shah and his replacement by a more nationalist figure like Mossadegh might open the way to Soviet influence in Iran, the United States began to increase its military support for the shah, so much so that by 1963 it had provided Iran with $1.3 billion worth of weapons. Then, at the end of 1967, Britain announced its intention to withdraw militarily from the Gulf by 1971, raising U.S. fears of a power vacuum that the Soviet Union could seek to take advantage of. Vietnam-era America was faced with three options: move in militarily and take on the role relinquished by Britain, do nothing, or support friendly states in the region capable of protecting the status quo and, with it, Western interests. With reference to the Vietnam War, in 1969 President Richard Nixon unveiled the Nixon Doctrine, which called for the United States to provide key regional allies with the military means required to defend themselves as an alternative to dispatching U.S. forces across the Third World to do it. In view of the British withdrawal, the Gulf region became a vital area for its application. The vehicle by which it would be applied in the Gulf was the "surrogate" or "twin pillars" policy. The principle underpinning this policy was that Iran and Saudi Arabia each represented a pillar acting on behalf of and supporting U.S. and Western interests in the region. The stated purpose of the policy was "to preserve access to oil and the stability of pro-Western regimes, while reducing opportunities for the Soviet Union to expand its influence." In securing these objectives, one pillar—Iran—came to be considered of much greater importance than the other.

There were a number of reasons for this. At this time, Saudi Arabia was not militarily capable of assuming such a role. Its army was small (around 30,000), geared toward internal security rather than external threat, and it did not have a navy. By contrast, Iran had an army of 150,000, impressively equipped by regional standards, and an established air force and navy. In addition, it was strategically better placed than Saudi Arabia, while Washington needed only to consult with one individual—the shah—to get a decision. "Iran's geostrategic location adjacent to the Soviet Union, Iraq, Pakistan and Afghanistan; its physical control of the Strait of Hormuz; its proven oil reserves, daily production and OPEC leadership; its large population; and the stated willingness of the shah to act aggressively on behalf of American interests whenever they might be threatened"[13] all combined to make Iran the more essential of the twin pillars in U.S. eyes.

This recognition necessitated a further expansion of U.S. military ties with Iran, which took a qualitative leap forward during an infamous May 1972 stopover in Iran, when President Richard Nixon and Henry Kissinger offered to sell Iran "virtually any conventional arms it wanted"[14]—the first time in history a Third World state had been offered its own selection of the latest U.S. military technology. Subsequently, the shah ordered 80 F-14 aircraft (estimated cost $2 billion) and a string of other major U.S. weapons systems, including 169 F-5E and F-5F fighter aircraft ($480 million), 209 F-4 Phantom aircraft ($1 billion), 160 F-16s ($3.2 billion), 202 Cobra helicopter gunships ($267 million), and 25,000 TOW and Dragon missiles ($150 million). This spending spree led Iranian spending on U.S. arms to jump from the comparative obscurity of $500 million in 1972 to an enormous $4.3 billion in 1974, at the same time firmly establishing Iran as the linchpin of U.S. security policy in the region.[15]

Although Iraq formally gained independence in 1932, in the immediate post-1945 period it remained one of the closest Western allies in the Arab world, so much so that the regional anti-Communist defense alliance was even known as the Baghdad Pact,[16] with Iraq the only Arab member alongside Britain, Iran, Pakistan, and Turkey. However, a sea change occurred in this relationship in the wake of the 1958 coup, which brought General Abdul Karim Qassim to power. Relations with the West worsened as Qassim established diplomatic relations with the Soviet Union and deteriorated further over Iraq's 1961 threat to the sovereignty of newly independent Kuwait, which Iraq claimed as an integral part of its territory.[17]

Neither did relations with the West improve with the 1963 coup, which brought the Ba'ath Party to power; and following the 1967 Arab-Israeli War, Iraq severed diplomatic relations with the United States. At the same time, the Ba'athists oversaw the development of ever-closer relations with the Soviet Union, culminating in the 1972 Treaty of Friendship and Cooperation, which allowed the Soviet Union access to Iraqi air and naval facilities. As a consequence of these ties, by the mid-1970s, Soviet arms supplies accounted for 95 percent of Iraq's holdings and included, for example, SCUD missiles and TU-22 bombers—the first time the latter had been deployed outside the Warsaw Pact.[18]

A further indication of how far outside the Western orbit Iraq had strayed came in 1978 when the Carter administration placed it on its list of states sponsoring terrorism for providing funding, training, and other support to the PLO and other Palestinian terrorist groups. Such a placing carried with it rigorous economic sanctions and further increased Iraq's isolation from the United States.

Table 1.5

Suppliers of Iraqi Major Weapons Imports, 1950–1980 (%)

	USSR	USA	France	UK	Italy	China	Third World	Other	Total (millions of $US)
1951–55	—	—	—	100	—	—	—	—	71
1956–60	78	4	—	10	—	—	8	—	257
1961–65	75	—	—	25	—	—	—	—	729
1966–70	88	—	4	2	—	—	—	6	787
1971–75	97	—	2	—	—	—	—	—	2,042
1976–80	85	—	10	—	—	—	3	2	5,559

Source: Michael Brzoska and Thomas Ohlson: *Arms Transfers to the Third World, 1971–85*, Oxford, OUP/SIPRI, 1987, p. 344.
Note: Totals are in 1985 dollars. Totals may not add up to 100 percent because of rounding.

◆ Arms and the Shah

At the same time, Western relations with Iraq's historical rival, Iran, had never been closer.[19] As Iraq was withdrawing from the Baghdad Pact in March 1959, Iran was signing a military cooperation agreement that pledged U.S. support for the shah in the event of foreign aggression. As Dilip Hiro has noted, by the mid- to late 1970s:

> Iran regarded itself as the gendarmerie of the region and its monarchical Arab regimes, whereas Iraq perceived itself as the standard-bearer of militant, republican Arab nationalism in the Gulf. The conflict between the pro-West, conservative Iran, determined to maintain the status quo, and the pro-Soviet, radical Iraq, committed to revolution, was sharp and irreconcilable.[20]

The West invested heavily in the shah throughout the decade, as he built up a vast array of Western arms with which to defend his position. Between 1970 and 1978 he ordered $20 billion worth of military equipment from the United States, accounting for 25 percent of all U.S. arms sales in this period.[21] His dependence on the West was rivaled only by his apparent lack of interest in the Arab question, which, whether a function of his debt to the West or not, helped to make him the ideal focus of Western strategy in the region. It all contributed toward making Iran "the salesman's dream. . . . The Shah of Iran was the kind of patron that salesmen dream of—a warlord who understands the same shoptalk, as fascinated by gadgets as they are."[22]

However, the shah used the West's focus to develop a military apparatus designed more to secure his personal position than to hold back a Soviet advance, producing "an expensive army too large for border incidents and internal security and of no use in all out war . . . [it] resembled the proverbial man who was too heavy to do any light work and too light to do any heavy work."[23] As a result of this strategy, by the middle of the decade, the West—overwhelmingly the United States—had created an enormous military machine under the shah's control. However, the British contribution was not insignificant. In 1975, for example, Iran possessed 300 Chieftain tanks, with a further 1,680 on order; 860 other Western tanks; 250 Scorpion light tanks/APVs on order; three destroyers, with a further six and three submarines on order; and 238 combat aircraft, with a further 349 on order. In addition, throughout the 1970s, Britain sold the Rapier missile system; Tigercat, Sea Killer I and Sea Killer II, and Swingfire missiles; Westland Sea King helicopters; and military hovercraft and fleet support ships. At the same time France

Table 1.6

Iranian Dependence on US (and UK) for Major Weapons Imports,
1950–1980 (%)

	US(%)	UK(%)	Combined Value (millions of $US)	Value of 100% (millions of $US)
1951–55	99	—	53.5	54
1956–60	52	—	248.5	478
1961–65	100	—	1,203	1,203
1966–70	85	2	2,493	2,866
1971–75	67	28	9,256	9,744
1976–80	89	1	94,267	10,473

Source: Michael Brzoska and Thomas Ohlson: *Arms Transfers to the Third World, 1971–85*, Oxford, OUP/SIPRI, 1987, p. 343.
Note: Values are in 1985 dollars.

supplied missiles, West Germany naval equipment, and Italy helicopters, albeit in less significant quantities.

Some of the consequences of this close relationship were later forced into the open at the Old Bailey at a corruption trial of former employees of Racal, which revealed something of the scale of corruption that a market this size invited.[24] Clearly, a market of this magnitude was a breeding ground for corruption, but it was also one in which neither the United States nor Britain could afford to turn down the shah's requests. This created an era of unbridled enthusiasm for a slice of an arms market of unprecedented size on the part of the British government's International Military Services (IMS)[25] and Defence Sales Organisation (DSO).[26] This feeding frenzy was not free of controversy, as one commentator described:

> Some in the Foreign Office still recall with dismay "excesses" of the Defence Sales Organisation during the multifarious and lucrative deals with Iran during the mid to late 1970s. Evidently, for instance, the Foreign Office was not consulted when Sir Ronald Ellis, then the Head of Defence Sales, concluded an approximately £1 billion deal for an Iranian military installation during a personal meeting with the Shah, agreeing to accept payment for the project in oil.[27]

The irony is, of course, that rather than secure the shah's position, his gorging on Western arms seems to have fatally undermined it—a process well captured by Michael Klare. The unavoidable consequence of this was, as Klare says, to leave "a huge stockpile of modern arms in the hands of people with a pronounced anti-American bias" once the shah was overthrown.[28]

◆ Impact of the Iranian Revolution

The 1979 Iranian Revolution was a seismic event for the West. The key pillar of U.S. Gulf strategy crumbled overnight. The full implications for U.S. and Western influence and protection of its interests elsewhere in the region were realized when seventy-six members of the U.S. embassy staff in Tehran were seized as hostages in November 1979. This combination of events altered Western perceptions of Iraq and also affected Iraq's own outlook. As Hiro comments, this changed situation also shifted the basis of the traditional rivalry between Iran and Iraq: "It was ironic that a pro-Western, conservative, secular Iranian regime had been transformed into a revolutionary proselytizer threatening the status quo which the erstwhile radical, pro-Soviet Iraqi regime was keen to preserve in the region."[29]

The revolution also left Britain and the United States with a mountain of arms orders from Iran, which the new revolutionary government canceled. Most notably for the United Kingdom, the Chieftain tank order was eventually taken up by Jordan. However, the revolution did not result in such an immediate break in relations with Britain as is commonly assumed. Despite the largely formal application of an embargo, it was the revolutionary government's cancellation of contracts that was the more significant move in rupturing Anglo-Iranian trade, which had been of considerable economic as well as strategic importance for Britain, and which Britain would therefore prefer to hang on to if possible.[30]

In 1980 the *New Statesman* exposed some of the government's work in this direction:

> Despite the cancellation of most of IMS's contracts by the new government, the MOD [Ministry of Defence] have not given up. In November, MOD Under-secretary Braden visited Tehran and returned with a new "Memorandum of Understanding." The Iranians then coughed up a further £2.5 million prepayment for ammunition they badly wanted. After the American hostages were seized, however, the Foreign Office ordered trading links to be cut off. IMS still retain this cash—and forlorn hopes of going back into business with Iran. Throughout the period the hostages have been held in Tehran, IMS have been quietly running a local office with locally recruited staff to keep "contact" with the new military leaders, despite government policy on trading sanctions against Iran.[31]

The taking of the U.S. hostages complicated but did not itself lead to the termination of Britain's attempts to revive its lucrative arms trade. Gary Sick, author of *October Surprise*, cites Ali Reza Nobari, a former head of the Central Bank of Iran, as saying: "The British were not loyal to [the United States] during the hostage crisis. The U.K. ambassador came to me at that time and since I was rather naive he had to put it to me very clearly. He told me that the British were prepared to sell military equipment to us despite the embargo."[32] Neither was Britain alone. France, Iraq's foremost Western supplier of arms at the time, also allowed arms to reach Iran via Israel.[33] Moreover, a number of arms dealers have alleged that during 1980 and 1981 the United States itself facilitated deliveries of arms of U.S. origin to Iran via Israel as part of a deal by elements within the Reagan-Bush campaign team to prevent the release of the American hostages until after the 1980 presidential election (the "October surprise" idea). One, Arif Durrani, claimed that NATO arms were flowing out of Europe to Iran and that on one occasion thirteen Cobra helicopters were sold to Iran from a U.S. base in West Germany, using Zaire as a conduit. A second arms dealer, Hushang Lavi, told a similar story, claiming: "Anything that they could not supply from Israel, they would supply from Belgium. The Iranians would come there, they would be taken to NATO bases, particularly the bases in the border in between Belgium and Germany, and they would pick up whatever they want, and . . . the Belgians would ship it to Iran."[34] Certainly, Belgium was to play a key role in the arming of Iraq and Iran during the next decade.

At the same time that British and Western relations with Iran were declining, British relations with Iraq began to improve. There had been low-key military links between Britain and Baghdad even before the fall of the shah. For example, in 1976 the Royal Air Force (RAF) had begun training Iraqi pilots in Britain, even though the Iraqi air force was equipped almost completely with MIGs and other Soviet aircraft.[35] Then, on 4 July 1979, two months to the day after Mrs. Thatcher's first general election victory, Iraq lifted its selective business embargo against Britain.[36] The embargo had been one of the consequences of the previous Labour government's expulsion of eleven Iraqi diplomats in July 1978 following the murder in London of former Iraqi Prime Minister Abderrazak Nayif. Its lifting came at a time when the denial of the Iraqi market[37] was becoming increasingly significant because of the loss of the Iranian market. The embargo's removal was sealed during a visit to Baghdad by Lord Carrington, the foreign secretary. The much-travelled trade minister, Cecil Parkinson, followed this up with a visit in October 1979, timed to coincide with the Baghdad Trade Fair; and his secretary of state, John Nott, arrived a month later. These were the earliest in what became a constant stream of visits during the Thatcher years.[38]

Hence, for the bulk of the cold war years, the West armed Iran under the shah so that it could fulfill a role characterized in the United States as that of a regional *gendarme* but more accurately described as that of a heavily armed buffer state, as part of a twin pillars strategy. However, this strategy collapsed with the 1979 Iranian revolution. Although the break with the West was perhaps not as quick and complete as is sometimes assumed, by the early 1980s Western interests in the region had been redefined. For the United States they now lay in arming Iraq in its war with Iran so as to prevent an Iranian victory and contain the spread of Islamic fundamentalism, which, it was assumed, threatened to disrupt the carefully preserved status quo throughout the region. France's policy now was to cement a relationship with its key regional ally, Iraq. A balance of power was equally important to Britain's interests, given the allegiances of its main allies in the region, even though it did not openly share the same anti-Iranian paranoia that came to characterize U.S. foreign policy (at least, publicly) in the 1980s. However, in practice this interest also came to mean preventing an Iranian victory through support for Iraq. By arming Iraq, covertly where necessary, the West could nurture a prolonged, exhaustive conflict following which neither belligerent would emerge dominant but both (particularly Iran) would be too materially exhausted to threaten the lower Gulf states. In this assumption, with hindsight, the strategy was clearly flawed. As a consequence of the material exhaustion brought about by the long war, in August 1990 Iraq turned on its smaller Gulf neighbor, Kuwait, with arms and military know-how that the West had supplied.

N O T E S

1 It is beyond the scope of the present study to analyze the history of this rivalry. On this see Dilip Hiro: *The Longest War: The Iran-Iraq Military Conflict*, London, Paladin, 1990. On the British decision to withdraw from the Gulf, see Donald Cameron Watt: The Decision to Withdraw from the Gulf, *Political Quarterly*, Vol. 39 No. 3 1968, pp. 310–321. See also F. Gregory Gause III: British and American Policies in the Persian Gulf, 1968–1973, *Review of International Studies*, Vol. 11 No. iv 1985, pp. 247–273.

2 These figures are taken from James A. Bill and Robert Springborg: *Politics in the Middle East*, 4th ed., New York, HarperCollins, 1994, p. 386.

3 Yahya Sadowski: Scuds Versus Butter: The Political Economy of Arms Control in the Arab World, *Middle East Report*, July–August 1992, p. 4.

4 Stephen Gill and David Law: *The Global Political Economy: Perspectives, Problems and Policies*, Hemel Hempstead, Harvester-Wheatsheaf, 1988, p. 256.

5 In 1991, on the eve of the Gulf War, the Japanese consul general in the United States Mosamichi Hanabusa, commented that "who will control the oil is a serious issue for the US at this time. But it is not a serious issue for Japan. It is of course better that oil is in friendly hands. But experience tells us that whoever controls oil will be disposed to sell it." Although much can be read into this, it suggests that price stability was the key issue for Japan, although given Japan's dependence on imports, control is also clearly an issue. Cited in Edward N. Krapels: The Commanding Heights—International Oil in a Changed World, *International Affairs*, Vol. 69 No. 1 1993, p. 71.

6 Joe Stork and Ann M. Lesch: Why War?, *Middle East Report*, Nov–Dec 1990, p. 13.

7 *Newsnight*, 3.30.95. My emphasis.

8 Yahya Sadowski: Scuds Versus Butter, p. 4.

9 Quoted in K. Matthews: *The Gulf Conflict and International Relations*, pp. 199–200. NB: I have used pre-1990 figures here to present the picture at the end of the Iran-Iraq War, and also in preference to more current figures to indicate the significance of Iraq as a producer and exporter, a factor that is distorted in post-1990 data by the effects of the embargo.

10 Figures taken from the *BP Statistical Review of World Energy*, June 1995.

11 This is not, of course, an indication of a state's or region's *dependence* on oil, which would require parallel consideration of its use of oil for energy in relation to its use of gas, coal, nuclear, and hydroelectric power. In 1994, on this basis, U.S. dependence on oil for its energy was just under 40 percent (38 percent for U.K. 56 percent for Japan). Hence, in 1994 the United States was dependent on oil imports for over 20 percent of its energy needs.

12 Inquiry into Exports of Defence Equipment and Dual Use Goods to Iraq (henceforth, Scott Inquiry)—Day 1: Evidence of Sir Richard Luce, p. 3.

13 Howard and Gayle Radley Teicher: *Twin Pillars to Desert Storm: America's Flawed Vision in the Middle East from Nixon to Bush*, New York, William Morrow, 1993, p. 29. As early as 1969, the Georgetown University Center for Strategic and International Studies had warned: "The strategic interests of the non-communist world would be in grave jeopardy if freedom of movement in and out of the Gulf were curtailed or denied." Georgetown University CSIS: *The Gulf—Implications of the British Withdrawal*, Washington, D.C., 1969. Cited in Michael T. Klare: *American Arms Supermarket*, Austin, University of Texas, 1984, p. 113.

14 U.S. Senate: U.S. Military Sales to Iran, July 1976, p. 41.

15 Michael T. Klare: *American Arms Supermarket*, pp. 116–117.

16 Formally, it was the Middle East Treaty Organisation, established in February 1951.

17 Since the 1991 Gulf War, there was been much written on the Iraqi-Kuwaiti border dispute. By far the best guide is Dr. W. Hamdi (ed.): *Kuwait-Iraq Boundary Dispute in British Archives*, *Vols. 1 & 2*, London, Quick Print, 1993. On the 1961 Iraq-Kuwait crisis and the British reaction, see Mustafa M. Alani: *Operation Vantage: British Military Intervention in Kuwait 1961*, Surbiton, LAAM, 1990.

18 Oles M. Smolansky and Bettie M. Smolansky: *The USSR and Iraq: The Soviet Quest for Influence*, Durham, N.C., Duke University Press, pp. 18–19.

19 For a good account of the U.S.-Iranian relationship under the shah, see Barry Rubin: *Paved with Good Intentions: The American Experience and Iran*, New York, Penguin, 1981—particularly chapter 6 on the arms relationship.

20 Dilip Hiro: *The Longest War: The Iran-Iraq Military Conflict*, p. 15.

21 These figures are for orders. However, by the time of the shah's fall, only $10 billion worth had actually been delivered.

22 Anthony Sampson: *The Arms Bazaar*, 2nd ed., Sevenoaks, Hodder & Stoughton, 1988, p. 16. The shah had his own pilot's license and even subscribed to *Aviation Week*.

23 Quoted in Sampson, *The Arms Bazaar*, p. 242.

24 Mark Phythian: The Politics of the Pay-Off: Commissions and Corruption in the Arms Sales Process, unpublished paper.

25 An arms-length, government-owned private company, directed to behave "as commercially as possible" in securing arms deals for British companies. See Mark Phythian and Walter Little: Administering Britain's Arms Trade, *Public Administration*, Vol. 71 No. 3 1993, pp. 259–277.

26 Renamed DESO (Defence Export Services Organisation) under Mrs. Thatcher.

27 Frederic S. Pearson: The Question of Control in British Defence Sales Policy, *International Affairs*, Vol. 59 No. 2 1983, p. 227.

28 M. Klare: *American Arms Supermarket*, p. 127. A good short account of the way in which the U.S. arming of the shah actually contributed to his overthrow rather than secured his position is also provided by Klare in Arms and the Shah—The Rise and Fall of the "Surrogate Strategy," *The Progressive*, Vol. 43 No. 8 1979, pp. 15–21. See also William D. Hartung: *And Weapons for All*, New York, HarperCollins, 1994, ch. 2.

29 D. Hiro: *The Longest War*, p. 28.

30 Sir Richard Luce told the Scott Inquiry that "in the long-term Iran [was regarded] as a very important nation with whom we would hope, even though there was a temporary decline in our relations . . . to be able to restore good relations both politically and from the commercial point of view as well." Scott Inquiry—Day 1: Evidence of Sir Richard Luce, pp. 4–5.

31 Duncan Campbell: The Bribe Machine, *New Statesman*, 10.17.80, p. 16.

32 Quoted in Gary Sick: *October Surprise: America's Hostages in Iran and the Election of Ronald Reagan*, London, I. B. Taurus, 1991, p. 108.

33 Ibid., pp. 109–113, and pp. 165–167.

34 Ibid., pp. 202–203.

35 *Guardian*, 7.7.76.

36 There were similarities between this and Malaysia's subsequent "Buy British Last" campaign, in that it did not prevent Iraq from purchasing goods it could not get elsewhere. In general, however, the Iraqi government refused to accept tenders from British companies for contracts worth over £35,000. See the *Financial Times*, 7.5.79.

37 Iraq's population of 12 million and estimated $11.4 billion balance of payments surplus in 1979 made it a very attractive proposition in its own right. *Financial Times*, 2.15.80.

38 See chapter 3.

The United States, the West, and the Geopolitics of the Iran-Iraq War

Why did Iraq attack Iran on 22 September 1980? Added to the long-term historical antagonisms, the ascent to power of Saddam in Iraq and Khomeini in Iran heightened tensions. Khomeini's rhetoric represented a potential threat to Saddam. With Tehran calling for Shia Muslims across the Gulf region to imitate the Iranian example, the possibility of a Shia insurrection in Iraq aided by Iran was much increased. In terms of more immediate factors, it was an ideal time to take on Iran on behalf of the Gulf states, given the upheaval of the revolution. Success would bring economic as well as political influence. As Howard and Gayle Teicher point out, if Saddam had seized Khuzestan Province and Kharg Island, he would have almost doubled Iraqi oil production to around 11 million barrels per day—around 20 percent of world consumption.[1] The stakes, therefore, were high. Furthermore, as tensions increased during 1980, it seemed that the Iranians were remarkably ill prepared for a war, since their army had been weakened by the purges that had followed the revolution. As Gary Sick notes, the view was that the "new Revolutionary Guards Corps was little more than a ragtag band of zealous, inexperienced youths."[2] Part of Saddam's calculation was that he would be able to score a quick and decisive victory and that the conflict would not turn out to be protracted. In reaching this conclusion he was influenced by various analyses. First, both Jordan and Saudi Arabia passed on summaries of U.S. briefings indicating a decline in Iran's military capability. Howard Teicher, from his insider's position at the National Security Council (NSC), observed:

> Much of Washington's information which was used to brief the Saudis and Jordanians on the Iranian military was derived from the DOD's [Department of Defense] expectations that Iran's advanced military systems were not being properly used or maintained. The conclusion led the American government to believe that the Iranian military, already racked by numerous purges of the senior officers, would not be capable of sustaining modern combat for more than several days. Although US

officials did not intentionally provide military intelligence on Iran to the Iraqis, US officials were clearly aware that the American assessments would reach Baghdad. Given the significance the Arab leaders attached to these briefings, the United States had some responsibility for significantly contributing to Saddam's calculation that Iraqi power could overwhelm the remnants of the Iranian military.[3]

Iraq was also in receipt of regular intelligence from Iranian exiles opposed to Khomeini, all of which suggested that the Iranian military was in disarray. Moreover, by September 1980, Iran was diplomatically isolated. Its most important ally and arms supplier, the United States, had cut off links in response to the hostage situation, its relations with Moscow had deteriorated following the Soviet invasion of Afghanistan, and the conservative states of the Gulf were fearful of its fundamentalist rhetoric and suspicious of its intentions. Conversely, Iraq's relations with the conservative Gulf states were very good, and Saddam had even visited Saudi Arabia and Kuwait to gauge reaction to his plan to invade Iran. It was a plan that, if successful, would bring Iraq recognition as the leader of the Arab world.

◆ The Course of the War

Broadly speaking, for the first two years of the conflict the war was conducted largely inside Iranian territory, but thereafter the front line moved inside Iraqi territory for the bulk of the time. Once Saddam had invaded, it became apparent that some of the more pessimistic assessments of Iran's military strength were not based on reality but perhaps stemmed more from the personal agendas of the Iranian exiles who had mostly provided the assessments (directly and via the United States) than from impartial analysis. In particular, that the Iranian air force could function at all seemed to take the Iraqis by surprise; in fact it was able to undertake a number of sorties over Baghdad and strike at strategic installations. That this was the case was also at least partly due to the decision of the Reagan administration to allow Israel to channel arms of U.S. origin to Iran to prevent an easy and early Iraqi victory (as discussed in more detail below) and to the fact that, as Anthony Cordesman has pointed out, Iraq, with a population of some 16 million compared with Iran's 46 million, had little "strategic depth" with which to defend its long Iranian border.[4] Iran's population advantage was borne out by its political ability to withstand enormous casualties. This was a luxury Saddam did not have, and Iraq eventually began placing limits on the number of public funerals to help conceal its heavy losses.

Hence, although the initial Iraqi advance made some progress—capturing towns like Mehran and Qasr-e-Shirin—the Iranian response was stronger than anticipated. When its army bombed the Iraqi city of Basra,[5] Iraqi forces dug in rather than continue their advance, allowing Iran to prepare for a counteroffensive that succeeded in prizing the Iraqi forces out of Khorram-shahr in June 1982. From there the Iranians targeted Basra again and made numerous attempts to take the highway joining Basra to Baghdad, which would have effectively cut Iraq in two and possibly brought the conflict to an end with an Iranian military victory. In 1985 a small Iranian force actually succeeded in seizing control of the highway before being forced to with-draw—a major shock for the Iraqis.

In this classic land-war scenario, long-range artillery played a crucial role. By 1984 the military balance once again lay in Iraq's favor. The Soviet Union, which at one point had suspended deliveries of arms (see below), resumed the flow. France began to emerge as the leading Western supplier of choice. Regional allies like Egypt provided Baghdad with small arms and ammuni-tion; and at the same time, Operation Staunch began to have an effect on Iran's capacity to wage war. By 1987 Iraq had become the world's leading arms importer. By contrast, Iran was finding resupply problematic and was now obliged to rely more heavily than Iraq on covert supplies. Iran's arsenal of American arms—once the most sophisticated outside NATO—became of increasingly limited use as spare parts were no longer openly available. This was the environment that spawned the original Iranian arms component of the Iran-Contra scandal and persuaded Israel of the need to channel spare parts for U.S. equipment to Iran on a regular basis. As the war progressed, the Iranian requirement for the kind of integrated defense systems that the "black" and "gray" markets could not guarantee led them to look increas-ingly to China and North Korea for their arms purchases. In addition, Brazil proved a willing source of both weapons and false end-user certificates, while Singapore proved an invaluable transshipment point. Furthermore, there was one country willing and able to sell arms of U.S. origin: Vietnam. It is thought to have sold Iran a number of M-48 tanks, M-113 APCs, and F-5 fighter aircraft, as well as various parts and ammunition. However, Vietnam could only supply what it had by way of captured weapons. Hence, the Viet-namese connection alone could not provide the solution to the problem of finding the consistent supply and comprehensive range of spares that Iran needed for its shah-purchased U.S. weaponry.

◆ **Iraqi Long-Range Missiles and the "War of the Cities"**

January 1987 saw an Iranian offensive on Basra that the Iraqis blocked just outside the city itself, and in March Iran launched an offensive in the north of Iraq. But in 1988 Iraq introduced two new military dimensions to the conflict. These were to bring to a conclusion a conflict that had seemed without end, and were to have an important influence on Iraq's postwar militarization drive. In February 1988 a new War of the Cities broke out in which Iran deployed its new SCUD missile technology, hitting Tehran—some 350 miles from the Iraqi border—for the first time and thus delivering a major psychological blow to Iran from which it did not fully recover. Although the lengthening of the Soviet SCUD to create the Al-Hussein, which had given the Iraqi variants their extended range, allowed the missiles to reach Tehran, they bought range at the expense of accuracy. As illustrated again during the 1991 Gulf War, the longer body made the missiles unstable in flight, and during the War of the Cities probably only half the missiles landed within a mile of their target. On the other hand, their somewhat indiscriminate nature made the SCUD the ideal terror weapon—the antithesis of SMART technology. This phase of the war continued into April, when Iraq deployed chemical weapons against the Kurds of Halabja, reportedly killing around five thousand of its inhabitants in the attack. This act led the Iranians to believe that chemical weapons might be deployed against them, and they began to fall back in the face of every Iraqi advance, allowing Iraq to retake the Fao Peninsula and further territories. Combined with the effects of the long-range bombing of Tehran, this fear reportedly caused the Iranian military to persuade a reluctant Khomeini to accept a cease-fire, to take effect from August 1988. In terms of the future, the success of this combination was to give Saddam a strongly held belief in the importance of long-range weapons and in the demoralizing effect of chemical weapons. If the two could be combined, their military significance would be even greater.

One early Iraqi exploration of the potential of long-range missiles had taken the form of involvement in the Condor II ballistic missile program. This program had been set up in Argentina in the late 1970s with West German help, particularly from Messerschmitt-Bolkow-Blohm (MBB), which preferred to describe the project as being for a "meteorological rocket."[6] When Iraq joined the program, it brought in Egypt as an acceptable front: "Technical know-how obtained by the Egyptians would be shared with their Iraqi colleagues. Materials would be cross-shipped from Cairo to Baghdad. Iraq, with Saudi help, would pay the bills."[7] Iraq's desire to manufacture the Condor missile represented a qualitative advance in its military ambition. It looked beyond the current conflict to a time when Iraq would represent the arsenal of the Arab world. With its 650-mile range, the Condor II would bring within range not just Iran and Israel but also Iraq's current allies— Kuwait, Saudi Arabia, Oman, Bahrain, and so on. It was a program that should have concerned the British government more than it did and should have made British officials more aware of the risks inherent in equipping Iraq with the means of developing an indigenous arms industry. Given the Argentine involvement, it would have been likely for the Condor II to have been produced in Argentina as well as the Middle East, and from there the Falkland Islands would have been within its range.[8]

◆ Arms Sales to the Belligerents

If arms are the fuel of war, then war fuels the arms industry. In an era other-wise marked by a depression in the international arms market, the Iran-Iraq War was a long, protracted war that generated an insatiable demand for a full range of arms and military equipment. It wasn't just the biggest game in town, it was the only game in town. Hence, despite the existence of various national restrictions on the sale of arms, the arming of Iran and Iraq was truly global in nature. As Chris Cowley, the project manager for Project Babylon (the supergun program) has observed:

> Many people live under the illusion that arms deals are struck by shadowy entrepre-neurs operating on the margins of the law. This may be true of light weapons . . . [but] contemporary wars cannot be won with assault rifles, machine guns and gre-nades. The eight-year Iran-Iraq conflict consumed hundreds of advanced fighter aircraft and helicopters, thousands of battlefield tanks and artillery guns, millions of modern rockets, shells and bombs, and for most of these the only realistic sources of supply are the state-regulated arms industries of the industrialised na-tions.[9]

In reality, private arms dealers have been used by governments to supply arms to areas where they are constrained from acting openly. The dealers provide deniability and in return gain a lucrative profit on an approved deal— unless it is exposed. Then they are abandoned and portrayed as rogue op-erators. Gerald Bull suffered this fate over South Africa, while Sarkis

Soghanalian was among several arms dealers arrested over the "Irangate" affair in the United States.

In 1986, three-quarters of the way through the war, the Stockholm International Peace Research Institute (SIPRI) estimated that twenty-eight states had supported both Iran and Iraq militarily at some time since the conflict began. (Within Europe, for example, Italy made frigates for Iraq while sending mines to Iran; Spain exported ammunition to both sides, with Spanish ammunition for Iraq being routed through Saudi Arabia.) Sixteen more nations had supported only Iran militarily, and nine had favored just Iraq. In all, forty-four states were identified as having supported Iran and thirty-seven Iraq. Of the twenty-eight states equipping both belligerents, all but Ethiopia and Saudi Arabia were considered to have passed on or sold major weapons systems, although evidence has since emerged to suggest that Saudi Arabia too passed on major weapons to Iraq. This is not to say that these states backed both sides equally. For example, France, Spain, Italy, the United States, and the United Kingdom all sent military equipment to Iran, but each enjoyed a more extensive military relationship with Iraq during the war. Why did so many states arm both sides? Essentially, these states had no immediate strategic interest in the conflict—it did not affect them directly. The art of arming both sides could be interpreted as hedging their bets, but it is in fact better explained as the application of the ultimate commercial logic in the arms sales environment, a logic that most of these states had no qualms in applying given their general perception of both governments as equally odious. In somes cases, however, most notably the United States, arming both sides represented a conscious policy decision intended to influence the outcome of the conflict.

◆ Iraqi Arms Procurement Strategy

The Iraqi arms procurement operation of the 1980s consisted of two planks, one reflecting the immediate needs brought about by the war with Iran, the other Iraq's long-term ambition to develop an indigenous defense base and become the leading Arab military power.[10]

The former was an overt strategy, requiring the importation of major weapons systems, spares, and training from leading Eastern and Western states. Once Iraq came to the conclusion that the Soviet Union was an unreliable supplier, and given the tendency of major weapons exporters to restrict supplies at times of war, Iraq turned to more commercially oriented Third

Table 2.1

Arms Supply and Other Support to Iran and Iraq, 1980–1986

Country	Iran		Iraq	
	Weapons	Other Support	Weapons	Other Support
Supporting Both Iran and Iraq				
Austria	x		x	
Belgium	x		x	
Brazil	x	x	x	x
Bulgaria	x	x	x	x
Chile	x		x	
China	x	x	x	x
Czechoslovakia	x	x	x	x
East Germany	x	x	x	x
Ethiopia		x	x	
France	x		x	x
Greece	x	x	x	x
Hungary	x	x	x	x
Italy	x	x	x	x
Netherlands	x		x	
North Korea	x		x	
Pakistan	x	x	x	x
Poland	x	x	x	x
Portugal	x		x	
Saudi Arabia		x		x
South Africa	x		x	
Soviet Union	x	x	x	x
Spain	x		x	x
Sweden	x	x	x	
Switzerland	x		x	
United Kingdom	x	x	x	x
United States	x	x	x	x
West Germany	x	x	x	x
Yugoslavia	x	x	x	x
Supporting Iran Only				
Algeria	x	x		
Argentina	x	x	(x)	
Canada	x	x		
Denmark		x		
Finland	x	x		
Israel	x	x	(x)	
Kenya		x		
Libya	x	x		
Mexico	x	x		
Singapore		x		
South Korea	x	x		
South Yemen		x		

(continued)

| Table 2.1 (continued) |

	Iran		Iraq	
Country	Weapons	Other Support	Weapons	Other Support
Syria	x	x		
Taiwan	x	x		
Turkey	x	x		
Vietnam	x			
Supporting Iraq Only				
Egypt			x	x
Jordan			x	x
Kuwait				x
Morocco				x
North Yemen				x
Philippines			x	x
Sudan				x
Tunisia				x
United Arab Emirates				x

Source: Armaments and Disarmament: SIPRI Yearbook 1987, Oxford, OUP/SIPRI, pp. 204–205.[11]
Notes: (1) "Weapons" includes major weapons, small arms, ammunition, and explosives; (2) "Other Support" includes military transport vehicles (jeeps, trucks) spare parts, training, military advisers, logistic support, and financial support. In this way, the SIPRI categorization nicely mirrors the lethal/nonlethal distinction implicit in the Howe Guidelines. (3) "(x)" = unconfirmed.

World suppliers with fewer or nonexistent restrictions—Chile being the epitome of these exporters. This approach reflects two realities. First, in order to establish themselves in what by the early 1980s was already an overcrowded and declining world arms market, emergent exporters had to be prepared to sell in cases where other states chose not to. Second, Third World leaders could expect to reap enormous financial rewards, either directly or via their political parties, through commissions on sales or fees levied to allow their state to be used as a transshipment point or on end-user certificates in covert sales.

The latter plank was largely covert, although a covert strategy on such a large scale could not go unnoticed. It was accelerated after the cease-fire in the Iran-Iraq War and centered on the Ministry of Industry and Military Industrialization headed by Saddam's son-in-law, Hussein Kamel. While this was the less visible and relatively less expensive side of the procurement operation, its long-term significance was considerable. This more covert level is the one at which the British contribution was uncovered by the Matrix Churchill scandal, and also much American support was pitched.

It is also worth noting that Iran's difficulty over resupply led it to many of the same conclusions regarding the necessity of developing an indigenous arms industry, although without the same dramatic consequences. As an indication of this, in September 1995 Iran's minister of defense and armed forces logistics, Mohammed Forouzandeth, announced that Iran was now "exporting arms and ammunition to 14 countries and . . . even transferring technology."[12]

◆ The Role of the Soviet Union

The Soviet Union dominated the Iraqi arms market throughout the 1970s. Between 1971 and 1975 it provided 97 percent of all Iraqi major weapons imports and still provided 85 percent of them between 1976 and 1980. Although it increasingly lost ground to France, Italy, and other countries after 1980, between 1981 and 1985 it nonetheless accounted for 55 percent of Iraqi major arms imports.[13]

Crucially for Iraq, the Soviet Union did not support its war with Iran, viewing the outbreak of war as a disaster.[14] For the Soviet Union as for the United States, geostrategically Iran was potentially of greater value as an ally, and given the state of Iran's relations with the United States at that time, the Soviet Union could reasonably have hoped for improved relations. Furthermore, Iraq embarrassed the Soviets by giving the impression that they had little control over their client states. Because of this, Soviet arms shipments to Iraq proved highly unreliable from the outset of the war and were even suspended for a time. To the dismay of the Iraqis, the Soviet Union publicly adopted a position of neutrality in the war and privately even sought to use the opportunity to build better relations with Iran, reportedly going so far as to offer arms. Nonetheless, during this period Iraq was still able to acquire Soviet-type arms from Czechoslovakia (mainly small arms and ammunition); Hungary, Poland, and Romania (mainly armored vehicles and ammunition); and Egypt, China, and Yugoslavia. However, the Soviets' maneuvering led the Iraqis to question the wisdom of reliance on outside arms suppliers, and the experience was to prove an important factor in Iraq's drive to develop its own arms industry.

Meanwhile, the Iranians having shown little interest in the Soviet approach, by 1981 Moscow was willing once more to provide Iraq with arms as a way of mending fences, although without renouncing its public position of neutrality in the war. There also remained the suspicion that the Soviet Union was continuing to hedge its bets by facilitating the arming of Iran via

Syria and Libya. However, from an Iraqi perspective its relationship with Moscow was more than ever now a short-term marriage of convenience, creating fertile ground on which the Reagan administration could make a pitch to wean Iraq away from the Soviet orbit.

The military lessons that Iraq drew were not that it should shift dependence on arms imports from the East to the West but that it should end its dependence on such imports altogether by developing its own arms industry,[15] an aim that was firmly established by the early stages of the Iran-Iraq War. Although initially the war made the acquisition of arms a more immediate priority for Iraq than the development of an indigenous arms industry, its long-term aim was not entirely neglected, and it began to gather momentum toward the end of the conflict. Once that war ended, Saddam was able to concentrate even greater resources on an ambitious military industrialization drive. Hence, rather than demilitarizing after the conflict, Saddam aimed to expand Iraq's military-industrial base further, confirming Iraq not only as the Arab world's preeminent military power but also as a potential threat to the smaller Arab states of the lower Gulf. Documents released to the Scott Inquiry show that Saudi Arabia and the Gulf states were acutely aware of this plan, which involved closely aligning industrial activity with military needs. A July 1990 U.S. intelligence report warned:

> In May 1989, Hussein Kamel, the head of the Ministry of Industry and Military Industrialization, proclaimed publicly that Iraq was implementing a defense industrial program to cover all its armed force needs for weapons and equipment by 1991. He stated that Iraq's industrialization program was intended to provide all of Iraq's basic industrial supplies from indigenous sources.[16]

◆ France and the Arming of Iraq

Iraq had never been a traditional Soviet client. Aside from its marked reluctance to identify itself with Soviet foreign policy aims, it had also sought to diversify its supply of arms so as not to be vulnerable to shifts in Soviet foreign interests. To this end, from the mid-1970s Iraq had turned increasingly to France, whose independent, Gaullist foreign policy translated into an independent position on arms sales. The relationship was to make France Iraq's second-largest supplier of conventional arms after the Soviet Union.

Initially, this relationship extended to facilitating Iraq's "civilian" nuclear research program by selling it the Osirak reactor, which Israeli aircraft destroyed on 7 June 1981 in a mission planned with the aid of U.S. satellite photography available under an American-Israeli intelligence-sharing agreement.[17] In September 1983, just over a year after the Falklands War, in which the French Exocet missile had proved itself to devastating effect, France was due to deliver five Super Etendard aircraft armed with Exocets to Iraq. The aircraft, which had to be taken from use on the aircraft carrier *Foch* off the Lebanese coast, were leased for two years in the first instance.[18] They were delivered on 7 October 1983 and returned by September 1985.[19] France justified this deal as representing such a significant enhancement of Iraq's military capability that the sale would force Iran to the negotiating table and thereby bring about an end to the conflict. In addition, France sold Iraq Mirage and Mystère fighter aircraft, a range of military helicopters (Alouette, Gazelle, Puma, and Super Frelon), antitank and antiship missiles (including the Exocet), and a number of armored vehicles and tanks. As a consequence, France was in a highly vulnerable position when Iraq began to have difficulty in paying and had to renegotiate the payment of its debts. The French feared that any military setbacks that might lead to the fall of Saddam would leave those unpaid, a concern that propelled it toward an ever-closer relationship with Baghdad. Not that this closeness concerned the French defense industry. As a Dassault representative told Kenneth Timmerman at the 1989 Baghdad International Military Exhibition: "Don't confuse a poor country with one that has a budgetary problem. Iraq has oil resources almost equal to those of Saudi Arabia. This is a rich nation, even though it has temporary problems paying its bills."[20] This confidence was borne out by negotiations in 1989 for the sale of fifty Mirage 2000 and fifty Alpha trainer aircraft (in a direct competition with the British Hawk)—an order of key importance to Dassault, which was feeling the effects of the recession in the market and of losing out to Britain, inexplicably as far as the French were concerned, over the highly lucrative Saudi Arabian Al Yamamah project. Hence, these negotiations went ahead even though Iraq owed France over 25 billion francs and was refusing to pay due installments, with delivery being linked to success in rescheduling the Iraqi debt.

◆ The West German Contribution

West Germany, despite its notionally stricter arms export regulations and sensitivity toward the sale of arms that could be used against Israel, was heavily involved in the supply of chemical weapons equipment and infrastructure

| Table 2.2 |

Imports of Major Weapons Systems by Iraq, 1980–1989
(in millions of $US)

Exporter	1980	1981	1982	1983	1984	1985	1986	1987	1988	1989
Soviet Union	1,336	965	1,075	992	2,162	1,541	1,156	3,197	852	120
France	188	951	189	778	864	722	757	234	271	100
China	—	—	111	258	228	228	228	294	317	—
Brazil	118	118	118	138	108	68	18	163	160	112
Egypt	21	33	44	314	94	118	150	190	101	43
Czechoslovakia	20	107	98	79	79	79	38	38	38	38
Jordan	—	12	42	201	94	—	16	—	—	—
Poland	—	204	68	—	—	20	20	—	—	—
United States	—	—	—	—	—	—	—	46	192	—
Spain	—	—	38	38	25	25	21	21	17	—
Denmark	—	—	—	189	—	—	—	—	—	—
South Africa	—	—	—	—	—	40	40	40	40	—
Italy	—	—	39	19	40	23	—	4	7	—
Romania	—	—	34	34	34	—	—	—	—	—
Switzerland	5	17	10	38	—	—	—	21	5	—
Libya	—	—	—	80	—	—	—	—	—	—
Yugoslavia	—	50	—	—	—	—	—	—	—	—
Hungary	—	37	—	—	—	—	—	—	—	—
Kuwait	—	—	—	—	36	—	—	—	—	—
West Germany	—	—	12	4	3	6	—	—	—	6
United Kingdom	—	—	2	15	—	—	—	—	—	—
East Germany	—	14	—	—	—	—	—	—	—	—
Canada	—	—	—	—	—	—	—	—	6	—
Saudi Arabia	—	—	—	—	—	—	4	—	—	—

Source: Armaments and Disarmament: SIPRI Yearbook, 1991, OUP/SIPRI, Oxford, p. 202.
Note: Amounts are estimates in 1985 dollars.

to Iraq. Between 1982 and 1990, sixty-eight German companies supplied equipment or undertook infrastructural work on the Iraqi militarization program.[22] They also supplied arms like military trucks more overtly.[23]

One company that was heavily involved in this area was Water Engineering Trading, which sold 58 tons of precursor chemicals required for the production of Tabun. It exported machines to Falluja in 1986 that were intended to produce poison gas, and it sent equipment to both Salman Pak and Samarra—two of the centers of the Iraqi chemical weapons program. This company was not alone. Pilot Plant, a company based in Dreieich, actually built Samarra along with five other chemicals production facilities.[24]

MBB, one of Germany's leading arms manufacturers, was also a leading supplier of military technology to Iraq, although not directly.[25] As *Der Spiegel* commented, the company itself never made an appearance. "Whether with rocket projects or the superbomb for Iraq, MBB only researches and develops; the murderous hardware itself is sent by NATO allies to foreign countries. The dirty work in Iraq is mainly done by firms which are run by former MBB people; the company itself remains outwardly clean."[26]

There is also the suggestion of an intelligence link. At least three of the German businessmen arrested over the export of chemical weapons–related material to Iraq are said to have been at one time on the payroll of the West German foreign intelligence agency, the BND. Peter Leifer, the manager of the heavily involved Water Engineering Trading, is said to have been a BND agent from 1986.[27]

A leading West German company was also involved in one of the more complicated arms diversion maneuvers involving several states. Rheinmetall supplied Paraguay with a turnkey plant for the filling of 155mm shells. This was then transported to South Africa, where the shells were filled before being passed on to Iraq. The shells were apparently for use with the FH-70 howitzer, seventy-two of which Britain sold to Saudi Arabia in the early 1980s, from where they were allegedly passed on to Iraq.[28]

◆ Other Western European Contributions

A number of other Western European states participated in the arming of Iraq, and some of their involvements are discussed in more detail later. Spain and Portugal were convenient and willing transshipment points and issuers of false end-user certificates. After the 1991 Gulf War, the Swiss Socialist Party, part of the coalition government, named forty-eight Swiss companies—mainly dealing in dual-use technology—as having participated in the arming of Iraq, including some, like Schmiedemeccanica, in nonconventional weapons programs.[29] In addition, Switzerland supplied fifty Roland armored personnel carriers early in the war and over a hundred "training" aircraft during the course of it (PC-7s, PC-9s, and the AS-202 Bravo).[30] Dutch companies like Eurometaal were heavily involved. Eurometaal manufactured 220,000 propellant charges and 30,000 155mm shells and sold them to Poudreries Réunies de Belgique (PRB) in Belgium, which passed them on to Jordan, and from there to Iraq. In 1981 Iraq ordered a number of frigates, corvettes, and support ships from the Italian company Fincantieri at a cost of $2.86 billion. Ultimately, they were not handed over, however, because of a dispute over Iraqi debt servicing. Nevertheless, Italy also supplied a range of missiles, mines, and light armored vehicles.

Mention should also be made here of the South American contribution, which will be discussed at various points in this book. This took the form not only of straight arms transfers but also of other types of assistance. In particular, the links between the Brazilian manufacturer Engesa and Iraq were significant, as was the contribution of the Chilean Carlos Cardoen's Cardoen Industries, which by the end of the Iran-Iraq War conducted 95 percent of its business with Iraq. Such was Cardoen's personal gratitude that he hung a portrait of Saddam on the wall of his office.[31]

◆ The United States and Saddam

The clearest early indication that the United States sought to mend fences with Iraq and establish a relationship with which to replace that lost in Iran with the fall of the shah came when the Reagan administration removed Iraq from the list of states sponsoring terrorism,[32] despite evidence that it was still supporting groups like Abu Nidal. This change partly reflected the fact that the Ayatollah Khomeini had ascended to the top of the list of most-hated foreign leaders in American demonology. Not only had the fall of the shah led to the loss of a key regional ally, it had produced a new government that appeared hostile toward the United States, terming it "the great Satan," and had held U.S. nationals hostage for 444 days. Arguably, the tilt toward Iraq can even be traced back to the Carter administration, toward the end of which National Security Adviser Zbigniew Brzezinski advocated that the United States "compensate for the loss of its Iranian pillar by tilting toward Iraq."[33] He even publicly argued: "We see no fundamental incompatibility of interests between the United States and Iraq. We do not feel that American-Iraqi relations need to be frozen in antagonism."[34] However, the Carter administration did not attempt to remove Iraq from the list of states sponsoring terrorism.

From 1981, the Reagan administration was split over its policy toward Iran and Iraq, with one group within it seeking to prop up Saddam and another looking to repair relations with Iran. The Pentagon, Caspar Weinberger, George Bush, James Baker, and Richard Murphy backed Iraq, while Robert McFarlane and Oliver North were among those backing Iran. This lack of clear direction may help to explain the impression that "[b]efore the Reagan Administration was six months old, the intelligence network was humming with the word that the U.S. government wanted both sides to lose the Iran-Iraq war."[35]

The absence of a clear policy approach was further reflected in the administration's 1981 decision to allow Israel to supply Iran with spare parts, including those for its F-4s, on condition that specific lists be passed to the administration for approval prior to each shipment. But this arrangement soon grew beyond U.S. control, so much so that "Israeli and American intelligence officials acknowledged that weapons, ammunition, and spare parts worth several billion dollars flowed to Iran each year during the early 1980s."[36]

The United States had given Israel a "green light" to arm Iran,[37] and as a former U.S. ambassador to the Middle East told *Los Angeles Times* reporters Murray Waas and Craig Ungar, this made it difficult then to put an accurate figure on the volume or value of the arms Israel passed on: "The problem with this type of covert operation is that for officials to maintain their deniability," the ambassador told them, "they can do little to oversee the operation. In this case, it is probable that those who were to serve as their proxies—Israel and private international arms dealers—had agendas of their own, and the end result was that more arms were shipped than anyone in the Administration wanted."[38]

This early U.S. policy shift helped Iran launch its first successful counteroffensive against Iraq. However, the advantage bestowed by U.S. and Israeli arms and intelligence soon had to be balanced, as Iranian successes on the battlefield raised the specter of Iran overrunning Iraq and dominating the entire Gulf region. In response, from 1982 the administration came down increasingly on the side of Iraq. The administration reasoned that such support could represent a first step toward weaning Iraq away from reliance on the Soviet Union (by now a strained relationship) and bringing it into the Western orbit, from where it could play a role for the West similar to that played by the shah—a replacement pillar—and keep Iran occupied at the same time. From the NSC, Howard Teicher observed:

> Recalling the notion of Iraq as a counterweight to Syria and Iran during America's futile efforts in Lebanon, some representatives from State, Defense and Commerce argued that if the Iran-Iraq War could be brought to a peaceful end without victor or vanquished, a rebuilt and prosperous Iraq could assume the role that Iran once played to ensure the security of the Gulf, while co-operating with Saudi Arabia to maintain stability in the world oil markets. In other words, the United States should help Iraq replace Iran as America's pillar in the Gulf.[39]

In accordance with this approach, in November 1983 Iraq was removed from the list of "nations that support international terrorism," while in January 1984 Iran was added.[40] This change loosened export controls on Iraq and tightened those on Iran. At the same time, the new direction also involved sharing intelligence and supplying arms and technology, initially through Jordan. The intelligence-sharing initiative, an important development in a conflict in which neither side boasted a particularly developed intelligence capability, reportedly began as early as spring 1982, "after American intelligence agencies warned that Iraq was on the verge of being overrun by Iran," which was by then deploying weapons of U.S. origin supplied via Israel. It was expanded thereafter as the battlefield situation required.[41] This liaison was kept from both the Senate and House intelligence committees for fear that pro-Israeli members of Congress would attempt to end it. One official, quoted by Seymour Hersh in the *New York Times*, explained—in terms that could have come straight from British officials giving evidence to the Scott Inquiry: "It was agreed that the public policy of the Administration, to remain even-handed, was not in the national interest [but it was] decided that it was not in the national interest to publicly announce a change in the policy."[42] It eventually extended to providing direct assistance in the war with Iran, an involvement that cost the lives of thirty-seven crew members aboard the *USS Stark* (discussed below) when they were struck by another part of Iraq's Western inventory, a French Exocet missile.[43] This is not to suggest that the United States desired an Iraqi victory, just that U.S. interests lay in fostering a long and bloody conflict with no victor. In 1983, one State Department official was quoted as explaining: "We don't give a damn as long as the Iran-Iraq carnage does not affect our allies or alter the balance of power."[44]

Removing Iraq from the state terrorism list was a move of much greater significance than it may have appeared at the time. It was a prerequisite for exerting influence over Iraq. There could be little influence without contact, and while Iraq remained on the list, there could be little contact. Inclusion precluded Iraq from receiving U.S. government–financed export credits and meant that military and dual-use technology sales were prohibited by strictly applied export controls. The removal of Iraq from the list, therefore, did three things. It made Iraq eligible to receive U.S. government–backed credits and U.S. military and dual-use technology; and it foreshadowed a resumption of full diplomatic relations in the near future by testing the reaction of Congress and the public (largely indifferent) to closer relations.

A second dimension to the tilt was the spring 1983 launch of Operation

Staunch, aimed at restricting the flow of arms to Iran. To back it up, the Reagan administration sent Richard Fairbanks on a tour to persuade pro-Western states not to sell arms or militarily useful equipment to Iran. He recalled: "It might not have been a 100 per cent success, but we definitely managed to stop most major weapons from reaching Iran from U.S. allies. By the time I returned to private law practice in September 1985, Iran's major suppliers were almost all Soviet bloc countries."[45] Largely as a consequence of Operation Staunch, one of the features of the war would be Iraq's superiority of arms over Iran. Staunch denied Iran open access to spares for its established (mainly U.S.) weapons systems, and the range of suppliers it was forced to deal with left it with an array of weapons, compounding the original problem of access to spare parts. The Iranian response—to turn to covert suppliers and the black market—resulted in several shipments of what purported to be arms leaving for Iran, only to turn out on arrival to be anything but. In one case, when the Iranians opened a consignment of "arms," they discovered that they had in fact been sent a shipment of dog food.[46]

At the same time that Operation Staunch sought to deny Iran access to arms, in October 1983 a classified memo from the head of the U.S. interests section in Baghdad advocated "selectively [lifting] restrictions on third-party transfers of U.S.-licensed military equipment to Iraq." As a result, according to Waas and Ungar, "that year the Reagan Administration began secretly allowing Jordan, Saudi Arabia, Kuwait and Egypt to transfer United States weapons, including howitzers, Huey helicopters, and bombs to Iraq."[47] Turning a blind eye in this way to the diversion of weapons by Iraq's Arab allies was a phenomenon that was to be repeated across Europe, and nowhere more so than in the United Kingdom.

Then in January 1984 Assistant Secretary of State Richard Murphy wrote a memo advocating a line over arming Iran and Iraq that paralleled the way in which the Howe Guidelines were to be applied in the United Kingdom. It suggested further tightening controls on the sale of arms to Iran but relaxing those on Iraq so as to allow through dual-use equipment technologies:

Liberalizing export controls on Iraq:
     We are considering revising present policy to permit virtually all sales of non-munitions list dual use equipment to Iraq . . .
     Egyptian tank sales. In the context of recommending ways to improve our relations with Iraq, Egypt has suggested that we provide it additional M-60 tanks under FMS. Egypt would use the additional M-60s to replace used Soviet T-62s which it would sell to Iraq.

As with similarly duplicitous maneuvers in Britain, Murphy recognized that because his memo ran counter to stated policy, it would have to be kept from the legislature. Therefore, the memo recommended, any background briefings for Congress should emphasize U.S. "efforts to deter escalation and bring about a cessation of hostilities."

Sympathetic European allies were also approached and asked how they could help. According to Bruce Jentleson: "Washington had been nodding and winking for quite a while at French arms sales to Iraq. . . . It would later be revealed that Italy got not just a wink, but a 'request' to supply arms to Iraq."[48] Former Italian Prime Minister Giulio Andreotti subsequently confirmed that Reagan had asked Italy to help channel arms to Iraq.[49]

In 1986, the Reagan administration again sought to step up arms deliveries to Iraq via conduits to help realize its foreign policy goals in the region. This time the administration was trying to jump-start the Iran-Contra arms-for-hostages deal, which had temporarily stalled. To convince the Iranians of their need for further U.S. weapons, the administration tried to persuade Iraq to step up air attacks on Iran. However, the Iraqis were not keen, and so to encourage them further the administration then secretly authorized Saudi Arabia to transfer U.S.-made bombs (1,500 MK-84s were sent) to Iraq. However, as with the earlier U.S. arming of Iran, this bid to influence Iran had a circular logic. While it revived the arms-for-hostages swap, it provided Iran with more weapons to aid its war effort and had to be counterbalanced by deepening the U.S. intelligence-sharing program with Iraq.

◆ **The CCC Program**

In parallel with the facilitation of arms acquisition and early intelligence sharing was a scheme that allowed Iraq to free up currency to make further arms purchases. This was the U.S. Agriculture Department's Commodity Credit Corporation (CCC) guarantees program.[50] Credits that it extended could be used to purchase U.S. agricultural produce. These credits represented an important form of nonmilitary support for Iraq, which was dependent on imports for around 75 percent of all its food. However, the impact of Iraq's war with Iran was beginning to be felt, and the disruption to its oil production was hitting oil revenue so hard that it was becoming short of cash to import the food it needed. Hence, the extension of CCC credits was welcome news for Iraq and, on the domestic front, for U.S. farmers. At the time, U.S. agricultural exports were slumping, and the potentially large Iraqi market seemed an ideal vehicle for offsetting this slump. In 1983 Iraq was granted over $400 million in credits. The following year CCC guarantees for Iraq increased to $513 million—15 percent of the entire CCC program. By 1987 this figure had risen to $652.5 million—23 percent of the total program.

In 1990 a CIA report showed that the $4.7 billion extended in credit guarantees by the CCC between 1983 and 1990 ($2.6 billion of which was authorized in the first thirty months of the Bush administration) had transformed Iraq into the largest Middle Eastern market for U.S. agricultural produce (which represented a massive 85 percent of all U.S. sales to Iraq), enabling Iraq to divert funds needed for its military industrialization drive. Sarkis Soghanalian has even suggested that, among other things, Gerald Bull's supergun work was financed out of profits from the CCC program.[51] At the same time U.S. farmers came to have a vested interest in the maintenance of good relations with Iraq. Whenever Congress considered sanctions, the farmers mobilized to oppose such moves.

This relationship, and Baghdad's need to remain on good terms with Washington because of the significance of a good relationship in the court of world opinion, also led to a marked increase in U.S. oil imports from Iraq. By 1990 the U.S. market accounted for 24 percent of Iraq's oil exports—8 percent of net U.S. oil imports.[52]

◆ The Growth of U.S. Military and Intelligence Assistance

The removal of Iraq from the state terrorism list also freed the Reagan administration to aid Iraq militarily in its war with Iran. The first concrete expression of this new freedom was the decision to sell Iraq sixty Hughes MD-500 Defender helicopters and ten Bell UH-1 helicopters, ostensibly for civilian purposes. It was a proposal that caused a serious division within the administration.

The sale of "civilian" helicopters has long been a classic way of providing military support to a favored state or ally in the face of congressional opposition, and the ploy had been used before by the Reagan administration—with El Salvador, for example. Although exported as a civilian kit, the weaponization of a civilian helicopter requires only adding armored plating, strapping on a frame to support the weapons to be attached, attaching the weapons, and ideally adding an electronic integration system, all of which takes a matter of hours. Even where they are not weaponized, the helicopters can quickly ferry troops to remote or inaccessible areas, and as such have an important utility.

As the MOD's Lt. Col. Glazebrook told the Scott Inquiry: "There is basically no difference between a military helicopter and a civilian helicopter, except the colour it is painted."[53] As former NSC official Howard Teicher recalled:

> The tempo of commercial sales accelerated rapidly following the Hughes sale. Based on Hughes's quiet success, Bell Helicopters wanted to sell Iraq ten UH-1s, Vietnam-vintage transport helicopters, still in use in the US military. The NSC was asked to participate in the interagency dispute. I strongly opposed the sale of the UH-1s and argued that the civilian model could easily be modified by the Iraqis to carry machine guns and transport troops. . . . I was told that Secretary of Commerce Malcolm Baldrige and Secretary of State Schultz lobbied NSC advisor Clark hard over a period of weeks, leading him to acquiesce in August 1983 to authorize the issuance of licences. In an environment increasingly dominated by commercial and political considerations, licence requests for the sale of dual-use technologies to Iraq, and the accompanying interagency disputes became frequent and contentious.[54]

Although it was claimed at the time that the helicopters were needed to spray crops, it has been claimed since that they were used to spray Kurds with chemicals.[55] At the same time, pressure was being applied on the United States by Arab leaders to support Iraq to prevent an Iranian victory. Again, Teicher observed:

> As the bureaucracy continued to debate how far and at what pace to move with Iraq, Arab leaders, notably King Hussein of Jordan, President Mubarak of Egypt and King Fahd of Saudi Arabia, continued to encourage Washington to reach out to Baghdad at a political level. These and other leaders argued out of fear and hope—fear that Iraq would fall to the Iranians if the United States did not provide Baghdad with political, economic and material assistance, and hope that once the war ended, a stable Iraq with strong economic ties with the West could serve as the bulwark against radicalism in the Gulf.[56]

Chris Cowley saw the American UH-1 helicopters in Iraq in 1988 while overseeing testing on the supergun program. He was being taken northwest of Baghdad by Iraqi officials as they continued to look for a suitable test site for the prototype. En route, they stopped off to refuel at a military base, where Cowley saw "fifty or sixty" of them being worked on. The next time he stopped off at the base, they were gone. The Iraqi overseeing the supergun project, Brigadier Azzawi, told him that they had "gone south" (toward the front in the Iran-Iraq War).

Still, Iraq was not faring well in the war. In July 1986 Assistant Secretary Murphy warned that questions over "Iraq's ability to sustain its defenses [have] substantially risen over the past three weeks. . . . The trends in the war, developing at an ever faster pace since the Iranian success at Faw in February, underscore our long-held view that the longer the war continues, the greater the risk of an Iraqi defeat."[57]

The irony, of course, is that these Iranian advances were facilitated partly by the sale of weapons to Iran by the Reagan administration as part of the Iran-Contra initiative. When the Iran-Contra scheme was exposed by the Lebanese newsmagazine *Al-Shiraa*,[58] this served to tie the Reagan administration closer than ever to Iraq because it closed off alternative policy options involving an opening to Iran. It also made it necessary to reassure Saudi Arabia, and of course Iraq, of the U.S. commitment to their cause. One immediate expression of this was a move to loosen further U.S. export controls on dual-use technology. As Undersecretary of State Armacost advised acting National Security Adviser Alton Keel: "In light of recent events, Iraq and the other Gulf Arabs are looking for signs of American seriousness about their region. Tangible steps, such as breaking the logjam on licensing for Iraq, would give us something to point to as we attempt to reassure the Gulf states about U.S. policy in that region."[59]

Shortly thereafter, in the spring of 1987, the United States launched the Kuwaiti reflagging operation. This logical culmination of U.S. efforts thus far to support Iraq thereby prevented an Iranian victory and ensured the continuation of the pro-Western status quo. However, as Jentleson notes, it also marked a shift in the U.S. role. For the first time, the United States openly sided with Iraq militarily by defending Kuwaiti interests against Iranian attacks:

> Protecting Kuwaiti oil tankers under the American flag and with US Navy escorts . . . was consistent with the long-standing US commitments both to contain Iranian aggression against moderate Arab states and to defend the principle of freedom of the seas and the vital economic interests at risk from another major disruption of world oil supplies. Yet it must also be acknowledged that the reflagging of Kuwaiti oil tankers amounted to a de facto military alliance between the United States and Iraq. While Kuwait was not a declared party to the war, it also was not an innocent bystander. It was, after all, providing billions of dollars in financing to Iraq.[60]

At the same time, the U.S. provision of intelligence data to Iraq was increasing. The United States had identified weaknesses in Iraq's defenses and had learned of apparent Iranian plans to strike at them. As early as June 1982, the United States had offered Iraq satellite intelligence of its vulnerabilities and had even dispatched an intelligence officer to Baghdad to ensure that the images were fully understood. This had been the prelude to President Reagan's signing in 1984 of a national security directive formally authorizing a "limited intelligence-sharing program with Iraq." The information the United States thereafter supplied included satellite reconnaissance photographs of strategic Iranian sites for targeting bombing raids, data on Iranian air force and troop positions gathered from U.S.-manned AWACS based in Saudi Arabia, and communications intercepts. This intelligence sharing was to have tragic consequences. John Simpson, then the BBC's foreign affairs editor, who covered the Gulf War from Baghdad, wrote:

> By the beginning of 1987, if not before, American satellite and radar intelligence was being handed to Iraq in considerable quantities and the United States had become an active if secret partner in Iraq's battle against Iran. American intelligence officers plotted the movements of Iranian troops and planes and passed the information on to Iraq. According to an officer who served with them, two American warships, the USS *Stark* and her sister ship *Coontz* had the task of radioing the co-ordinates of targets which American intelligence officers themselves recommended to the Iraqis and guiding them on to the attack. On 17 May 1987 two Exocet missiles from an Iraqi Air Force Mirage homed in accidentally on the radio beam from the *Stark* which was directing the pilot to his target. Following the beam down, they struck the *Stark* amidships, killing 37 American crewmen and injuring dozens of others.[61]

The CIA played a key role in this provision of information, and both Bill Casey and Robert Gates were closely involved. John Simpson was one observer who felt that Iraq's newfound success at the front in early 1988 was facilitated by U.S. intelligence:

> On 17 April 1988, having spent most of the war on the defensive and refusing to attack even when the opportunity arose, the Iraqi army stormed the Faw Peninsula which two years previously had been captured by Iran. The Iranian positions were thinly manned by old men and reservists; it seemed remarkable at the time that the Iraqis, whose intelligence had never been very good, should have chosen their moment so well. In May the Iraqis recaptured land around Basra which had cost Iran 70,000 casualties during three weeks' bitter fighting the previous year. Again the Iraqis chose their moment with extraordinary perception and the battle lasted only seven hours.[62]

Even as late as 16 May 1990, the State Department's Near East and South Asia section produced an "Options Paper on Iraq," which revealed that Iraq was still in receipt of U.S. intelligence: "Intelligence exchanges have waned since the Gulf war cease-fire. PRO: They still provide Iraq with limited information on Iranian military activity that would be missed. CON: Ending this contact would close off our very limited access to this important segment of the Iraqi establishment." Previously, the Senate Intelligence Committee had been given the impression that such intelligence sharing had come to a halt with the end of the Iran-Iraq War.[63]

This level of assistance necessitated a degree of revisionism on the part of leading figures in the Reagan and Bush administrations following the Iraqi invasion of Kuwait. As Teicher noted: "During testimony before the House Foreign Affairs Committee in 1987, Weinberger boasted of the extensive assistance the United States was providing to Iraq. But when questioned in late 1991 about the support given to Iraq, prior to its 1990 invasion of Kuwait, Weinberger categorically denied that the United States had helped Iraq in any significant way."[64]

Hence, during the war years, the U.S. tilt was complete. While Operation Staunch aimed to prevent Iran from acquiring much-needed arms (notwithstanding the Iran-Contra initiative), the United States provided battlefield intelligence to the Iraqis (at a cost measured in American lives); encouraged allies to arm Iraq; permitted the export of dual-use goods, despite knowing that they were destined for weapons establishments (discussed below); and increased both the value of ccc loans to Iraq and U.S. oil purchases from Iraq. After the war, this relationship continued. It was given its highest expression in NSD-26, the national security directive signed by President George Bush in October 1989. This outlined the principles governing the Bush administration's approach to Iraq and effectively also delineated the rationale underlying the policy of successive administrations since at least 1983. It also illustrated how far U.S. policy toward the Gulf was still dominated by the cold war framework of the Nixon Doctrine. The released version, partly blacked out, reads:

> Access to Persian Gulf oil and the security of key friendly states in the area are vital to U.S. national security. The United States remains committed to defend its vital interests in the region, if necessary and appropriate through the use of U.S. military force, against the Soviet Union or any other regional power with interests inimical to our own. The United States also remains committed to support the individual and collective self-defense of friendly countries in the area to enable them to play

a more active role in their own defense and thereby reduce the necessity for unilateral U.S. military intervention. The United States also will encourage the effective support and participation of our western allies and Japan to promote our mutual interests in the Persian Gulf region.
(section blacked out)

Iraq
Normal relations between the United States and Iraq would serve our longer-term interests and promote stability in both the Gulf and the Middle East. The United States Government should propose economic and political incentives for Iraq to moderate its behavior and to increase our influence with Iraq. At the same time, the Iraqi leadership must understand that any illegal use of chemical and/or biological weapons will lead to economic and political sanctions, for which we would seek the broadest possible support from our allies and friends. Any breach by Iraq of IAEA [International Atomic Energy Authority] safeguards in its nuclear program will result in a similar response. Human rights considerations should continue to be an important element in our policy toward Iraq. In addition, Iraq should be urged to cease its meddling in external affairs, such as in Lebanon, and be encouraged to play a conservative role in negotiating a settlement with Iran and cooperating in the Middle East peace process.

We should pursue and seek to facilitate, opportunities for US firms to participate in the reconstruction of the Iraqi economy, particularly in the energy area, where they do not conflict with our non-proliferation and other significant objectives. Also, as a means of developing access to and influence with the Iraqi defense establishment, the United States should consider sales of non-lethal forms of military assistance, e.g., training courses and medical exchanges, on a case by case basis.

◆ The United States and Dual-Use License Applications

A further plank of U.S. policy toward Iraq under the Reagan and Bush administrations was the approval of licenses for the export of dual-use equipment to Iraq, even where the destination was known to be involved in military work. This was also an important device used by the British government, as well as by other European countries such as West Germany and Switzerland. In this respect, March 1985 is a further significant date in the United States–Iraqi relationship. This was when high-technology/dual-use export license applications, which up until this point had generally been refused, began to be regularly approved.[65] The approvals did not occur without some opposition being voiced, but ultimately the decision reflected the administration's view that there would be no Iraqi nuclear weapons program for the foreseeable future, and so proliferation concerns (which, as with Britain, did not apply to the acquisition of conventional arms or arms-making technology) should not be allowed to stand in the way of more immediate strategic objectives. A new national security directive was issued "enjoining all government agencies 'to be more forthcoming' on Iraqi license requests."[66] In the last two years of the Reagan administration, only 6 out of 247 license applications for dual-use equipment were refused. As Congressman Henry Gonzalez charged:

> During the period 1985–1990, the Reagan and Bush Administrations approved 771 export licences for Iraq—239 of these approvals came from the Bush Administration. Much of the equipment shipped to Iraq under these licenses ended up enhancing Iraq's military capability . . . The Bush Administration was acutely aware of Iraq's intentions, and knew that the financial assistance it was providing to Iraq facilitated Saddam Hussein's ambitious military industrialization effort.[67]

An Iraqi tactic designed to enable Western states inclined to support it and to deceive others was to combine both military and civilian projects in the same complex. This made it difficult to prove that dual-use goods ordered for a civilian program at a complex would be diverted to a military program there. Where absolute proof rather than likelihood of occurrence was the measure used in deciding on export licensing for Iraq, as it was in both the United States and Britain, this Iraqi strategy provided the perfect alibi for the Iraqi, the U.S., and British governments. Henry Gonzalez compiled a list illustrating how, under this approach, all of Iraq's most important military centers had acquired U.S. dual-use equipment (see table 2.3).

Of these establishments, nine (Nassr, Badr, Saddam, SAAD 16, Salah al Din, Al QaQa, Hutteen, Al Qadisiyah, and Al Yarmuk) received BNL-Atlanta money. In addition, in 1989 three employees from Al QaQa were allowed to take part in a U.S. government–sponsored conference on nuclear detonation held in Portland, Oregon.

The Bush administration also approved export licenses for Gerald Bull's Space Research Corporation (SRC) to export high-tech computers and missile design software to Iraq,[68] after the State Department had been briefed by SRC personnel on its proposed activities in Iraq. These were then used by Bull and SRC to design the projectiles to be fired from the supergun and its more overtly military successor programs (see chapter 4), and in Iraq's SCUD modification program. The computers (two Iris Super 380 computers) and software package (ANSYS),[69] which cost $161,080, were also used in the design

Table 2.3

Major Iraqi Weapons Facilities Receiving U.S. Export Licenses

Establishment	Details
Nassr State Establishment for Mechanical Industries	Major player in nuclear weapons program; production of modified SCUD missiles and components; other ballistic missiles, conventional bombs, etc.
Badr General Establishment	Nuclear weapons program—development and testing of centrifuges.
Saddam State Establishment	Work on Condor II ballistic missile, nuclear weapons program, long-range guns, assembly of tanks, and other weapons-related activities.
Al Kindi Research Complex (formerly SAAD 16)	Main missile research center in Iraq; work on nuclear weapons program.
Salah al Din State Establishment	Iraq's major electronics complex. Military communications and guidance systems, radar, work for missile programs and other weapons programs.
Al QaQa State Establishment	Iraq's major explosives and rocket fuel factory. Filling station for ballistic missiles, work on Condor II ballistic missile, nuclear weapons program, and explosives for conventional bombs.
Hutteen State Establishment	Test site for Condor II ballistic missiles, nuclear weapons program, conventional weapons production.
Al Qadisiyah State Enterprise for Electrical Industries	Nuclear program; supergun.
Al Yarmuk State Establishment	Conventional weapons production, including mortars and small arms.
Auqba Bin Nafi State Establishment	Nuclear weapons program—machining of components for centrifuges; repair and production of tank parts.
Al Atheer, Tarmiyah, Al Tuwaitha Nuclear Research Center	Main complexes involved in secret nuclear weapons program. Prime development and testing site for various parts of nuclear weapons program.
Samarra, Salman Pak, Muthena, Al Qaim	Major production of chemical and biological weapons.

of the Al Abid rocket, which was "successfully" launched into space in December 1989, as well as the armored vehicles that carried the 155mm and 210mm self-propelled guns src was developing for Iraq. As Henry Gonzalez later explained:

> The export licenses for the computer and software were approved despite State Department knowledge that the Space Research Corporation was engaged in numerous military projects in Iraq and that Space Research and one of its affiliates had been identified in 1989 as important players in Iraq's military technology procurement apparatus. In fact, the US firm that received the license to sell the software to Space Research clearly informed the Commerce Department that the software could be used for missile and satellite design and other military uses. The end user for the computer was listed as the Al Qadisiyah State Enterprise. Prior to the license being approved the cia had identified this establishment as a weapons manufacturing complex. The end user for the software was listed as the Space Research Corporation of Belgium.[70]

Despite this and further evidence uncovered by the House Committee on Banking, Finance, and Urban Affairs investigation,[71] the report President Bush was obliged to compile on the U.S. contribution to the arming of Iraq as a provision of his belated Iraq Sanctions Act of 1990,[72] signed on 5 November, cleared the United States of any direct involvement and laid the blame for the arming of Iraq on European complicity. It concluded: "Reflecting both the US Government policy and responsible sales practices by American firms, United States suppliers did not contribute directly to Iraq's conventional or nonconventional weapons capability."[73] As Henry Gonzalez commented: "This claim is patently false. While there is no doubt that European firms provided Saddam Hussein with dangerous technology, that fact neither eliminates nor excuses the fact that US firms, at the urging of the Administration, played a considerable role in arming Iraq."[74]

◆ **BNL**

Another way in which the United States facilitated the arming of Iraq lay in the activities of the hitherto anonymous Atlanta, Georgia, branch of bnl. On 4 August 1989, just one year before the Iraqi invasion of Kuwait, the fbi raided the Atlanta branch. They discovered what was, until overtaken by the bcci (Bank of Credit and Commerce International) case, the most substantial case of bank fraud in U.S. history. Not only had the Atlanta branch, managed by the resourceful Christopher Drogoul, extended $270 million in CCC-backed credits to Iraq, it had also extended a further unauthorized $4 billion, largely in the form of unsecured loans.

Founded in 1913, with 424 branches worldwide, BNL was Italy's largest bank. The Atlanta branch was opened in 1982 and initially lost money. But when Drogoul was appointed in 1984, he transformed its fortunes through his approach to the CCC program. The secret of his success lay in the fact that he would offer very low interest rates—as low as .0625 percent above LIBOR (London Inter Bank Offering Rate), while using BNL's AAA bond rating (a rating only one American bank had) to borrow short-term at or below LIBOR. As a result, by 1985 BNL-Atlanta had 20 percent of the Iraqi CCC program. By 1987 it had 92 percent, by which time senior BNL figures in Rome were calling Drogoul "Mr. CCC."[75]

Official BNL policy at the time was to limit the bank's exposure on CCC lending to any single customer to just $100 million. Hence, when Iraq had reached this limit, and Drogoul had gone on to agree to an additional $556 million CCC-backed line of credit, he had contacted Rome and requested an increase in allowable exposure to cover his actions. This request was turned down, largely as a consequence of the ongoing dispute between the Italian and Iraqi governments over Iraqi payments on a $2.65 billion naval contract.[76] Hence, to conceal the full extent of his dealings with Iraq, Drogoul began to remove the amount of the Iraqi loan exposure from the monthly reports he was required to make to Rome, return this sum to the books the following day, and remove it again for his next report. As the branch's involvement deepened, the manner in which it was concealed had to be altered. As Drogoul recalled: "We went from not showing the loans one day to not showing them on any day."[77] This was Drogoul's "gray book" scheme, whereby all Iraqi loans were moved to a secret, parallel set of accounts. Jentleson summarized the importance of BNL-Atlanta to the Iraqi weapons program thus:

> The CIA estimated that at least $600 million of the BNL money was used for the acquisition and development of weapons technology . . . [including] about $53 million worth of technology and machinery for the Condor-II missile. BNL-Atlanta also financed numerous exports by European companies of equipment for nuclear centrifuges and other nuclear machines and materials, for the Condor-II missile, for SCUD missile enhancements, for the short-range Ababel rocket, for 210- and 155mm howitzers, for military night vision equipment, for the artillery fuse factory, and for numerous other weapons systems. Matrix Churchill was involved in many

of these, and BNL even made a $600,000 direct loan to Matrix Churchill for the company's own operating expenses.[78]

But how far had this been the outcome of an unaccountable and undetected rogue operation, as portrayed by the U.S. government? Certainly Drogoul's activities were an open secret in the banking world and had not escaped the attention of BNL-Rome. In dealing with Matrix Churchill in the United Kingdom (see chapter 7), and holding meetings with Matrix Churchill officials in London, BNL-Atlanta officials would have come within the scrutiny of an intelligence operation designed to keep an eye on the Iraqi-owned company and its directors—particularly Dr. Safa al-Habobi, known to be an official of Iraqi intelligence. Did the U.S. government also know what BNL-Atlanta was up to but allow it to continue because its actions, although illegal, were consistent with U.S. policy aims? After all, the affair came to light only because a tip-off from within the branch triggered off an FBI raid. It is certainly possible that the British intelligence source within Matrix Churchill at the time (Mark Gutteridge) could have been debriefed on the company's relationship with BNL during his numerous sessions with MI5. Information gained from him was used in a November 1989 CIA report on the repercussions of BNL.[79] In September 1992, Henry Gonzalez criticized the U.S. government's presentation of the BNL affair and considered this possibility:

From the very beginning, the Justice Department pursued the theory that BNL-Atlanta was a rogue operation that defrauded BNL-Rome. As it happens, this is politically a very convenient theory. . . . But the problem with the rogue bank theory is that it seems highly improbable that a tiny office in Atlanta could loan more than $5 billion to Iraq without some level of knowledge or assent from higher authority—namely BNL's headquarters in Rome.[80]

A CIA report prepared for Gonzalez in 1991 suggested that BNL-Rome must have known about the activities of BNL-Atlanta. It revealed that while Iraq had initially been willing to accept loans signed just by a BNL-Atlanta official, it later came to require authorization from BNL-Rome as the value of the loans gradually increased.[81] According to the CIA report: "BNL agreed to this request and the loans were then signed by bank officers in Rome."[82] On the CIA, Gonzalez argued: "While the intelligence community has remained silent on what it knew about BNL's activities prior to the raid on BNL-Atlanta in August 1989, it is safe to assume that it would have been highly unusual for our intelligence community not to have noticed thousands of communications between Iraq's highest profile military organisations and BNL in Atlanta, Georgia . . ."[83] This had also been a theme of testimony Drogoul gave to Congress in 1993. Before being jailed for thirty-seven months, Drogoul told Congress that U.S. government officials and BNL executives in Rome (named by Drogoul as Giacomo Pedde and Angelo Florio) had approved of his lending. He also cited a dinner held in Washington in October 1988, which he attended alongside U.S. and Iraqi government officials. There, he said, he heard the Iraqis being advised to sign up for further loan guarantees quickly, because "if Dukakis defeats Bush, the Democrats will cut you off." Drogoul claimed that BNL-Atlanta "was no more and no less than a tool of the U.S. government" and that Iraqi central bank officials had told him he had nothing to worry about "because [they had] been working with the CIA and U.S. intelligence for a number of years."[84] This impression was not entirely dispelled by Judge Marvin Shoob. In handing down sentences to four other BNL-Atlanta defendants, Shoob described them as "pawns or bit players in a far larger and wider-ranging sophisticated conspiracy that involved BNL-Rome and possibly large American and foreign corporations, and the governments of the United States, England, Italy and Iraq." He said the four defendants had been merely "functionaries" in a scheme that "furthered the foreign policy of the United States and Italy."[85]

◆ Postwar Relations with Iraq

Why did the United States continue to foster close relations with Iraq, even after the cease-fire in the Iran-Iraq War? There are a number of reasons. First, it did so to reassert its credibility after the exposure of the Iran-Contra scheme. Furthermore, because of the Iran-Contra revelations, any move toward Iran was politically impossible for the Reagan and Bush administrations. If the United States wanted a second pillar, it had no option but to continue to foster closer relations with Iraq.

Second, by the end of the war Iraq had become an important market for U.S. agricultural produce. It was the twelfth-largest market for U.S. agricultural exports and was second only to Mexico as a recipient of CCC credits. Another development was that during the course of the tilt toward Iraq, the United States had become a major customer for Iraqi oil. In 1981 the United States did not import any oil from Iraq. During 1987 it imported 30 million barrels. In 1988 this figure rocketed to 126 million barrels—one in every four barrels Iraq exported that year.[86]

Third, the loosening of export controls had contributed toward increased exports of U.S. manufactured goods, and billions of dollars worth of contracts had been signed covering contracts for steel, petrochemicals, and electricity generation. Collectively, these groups now formed a powerful lobby in the form of the U.S.-Iraq Business Forum,[87] opposed to any moves that would damage commercial ties with Iraq. For instance, if sanctions were applied in light of human rights abuses (for example over the use of poison gas at Halabja), markets would be lost and, worse still, U.S. companies—at this point in time ideally placed—would lose out on the anticipated postwar reconstruction bonanza just getting under way.

Finally, the original rationale continued to act as a constraint as well. Before Iraq had been an important market, it had been of strategic importance. Maintaining influence and persuading Iraq to remain (just) within the "family of nations" was a priority. Trade was just one expression of this policy, it was not the reason for it. The trade element had been one part of the wider political strategy. It flowed from it, but was never intended to dictate it.

These interests led State Department analysts to view postwar Iraqi intentions through the prism of U.S. aspirations for Iraq, which were governed by the "family of nations" principle.[88] This was a fatal form of self-delusion. Iraq was less interested in a sincere relationship than a marriage of convenience. A good example of this self-delusion can be found in a March 1988 memo, which erroneously (with hindsight, almost comically) identified various indicators that Iraq was moving further into the mainstream of the international community. These included the following points:

> In the likely case that the Iran-Iraq war ends in an armed truce rather than a peace treaty or a decisive victory, Iraq will be vulnerable, hence unlikely to embark on foreign adventures in the Gulf or against Israel.
> Iraq has developed good working relations with Kuwait and is no longer trying to encroach on Kuwaiti territory.
> Fears of Iraqi aggression seem exaggerated.[89]

As previously, reaching these conclusions involved minimizing the impact of behavior contrary to the trend identified as the dominant one, including the issue of Iraqi use of poison gas on the Kurds. During a debate on the wisdom of applying sanctions in light of these atrocities, the State Department argued that sanctions would "undermine relations and reduce US influence on a country that has emerged from the Gulf War as one of the most powerful Arab nations."[90] It could have added that this power was military, that it represented a threat to Iraq's neighbors, and that Iraq had assumed this position only through Western assistance, particularly in the field of arms and dual-use technology supply.

Were there no warning signals? If there were, why were they not acted upon? Some in the State Department did recognize the potential danger Iraq now represented. George Schultz claims:

> I came to regard Iraq, once again, as one of the enemy states of the responsible world community. By the end of the Reagan years, after our reflagging policy had turned the Gulf War [Iran-Iraq War] toward its conclusion, it was clear to me that no further reason existed for the United States to give Iraq the benefit of the doubt for balance-of-power purposes against Iran.[91]

The kind of balance-of-power considerations that had led the United States and the West to support Iraq so as to prevent it from being defeated during the war should now have dictated that they aim to contain Iraq, although in retrospect this could have proved fatal, as the damage had already been done in terms of facilitating Iraqi nonconventional weapons programs. Zalmay Khalilzad of the Policy Planning Staff wrote in 1988: "US interests in the Gulf have changed dramatically in the past two years. Where stability once rested on keeping Iran's relative strength in check by preventing it from defeating Iraq and exporting revolution, it is now based on bolstering an economically and militarily strained Iran from Iraqi exploitation."[92]

This classic balance-of-power prescription could not, however, be taken up by the United States because Iran had been so demonized, and the Reagan administration so heavily compromised by Iran-Contra, that it had little room to maneuver if it was to try to sustain its twin pillars approach to the region. Because normalizing relations with Iran was unthinkable for a president who had done so much publicly to stigmatize its leadership at the time of the hostages saga (and George Bush suffered here too as candidate and then vice president) and whose covert dealings with Iran had then come back to haunt him, Iraq was the only option. Hence, human rights considerations could not be allowed to intrude. The loss of Iraq would leave the United States without influence in the upper Gulf, shatter the twin pillars strategy, and increase the vulnerability of Saudi Arabia and the smaller Gulf states.

However, by 1989–1990, a relationship sustained partly by an image of Iraq as a significant market for U.S. commerce now faced a situation where Saddam's ambition had transformed Iraq into a debtor nation that was no longer able to afford its ambition (although this message had yet to sink home in Baghdad, as it pursued fresh lines of credit, albeit with diminishing success). In April 1990, at what was effectively the end of the West's fling with Saddam, the CIA summarized the transformation in Iraq's economic fortunes thus:

> Iraq's extensive use of foreign loans since 1982 has transformed it from one of the Third World's richest countries and net creditors into one of its problem debtors. The accumulation of debt stems from President Saddam Husayn's [sic] decision to continue pursuing an ambitious economic development program despite the outbreak of war with Iran in 1980. Iraq boosted civilian spending while military expenditures rose and oil exports fell sharply because of the war. This "guns and butter" policy rapidly drained Iraq's foreign assets from $36 billion in 1980 to $7 billion in 1982 . . . We estimate Iraq's foreign debt increased from $5–6 billion—mostly short-term trade credits—before the war to about $45 billion by the end of 1989. Its Persian Gulf allies provided an additional $37 billion in wartime financial assistance, mostly oil sold on Baghdad's behalf that is unlikely to be repaid.[93]

It went on to record how Iraq regarded debt servicing as a lower priority than maintaining its high level of military spending, which was (and this was the background to the Matrix Churchill case) by this time turning increasingly to the development of an indigenous arms-manufacturing capability. Hence, during 1989 Iraq held discussions that enabled it to reschedule the almost $2 billion it owed to France, West Germany, and Italy and used oil to repay several other creditor states (including Brazil, Japan, and Yugoslavia) rather than use up scarce foreign exchange. Creditor states tended not to object openly to Iraqi rescheduling plans, given that they tended to be net oil importers and Iraq sat on the second-largest known oil reserves in the world. However, repayment of debts to the United States still tended to remain on schedule—a reflection of the crucial importance of the CCC program to Baghdad.

October 1989's national security directive, NSD-26, was the logical outcome of U.S. and Western strategy toward both Iran and Iraq during their eight-year war. The basic premise was that a friendly Iraq could be brought into the "family of nations" (a euphemism for U.S. and Western hegemony) and would then protect U.S. and Western interests in the Gulf region, as U.S. and Iraqi interests would become one and the same thing. Steps toward bringing Iraq into the Western circle had begun with the support it received during the war with Iran to ensure that it was not defeated. However, greater incentives were required in the postwar climate of reconstruction to make sure that Iraq—a stubborn and difficult ally, as the Soviet Union had discovered—signed up. These incentives took the form of facilitating a wide-ranging trade with Iraq, part of which was in the high-tech area of dual-use and military equipment through which Iraq intended to construct an indigenous Third World weapons industry. The problem was that once it had done this, it would no longer have to rely on what it considered alliances of convenience with the United States or the Soviet Union to maintain a weapons flow. It would be able to act truly independently.

Hence, the West's logic was seriously flawed in at least three respects. First, Iraq could never truly be drawn into the international community, because that was never its real intention or goal. Its apparent interest in better relations with the United States and the West was purely a consequence of its desire to obtain advanced technology. The U.S. government was engaging in a self-deception. It seemed to believe that, because it sought to bring Iraq into the world "family," Iraq would automatically welcome this, and that every subsequent apparent advance in this direction was progress toward this inevitable goal, while every Iraqi excess could be explained away as being no more than a tolerable deviation from the path that led inexorably toward the Western orbit.

Second, the need to provide additional postwar incentives created a significant pro-Iraq lobby across a number of sectors in the United States and Western Europe. The existence of this lobby made it more difficult to make a clean break with Iraq when the realization that Saddam Hussein had intended a marriage of convenience rather than a sincere international relationship finally, undeniably, began to hit home. Nowhere is this better illustrated than in the Matrix Churchill saga.[94]

Third, just as Iraq's nonconventional aspirations became more apparent (or could no longer be ignored) in 1989 and early 1990, and just as the State Department and the Department of Defense (DOD) were starting to pull back and advise against licensing for destinations like Nassr, NSD-26 came along and produced a contradictory tension between its rejoinder to increase trade with Iraq on the one hand and fears over missile and nuclear proliferation on the other. In this contest, NSD-26 proved the winner. One case in particular illustrates this well. On 12 February 1990, the State Department sent a "secret" cable to various U.S. embassies[95] to alert them to Iraq's nonconventional procurement activities and to urge them specifically not to export carbon and glass fiber technology to Nassr. The cable informed the embassies that companies in their countries possessed this technology and went on to note: "A number of companies in the US manufacture these items: the

USG is exercising special caution to ensure that those companies are aware that a license is required for their export. Those companies are also being told that, given US policy, licenses for the export to Iraq of these particular items would not be granted." Yet just three months later, on 30 May 1990, the Commerce Department informed Matrix Churchill (Cleveland, Ohio) that it did not even need an export license to send "equipment to be used to control a glass fiber production line with a capacity of 15 tons a day" to Iraq's Technical Corporation for Special Projects (TECO), even though it knew that Matrix Churchill, Ohio, was effectively an Iraqi front company that made machines to make (amongst other things) missile casings and that TECO was involved in missile projects.

The way in which NSD-26 overpowered all other considerations can also be seen in the debate within the Bush administration over the level of CCC credits for Iraq for 1990. The Department of Agriculture had proposed an additional $1 billion line of credit. At a meeting on 3 October 1989

The Treasury desk officer for Iraq, noting that the CCC and the US and UK export financing agencies were the only official credit institutions open in Iraq, said that Iraq's international creditworthiness was very low. . . . He continued by saying that it was well known in the international financial community that Iraq only paid those creditors from which it received new credits and, viewed in this manner, the CCC could be contributing to a Ponzi-type scheme.[96]

However, the State Department argued in favor, on the basis that "Iraq had great strategic importance to the United States."[97]

Three days later, on 6 October, Secretary of State James Baker met with Tariq Aziz. Aziz gave various assurances to Baker: "Iraq has said clearly that it wants to maintain the whole region intact—including the individual countries—and that it has no bad intentions against any of them. [Aziz] stressed that Iraq's objective was and is good relations with them all, particularly Saudi Arabia and Kuwait."[98] The Bush administration needed to believe this for its policy to have any logic. It did. The die was cast. Less than ten months later, Iraq invaded Kuwait.

NOTES

1 H. and G. R. Teicher: *Twin Pillars*, pp. 64–66. "As with Iraq's later invasion of Kuwait in August 1990, the fundamental rationale for Saddam's invasion of Iran in September 1980 was to take over Iran's oil and thereby wield the financial and political power that flowed from it."

2 G. Sick: *October Surprise*, p. 42.

3 H. and G. R. Teicher: *Twin Pillars*, p. 103. Also, on the idea of a U.S. "green light" for the invasion, see G. Sick: *October Surprise*, passim. However, in a letter to the *Wall Street Journal* dated 6.18.91, Zbigniew Brzezinski wrote: "It is . . . false to suggest that the Carter administration in any fashion whatsoever, directly or indirectly, encouraged Iraq to undertake a military adventure against Iran." Sick, op. cit., p. 254.

4 Anthony H. Cordesman: *The Iran-Iraq War and Western Security, 1984–87*, London, Jane's, 1987, p. 20.

5 It is not the intention of the present work to provide a blow-by-blow account of the Iran-Iraq War. For detailed studies see, for example, D. Hiro: *The Longest War*; Efraim Karsh: *The Iran-Iraq War: A Military Analysis*, Adelphi Papers, London, IISS, 1987; and Shahram Chubin and Charles Tripp: *Iran and Iraq at War*, London, I. B. Taurus, 1988.

6 Kenneth R. Timmerman: *The Death Lobby: How the West Armed Iraq*, London, Fourth Estate, 1992, p. 152.

7 Herbert Krosney: *Deadly Business: Legal Deals and Outlaw Weapons—The Arming of Iran and Iraq, 1975 to the Present*, New York, Four Walls Eight Windows, 1993, pp. 140–141.

8 This possibility was raised by the persistent Lt. Col. Glazebrook within the U.K. regulatory machinery. See Scott Inquiry—Day 39: Evidence of Alan Barrett, p. 45.

9 Chris Cowley: *Guns, Lies and Spies*, London, Hamish Hamilton, 1992, p. 107.

10 Iraq's director general of information was quoted as asking: "Should we wait for arms to be sent from other states? The only solution to the threat to our very existence is to establish our own military industry and to provide our armed forces with Iraqi arms." *Financial Times*, 9.11.89. See also the *Financial Times*, 9.9.89. There are indications that even prior to the outbreak of war, Iraq intended to take this route, largely in response to the shah's attempts to establish an indigenous Iranian arms industry with U.S. and U.K. assistance.

11 Although the figures gloss over the illegality that often accompanied the arming and do not include certain states that acted as conduits, they do indicate clearly the global reach of Iranian and Iraqi procurement operations, the political interest in the war's outcome, and of course the enormous profits to be made selling arms to warring parties regardless of national or international restrictions.

12 Cited in the *Independent*, 9.30.95.

13 M. Brzoska and T. Ohlson: *Arms Transfers to the Third World, 1971–85*, p. 17.

14 For a useful perspective on Soviet thinking, see Jerrold D. Green: The Soviet Union, the Persian Gulf, and the Iran-Iraq War, in Edward A. Kolodziej and Roger E. Kanet (eds): *The Limits of Soviet Power in the Developing World*, Basingstoke, Macmillan, 1989, pp. 255–274. See also Alexander J. Bennett: Arms Transfers as an Instrument of Soviet Policy in the Middle East, *Middle East Journal*, Vol. 39 No. 4 1985, pp. 745–774.

15 In the summer of 1990, the CIA noted how "Iraq's desire for a large arms industry has grown during the past decade. President Saddam Hussein apparently believes an expanded arms industry will enhance Iraqi prestige and help solve security problems identified during the war such as lack of reliable arms suppliers." Quoted by Henry B. Gonzalez: *Bush Administration Had Acute Knowledge of Iraq's Military Industrialization Plans*—Floor Statement, 7.27.92, p. 5.

16 Ibid. A June 1989 Eximbank Report illustrated the intensity of this effort in revealing that in 1988 Iraq spent a massive 42 percent of its oil revenue on military-related procurement.

17 Bob Woodward: *Veil—The Secret Wars of the* CIA, 1981–87, London, Headline, 1988, p. 181. On the attack, see Amos Perlmutter, Michael Handel, and Uri Bar-Joseph: *Two Minutes over Baghdad*, London, Corgi, 1982.

18 *Guardian*, 9.13.83.

19 *Flight International*, 9.21.85.

20 K. Timmerman: *The Death Lobby*, p. 337.

21 As mentioned in note 11, the shortcomings of data of this kind brought about by Iraqi modes of acquisition are obvious. While they indicate something of the global nature of the Iraqi arms procurement operation, the data are quantitative and not qualitative. They offer no indication of usefulness as a conduit, do not consider dual-use equipment or deals worth less than US$1 million—of particular importance since one element of Iraq's twin-track procurement policy was to create the basis for an indigenous Iraqi arms industry—and of course cannot take account of covert procurement operations, some because of their secrecy, some because dual-use items were represented as being intended for a civilian application when in reality they were for military use.

22 For more details of the West German contribution and the Iraqi chemical weapons program, see K. Timmerman: *The Death Lobby*; H. Krosney: *Deadly Business*; and Adel Darwish and "Gregory Alexander": *Unholy Babylon—The Secret History of Saddam's War*, London, Victor Gollancz, 1991.

23 *International Herald Tribune*, 11.1.80. On West German arms export regulations, see Herbert Wulf: The Federal Republic of Germany, in I. Anthony (ed.): *Arms Export Regulations*, Oxford, OUP/SIPRI, 1992, pp. 72–85.

24 The involvement of German companies in the Iraqi chemical weapons program has been followed quite closely by *Der Spiegel*. See, for example, articles in the 8 October 1990 issue.

25 Ironically, MBB is owned by Daimler-Benz, in which Kuwait holds a 14 percent stake.

26 *Der Spiegel*, 8.27.90, p. 99.

27 Jochen Hippler: Iraq's Military Power—The German Connection, *Middle East Report*, Jan–Feb 1991, p. 30.

28 A. Darwish and "G. Alexander": *Unholy Babylon*, p. 146.

29 *Economist*, 9.7.91, p. 92.

30 On the Swiss role, see *Dispatches*: The Swiss Connection, Channel 4, 11.13.91.

31 *Independent on Sunday*, 8.26.90. The report noted that Cardoen "is one of the richest men in Chile. He lives in a mansion in Santiago where the walls are said to be lined with silk, has his own army, and runs one of the biggest private arms companies in Latin America. He is probably worth $400m."

32 At the Scott Inquiry, Foreign Office Minister William Waldegrave was asked whether Iraq's support for terrorism had not been a barrier to good relations with the United Kingdom:
A: Yes, there had been terrorism, but they had not supported terrorism against us. . . .
Q: Had there not been an assassination in this country?
A: Some time ago, but they had, as far as I remember, expelled somebody subsequent to that. They had assassinated what they regarded as their own people.
Q: In this country?
A: And we had a man in jail for it.
Scott Inquiry—Day 30: Evidence of William Waldegrave, p. 149.

33 H. and G. R. Teicher: *Twin Pillars*, p. 61. See ch. 2 on the first indications of a tilt toward Iraq.

34 *New York Times*, 5.5.80. Quoted in Bruce W. Jentleson: *With Friends like These: Reagan, Bush, and Saddam 1982–1990*, New York, W. W. Norton, 1994, p. 34.

35 Ibid., p. 15.
36 Seymour Hersh, cited in Murray Waas and Craig Ungar: In the Loop: Bush's Secret Mission, *New Yorker*, 11.2.92, p. 67.
37 Anthony Cordesman cites deliveries from Israel to Iran of 360 tons of spare parts for U.S. tanks; various arms captured from the PLO in the 1982 invasion of Lebanon; at least 500 TOW missiles; and a range of ammunition including 100,000 155mm shells, 150,000 203 mm shells, 50,000 105mm shells, and 100,000 rounds of 106mm rifle shells—all between 1982 and 1985. Anthony Cordesman: Arms to Iran—The Impact of U.S. and Other Arms Sales on the Iran-Iraq War, *American-Arab Affairs*, Spring 1987, p. 22.
38 M. Waas and C. Ungar: In the Loop, p. 67.
39 H. and G. R. Teicher: *Twin Pillars*, p. 330.
40 This latter move was mainly motivated by the 23 October 1983 suicide bombing of the U.S. Marine barracks in Beirut by Shia militants, in which 259 U.S. service personnel were killed.
41 *New York Times*, 1.26.92. See also the *Washington Post*, 2.20.87.
42 *New York Times*, 1.26.92.
43 On the U.S. role in the *USS Stark* incident, see John Simpson: *From the House of War*, London, Arrow, 1991, pp. 44–45. On the U.S. tilt, see A. Friedman: *Spider's Web*, passim, and D. Hiro: *The Longest War*.
44 Cited in D. Hiro: *The Longest War*, p. 121.
45 Quoted in Kenneth R. Timmerman: Europe's Arms Pipeline to Iran, *The Nation*, 7.18/25.87, p. 47.
46 Cited in A. Cordesman: Arms to Iran, p. 19.
47 M. Waas and C. Ungar: In the Loop, p. 70.
48 B. W. Jentleson: *With Friends like These*, p. 45.
49 See A. Friedman: *Spider's Web*, pp. 81–84.
50 A detailed account of this can be found in P. Mantius: *Shell Game*. See also A. Friedman: *Spider's Web*.
51 *U.S. News and World Report*, 5.18.92, p. 43. On the CCC program, see also Murray Waas and Douglas Frantz's articles in the *Los Angeles Times*, esp. 2.25.92 (Loans: U.S. Gave Help to Baghdad in Arms Build-Up), and 7.22.92 (Abuses in Iraqi Aid Program Overlooked); and Dean Baquet: Documents Charge Pre-War Iraqi Swap: U.S. Food for Arms, *New York Times*, 4.27.92.
52 CIA: *Iraq: No End in Sight to Debt Burden*, 4.12.90, p. 5.
53 Scott Inquiry—Day 5: Evidence of Lt. Col. Glazebrook, p. 27.
54 H. and G. R. Teicher: *Twin Pillars*, p. 275.
55 *Guardian*, 3.12.91.
56 H. and G. R. Teicher: *Twin Pillars*, p. 276.
57 State Department memorandum, cited in B. W. Jentleson: *With Friends like These*, p. 56.
58 According to Defence Intelligence Agency (DIA) operative Lester K. Coleman, as a result of information leaked by the DIA as part of an intelligence turf war. See Donald Goddard and Lester K. Coleman: *Trail of the Octopus: Behind the Lockerbie Disaster*, London, Bloomsbury, 1993, ch. 10.
59 Letter dated 12.12.86, quoted in B. W. Jentleson: *With Friends like These*, p. 60.
60 Ibid., p. 61.
61 John Simpson: *From the House of War*, p. 44.
62 Ibid., p. 41.
63 See U.S. Senate Committee on Intelligence: Nomination of Robert M. Gates to be Director of Intelligence, 10.24.91.
64 H. and G. R. Teicher: *Twin Pillars*, p. 392.
65 K. Timmerman: *The Death Lobby*, p. 202.

66 Ibid., p. 241.

67 Floor Statement of Henry B. Gonzalez, 7.27.92.

68 The export license was approved on 21 September 1989.

69 On this episode, see *Los Angeles Times*, 10.27.92, *Wall Street Journal*, 10.27.92, *U.S. News and World Report*, 11.2.92. The computer was manufactured by Silicon Graphics and the software package by Swanson Analysis Systems, Inc.

70 *U.S. Export Licensing Process Used to Enhance Iraq's Military Capability*—Statement of Henry B. Gonzalez, chair, Committee on Banking, Finance, and Urban Affairs before the Senate Committee on Banking, Housing, and Urban Affairs, 10.27.92, p. 5. As Gonzalez pointed out, this approval was hardly compatible with a State Department press release, 11 February 1991, which stated: "The Department of State has not approved any exports of equipment or technology by Bull or companies associated with Bull to Iraq."

71 House Committee on Banking, Finance and Urban Affairs: *The Banca Nazionale del Lavoro (BNL) Scandal and the Department of Agriculture's Commodity Credit Corporation (CCC) Program for Iraq, Parts I & II*, 5.21.92.

72 The provision required Bush to "conduct a study and report on the sale, export, and third party transfer or development of nuclear, biological, chemical and ballistic missile technology to or with Iraq."

73 Statement of Henry B. Gonzalez, 10.27.92, p. 2.

74 Ibid.

75 Cited in P. Mantius: *Shell Game*, p. 29.

76 See K. Timmerman: *The Death Lobby*, pp. 227–228.

77 A. Friedman: *Spider's Web*, p. 103.

78 B. W. Jentleson: *With Friends like These*, pp. 125–126.

79 Paul Henderson: *The Unlikely Spy: An Autobiography*, London, Bloomsbury, 1993, pp. 171–172.

80 *The Banca Nazionale del Lavoro Scandal—High Level Politics Try to Hide the Evidence:* Statement of Henry B. Gonzalez, chair, Committee on Banking, Finance and Urban Affairs, 9.14.92.

81 On BNL-Rome's state of knowledge, see P. Mantius: *Shell Game*, ch. 8.

82 Ibid.

83 Floor statement of Henry B. Gonzalez, 7.27.92.

84 *Financial Times*, 11.10.93.

85 *Guardian*, 9.10.93.

86 Cited in B. W. Jentleson: *With Friends like These*, pp. 81–82.

87 Members of the U.S.-Iraq Business Forum included Amoco, Mobil, Exxon, Texaco, and Occidental (all involved in importing discounted Iraqi oil) as well as Lockheed, Bell, General Motors, Bechtel, and Caterpillar.

88 This was the phrase used by President Bush on ABC's *Good Morning America* on 28 October 1992. He went on:

The guy that's holding the hearings in the House, Chairman Henry B. Gonzalez, at the time of the war, filed impeachment papers against me, impeaching me as President, not because of any malfeasance but because I committed this country to do the right thing. . . . And yes, we did try to bring Saddam Hussein into the family of nations and we failed on that, but it was worth the effort. And our allies in Saudi Arabia and Kuwait, those that stood shoulder to shoulder with us later on, were saying, try this, we don't want instability in the Middle East. And we tried and it didn't work.

89 State Department memorandum: *Iraq's Foreign Policy: Deeper into the Mainstream*, 3.3.88.

90 State Department memorandum: *U.S.-Iraqi Relations: Implications of Passage of Economic Sanctions Bill*, 10.18.88.

91 George Schultz: *Turmoil and Triumph*, p. 243.

92 Zalmay Khalilzad: A Geo-Strategic Overview: Stability or New Aggressive Coalitions, in *Proceedings of the Washington Institute*, Third Annual Policy Conference, "US Policy in the Middle East: Toward the Next Administration," 9.16–18.88 Washington, D.C.: Washington Institute for Near East Policy, 1988, pp. 12–13. Quoted in B. W. Jentleson: *With Friends like These*, p. 91.

93 cia: *Iraq: No End in Sight to Debt Burden*, 4.12.90.

94 See chapter 7.

95 It was sent to the British, German, French, Japanese, Swiss, Dutch, and Spanish embassies.

96 Minutes, nac Staff Committee, 10.3.89, quoted in B. W. Jentleson: *With Friends like These*, p. 128.

97 Ibid.

98 *Congressional Record*, 3.2.92, H864–66.

CHAPTER THREE

Arming Iraq

While the United States played a leading role in facilitating Iraq's militarization drive, and while France openly provided Iraq with major weapons systems, Britain also played a very significant role in the arming of Iraq, albeit one that was somewhat concealed by the operation of the Howe Guidelines.

◆ The Howe Guidelines

The very fact that Iraq and Iran were at war meant that the British government, along with most of the international community, sought to apply restrictions to the export of certain types of military equipment. This was done informally until 1984 and thereafter through the application of what became known as the Howe Guidelines. These were formulated in November 1984 and finally revealed to Parliament in a written answer to a parliamentary question—a much-favored, low-key way of making sensitive information public when necessary—from Sir David Steel, MP in October 1985. They stated:

> The United Kingdom has been strictly impartial in the conflict between Iran and Iraq and has refused the supply of lethal defence equipment to either side. In order to reinforce our policy of doing everything possible to see this tragic conflict brought to the earliest possible end, we decided in December 1984 to apply thereafter, the following guidelines to all deliveries of defence equipment to Iran and Iraq:
>
> i) We should maintain our consistent refusal to supply lethal equipment to either side;
> ii) Subject to that overriding consideration, we should attempt to fulfil existing contracts and obligations;
> iii) We should not, in future, approve orders for any defence equipment which,

in our view, would significantly enhance the capability of either side to prolong or exacerbate the conflict;

iv) In line with this policy, we should continue to scrutinise rigorously all applications for export licences for the supply of defence equipment to Iran and
Iraq.[1]

The purpose of the guidelines, then, was to allow the British government
to be seen to be moving—along with the United States—to restrict the flow
of arms to a war zone, fulfilling expectations based on the responsibility of
the West and Britain's proclaimed neutrality in the conflict. In practice, by
vaguely defining a prohibition on the export of major weapons systems,
which Britain did not then export to Iraq or Iran, they in fact legitimized the
export of a wide range of dual-use and support equipment under the guise of
closer control.[2]

Why was the existence of the guidelines kept from Parliament for so long?
The answer lies in the fact that Britain, unlike the United States, had not
completely written off Iran, and the FCO did not share the U.S. belief that
Iraq could perform the twin pillar role as effectively as Iran had. Nevertheless, Britain had no desire to see Iran emerge victorious from the Iran-Iraq
War and hence tilted toward Iraq to maintain a status quo in the conflict and
ensure that there was no victory on either side. But this tilt took place, after
1984, largely within the framework of the Howe Guidelines, which were
notionally committed to an "evenhanded" approach. They allowed Britain
to favor Iraq within a policy stance that emphasized Britain's neutrality in the
conflict (really a neutrality of desired outcome), and so did not risk alienating
Iran. But this also meant that the policy, neutral in name but not in application, could be misunderstood by Iraq and allies keen that Britain should back
Iraq. Hence, the guidelines had to be kept from the British public and Parliament so that they could be kept from Iraq, the Gulf states (particularly Saudi
Arabia), and even the United States. As Sir Adam Butler noted: "America was
just as insistent as anybody else with regard to supplying Iraq. At that time
they had shifted very strongly in favour of Iraq for some understandable reasons."[3]

The decision not to publicize was taken partly on the advice of the British
ambassador in Baghdad, Sir John Moberly, who wanted to avoid straining
relations with Iraq. Before they were eventually announced, Sir Richard Luce
flew to Baghdad to explain them to senior Iraqi officials, and Sir Stephen
Egerton was dispatched to explain British policy to other interested parties—
the French and Italian foreign ministries and the U.S. State Department, for
example. As he told the Scott Inquiry:

. . . I had to go round telling many allies, particularly of course the United States but also in Europe, what we were going to do, and they either laughed kindly at me or else expressed great indignation. Some people were extremely annoyed that we were planning to continue with some existing contracts to Iran because Iraq was in danger of losing the war and a lot of our allies and friends were determined that that should not happen. . . .[4]

This difference of approach to the conflict did not mean that Britain was less keen than any of its allies that Iran should not win the war, merely that the British assessment of the situation—that Iraq was unlikely to be defeated by Iran—was different.[5]

The guidelines, then, reflected political rather than ethical considerations, and a perceived need to fall in line with the policy of neutrality publicly adopted by the United States and many of Britain's European partners. They were also intended as a general insurance against public opinion, which might be critical of unrestrained arms sales to a wartorn area. After all, would not the normal licensing procedures have produced the same results as the guidelines? Given that exports of arms and militarily useful equipment are subject to political control through the need to secure an export license, were there any products not available for sale to Iraq as a result of the application of these guidelines that would otherwise have been sold? In practice, the guidelines were clearly flawed in several respects. Close inspection reveals numerous qualifying phrases that render them so elastic as to be meaningless. The idea underpinning them—that an effective distinction can be made, especially in time of war, between lethal and nonlethal equipment—is inherently weak. It is a distinction treated with scepticism within the arms industry, which (with some justification) views its aim as being to allow as high a level of trade as possible. Point iii) of the guidelines is key in this respect. It talks of refusing to sell defense equipment that *in the government's view* would significantly enhance either side's ability to "prolong or exacerbate the conflict." Not only does this point introduce four qualifiers offering considerable latitude in interpretation (*significantly, enhance, prolong,* and *exacerbate*), it also introduces the element of subjectivity upon which the government's case could rest should an export have been proved to have had a lethal application ("in our view"). During his testimony at the Matrix Churchill trial, Alan Clark remarked: "By their very nature the guidelines were elastic—the wording was a matter for interpretation and argument."[6] And he told the Scott Inquiry: "The whole of iii) is magnificent—it is a brilliant piece of drafting, because it is far from being restrictive, it is open to argument in respect of practically every one of its elements."[7] The guidelines were "capable of very flexible interpretation because they [were] not specific, and [were] full of adjectival adverbial qualification which is itself put in to give them additional flexibility."[8] Even Sir Geoffrey Howe's letter to Prime Minister Thatcher informing her of their adoption recognized that point iii) in particular, "enables us to maintain a modicum of flexibility"—a classic understatement. So elastic were they that, had they so desired, ministers could have justified the sale of the British Aerospace [BAE] Hawk "trainer" aircraft and the export of the barrels for the supergun project under the terms of the guidelines. This elasticity of interpretation was quite deliberate and gave the government a complete alibi. Lord Trefgarne, a key figure in the Iraqgate scandal in the United Kingdom, was asked whether the guidelines should have been followed by officials: "Officials were to be guided by the guidelines and could be guided flexibly," he explained.[9] In December 1988, in a briefing note for Lord Trefgarne, Alan Barrett of the MOD reflected: "The Guidelines have served UK policy well. They have been and remain capable of being interpreted flexibly and in a way which we could always justify to Parliament, the press, industry and the public."[10] As a piece of drafting, the guidelines were little short of masterly. Undebated by the House, their studiously ambiguous and qualified language gave government spokespeople all the flexibility they needed. For Mark Higson at the FCO, they were "moveable goalposts."[11] They were as watertight as the government wanted them to be and at the same time as leaky as desired.

Furthermore, because they were only *guidelines*, they had no legal force, and hence breaching them had no legal consequences. Mrs. Thatcher made this clear to the Scott Inquiry: "The guidelines are for the guidance of officials to be consistent. Of course they have to be followed, but they are not strict law. That is why they are guidelines and not law."[12] And as Lord Trefgarne explained:

> The Guidelines . . . were not of course the only considerations taken into account in considering exports to Iran and Iraq. They did not, on their own, constitute policy, and they did not have any legal force. The Guidelines were an aid to those considering Export Licence applications in respect of Iran and Iraq and a summary description of the Government's approach to exports to those countries of equipment which might have defence applications . . . I and my colleagues were, above all, responding in difficult and changing circumstances to the often conflicting interests of British foreign policy, British trade and British security. It is the amalgam of these three that represents the national interest.[13]

Notwithstanding the "evenhanded" approach said to be implicit in them, the guidelines represented a military tilt toward Iraq because of the "significant enhancement" clause. This clause meant that in practice, because Iraq was already more heavily armed than Iran, the supply of military equipment to Iraq could be construed as not representing a "significant enhancement," whereas for the more lightly and motley-armed Iran, even small-scale or low-level exports could be said to amount to a "significant enhancement." Take, for instance, this exchange at the Scott Inquiry between Presiley Baxendale, counsel to the inquiry and chief interrogator of witnesses, and Ian Blackley, a former assistant head of the FCO's Middle East Department:

> **Q:** . . . At that point Iraq had much more military equipment than Iran, so a piece of equipment for Iraq might easily not be a significant enhancement, which it would be for Iran?
> **A:** That could be.
> **Q:** Is that how you understood *evenhanded* ?
> **A:** Yes, I think so.[14]

Tim Renton, a former FCO minister, conceded that "one cannot avoid it, that something could be a significant enhancement to Iran that was not to Iraq."[15]

Moreover, the guidelines began by stating that the government's overriding concern lay in bringing an end to the Iran-Iraq War. However, many observers considered that in geopolitical terms Western interests were best served by having the conflict continue. A prolonged war would ensure that, regardless of the final outcome, neither side could score a sufficiently rapid military victory to keep the bulk of its forces intact and powerful enough to dominate the Gulf and threaten the lower Gulf states. In effect, this approach was a form of dual containment (and would become official U.S. policy toward Iran and Iraq after the 1991 Gulf War).[16] In 1992 Alan Clark suggested that such a policy had been in effect, arguing: "Iran was the enemy—and still is—and it was clear to me that the interests of the West were well served by Iran and Iraq fighting each other."[17] Blackley told the inquiry: "I think the context of this is that the government's view was that British interests would best be served if neither side won the war. That is the context in which we were operating. We did not want Iraq to win and we did not want Iran to win. We were possibly more worried about Iran winning."[18] This led Lord Justice Scott to observe:

> So far as neither side winning is concerned, that has the implication that if one or other side seemed to be getting the upper hand, a more liberal approach to the one that was on the underneath might then be adopted.

A: That would be a possibility for Ministers to look at.
Q: Nothing to do with the Guidelines?
A: Everything is to do with the Guidelines.[19]

The guidelines were effectively altered in December 1988 following the cease-fire in the Iran-Iraq War, although the change was deliberately withheld from Parliament. From then on, point iii) stated that weapons would not be exported if they were considered to be of "direct and significant assistance to either country in the conduct of offensive operations in breach of the cease-fire." This represented a relaxation in policy. It incorporated a variation on the lethal/nonlethal distinction, and hence retained a sufficient degree of ambiguity and subjectivity over all weapons except military equipment that clearly fell in the margins. Furthermore, like the original point iii), it contained the fail-safe wording *significant* (i.e., if invoked, equipment would have to provide both direct *and* significant assistance). This required a subjective assessment that could change as the course of the war did, while loose interpretation could be used to legitimize a wide range of militarily useful exports. In addition, a point v) was added to note that the guidelines would continue to be reviewed in the light of developments in the peace process.

When is an alteration not a change? Parliament was not advised of the alteration, even though it should have been informed of any shift in policy. This question would produce some of the most circular discussions, marked by some of the most obstructive answers, of the whole Scott Inquiry. If the guidelines had been changed, then, because Parliament had not been informed, ministers would have acted improperly. However, if this alteration could be said not to have amounted to a change, then there would have been no reason to make any announcement to Parliament, and ministers could not be said to have acted improperly. From the time of the change, Parliament was told that the guidelines were "being kept under constant review in the light of the cease-fire and developments in the peace negotiations."[20] Alan Clark admitted to the Inquiry that "it denies the ordinary meaning of words to argue that the guidelines were not 'changed' " but that "by stretching the meaning of words you could say they had not changed."[21]

Various ministers, most notably William Waldegrave, argued in the face of common sense that the guidelines had not been changed in 1988. However, those who wished to take this line had a difficulty to overcome. In January 1992, John Goulden of the FCO had told the Trade and Industry Select Committee (TISC) investigating the supergun affair that the guidelines had been "amended" in 1988. The MOD's Nicholas Bevan told the Scott Inquiry that he thought Goulden had been wrong to say there had been a change to the guidelines. Sir Robin Butler, the Cabinet secretary, agreed, explaining that "the papers that Mr Goulden looked at caused him . . . to mislead himself."[22] But, Presiley Baxendale suggested, Goulden's brief had been approved by the FCO, the MOD, and the Department of Trade and Industry (DTI), so surely what Butler was outlining was a situation in which they were "all misleading themselves"? By the time Butler agreed that this must indeed have been the case, the inquiry had once again crossed the boundary between detailed probing and high farce that senior civil servants seemed intent on exploring. Butler also told the Scott Inquiry that the fact that the TISC did not react to Goulden's revelation of a change—that, as Butler put it, "the dog in the night did not bark"—was indicative that it "and then the House to which it reported, did not appear to believe that the Government had behaved unreasonably" and that this was "a fact to which the Inquiry should give weight."[23]

What Goulden's presentation of the shifting basis of policy did was to open the way for a catch-all defense of the Government's actions. While on one level the government argued that the guidelines had not been changed, that government policy was merely exploring the flexibility inherent in them, and that there was therefore no need to announce a change (because none had occurred!), at another level it was arguing that if a change had in fact occurred, then it had already been announced by Goulden at the TISC and so no further announcement was necessary! Either way, the government had not acted incorrectly in making no announcement. William Waldegrave's assertion that the guidelines had not changed rested on an even more ingenious formula. He told the Scott Inquiry that "it is perfectly clear that the guidelines are never changed." Lord Justice Scott tried valiantly to outline the logic of Waldegrave's argument:

> There is a problem about this, which has been keeping me awake at night. The proposition that seems to come from your paper is that the guidelines were announced in 1985. The guidelines could not be changed without the proposal going to senior Ministers, the Prime Minister and being announced in Parliament. None of those things ever happened. The guidelines were never changed.[24]

Waldegrave was undeterred, and the next day returned to this theme, explaining thus: "After the collapse of the Matrix Churchill trial . . . I looked at this and others looked at this, and I remember talking to Sir Robin Butler about it at the time saying I do not remember changing the guidelines. Into the papers we dived and find, actually, that is not what happened." But as Presiley Baxendale was quick to point out: "You dive into the papers and you find it is not what happened. We have dived into the papers and we have seen that in practice that is what happened."[25]

At the inquiry, different ministers and officials had different explanations and interpretations of what the guidelines were intended for, a contrariety that itself tends to lend credence to the idea that their intention was to be sufficiently vague and imprecise to allow whatever trade the government deemed desirable and justify blocking that which it did not. The result was that the Scott Inquiry spent much of its time during the earlier public sessions pursuing a circular debate; officials basked in it, but the inquiry seemed to have failed to grasp this fundamental point.[26]

Gradually, the suggestion emerged that the guidelines existed in order to legitimize arms and dual-use equipment export decisions by being able to show that they were consistent with a stated restrictive export policy—what Alan Clark referred to at the Matrix Churchill trial as "Whitehall cosmetics." The FCO's Sir David Miers, for example, wrote in a memo dated 4 July 1986:

> I believe the Guidelines should be regarded primarily as a set of criteria for use in defending against public and parliamentary criticism and criticism from the Americans and Saudis, whatever decisions we take on grounds of commercial and political interest. In following these concrete interests, we have to make sure that our decisions are consistent with the Guidelines, but the war poses too many problems and our interests are too finely balanced to allow mechanical application of the Guidelines to dictate our policy.[27]

This could certainly be seen to be the case in the 1986 debate over whether or not to allow the export to Iran of small inflatable boats, which could be used in their offensive in the southern marshlands of Iraq. This decision seemed to be made not on the grounds of whether this would represent a "significant enhancement" (although it could have been argued to be such under the guidelines) but on political grounds. In particular, the decision rested on the extent to which it would put at risk the highly lucrative and politically important Al Yamamah/Tornado agreement with Saudi Arabia. As Miers noted in July 1986: "The real argument against supply is that the Saudis, and perhaps the Americans, will object and the Tornado financing package could be jeopardised . . . It is a pity that we have to take a decision when the Tornado contract is apparently at a critical stage."[28]

A further flaw was that, as former Foreign Office Minister David Mellor pointed out, the guidelines could not be interpreted too strictly initially, as to do so would create a series of precedents that would be difficult to ignore in the future if and when a more flexible approach was desired.[29] As Miers had observed in 1986 over the inflatable boats issue: "If the guidelines were very strictly and uncritically applied, they would result in our blocking almost all exports to each side."[30]

The flexibility inherent in them proved a problem for those arguing for restraint. The MOD's Lt. Col. Glazebrook, the most consistent advocate of restraint to appear before the Scott Inquiry, recalled one case in particular:

> In the days before the conflict started, the UK had supplied a fair number of combat aircraft to both Iran and Iraq. Fighter aircraft, and indeed bombers of that sort, are fitted with ejector seats whereby, if the plane becomes irreparably damaged, the pilot and the other crew members can eject themselves and hopefully come down safely by parachute. The plane, without the pilot, actually crashes.
>
> It was argued on the one side that, if the pilot ejected and parachuted to earth unharmed, this was humanitarian saving of life and, because the aeroplane had crashed, it could not be used again, and therefore our aims were satisfied.
>
> On the other hand, some of us, especially my colleague in the Royal Air Force, argued very strongly that if you did not provide him with spares for the ejector seats, the aeroplane would never have been available for lethal missions before it was actually attacked and crashed.[31]

As a result of the application of the Howe Guidelines, between 1987 and the invasion of Kuwait, Iraq was able to receive an entire inventory of military and militarily useful equipment from the United Kingdom, the sale of which had been legitimized by the guidelines' existence. Iraq was sent items such as aircraft engines, equipment and parts; body armor; depleted uranium; ejection seats and spares; fast assault craft; helicopter engines; radar systems and equipment; an air defense simulator; armor vehicle spares; boats; CNC lathes; explosive detectors; explosives; gas respirators; naval spares; night vision equipment; pistols, rifles, and shotguns; plutonium; portable explosive detectors; and secure telephone systems and spares.[32]

Although ministers and officials were careful to avoid telling lies to Parliament, their studiedly formulated answers did not tell the full truth, and certain witnesses to the Scott Inquiry made it clear that they did not think the whole truth was required. This approach was in itself inherently dishonest because it was intended to frustrate legitimate enquiry. But while the government had hoped to produce a position it could sell as principled, it appeared instead, to those in a position to observe it, to be merely hypocritical. For example, for Chris Cowley:

> British government hypocrisy took on a special meaning during the 1980s. Fighter pilots were to be trained in Britain, however certain types of aircraft could not be sold to Iraq. Spares to maintain British fighter aircraft could be supplied but not aircraft. Export licences for fighter aircraft ejector seats were approved because they formed part of aircraft safety equipment. Licences to export engines for battle tanks received official approval, being the non-lethal part of the tank. Battle field radar was sold because it had a defensive capability. Tens of millions of pounds worth of machine tools were provided to Iraq, the same machinery as that used to produce weapons and ammunition in British factories.[33]

◆ The British Government and Arms Sales to Iraq

Why and at what stage during the Iran-Iraq War, then, did the British government begin to lean toward Iraq? Although Britain had publicly declared its neutrality in the Iran-Iraq War in 1980, this question of whether and how far to favor Iraq was one that came up repeatedly, especially in view of the U.S. policy shift that had resulted from similar debates in Washington. A record of an FCO meeting of 7 March 1984, for example, says: "Mr Luce could not see how, under present circumstances, we could justify a policy of tilting in favour of Iraq." On 30 April another meeting recorded the first sign that the departmental agonizing and pressure from Gulf allies[34] (not to mention the United States) had resulted in a change in the direction of Iraq: "Ministers . . . agreed that though lethal arms and ammunition should not be supplied to either side, every opportunity should be taken to exploit Iraq's potential as a promising market for the sale of defence equipment, and to this end lethal items should be interpreted in the narrowest possible sense and the obligations of neutrality as flexibly as possible."[35]

Former Foreign Office Minister Tim Renton revealed something of the mindset of the FCO with regard to Iraq and Iran at this time when he told the Scott Inquiry that "although Iraq had started the war, Iran was seen at that stage as really the aggressor. The pressure was on to get Iran to agree to a cease-fire, recognition of international borders and deal with the prisoner of war question. In our, if you like, mentality towards the two, I do not think there was strict impartiality."[36]

This reflected not just the enormous strategic potential of Iraq in terms of the role it could play in "containing" Iran and preserving the pro-Western status quo across the Gulf region (the primary U.S. concern) but also the enormous potential, given its oil wealth, of Iraq as a market for British and Western goods. As David Mellor told the inquiry, Iraq's problem (from a U.K. perspective) was that it was "a badly run country, but [one] which has a potential as great as Saudi Arabia. If you look at their oil resources, particularly if you look at what their oil resources would be if they explored all the likely oil-bearing land . . . then you have to bear in mind that Iraq was a big market for British goods."[37]

At the same time, unencumbered by the legacy of a hostage crisis, the British government was freer to keep the door open to Iran, and even tolerated the operation of the Iranian arms procurement network, from which Iran conducted its worldwide search for weapons, under the guise of the Iranian National Oil Company at 4 Victoria Street, London. This was closed down only on 23 September 1987, following an Iranian attack on a British-flagged ship in the Gulf during the tanker war. It was not even the case that the operation of this office was unknown at the time. At best its existence and role were open secrets. For example, an article published in spring 1987 by Anthony Cordesman discussed its activities:

Iran has contacted virtually every possible source of arms in the West, legal and illegal. It has organised a large Logistic Support Centre in the Iranian National Oil Company building in London. . . . This office co-ordinates Iran's arms purchase efforts in Europe and aids in its illegal and covert purchase efforts in the United States, Israel, the Arab world and Latin America. This office has succeeded in obtaining important supplies, such as new engines for some of Iran's British-made Chieftain tanks. It also, however, has been trapped in numerous frauds, including a false effort to sell some 8,000 TOW missiles.[38]

Although the Iran-Iraq War started with a clearly defined event in 1980, the British government did not formulate any specific policy to guide military sales (other than that sales were to be decided on a case-by-case basis) until some time later. At the end of October 1980, E.U. foreign ministers met and, at the urging of France in particular, decided not to institute any embargo on sales to the belligerents, but to leave such decisions to individual member states, giving all those with an interest in the region the scope to profit from wartime requirements. One month after the Osirak attack, in July 1981, a team of twenty Iraqi technicians arrived in Britain to visit BAE as part of a bid to secure a deal allowing them to manufacture three hundred Hawk "trainer" aircraft in Iraq under license, although the Thatcher government had ruled out such a deal until after the end of the war. That the Iraqis were there at all reflected their frustration with the Soviet Union, which had suspended arms deliveries by this time. This frustration represented a window of opportunity for Western states to displace the Soviet Union as a leading supplier of military equipment to Iraq, lessen Soviet influence, and bring Iraq back firmly within the Western orbit. In doing so, there would also be enormous economic benefits. This was the logic of NSD-26, but it also reflected British thinking toward the region.

This Iraqi frustration with the Soviet Union was exploited by then Minister of State at the Foreign Office Douglas Hurd, who visited Baghdad in July 1981 to attend the anniversary celebration of the 1963 revolution that had propelled the Ba'athists to power.[39] Hurd was seen as acting as a "high-level salesman"[40] at a time when BAE was pushing for the sale of the Hawk. After all, despite the official stance of neutrality, in 1981 British companies had signed £250 million worth of contracts for arms-related, but nonlethal, equipment.[41] This marked the beginning of the commercial dimension to the pro-Iraqi shift in policy.[42] Hurd was followed in September by Trade and Industry Secretary John Biffen. At these meetings, the United Kingdom–Iraq Joint Commission was established; it was to meet annually from then on to discuss bilateral trade relations. Biffen subsequently reflected on his role at this time, remarking: "Being a trade minister is rather like being a door-to-door salesman. You find yourself saying things like: 'How are you off for aircraft?' and that sort of thing. I was always selling Hawk trainer jets to anybody I bumped into."[43]

In 1982, IMS facilitated the signing of an order for 1,000 military-specification Land Rovers, fifty Range Rovers and sixty other vehicles fitted with radio equipment. The total value of the package was £28 million.[44] During the same year IMS was given permission to repair British-made Chieftain tanks captured by Iraq during the war.[45] An MOD spokesman explained that this would not affect Britain's policy of neutrality in the war, as Britain would be prepared to supply tank spares to either side, but not ammunition. Another sign of the emerging bias was Douglas Hurd's decision, while undertaking a four-nation Gulf tour, to accuse Iran of harboring groups trying to destabilize the region—despite Western intelligence suggesting that Iraq was doing precisely the same thing.[46] This was followed in March 1983 by the extension of a £150 million line of credit to Baghdad to facilitate the completion of projects involving British companies. Then, on 6 October 1983, Mrs. Thatcher signed a £250 million trade deal with Iraq, which by this time had

Table 3.1

Visits to Iraq by Government Ministers and Conservative MPs, 1979–1989

Date	Details of Visit
5 July 1979	Lord Carrington, foreign secretary
October 1979	Cecil Parkinson, trade minister
November 1979	John Nott, trade and industry secretary
July 1981	Douglas Hurd, Foreign Office minister
30 Sept.–5 Oct. 1981	John Biffen, trade and industry secretary
1982	David Mellor, Foreign Office minister
April 1984	Robert Hicks, MP—as a guest of the Gulf Research Center
3–6 November 1984	Paul Channon, trade and industry secretary
8–10 November 1986	Alan Clark, trade minister
February 1988	David Mellor, Foreign Office minister
19 February 1988	Tony Marlow, MP Sponsored by the Gulf
	Robert Adley, MP Center for Strategic Studies
	Michael Brown, MP
	Nicholas Budgen, MP
	Robert Hicks, MP
	Roger Moate, MP
	Richard Page, MP
	John Cummings, MP (Lab)
	Bob Parry, MP (Lab)
	David Young, MP (Lab)
25 Sept.–2 Oct. 1988	Terry Dicks, MP
5–7 November 1988	Tony Newton, trade minister and chancellor of the Duchy of Lancaster
13 February 1989	William Waldegrave, Foreign Office minister
18–22 Sept. 1989	Tony Marlow, MP Parliamentary delegation
	Nicholas Bennett, MP
	Hugh Dykes, MP
	Anthony Nelson, MP
	Tim Smith, MP
	Timothy Wood, MP
12–15 October 1989	John Wakeham, energy secretary

Source: John Sweeney: *Trading with the Enemy*, London, Pan, 1993.

grown to become Britain's second-largest Middle Eastern market after Saudi Arabia.

The shift toward Iraq, then, emerged at roughly the same time as the U.S. tilt and was motivated by several factors, among them the same kind of cold war thinking that influenced U.S. policy. Lt. Col. Glazebrook explained to the Scott Inquiry that "[the] USSR was, at that time, our enemy, as it were . . . and anything that could reduce the linkage between Iraq and the USSR was considered a good thing."[47] Second, conservative Arab states with which Britain had a long-standing and close relationship, particularly Saudi Arabia, were also backing Iraq (although as Saudi concerns over Iraq grew after 1988, so British policy changed to accommodate them). This factor was to become more important for the British government as the decade wore on; it signed major arms deals with a number of Arab states, but Saudi concerns were always of paramount importance, and the Al Yamamah deal gave Saudi Arabia considerable reverse leverage over British policy in the region. One indication of this is found in a letter sent from the prime minister's office to the DTI and FCO on 19 August 1986, which rejected anything other than a strict interpretation of the guidelines for Iran. Anything less than this "would mean going back on the assurances which the Prime Minister has given on many occasions to Arab countries."[48]

If Saudi Arabia itself wanted to pass arms and related technology on to Iraq, the British government was unlikely to interfere for other, very good reasons. First, such an operation would have been "deniable," operating on the "arms-length" principle. All the paperwork for Saudi Arabia would be in order. In addition, the whole subject of Al Yamamah was a very delicate one across Whitehall, not least because of the alleged involvement in the deal of the prime minister's son, Mark Thatcher, who is thought to have taken a multimillion-pound commission out of it to cover his role.[49] The annual *Sunday Times* survey of the 500 richest people in Britain in 1993 placed Mark Thatcher, a failed accountant, at joint 219th with an estimated wealth of £40 million, commenting that he had "made his fortune from his Middle East and American business dealings."[50] By 1994 he had dropped to 303rd and was being described as "a Mr Fixit in the Middle and Far East, . . . reckoned to have made lucrative commissions on deals he helped secure."[51] Others have been more specific in explaining how Mark Thatcher amassed so much in so short a time. For example, Howard Teicher recalled his knowledge of Mark Thatcher's activities for a television documentary in 1992:

> I read of Mark Thatcher's involvement in this arms deal [Al Yamamah] in diplomatic dispatches from our embassy in Saudi Arabia, from intelligence reports that were gleaned in Saudi Arabia and Europe, and in diplomatic dispatches from other European capitals. I considered these dispatches totally reliable, totally accurate. I did not think that people would loosely accuse the son of the Prime Minister of being involved in such a transaction unless they were certain it was the case. And the fact that I saw his name appear in a number of different sourced documents

convinced me of the authenticity of at least the basic involvement on Mark Thatcher's part. . . . He was clearly playing some kind of role to help facilitate the completion of a transaction between the two governments.[52]

Subsequently, the *Sunday Times* published further evidence suggesting that Thatcher involved himself in the arms deals signed by his mother while she was prime minister. Adnan Khashoggi confirmed that "Wafic [Said] was using [Mark] Thatcher for intelligence. His value to Wafic was his name, of course, and that whenever Wafic needed a question answered, Thatcher could go directly to his mother for the answer."[53]

Syrian financier Wafic Said, the middleman who helped BAE secure the Al Yamamah deal, is certainly well connected. In addition to his friendship with Mark Thatcher, he has impeccable Swiss banking connections and owns a third of the investment company Aitken Hume, of which Jonathan Aitken, another intimate of the Saudi royal family, was deputy chairman until he took up his first ministerial post at Defence Procurement. In addition, Said has attended Conservative Party social functions and has made contributions to Conservative Party funds. Although he guards his privacy closely, he surfaced in 1992 to sue Misbah Baki for impugning his honor, and to be photographed with the Thatchers outside the premiere of the film *The Fourth Protocol*, which he financed.

Britain's position was also influenced by pressure applied by the United States, despite the fact that its analyses on several key issues varied from those of the FCO. The FCO did not think Iraq would lose the war with Iran. It did not think Iraq could play the role abdicated by Iran, and it did not consider Iraq to have been as much of a Soviet client as the United States did. Nevertheless, together with Saudi pressure, U.S. policy considerations seem to have prompted Britain to allow military equipment to go to Saudi Arabia and Kuwait, thence to be passed on to Iraq. Such pressure would account for the stories of British involvement in U.S.-inspired covert efforts to get propellant, explosives, and military equipment to Iraq. Finally, Britain's decision to favor Iraq was influenced more by trade considerations than was that of the United States. As a number of ministers and former ministers told the Scott Inquiry, after the war was over, Iraq would need to undertake a massive reconstruction program, which, because of its mineral wealth, it would be well able to pay for. Britain was one of several states that adopted the policy it followed during the war partly to jockey for position once it ended.

Reports of Iraqi use of chemical weapons had been a feature of the war with Iran since early 1981, and a 1980 U.S. Defense Intelligence Agency (DIA) report claimed that Iraq had been "actively acquiring" a chemical warfare capability since the mid-1970s.[54] An Iraqi spokesman had denied these allegations, saying: "This is Iranian blackmail and we deny it, the Iranians would like to use these weapons themselves and are trying to buy them on the black market."[55] Nevertheless, in December 1983, the *New Scientist* reported that in 1981 the DSO "channelled" 10,000 custom-made chemical weapons protection kits (including protective suits and breathing equipment) to Iraq in a contract worth $500,000.[56] Brian Hobbs, managing director of PMA Ltd., the kits' supplier, explained: "We liaised with the Chemical Defence Establishment at Porton Down in the development of the kits, but they were for civilian protection. We worked with the MOD's defence sales organisation and they marketed them."[57]

Interest in the British role in Iraq's chemical and biological warfare plans was revived in March 1984, when Iran accused Britain of supplying Iraq with chemical weapons that had been used on its soldiers. On 15 March, when Labour MP Tony Banks asked if the government would move to "ban the export of anti-nerve gas kits, gas masks and protective suits to Iran and Iraq whilst a state of war exists between those countries," he was told by Geoffrey Pattie that "export of these items is kept under close scrutiny. I can confirm that we do not intend to authorise the supply of any item which might assist Iran or Iraq to wage chemical warfare during the current conflict."[58]

On 29 March Foreign Office Minister Raymond Whitney confirmed this: "A team of specialists appointed by the United Nations Secretary General has concluded that chemical weapons have been used in the conflict between Iran and Iraq . . . we are glad to note that the report provides no evidence to substantiate the wholly unfounded claim that the United Kingdom has supplied chemical weapons to Iraq."[59] Nevertheless, on 12 April, Trade Minister Paul Channon outlined a tightening of the regulations surrounding the export of chemicals, just as the United States announced similar measures.[60] More positively, as a result of an agreement by the Anglo-Iraqi Joint Trade Commission reached the previous year, in April Morgan Grenfell secured approval to extend a £275 million line of credit for nonmilitary goods to Baghdad, guaranteed by the Export Credit Guarantee Department (ECGD).[61]

Following Paul Channon's 1984 trip to Baghdad, it was announced that Britain was to extend a further £300 million line of credit to Iraq, with Channon explaining: "The new credit agreement reflects the importance the UK attaches to its trade with Iraq, and the agreement will help generate business worth over £660 million for British companies and welcome employment for British workers."[62] With this level of governmental support, Anglo-Iraqi trade relations flourished. Governmental support was also expressed in the DTI's financial support of British companies exhibiting at the annual Baghdad International Fair—the principal shop window through which to sell to Iraq.

Growing disquiet about Iraqi violations of human rights was not to be allowed to get in the way of this trade. As Trade Minister Alan Clark told the House of Commons in 1988:

> The Government [is] concerned by the denial of human rights wherever this oc-
> curs, and has consistently made our views clear to the Iraqi government on this
> subject. We have also made clear to the Iraqi government our condemnation of the
> use of chemical weapons. We will continue to do so. At the same time, we should
> not lose sight of the importance of developing political and economic relations
> with Iraq, and the provision of export credit is a major contribution to this.[63]

However, Anglo-Iraqi trade relations were faltering by late 1989, so much so that the meeting of the Joint Commission was postponed.[64] Although the imprisonment of Briton Ian Richter on corruption charges, the detention of British nurse Daphne Parish, and the detention and execution of *Observer* journalist Farzad Bazoft all contributed to this deterioration, the main force behind it was the fact that Iraq had fallen behind in its payments. By October 1989 it was estimated that it owed around £80 million.[65] Energy Secretary John Wakeham was sent to Baghdad in October 1989 in an effort to improve

Table 3.2		
British Trade with Iraq, 1980–1990		
Year	Value (£'000s)	No. of British companies at Baghdad International Fair
1980	322,105	45
1981	623,890	130
1982	873,665	153
1983	399,920	70
1984	343,120	63
1985	444,749	70
1986	443,817	65
1987	271,655	30
1988	411,752	45
1989	450,998	69
1990	293,393	canceled

Source: TISC: *Exports to Iraq: Memoranda of Evidence*, Session 1990–91, HC 602, pp. 23–25.

relations, and as a result, at the December meeting of the Joint Commission, a new credit limit of £250 million was agreed.

◆ The BAe Hawk

One area of prevailing interest throughout the 1980s was the apparent Iraqi interest in buying the Hawk "trainer" aircraft. As we have seen, in 1981 twenty Iraqi technicians visited Britain to discuss a £1 billion contract to construct 300 Hawks under license in Iraq as a first step toward creating an indigenous aircraft industry.[66] BAe personnel had also visited Iraq to discuss the proposal. In March 1982, Defence Minister Geoffrey Pattie announced that "British Aerospace is negotiating with the Government of Iraq for the sale and local assembly of Hawk aircraft. No agreement has yet been reached."[67] However, BAe was informed that offensive military equipment could not be supplied while the war with Iran continued. Hence, the 1988 cease-fire that marked the end of the war also created a second opportunity for BAe to sell the Hawk. For some in the FCO, the sale of the Hawk represented a further step in the "family of nations" strategy, tying Iraq more closely to the West for its military needs. David Gore-Booth explained how ". . . my mind set at the time was that we were looking for ways to gain influence over the Iraqis, and it seemed to me that this was a big enough potential contract to act as a means of gaining influence over the Iraqis, which might influence them in other areas of direct interest to Britain."[68] FCO Minister William Waldegrave too came out in favor of the sale in a memo to the foreign secretary, which also outlined a number of problems that such a sale would create for British foreign policy in the region:

> There is no plausible political cover story for this deal. We cannot say, as with Saudi, that Iraq is a responsible force for moderation in that region, nor a bastion against the Soviets. She is a country which launched an irresponsible war which caused a million deaths. . . .We will not sell front-line weapons to Iraq, at least for the foreseeable future, and it cannot lead to an Al Yamamah or equivalent. . . . [However] . . . Iraq is soon going to be the second market in the Middle East [for British goods]. . . . Oddly she still regards herself as having something of a special relationship with us. We have a major long-term interest in retaining our position in this market, and weapons are what the regime uses as a touchstone of reliability in a trading partner.[69]

Such was the sensitivity of the proposal that a decision on the sale went all the way up to Cabinet Committee level—a relatively rare occurrence. It was decided on 27 July 1989, at a meeting of the Overseas and Defence Policy Committee, chaired by Mrs. Thatcher. The DTI and MOD had argued prior to the meeting that approval should be given to enable Britain to gain an important foothold where the French had previously been dominant, to secure jobs and the continued viability of BAE, and to capitalize on the "favored nation" status that Iraq had bestowed on Britain in recognition of the successive lines of credit that had been extended throughout the 1980s. Furthermore, the sale could be said to be compatible with the Howe Guidelines because Iraq already had 800 military aircraft, so the sale of 63 Hawks would hardly be the "significant enhancement" that the guidelines prohibited! A further argument advanced in favor of the sale was that the Hawk was only a "trainer" aircraft.

However, the labeling of the Hawk as a "trainer" aircraft appears to be partly a device designed to stop what might otherwise be a negative reaction, for example, on human rights grounds. BAE's own publicity did little to ease anxieties in this area by boasting that "[in] the Hawk 100 the distinction between an aircraft designed for advanced training duties and one designed solely for combat becomes extremely blurred."[70] Whereas normally the design of a "trainer" trades weaponization and armor plating for range— working on the basic assumption that flying time is the key requirement—the Hawk was somewhat different in this regard; it was the ultimate "dual-use" weapon.[71] Chris Cowley, on the basis of his observations between 1988 and 1989 when he was resident in Baghdad, recalled

> the close, if not fawning, attentions given by members of the [British] Embassy staff to representatives of British Aerospace who spent a long time in Baghdad putting together the sale of the Hawk aircraft to Baghdad . . . I have seen the specifications for these "training" aircraft. Their air frames and wings were reinforced in order to carry weapons for use as a ground attack aircraft . . . It was openly discussed that despite giving these aircraft the title of "training" the reality of it was that BAE, with the assistance of the Embassy, were trying to sell military attack aircraft where there would be follow-up orders for spares and weapons worth many millions of pounds.[72]

A briefing for the foreign secretary by David Gore-Booth on the question of whether or not to approve such an overt sale brought many of these issues to the fore:

> This is a very difficult decision. My own view is that the advantages of a sale in terms of relations with Iraq and our defence stake in the Middle East just outweigh

the disadvantages. . . . While we can argue that this contract would not contravene defence sales guidelines, we risk the accusation that we interpret the guidelines to suit our own convenience, e.g. would we be prepared to sell Hawk to Iran? Hawk will not be seen by the public as only a trainer aircraft. We are selling the Hawk 60 to Oman as a substitute for Tornado. And note Hawk is included in NATO's list of western combat capable aircraft. The trainer version is easily adaptable to carry all kinds of weaponry, including chemical weapons, although the Iraqis have a number of other delivery vehicles available already.[73]

At the July 1989 meeting, it was decided that the Hawk could not be sold to Iraq. Mrs. Thatcher's recollection of the meeting offers a small glimpse into the operation of Cabinet government in the 1980s. Even though the DTI and MOD had been supportive of the sale, at the meeting, Mrs. Thatcher recalled, "it took my colleagues . . . only about five minutes, and I eventually said to them: 'Does anyone wish to argue to the contrary?' Not a single person did. They smiled with great relief and agreed wholeheartedly."[74] In reaching this decision, Mrs. Thatcher was siding with the FCO, which had voiced concerns about any possible sale, and the Treasury, which was wary of the financial liability the sale could represent in view of Iraq's mounting economic difficulties.[75] The decision not to approve the sale was taken in the context of Iraqi use of chemical weapons on the Kurds, something Mrs. Thatcher would have read about in the Joint Intelligence Committee's (JIC) "red books." Clearly, there was a risk that the Hawk could be used at a future date to deliver chemical weapons. That this was a realistic possibility was reinforced by Masoud Barzani of the Kurdish Democratic Party who, lobbying against approval, pointed out that in the past Iraq had used the Swiss Pilatus PC-7 trainer to drop chemical weapons on the Kurds.[76]

◆ Training

Throughout the early stages of the war, British companies trained both Iraqi and Iranian pilots in the United Kingdom. Eighty Iraqi air force pilots were trained by Specialist Flying Training based in Carlisle. Iranian and Iraqi officers were trained in the use of the Skyguard air defense system at the Lincolnshire headquarters of the British Manufacture and Research Company (BMARC), purchased by Astra Holdings from the Swiss arms manufacturer Oerlikon Buhrle in 1988 (see chapter 5), even though the system had not been officially sold to Iraq. Gerald James, former chairman of Astra, explained:

It was normal practice to train ground crews i.e. military personnel belonging to the country who had purchased the system . . . The part of the Faldingworth site which was the training centre was sold back to Oerlikon . . . They explained that it was politically easier to train foreign gun crews in the UK than in Switzerland. Officially the Skyguard system was exported to Jordan, Saudi Arabia, Kuwait, the United Arab Emirates and other countries. It is common knowledge that this anti-aircraft system was heavily deployed in the defence of Baghdad. It is also common knowledge amongst anyone who had contact with the ground crews coming to Faldingworth for training that they were Iraqis, though often described as Saudis. In fact the former managing director of BMARC, Werner Leuch, explained to me that after 1984 only Iraqis came for training but prior to that it was both Iranians and Iraqis. He believed that there had been a policy decision in favour of Iraq after 1984.[77]

As James notes, at the end of 1984 the Iranians were denied this facility, although Iraqi pilots continued to be trained in Britain. In explaining this situation, Air Marshal Sir Peter Wykeham, then chairman of Specialist Flying Training, said: "Most of the RAF training schools were full up. There were some 4,000 Iraqi military personnel under training in Britain at one stage during that period."[78]

This is far from the only example of Iraqi military personnel being trained in Britain. In 1990, the Thorn-EMI house journal boasted of training Iraqi officers in the use of the Cymbeline radar, an arrangement that came to an end only following the execution of Farzad Bazoft. The government has not been particularly forthcoming about numbers, but it is known that at the time of Bazoft's execution, six Iraqis were being trained in Britain but were then expelled. Four were based at the Royal Military Academy at Sandhurst, and two on *HMS Dryad*, a Royal Navy training school off Portsmouth.[79]

◆ The (First) Baghdad International Exhibition for Military Production

On 28 April 1989, Saddam's birthday, 148 companies from twenty-eight countries gathered in Baghdad to exhibit their military products under the slogan "Defense Equipment for Peace and Prosperity."[80] A celebration of Iraqi military-industrial achievement, the Baghdad International Exhibition for Military Production was also a consequence of the inevitable mixed signals that flowed from Western policy. It should have been the clearest illustration to date of why the "family of nations" strategy was not working and why it was unlikely to do so. U.S. companies exhibited and U.S. Embassy staff attended, but the Bush administration was anxious to keep a low profile, even to the point of instructing the U.S. military attache to Baghdad not to wear his military uniform at the exhibition. Among the British contingent was the MOD's David Hastie, seconded back to his old company, BAE, so that he could attend while at the same time allowing the British government to maintain that there was no MOD representative there.[81] In addition to the leading U.S. and British companies, there were major exhibits from France, whose competition with Britain for Middle East arms markets was then at its fiercest following the British "victory" over Al Yamamah in controversial circumstances. Egypt, Italy, the Soviet Union, and Greece were among other major exhibitors. Also exhibiting were a number of machine tool manufacturers—a clear indication of Iraq's long-term intention to manufacture its own weapons. This ambition did not seem to pose a problem for the French salesmen. Dassault's Hugues de l'Estoile told one journalist in attendance that "the days of outright arms purchases by Iraq are over. Today, we have to sell the technology needed to build the arms, if we want to sell anything at all. We at Dassault are ready to play the game."[82]

The exhibition was also a way of showing off the advances that the fledgling Iraqi arms industry had made over recent years, extending to Iraqi-built ballistic missiles and a range of fuel-air explosives. On viewing these, General Maurice Schmidt, the French chief of staff, "began to wonder whether we hadn't gone a bit too far. I realized we had better begin paying closer attention to what the Iraqis were developing in the way of armament."[83] Although few seemed able to recall it later, also on display was a 1:100 scale model of Babylon—the first semipublic glimpse of the Iraqi supergun—made at a cost of £4,175 by Amalgam Design and Modelling Studio in Bristol, England.

◆ Allivane

The primary source of information about Allivane has been Frank Machon, the Glasgow-based businessman whose road haulage company, Polmadie Storage and Packing, had a contract to transport explosives for it. In 1988 Machon was contracted by Allivane to transport 1,000 metric tons of fuses and explosives for SRC's 155mm shells from Allivane's Scottish factories at Glenrothes and Cumbernauld to the Royal Ordnance (RO) plant at Bishopton. The final stated destination was Saudi Arabia.

Allivane went into receivership in 1988, by coincidence the same year that the Iran-Iraq war ended. When it did so, Allivane still owed Machon £68,000.

In his efforts to track this money down, Machon discovered a number of things about Allivane. One was the existence of papers for a company called Allivane International Group Ltd, apparently a subsidiary of Allivane, although inquiries to Companies House revealed absolutely no knowledge or record of this company ever having existed. It seems that Allivane International Group Ltd was solely a paper company used to disguise shipments of arms. In 1992 a "senior Customs investigator" told a national newspaper that this name was used "with the Government's knowledge, on documents relating to shipments of 155mm shells to Saudi Arabia and . . . to both sides in the Iran-Iraq war."[84] An "American intelligence officer" told journalist Alan Friedman: "Allivane was a facilitator, used in covert weapons shipments to Iraq, and at times to Iran as well."[85]

Customs officials were certainly in a position to know, having raided Allivane's London offices in 1987 after a tip-off from Dutch customs officials following their raid on cartel member Muiden-Chemie (see below). In 1988, after a former Allivane director, John Heneaghan, alleged in court that the company had been involved in illegally shipping arms to Iran, its Scottish offices were raided. No prosecutions followed.

Allivane had been set up in the early 1980s by Terry Byrne, Jr., who had previously worked alongside fraudster James Guerin. During the Iran-Iraq War, Allivane was contracted by Gerald Bull to supply Iraq with a fuse production line to manufacture fuses for his 155mm artillery shells. According to a former Allivane manager: "We never had any problems co-operating on the Iraqi fuse facility we negotiated with Dr Bull. We informed the Defence Ministry of exactly what we were doing. Somebody up there in the government loved us."[86] After the cease-fire and the contemporaneous closure of Allivane, this project was taken up by Ordtec (to be routed through Jordan), and resulted in the Ordtec prosecution.[87]

When he first realized the potential significance of the information he had, in December 1988 Machon wrote to Prime Minister Margaret Thatcher, warning that "either Britain or America is funnelling war equipment through Allivane which is certainly destined for Iraq."[88] After this, he began to receive the attentions of VAT inspectors, similar to the attentions both Paul Henderson and Gerald James received from the Inland Revenue when they sought to draw attention to their cases. In Henderson's case, his preparation of his defense for his Old Bailey trial was impeded by the need to devote his attention simultaneously to these tax demands.[89] Like Astra, Machon's company, it appeared, was expendable in the cause of concealing Britain's role in arming Iraq and Iran. Nevertheless on 29 January 1991, he wrote to Prime Minister John Major, telling him:

> What does alarm me most of all is that Britain has been supplying Iraq and creating a funnel through which every arms manufacturing country, even Eastern Bloc countries, have had the facility made "available" to them to complete the shipment to the Gulf through Britain since 1983 up to 1990. . . . Since 1988 I have amassed thousands of documents, many in original form, which in the eyes of my Legal Counsel prove that we were to be sacrificed financially to safeguard the British secret. . . . I appeal to you . . . to offer me the opportunity of discussing these papers in detail with you.

In response, Charles Powell wrote: "The Prime Minister has asked me to thank you for your letters of 29 January and 21 February. He has asked me to pass on to you his regrets that his diary commitments are such that he is unable to accept your invitation to meet."[90]

◆ Neutrals as Gunrunners: The Cases of Austria, Sweden, and the Propellant Cartel

Something of the extensive and illicit role of "neutrals" as suppliers of military goods to Iraq and Iran was exposed through the efforts of the Swedish authorities in the mid-1980s. While Iraq had been able to take advantage of the benign attitude toward it displayed by most "neutrals," was able to get major arms from a range of sources, and could receive notionally prohibited equipment via neighboring allies acting as conduits, Iran had experienced more difficulty in securing the means by which it could continue to prosecute the war. Following the outbreak of war, both belligerents developed an almost insatiable appetite for explosives and ammunition. For example, Iran has been estimated to have had an annual consumption during the war of 4,000 metric tons, firing between 500,000 and 1 million artillery shells each month, which amounted to a monthly requirement of between 50 and 100 metric tons. The Swedish Bofors affair revealed the extent to which both protagonists, but particularly Iran, were meeting this demand, with the assistance of a network of major European explosives manufacturers. These manufacturers had formed a propellant cartel[91] by means of which companies in Austria, Belgium, Britain, Finland, France,[92] Italy, Netherlands, Norway, Spain, Sweden, Switzerland, and West Germany illicitly supplied propellant to both Iran and Iraq during the 1980s. They used the tried and tested methods of false end-user certificates, conduits, and misleading descriptions of consignments of explosives as being for industrial rather than military use. Belligerent demand for gunpowder represented a volume beyond the capacity of individual manufacturers, and so the companies that made up the European Association for the Study of Safety Problems in the Production and Use of Propellant Powders (EASSP)[93] began to use their organization as a forum for allocating orders from Iran and Iraq within the member companies and devising means of getting these orders through to their prohibited destinations. The cartel's head office in Brussels, where EASSP's official business was conducted, also acted as a center for the cartel's unofficial business (although meetings tended to be rotated in hotels across Europe). The unofficial nature of the cartel makes it difficult to say with any certainty how many companies were involved. There seem to have been thirteen core members that drew on other companies' capacities when the need arose. For their part, Swedish customs and the Swedish commissioner for freedom of commerce (NO: Naringsombudsman) compiled a list of just seven members as a result of their investigations:

Table 3.3	
Propellant Cartel Members	
Company	**Country**
Bofors	Sweden
SNPE	France
Dyno	Norway
Biazzi (Dinamite)	Italy
Nobel Explosives (ICI)	Scotland
PRB	Belgium
SSE	Switzerland

In addition, a number of companies were named as being clearly involved with the cartel and occasionally participating in discussions and contracts. These include Rio Tinto in Spain, Muiden Chemie in the Netherlands and RO in the United Kingdom. The Swedish Peace and Arbitration Society cited thirteen members: Bofors, Muiden Chemie, Nobel Explosives (ICI), Kemira (Finland), Forcit (Finland), FDSP (Yugoslavia), SNPE, PRB, Raufoss (Norway), Rio Tinto, Vinnis (Switzerland), Vass A.G. (West Germany), and ERT (Spain). Documents obtained by Swedish customs suggest that the cartel performed three major functions. First, it reached price-fixing arrangements—agreeing common price levels for different markets (Europe, Africa, the Middle East, etc.). Second, it arranged "splits," the parceling out of large orders among the member companies. A Swedish customs official described the method:

> Cartel members in Sweden, France, Holland and Belgium would meet regularly to eat and drink together and plan how they would keep Iran and Iraq supplied with munitions. They knew that no single company would produce enough gunpowder to meet the enormous demand, without raising production quotas and attracting attention so they decided to spread the work around.[94]

Finally, the cartel also kept an eye on the activities of competitors outside the cartel, and any information obtained by one cartel member would be passed on to the rest. However, membership of the cartel was not fixed. New members could be nominated and then elected as, for example, the state-owned Swedish manufacturer FFV was in 1985.

In the case of Sweden, in many ways the nation dominating the propellant cartel, investigations during the 1980s uncovered a major operation by Nobel Kemi and Bofors—both subsidiaries of Nobel Industries, Sweden[95]—to supply Iran through several conduits (prominent amongst which was Singapore), in contravention of Sweden's prohibition on the export of arms to warring states. The scandal that resulted from this revelation developed further momentum when Admiral Carl-Fredrik Algernon, head of the Swedish War Materials Inspectorate, fell to his death in front of an oncoming train on the Stockholm underground on 15 January 1987, only days before he was due to give evidence to a special prosecutor. A number of senior Bofors officials subsequently resigned, including managing director Martin Ardbo, and an internal Nobel Industries inquiry confirmed that Bofors had made illegal shipments bound for Iran through conduits. However, Ardbo claimed government complicity in the exports, saying that the inspectorate knew of the exports and had recommended that Bofors route them through conduits like Singapore in order to avoid attracting attention.

Singapore was a much-favored conduit. Bofors notionally sold artillery shells, 155mm guns, 40mm naval guns, and at least 714 RBS-70 laser-guided anti-aircraft missiles to Singapore. These were then shipped on to Iran. So extensive was the use of Singapore that by 1985, on paper at least, Singapore had become the second-largest importer of Swedish arms in the world, accounting for 14.4 percent of all Swedish arms exports.[96] Another useful route was via Portugal and Spain. Spain was a channel favored by Gerald Bull's SRC for getting arms to Iraq via Saudi Arabia, while Portugal is estimated to have sent at least $150 million worth of arms to Iran between 1984 and 1987, as well as arms to Iraq. As well as favored conduits, the cartel also had preferred modes of delivery. One was to use Danish cargo ships; Swedish customs investigations came up with a list of nineteen that had been used to carry military equipment to Iran during the 1980s.[97] It has also been argued that the murder of Olaf Palme may have been linked to illegal sales of arms to Iran. One suggested scenario is that in 1985 Palme learned that howitzers were being exported to Iran and ended their export, another is that he knew of these exports and acquiesced in them.[98]

A crucial link from the Swedish companies to other cartel members and Iran and Iraq was provided by Karl Erik Schmitz's Malmo-based company, Scandinavian Commodity. In 1983 the company received an order for 4,340 metric tons of 105mm and 155mm ammunition from Iran, which was originally to be supplied by South Africa. However, when South Africa began to supply Iraq in 1984, it cut off supplies to Iran, leaving 1,400 metric tons still to be produced. Hence, Schmitz ("one of Iran's most capable arms brokers"[99]) turned to the state-owned Yugoslav company Federal Directorate of Supply and Procurement (FDSP), which could supply 500 metric tons itself, and was persuaded by Schmitz to buy in the remaining 1,000 metric tons from Bofors, Muiden Chemie, Kemira, Raufoss, ICI-Nobel, and Expro in Canada to complete the Iranian order. When an order placed with the cartel by the Italian company Tirrena via PRB and SNPE fell through[100]—only 150 metric tons of a 5,300 metric ton order left Italy—the cartel members agreed to allow Schmitz to take over this order, routing it through Yugoslavia. Schmitz completed the entire contract for 5,300 metric tons using conduits and false end-users. The powder would be loaded at various European ports like Nordenham and Zeebrugge, from where it would sail to Bar in Yugoslavia. The powder would then go through the Suez Canal to Bandar Abbas in Iran, using false Kenyan end-user certificates so as not to be stopped by the Egyptian authorities. Schmitz was questioned about this process by Swedish customs officials following his arrest:

S: When we pass through the Suez Canal they want to know the destination of these goods and the Yugoslavs then say we need basic documentation to avoid being left naked. Here therefore an EUC-confirmation has been made on Kenya against Y. This is what they wanted for each contract. There are ships destined for Iran that have been sequestered. All contracts receive a document from Kenya—not that we've deceived them—all cargoes need a document that can be produced at the Channel so that that product is not stopped.

Q: We have encountered a number of EUCs issued by the appropriate Kenyan authority.

S: These certificates are issued to all and sundry. You merely go to the embassy and say that you need one.

Q: The embassy in Stockholm?

S: No, it is the President himself. Count them all and you have an army on par with the Russian. But the documents are for the canal only.

Q: Do you pay Kenya for this service. A rhetorical question perhaps?

S: Of course, US$10,000.[101]

Thereafter, Iran would place orders with Schmitz, who would buy from FDSP in Yugoslavia (generally also the identified end-user), which in turn, because of the volume involved, would buy from Bofors, which would then parcel out the order to other members of the cartel, like Muiden Chemie. When Bofors placed part of the fall 1984 order with Muiden Chemie, it telexed the Dutch company to warn them of the need for discretion:

> Great Men like you are not easily shaken so keep fighting for the other parties until 12th October . . .
> PS: When you telex Nobel Krut, please use telex nr 73346 BONOBEL. The other (73419 BOFINK) goes to the purchasing department of the artillery division, which delays communications and draws in unnecessary attention to our small "wheelings and dealings."[102]

In 1987, the *Wall Street Journal* reported that, in addition to this activity, Schmitz had also delivered two consignments of explosives to Iran in 1985 via St. Lucia Airways—a CIA-linked company that Oliver North was using just three months later to ferry U.S. missiles to Iran. The first flight, on 24 July 1985, carried explosives from Muiden Chemie and PRB, complete with false Yugoslav and Greek end-user certificates; the second, on 14 August, went from Israel to Lille and then on to Iran.[103] In May 1987 Schmitz was indicted on forty-two separate counts concerning the illegal sale of explosives and gunpowder with a value of 74,800,000 kronor between 1981 and 1985.[104]

There were also a number of British links to the cartel, despite the existence of the Howe Guidelines. ICI-Nobel (Nobel Explosives Company—NEC) in Scotland was a member of the cartel and participated in its meetings regarding arming Iran. For example, it was allocated 900 metric tons of the Tirrena order, to be shipped via Yugoslavia by Schmitz. However, in a travel report dated June 1984, Mats Lundberg of Bofors conveyed some of the ICI management's concern at the involvement of this ICI subsidiary in the activities of the cartel: "Harvey-Jones [managing director of ICI] forbids continued participation in our meetings and therefore Frank cannot participate, but wants individual contacts with the members. Someone will contact Frank before each meeting."[105] What senior management wanted and what actually happened were clearly not always the same thing in the lucrative field of arming Iraq and Iran. A second link is provided by RO—at this time still a government-owned company. In a number of cartel travel reports, RO is named as a competitor to the cartel, but at a cartel meeting in October 1984 "Guy" (Guy Chevallier) of SNPE informed the meeting that "Truman" of RO had promised "market co-operation" with the cartel.[106]

A third link is provided by the operation of the Iranian arms procurement office in London under the cover of the National Iranian Oil Company. The procurement operation, based on the sixth floor, involved thirty to forty senior Iranians at any one time. Inside, the Iranian army, air force, and navy each had its own procurement department. The Iranians were under surveillance, and those who entered and left the building were photographed.[107] According to journalist James Adams, via Government Communications Headquarters (GCHQ), MI5 "was able to routinely listen to all telephone calls, intercept all telexes and facsimile messages and, using other systems, observe and listen to conversations between arms dealers and the Iranians."[108] When Britain closed this office in September 1987, the thirty-three Iranians then involved in this work were expelled. Iran simply moved the entire operation to Frankfurt.

◆ Austria

In addition to the activities of small and "neutral" European states in the cartel, Austria also sold arms to Iran and Iraq, despite the existence of a restrictive arms export regime similar to that of Sweden. It did so through the state-owned arms manufacturer Voest Alpine, to which Gerald Bull had sold designs for a towed 155mm gun (designated GHN-45) in 1978 for a one-time fee of just $2 million. To get around Austrian neutrality laws, which prohibited the sale of arms to states at war, Voest Alpine sold Iraq the Bull-designed 155mm guns through Jordan. As a consequence, on paper, between 1981 and 1990, Jordan was Austria's largest market for arms, importing $320 million worth of major weapons. The company reported sales of two hundred GHN-45s to Jordan in 1982 alone. According to one report, Saddam even met with the Austrian interior minister in April 1982 to try to speed up their delivery.[109] On paper, Jordan was a formidable military force.

The United States encouraged the Voest Alpine sales to Jordan (i.e., Iraq), but when Austria began to sell to Iran as well,[110] the United States, under Operation Staunch, moved to prevent such sales:

> In an unusual move in early April 1986, CIA and State Department officials showed Austria's ambassador to Washington classified satellite photographs of 15 GHN-45s at Iran's Isfahan artillery training center. A CIA narrative stamped TOP SECRET— SENSITIVE accompanying the photos declared, "[W]e believe that significant amounts of the extended-range full-bore ammunition were purchased along with the guns." But the Iranians got an estimated 180 GHN-45s anyway.[111]

Some of these were notionally intended for Libya (and at one point were intercepted by suspicious Austrian customs officials), but none went near, and all ended up in Iran. The whole ruse was eventually exposed, and on 26 January 1988, Peter Unterweger, general director of Noricum, staged a press conference to admit that Noricum/Voest Alpine had sold Sch 4,000 million worth of arms to Iran between 1984 and 1986 in contravention of Austrian arms export regulations.[112] This led to the most extensive criminal investigation in Austrian history in 1990–91, implicating two former Austrian chancellors and several cabinet ministers.

◆ Paraguay

The trick with false end-users, as distinct from conduits, is to use states that are (1) friendly, that is, pose no threat themselves if they have the equipment, so there is no outcry that they are a recipient and (2) geographically remote from areas of tension, so avoiding the kind of scrutiny that would later reveal that they did not actually have the equipment for which they issued an end-user certificate. During the Iran-Iraq War, South American states were well placed to perform this function. Brazil was heavily involved on behalf of Iran, while Paraguay was ideally situated to revive a role previously played in relation to beating the embargo on South Africa. On paper at least, Paraguay ordered an impressive quantity of military equipment. In practice, this went nowhere near Paraguay but was sent instead to Iran. Between 1980 and 1984, Paraguay was involved in at least $700 million worth of covert arms deals, prominent among which were deals involving twenty-three U.S. F-4E aircraft and 90,000 Italian mines.[113] The F-4 deal was brokered by a London-based company (operating from offices at 47 Brunswick Place) called Kindrib Ltd, on behalf of the Iranian Ministry of Defence. The company was set up in 1982, just before it brokered the deal, and was dissolved in 1987. This particular deal is one of the best illustrations of the transparent nature of much of the illicit arms trade. These U.S. aircraft were notionally ordered by a state whose cold war political development was shaped by the United States. Even its transition to democracy coincided with U.S. calls for a political opening. Its armed forces were not designed nor able to defend Paraguay from likely external threats from powerful neighbors like Brazil and have instead been directed toward internal policing. By the end of the Iran-Iraq War, the Paraguayan air force had just sixteen combat aircraft—nine of which were Brazilian EMB-326s. Despite this, the U.S. State Department approved the sale. While it is apparent that there are not twenty-three U.S. F-4Es in Paraguay, the State Department does not seem to have required an explanation from Paraguay as to what happened to them.

Hence, while the arming of Iraq and Iran was largely coordinated through Europe and facilitated by the United States, it was a global operation. No one person or company illustrates this better than Dr. Gerald Bull and src. Bull was a Canadian with U.S. citizenship, based in Europe, whose companies established an international network of links to fulfill their contracts with Iraq. Bull was also the ballistics genius behind the most audacious and controversial part of the whole Iraqi procurement operation: Project Babylon, the supergun.

NOTES

1 *Hansard*, 10.29.85, col. 454.
2 Indeed, between 1985 and 1990, the Inter-Departmental Committee (IDC) set up to vet license applications for Iraq and Iran approved a higher proportion of license applications received for Iraq than for Iran. For a breakdown of the figures, see *Hansard*, 6.24.93, cols. 263–264.
3 Scott Inquiry—Day 6: Evidence of Sir Adam Butler, p. 63.
4 Scott Inquiry—Day 11: Evidence of Sir Stephen Egerton, p. 11. Egerton told the inquiry that when he suggested that they should employ similar guidelines, "of course they all laughed." Ibid., p. 12.
5 See Scott Inquiry—Day 11: Evidence of Sir Stephen Egerton, pp. 13–15.
6 Quoted in the *Guardian*, 11.5.92.
7 Scott Inquiry—Day 49: Evidence of Alan Clark, p. 7. In his statement to the inquiry he had

said: "It must be understood that the Guidelines were an extremely useful adjunct to foreign policy offering a form of words elusive of definition, which offered the point of stick or carrot in policy terms." Ibid., p. 56.

8 Ibid., p. 112.

9 Scott Inquiry—Day 81: Evidence of Lord Trefgarne, p. 15.

10 Ibid., p. 58.

11 Scott Inquiry—Day 17: Evidence of Mark Higson, p. 80.

12 Scott Inquiry—Day 48: Evidence of Lady Thatcher, p. 4.

13 Scott Inquiry—Day 81: Evidence of Lord Trefgarne, pp. 3–8.

14 Scott Inquiry—Day 20: Evidence of Ian Blackley, p. 45.

15 Scott Inquiry—Day 24: Evidence of Tim Renton, p. 70.

16 See, for instance, F. Gregory Gause III: The Illogic of Dual Containment, *Foreign Affairs*, March/April 1994, pp. 56–66. In Anthony Parsons: Iran, Iraq and the West's Policy of Demonisation, *Middle East International*, 6.11.93, p. 16, Parsons termed this policy one of "equality of demonisation."

17 Quoted in the *Independent*, 11.6.92.

18 Scott Inquiry—Day 20: Evidence of Ian Blackley, p. 46. Blackley also told Scott: "If the war were prolonged, it is possible that one of them might have won. Our policy was also to work to bring the war to an end." As Scott noted: ". . . not wanting either side to win is an understandable concept, and it is not the same concept as not wanting the war to be prolonged." Ibid.

19 Ibid., p. 48.

20 *Hansard*, 1.18.89, col. 241.

21 Scott Inquiry—Day 49: Evidence of Alan Clark, pp. 117–119.

22 Scott Inquiry—Day 62: Evidence of Sir Robin Butler, p. 78. William Waldegrave backed up this assertion, telling the inquiry that Goulden's evidence, "though given in good faith," was not "quite right." Scott Inquiry—Day 27: Evidence of William Waldegrave, p. 18.

23 Ibid., pp. 73, 74.

24 Scott Inquiry—Day 26: Evidence of William Waldegrave, pp. 113–114. Waldegrave later revisited this assertion, telling a disbelieving Scott: "The more I looked at it, the more the truth is that we never actually changed the guidelines." Ibid., p. 197.

25 Scott Inquiry—Day 27: Evidence of William Waldegrave, p. 17.

26 The Howe Guidelines are considered in Mark Phythian and Walter Little: Parliament and Arms Sales: Lessons of the Matrix Churchill Affair, *Parliamentary Affairs*, Vol. 46 No. 3 July 1993, pp. 293–308.

27 Scott Inquiry—Day 48: Evidence of Lady Thatcher, p. 31.

28 Scott Inquiry—Day 24: Evidence of Tim Renton, p. 31.

29 Scott Inquiry—Day 25: Evidence of David Mellor, pp. 13–15.

30 Scott Inquiry—Day 18: Evidence of Sir David Miers, pp. 82–83.

31 Scott Inquiry—Day 4: Evidence of Lt. Col. Glazebrook, pp. 22–23.

32 For a full listing, see House of Commons Trade and Industry Committee: *Exports to Iraq—Memoranda of Evidence, 17 July 1991*, pp. 43–48.

33 TISC: *Exports to Iraq*, Evidence of Christopher Cowley, HC86-iv, EQ31, p. 191.

34 Sir Richard Luce told the Scott Inquiry that the member states of the Gulf Co-operation Council, "who were almost all very close in relations with Britain and other western countries, certainly put very strong pressure on the British Government to be as sympathetic and as supportive as possible to Iraq." Scott Inquiry—Day 1: Evidence of Sir Richard Luce, p. 25.

35 Scott Inquiry—Day 1: Evidence of Sir Richard Luce, pp. 19–20.

36 Scott Inquiry—Day 24: Evidence of Tim Renton, p. 69. As he also noted, "in the context

of . . . political contact, ministerial visits, diplomatic representation, clearly the two were not at that time on the same footing." Ibid., p. 71.

37 Scott Inquiry—Day 25: Evidence of David Mellor, p. 56.

38 A. Cordesman: Arms to Iran, p. 18.

39 *Guardian*, 7.17.81. See also John Pilger: Salesman Hurd, in Pilger: *Distant Voices*, London, Vintage, 1992, pp. 136–139.

40 Ibid.

41 *Financial Times*, 3.31.83.

42 At the Scott Inquiry, Sir Stephen Egerton, a former U.K. ambassador to Saudi Arabia, admitted that there had been such a British tilt in the early 1980s. Scott Inquiry—Day 11: Evidence of Sir Stephen Egerton, p. 14.

43 Quoted in John Sweeney: *Trading with the Enemy: Britain's Arming of Iraq*, London, Pan, 1993, p. 100.

44 Ibid.

45 See the *Guardian*, 2.23.82, and *Hansard*, 3.24.82, col. 196. In the event, no order for repair was forthcoming from Iraq, although it did attempt to acquire spare parts from Britain via Jordan.

46 *Financial Times*, 2.23.82.

47 Scott Inquiry—Day 4: Evidence of Lt. Col. Glazebrook, p. 81.

48 Scott Inquiry—Day 48: Evidence of Lady Thatcher, p. 34.

49 See Paul Halloran and Mark Hollingsworth: *Thatcher's Gold: The Life and Times of Mark Thatcher*, London, Simon & Schuster, 1995, ch. 6. Discussion of his "cut" of the Al Yamamah deal is at pp. 184–186.

50 *Sunday Times Magazine*, 4.4.93, p. 47.

51 *Sunday Times:* Britain's Richest 500 Supplement, 4.10.94, p. 41. His wealth was still estimated at around £40 million.

52 *Dispatches:* The First Thatcherite, Channel 4, 11.25.92.

53 *Sunday Times*, 10.9.94.

54 *Financial Times*, 2.23.82.

55 Ibid.

56 *New Scientist*, 12.22/29.83.

57 *Guardian*, 12.22.83. An MOD spokesman confirmed that the sale was consistent with stated government policy: "The kit which was supplied—if indeed it was supplied—through the defence sales organisation was of a defensive nature."

58 *Hansard*, 3.15.84, col. 214.

59 *Hansard*, 3.29.84, col. 286.

60 This was done through the Export of Goods (Control) (Amendment No. 6) Order, making chloroethanol, thiodiglycol, dimethylamine, phosphorous oxychloride, methyl phosphonyl difluoride, methyl phosphonyl dichloride, dimethyl methylphosphonate, and potassium fluoride licensable. *Hansard*, 4.12.84, cols. 339–340. West Germany, far more deeply implicated in the export of chemicals to Iraq, responded by tightening its regulations on the export of chemical manufacturing equipment in August 1984. *Guardian*, 8.8.84.

61 *Financial Times*, 4.16.84.

62 *Financial Times*, 11.9.84.

63 *Hansard*, 11.4.88, col. 787. The *Guardian* had described the extension of a further £200 million line of credit in 1988 as representing "a victory for Clark in the face of Foreign Office misgivings about the timing." *Guardian*, 9.24.87.

64 *Financial Times*, 10.14.89.

65 Ibid.

66 *Sunday Times*, 7.5.81.

67 *Hansard*, 3.25.82, col. 401.
68 Scott Inquiry—Day 21: Evidence of David Gore-Booth, p. 139.
69 Scott Inquiry—Day 27: Evidence of William Waldegrave, pp. 103–105.
70 BAE: *Hawk Focus 3*. Quoted in CAAT: *Arming Saddam*, p. 6.
71 At the Scott Inquiry, the FCO's Ian Blackley admitted, "it was what you might call a dual purpose aircraft." Scott Inquiry—Day 20: Evidence of Ian Blackley, p. 44.
72 Scott Inquiry: Statement of Christopher Cowley, pp. 5–7.
73 Scott Inquiry—Day 21: Evidence of David Gore-Booth, pp. 143–146.
74 Scott Inquiry—Day 48: Evidence of Lady Thatcher, pp. 146–147.
75 See Scott Inquiry—Day 15: Evidence of Robin Fellgett, passim.
76 *Hansard*, 3.25.82, col. 401.
77 Scott Inquiry: Statement of Gerald James, pp. 9–10. See also the report in the *Observer*, 4.1.84.
78 See *Flight International*, 4.28.84, the *Observer*, 8.26.90 and 1.27.91.
79 *Times*, 3.16.90.
80 K. Timmerman: *The Death Lobby*, p. 331.
81 On Hastie's controversial presence at the exhibition, see Scott Inquiry—Day 34: Evidence of Ian McDonald, pp. 205–215. A Whitehall memo on the Hastie visit, dated 4 March 1989, stated: "FCO not pleased, potential embarrassment, Hastie instructed to keep a low profile." Ibid., p. 209. Despite this, Hastie spoke freely with journalist Kenneth Timmerman and makes an appearance in Timmerman's book, *The Death Lobby*.
82 K. Timmerman: *The Death Lobby*, p. 338.
83 Ibid., p. 334.
84 *Guardian*, 5.4.92.
85 A. Friedman: *Spider's Web*, p. 75.
86 Ibid., p. 78.
87 See chapter 6.
88 The letter is reproduced in A. Friedman, *Spider's Web*, p. 358.
89 See chapters 5 and 7.
90 *Hansard*, 11.23.92, col. 680.
91 The following draws on material contained in the Swedish Peace and Arbitration Society: *International Connections of the Bofors Affair*, Stockholm, December 1987.
92 Although apparently outside the cartel's arrangements, the French company Luchaire supplied Iran with around 4,500 artillery shells between 1982 and 1986 in exchange for the release of French hostages held in Lebanon by pro-Iranian groups.
93 This was formed in 1975 as a forum for the discussion of safety, transport, and related issues. Its role in arming Iran (and Iraq) was first uncovered following a November 1984 Swedish customs raid on Nobel Chemie.
94 Quoted in Kenneth R. Timmerman: Europe's Arms Pipeline to Iran, the *Nation*, 7.18/25.87, p. 48.
95 Concurrently, Nobel was involved in controversy over Bofors' payment of bribes/commissions to Indian officials to secure a 8,400 million kronor deal for howitzers. On the Indian scandal, and speculation about Palme's death, see Henrik Westander: *Classified: The Political Cover-Up of the Bofors Scandal*, Bombay, Sterling Newspapers, 1992.
96 K. Timmerman: Europe's Arms Pipeline to Iran, p. 50.
97 These were Arrebo; Danalith; Dejro; Erria; Jotun; Karen Klipper; Lottelith; Marie TH; Othonia; Pia Vesta; Sea Star; Sea Trader; Svendborg Bay; Svendborg Pearl (renamed Vola, Jan. 1985); Vinderlevsholm; Ardal; Anne Lise Oltmann; Fylke (renamed Sea Star); Mercandian Ambassador 2; Mercandian Exporter 2; Mercandian Supplier 2; Pia Arre; Svendborg Galant (renamed Nuptse).

98 See *Keesing's,* Volume XXXIII, August 1987, pp. 35, 334–335, 336.

99 K. Timmerman: Europe's Arms Pipeline to Iran, p. 48.

100 SNPE, PRB, Bofors-Nobel, ICI-Nobel in Scotland, and Muiden Chemie were, according to Swedish customs, the five companies in the cartel that had agreed to handle the Tirrena deal.

101 Cited in *International Connections of the Bofors Affair,* p. 35.

102 Ibid., p. 28.

103 *Wall Street Journal,* 9.10.87.

104 At the time one dollar = 6.349 kronor.

105 *International Connections of the Bofors Affair,* p. 20.

106 Ibid., p. 21.

107 See the experiences of John Anderson in chapter 5.

108 James Adams: *Trading in Death,* London, Hutchinson, 1990, p. 129. Adams cites interviews with those involved as his source for this.

109 *Washington Post,* 2.10.91.

110 For example, in a deal worth $60 million, Austria supplied Brazil with 155mm barrels via Yugoslavia. Of course, once these left Yugoslavia they went to Iran and did not go anywhere near the continent on the end-user certificate, let alone the country.

111 *Washington Post,* 2.10.91.

112 These are governed by the KMG (Bundesgesetz uber die Ein-, Aus- und Durchführ von Kriegsmaterial), which prohibits arms exports to areas of tension or war or where serious human rights violations have taken place.

113 *Assignment:* Secrets of the Generals, BBC2, 5.4.93.

The Supergun

Project Babylon was to be the culmination of the work that Gerald Bull had begun in the 1960s on the High Altitude Research Project (HARP). The assumption underlying the project was that satellites could be fired into orbit from the barrel of a large gun at relatively low cost. Bull was convinced of the viability of the project, but by the end of the 1960s his funding had dried up and he was forced to suspend his work in this area. Twenty years later, early in 1988, Iraq expressed an interest in allowing Bull to resume his HARP work and build a big gun capable of launching a satellite from inside Iraq.

Gerald Vincent Bull was born in North Bay, Ontario, Canada, on 9 March 1928. In 1948 he graduated from the University of Toronto with a degree in aeronautical engineering, and in 1951 became the university's youngest ever Ph.D. at the age of twenty-three. From then until his resignation in 1961, he worked for the Canadian Armament, Research and Development Establishment (CARDE) on the Velvet Glove missile and other programs. At 34 Bull became the youngest ever full professor to be appointed by McGill University, where he developed his interest in using long-range guns as satellite launchers and began work on HARP.

HARP was funded by McGill, the U.S. Army, and later, although without any real commitment, the Canadian government. The project was set up in Barbados, where McGill already had other facilities and where shells could be fired harmlessly into the sea. The project's most important equipment, supplied through Bull's contacts in the U.S. Army, was a 40cm, 21m-long gun barrel christened Betsy. In 1962 Bull developed the Martlet I, an experimental missile capable of carrying scientific equipment in its nose cone. This was fired from Betsy to a height of 15 miles at its first firing in 1963. In June of that year an improved missile—Martlet II—was fired almost 60 miles. These were the days immediately after the Cuban missile crisis, and when the government of Barbados expressed concern that the Cubans could well mistake Bull's research for a military program and launch a preemptive strike against it, Bull reassured them that the program made no sense militarily, and that its fixed position made it so vulnerable that the Cubans would easily recognize this.

In 1965, just as he would later do with Project Babylon, Bull put together a 40cm horizontally mounted gun (christened Betsy junior) on which to conduct tests. However, by this time, the limitations presented by Betsy's barrel length, which in practice meant that the 60-mile record could not be much improved upon, were becoming obvious. Bull therefore extended the barrel length to 36m and in so doing made Betsy the longest working gun in the world. In July 1965 this extended gun fired a Martlet II to a height of almost 90 miles, a new record. Shortly afterward, though, the Canadian government began to distance itself from HARP and, despite Bull's successes, in 1967 withdrew its financial support, bringing the project to a close. An ironic endnote to the HARP program is that while the U.S. Army supported HARP, it did so only because it was interested in the military applications of a gun that could fire projectiles over long distances. Hence, in both the HARP and later Babylon programs, while Bull was building a satellite launcher, both his major sponsors—the Pentagon and then the Iraqi government—were more interested in the military value of his work.

In 1968, with HARP on ice, Bull formed SRC as an independent vehicle for his ballistics expertise, and based it at his expanding Highwater estate, which straddled the U.S.-Canadian border. It was at this point that he began work on 155mm guns, setting out to design a 155mm shell that would exceed the 12½-mile range of the typical 155mm shell. In 1973 Bull and SRC joined forces with Belgium's PRB to create Space Research Corporation International (SRC-I), based in Brussels, an association that marked a definite shift for Bull into the world of the international arms dealer. Now Bull moved from designing just shells to designing entire artillery systems. The GC-45 155mm gun that he designed would be able to fire a shell over 16 miles, giving it a superiority of more than 6 miles over existing 155mm systems.

Bull's ultimately fatal liaison with Iraq had parallels in his earlier work. In each case, Bull was to deal with states with which the U.S. government and the West (for the most part) publicly had no direct military dealings and to which, notionally, they did not want to see arms and Western technology sent. Yet in each case, wider interests caused them either to encourage Bull to supply these countries or to give him consent to supply them. The first of these cases brought Bull and SRC into contact with South Africa and led to his imprisonment.

In February 1975 Bull was contacted by an American named Jack Frost and asked to supply Israel with 15,000 of his extended range full-bore (ERFB) 155mm shells. The shells were manufactured in Pennsylvania by Chamberlain Manufacturing, cleaned up at Highwater, and shipped to PRB in Belgium to be filled with explosive. From there they were sent to Israel, and passed on to South Africa to be used to support the National Union for the Total Independence of Angola (UNITA) in the Angolan civil war—a cause in which the CIA was to become heavily involved.[1] Bull's biographer, William Lowther, claims: "From an early date in the course of the South African deal, at least some officials within the CIA, the State Department and the Pentagon knew everything. They did not want the Marxist government in Angola, backed by Cuban troops, to succeed in squashing the pro-Western UNITA force. And if that meant arming South Africa to prevent a Communist take-over, then so be it."[2] Bull's son, Michel, has said that his father was "led to believe it was the thing to do . . . that the US had a passive policy to more or less favor these type of things in order to save the last bastion of capitalism in Africa."[3]

Bull's shells performed well, and in 1976 officials from ARMSCOR, the South African state armaments manufacturer, met with SRC-I's Luis Palacio in Brussels to discuss the possibility of collaboration on a South African 155mm gun and shell. On 7 April 1976, ARMSCOR signed a contract to buy 35,000 of Bull's shells with an option on a further 15,000, while SRC-I also began working with the South Africans on a 155mm gun, with SRC-I staff like Alec Pappas and Steve Adams being sent to work in South Africa to oversee development and testing. In terms of the South African order for shells, Bull would buy rough shell casings from the United States and clean them up at Highwater, just as he had previously. However, this time they would be shipped to Bull's testing facility in Antigua (to which Bull had moved from Barbados) from where, rather than be used in tests, they would be picked up by a cargo ship (*SS Tugeland*) and taken to Cape Town. While this operation worked smoothly at its inception, it ultimately ran into trouble under the changed foreign policy priorities of the Carter administration.

Bull's South African operation began to come unstuck in 1978, after he announced a contract with the Spanish government to buy 21,624 155mm shells. In March of that year a Danish cargo ship took them from Antigua to Barcelona, where a Dutch ship picked them up in May and shipped them to Durban, South Africa. This deal revived official interest in Bull's activities. An inspection of the Antigua facility revealed that, while 30,000 shells had been sent to Antigua, there were just 2,508 shells in stock of which no more than 2,000 had been fired. Where were the missing 25,492?[4] Later in the year, the entire operation was exposed, and in 1980 Bull pleaded guilty to exporting shells, gun barrels, and radar equipment in violation of the U.N. embargo on South Africa and U.S. law. On 16 June 1980 he was sentenced to a year in prison, with six months suspended.[5]

For South Africa, the outcome of its relationship with Bull was the development of the G-5 towed 155mm gun—subsequently sold to Iraq during the Iran-Iraq War—and by 1982 the G-6 155mm self-propelled gun, capable of traveling at speeds of up to 65mph, earning it the nickname Kalahari Ferrari. It also boasted a range of around 25 miles, comfortably outdistancing NATO's own 155mm guns.

Bull was released from the Allenwood prison camp in Montgomery, Pennsylvania, in February 1981 after serving over four months of his sentence, and he soon began the task of reconstituting SRC from a European base in Brussels. He had resumed negotiations, seemingly initiated by George Wong, a banker with alleged connections to British intelligence,[6] prior to his imprisonment over the possibility of carrying out some work for China—the second notionally prohibited destination in which Bull was to work. China, which was subject to Co-Ordinating Committee for Multilateral Export Control (COCOM) restrictions,[7] was looking to upgrade its artillery to counter the longer-range Soviet 130mm artillery it faced across their long shared border, which had been the scene of an estimated 5,000 clashes between 1964 and 1969. Bull visited China shortly after his release from Allenwood where, after the degrading experience of prison and (as far as Bull was concerned) abandonment by a government whose bidding he was doing, the contrast could hardly have been greater. As James Adams describes, "he was treated with great respect, something close to veneration, by the military leaders and scientists he met. He found that the officials were familiar with his work, had read his reports on the HARP program, and had followed with interest his work on new artillery systems."[8]

Bull suggested that the Chinese combine the Voest Alpine version of his 155mm gun—the GHN-45—with his new "base-bleed" ammunition, which would give a range of around 25 miles. However, the Chinese wanted a complete, indigenous, 155mm production facility, and this is what Bull and SRC undertook, under a 1982 contract, to produce. By this time Bull's son, Michel, had joined his father as an SRC executive. Once the Chinese contract was signed (with Norinco), Michel flew to Washington and briefed the Office of Munitions Control on the plan. Although China was COCOM-proscribed, the Office of Munitions Control approved the deal, thus reflecting the realization that there were several foreign policy advantages to be derived from seeing China armed in this way. The first was the intelligence that could be gleaned on the Chinese arms industry. Before leaving for a visit to China, American SRC staff would visit the U.S. Embassy in Brussels, and they would go back there on their return to be debriefed. They would be asked what they had seen, what they had been doing, and what the next stage of their work would involve. From an SRC perspective, they were making sure that the South African situation did not recur. Chris Cowley, who worked alongside Bull in China, considers that in addition, George Wong, who was often present in China, was used to pass on information to British intelligence:

> Every time any engineer came out [of China], we wrote a Visit Report. I would keep a diary—what was going on, who I had seen, what was discussed—and that Visit Report was given to George Wong. Now what the hell is it being given to George Wong for? George Wong is the banker! And when we queried this with Bull, Bull said, "ah well, George is going to interpret what's going on," but half the time these documents were covered in mathematical equations!⁹

Second, the U.S. assessment seems to have been that the Soviets would have to respond to the introduction of these guns, which would comfortably outrange their 130mm guns, along their border, and that the only way for them to do this would be to transfer a number of divisions out of Europe to reinforce their Chinese border. Indeed, this is precisely what appears to have happened.

In 1983 SRC's (one-year) Chinese contract was renewed. It was renewed again in 1984 (this time for a further three years), helping to establish SRC on a secure financial footing and to finance the development of the company's Brussels base. At the same time, Bull appears to have revived his interest in his old HARP work, and in November 1985 he gave a paper on HARP at a conference on military applications of big guns organized by the Pentagon. From the range of work presented there, it was clear to Bull that progress had been made on what had been the thorny question of guidance systems. What was perhaps less clear was the military agenda that the scientists present had for gun-launched projectiles. After the conference, Bull was formally asked by the Pentagon's Defense Advanced Research Projects Agency to produce a formal proposal for a big gun that could fire a payload over 625 miles—implicitly for a military purpose—to act as a cheap intercontinental ballistic missile-launching system. Bull submitted his proposal in 1986 but heard nothing more of it.

Meanwhile, with the Chinese contract approaching completion, Bull had to find other work to keep SRC going. The company secured a contract with Spain's Rio Tinto, a member of the propellant cartel, to design a 155mm gun (the FGH-155). For the Yugoslav army, Bull designed a conversion kit, swapping the old Soviet-designed barrels for 45-caliber barrels, which allowed them to fire 155mm ammunition and achieve greater range. These guns have been much in evidence pounding towns and cities throughout the war in Bosnia. As each of these contracts reached completion, SRC was once again looking for work, and in early 1988 the Iraqi government made contact.

Immediately prior to beginning work for Iraq, SRC had been doing design work on a £700–800 million turnkey artillery production project for Iran and had held negotiations in Rio de Janeiro at the beginning of 1988 with representatives of the Iranian government. This was to be built to SRC specifications by the German company Mannesmann De Mag in Brazil, from where it would produce munitions for Iran. Suddenly, despite the months of work that had gone into the project, in early 1988 Bull announced that the project was being canceled in favor of a similar one in Iraq.

In January 1988 Bull had visited Baghdad and met Hussein Kamel, Saddam's son-in-law, soon to be appointed minister of industry and military industrialization. Bull had visited Baghdad previously, and on both occasions the Iraqi interest that had prompted the visit was the same: Bull's artillery expertise. Bull's guns were well known to Iraq (and Iran) by this time. Iraq had deployed his artillery, supplied by South Africa and Austria, in the war with Iran,[10] and now the Iraqis wanted their own versions of the Bull 155mm gun, in keeping with the logic of their drive for military self-sufficiency. While negotiating these contracts, Bull took the opportunity to run through his satellite-launching gun sales pitch, something he had tried on Israel without success back in 1983. However, the Iraqis seemed receptive, and by March 1988 they were willing to finance it. Whether or not this was the extra carrot that bought Bull's expertise and at the same time denied it to Iran is unclear. What is clear, though, is that in terms of the design work, Bull's vision was comparatively cheap. The Iraqis had been interested in a satellite capability for some time. As noted earlier, for much of the Iran-Iraq War, Iraq had benefited from U.S. satellite intelligence, but the Iraqis were acutely aware that this facility was likely to be withdrawn or reduced once the war ended. Perhaps it had proved so useful to the Iraqis that they decided they could not afford to be without it. Perhaps it cost so little that it was worth committing to in order to secure Bull's involvement in the area where his track record was so impressive and their need more immediate, namely, long-range artillery.

Under the terms of the contract, finally signed on 10 June 1988 (and subject to annual review in light of progress made), a prototype gun would be
set up in one year, and a first satellite launched by 1993. It was a highly
ambitious schedule, but it marked the formal start of Project Babylon. From
a design perspective, the starting point was the size of the payload that Bull
intended to put into space. This would determine the size of the gun. It was
decided that the gun would need to be 156m long, including its recoil system,
which meant it would weigh 2,100 metric tons. A "model" (i.e., a scaled-
down working version) would be built for testing purposes, just as in the
earlier HARP program. This would be roughly a third the size of the actual
gun, 46m long, with a barrel that weighed 113 metric tons.

Bull then formed the Advanced Technology Institute (ATI) to handle Project Babylon and thereby keep it separate from SRC's other work. The institute
was registered in Athens, but although it moved out of the SRC offices, it
remained in Brussels, housed above the Bolivian Embassy. The project was
handled on the Iraqi side by a team led by Shabib Azzawi, who, like several
key figures involved in Iraqi weapons programs, had done postgraduate work
at an English university; he had an M.Sc. from Liverpool University. Azzawi
reported to Dr. Amir Saadi, who was Hussein Kamel's deputy.

The military industrialization program that Iraq was following, and of
which Bull and SRC were a key part, was very much modeled on the approach
of South Africa from the mid-1960s. The states that had followed the South
African example during the 1970s—countries like Israel, Brazil under the
generals, Argentina, and to a lesser extent Chile—were by this time themselves exporting arms. The Iraqis wanted Bull to design a version of the
155mm Kalahari Ferrari, to be designated Majnoon, as well as a 210mm self-
propelled gun, designated Al Fao (both named after battles in the Iran-Iraq
War). In addition, Bull agreed, following a visit to the SAAD 16 plant, to assist
the Iraqis with the nose cone design of their Al-Abid three-stage ballistic
missile program.[11]

Iraq certainly had found a need for long-range artillery in its war with Iran.
At the start of the war, both Iran and Iraq had Soviet SCUD B missiles,
which had a range of around 175 miles. Baghdad was close enough to the
Iranian border to allow Iran to shell it with its SCUD Bs. However, Tehran
was so far away from the border as to be beyond reach from inside Iraq.
Hence, Iraq went to work modifying the SCUD. The version the Iraqis came
up with by February 1988, dubbed the Al-Hussein, had a range of up to 375
miles—putting Tehran, at around 350 miles away, within range from inside
Iraq for the first time. That month the so-called War of the Cities resumed;

over a seven-week period, Iraq fired 189 Al-Hussein missiles at six Iranian cities, not only bringing about an end to the Iranian bombardment of Iraqi cities but also draining the morale of the Iranians.[12] The results that long-range artillery had achieved had been impressive. So, too, had the impact on Iranian morale of the use of chemical weapons on the Kurds. This was where Gerald Bull's expertise could help make Iraq a formidable military force.

◆ Britain and the Supergun

It has generally been accepted that the British companies that became involved in the construction of the supergun did so thinking that they were being asked to participate in another export venture encouraged by the government and legitimized by the existence of the Anglo-Iraqi Joint Trade Commission and the Howe Guidelines. The two British companies that actually constructed the supergun barrels—Walter Somers, which constructed the prototype 350mm, or "model," gun (Baby Babylon), and Sheffield Forgemasters, which made the 1,000mm supergun barrel (Babylon)—portrayed their involvement as part of this expanding Anglo-Iraqi trade. Their first involvement came when they met with the newly appointed project manager for Project Babylon, Dr. Chris Cowley, at Somers's Halesowen office in June 1988.

Cowley had joined SRC in 1984. Initially, he had worked with Bull in China on the 155mm gun and base-bleed ammunition project (the GC 45). Between then and 1988, he worked in Austria, France, the Netherlands, South Africa, India, Yugoslavia, Brazil, the United States, and elsewhere for SRC. He remained with SRC until May 1989, by which time the design work for which he was responsible was largely complete. Cowley lived in Baghdad for most of the year following May 1988. As a result, he was extremely well placed to comment on British and Western military support for Iraq:

> During my year of residence in Iraq I saw many examples of British military support to Iraq, perhaps the most material example being the virtually new "Sea King" often allocated for my travel needs.
>
> Evidence of western arms sales and military technology transfer projects could be seen in abundance. These extended from American Bell UH-1 Iraqi helicopters fitted with air to ground missiles, and supplied as part of an agricultural programme . . . [to] German BO-105 helicopters, [while] French Mirage F-1C supersonic fighter aircraft dotted airfields. UK Saboteur APCs and Chieftain 5 main battle tanks

could be seen parked on the roads north of Baghdad. Iraqi soldiers were armed with Italian Aspide/Albatros missile launchers.[13]

At this first meeting of Somers, Forgemasters, and SRC/ATI, Cowley allegedly outlined a plan for constructing a petrochemical plant[14] in Iraq and the role of Somers and Forgemasters in the project. This meeting effectively marked their first involvement in what was to become a complex trans-European Iraqi procurement network to ensure the undetected and uninterrupted progress of Project Babylon, taking in Britain, Switzerland, Italy, Belgium, the Netherlands, Spain, and Greece. Cowley invited both companies to attend a further meeting at SRC's headquarters later in June. Before this, Forgemasters' representatives contacted their solicitors, having become suspicious as to why a defense company like SRC should have become involved in a petrochemical project, especially in Iraq. Nevertheless, Forgemasters sent representatives to the meeting in Brussels.

The basis of their suspicions lay in the technical specification to which the tubes had to be manufactured—forging steel with a high chrome, molybdenum, and vanadium content. This process gave the steel a strength far in excess of that required for the manufacture of pipes for the petrochemical industry. Cowley reassured the company that the intent was to construct a petrochemical plant, and that this was merely evidence of diversification on the part of SRC. The Forgemasters Engineering minutes of the meeting of 17 June records that they

asked Dr Cowley to reconcile the SRC involvement in petrochemical plant considering their brochure, which specifically relates to defence and military equipment . . . Dr Cowley was asked specifically if the tubes were for some form of weapon. He replied that they were not and that it would seem silly to fire things from a 150m length of tube bolted together and 1m diameter. The equipment was for a petrochemical plant aimed at improved efficiency of oil production.[15]

The two companies accepted the contracts. Forgemasters indicated that it would have to approach the DTI to see whether the order was licensable (i.e., required a license to be exported) and if so, whether a license would be granted. Cowley agreed to this. Cowley passed this information on to Bull, who was very blasé about it. Moreover, Cowley recalls, Somers officials did not tell him that they too were going to approach the DTI, but Bull knew all about this as well.

Cowley regarded the story of a petrochemical plant as a convenient fiction that both sides could maintain, but not an explanation that the companies themselves would really believe. He assumed this because steel is priced in direct proportion to its properties; and because Cowley's specifications were much more exacting (because of the high-impact properties required of the steel for a gun) than those required for a petrochemical plant, the Iraqis would be paying much more than was necessary for petrochemical piping.

A Forgemasters representative subsequently called the DTI and was informed that piping for a petrochemical project would not require an export license. The company's directors then wrote to the DTI's Export Licensing Unit (ELU)—the section of the DTI that actually issues export licenses—supplying details of the tubes' specifications and a copy of an Iraqi order dated 14 July 1988 for twenty-six tubes. An ELU official passed this on to the DTI's Industrial, Mineral and Metals (IMM) division for advice. IMM too advised that a license would not be required. However, the misrepresentation of the purpose of the tubing had led to its circumvention of the arms and related products regulation process and its diversion from the military to the industrial process. However, even here officials should have noticed that the material from which the tubes were to be constructed was of a higher standard than that required for petrochemical purposes. Because, apparently, no such suspicions were raised, the application was not passed to the MOD for checking.

However, ICI, which was asked to analyze drawings by the TISC investigating the supergun affair, concluded:

> Although we cannot be certain that pipework of this type is not present on any existing petrochemical plant, it would in our view be most unusual . . . anyone with significant experience of the petrochemical industry would have recognised that this particular order was a highly unusual one.[16]

Nevertheless, Forgemasters had behaved properly in seeking clearance and had been given the go-ahead, even though the company did not openly voice its suspicions, due to SRC's involvement, that it was being asked to take part in a military project in a sensitive destination.

On learning that the order was destined for Iraq, Walter Somers also sought confirmation from the DTI that the company would not be contravening export control legislation in producing its order for 350mm tubes. In fact, Somers went to greater lengths than Forgemasters. In June 1988 SRC had contacted Somers and altered the specifications of the tubes on order. The new specifications aroused the suspicions of the managing director, Dr. Rex

Bayliss, as they had been upgraded close to a grade of steel—H65—that is a standard for gun manufacture. He contacted local Conservative MP Sir Hal Miller, who in turn contacted the relevant government departments on Bayliss's behalf. As Miller later recalled to the House of Commons: "[at the time] I made an offer [to the DTI], the Ministry of Defence and, I believe, to a third agency, on behalf of Walter Somers, to withdraw from the contract, to meet the contract and enable it to be traced, or to carry on with the contract."[17]

Following Miller's enquiry, an ELU official contacted the MOD, which in turn contacted Somers. Bayliss told the investigating TISC that after studying the initial Iraqi request, he thought it looked "like a giant pea-shooter that might be used for launching missiles."[18] Miller had passed on to him the name and telephone number of an official at the MOD, Bill Weir, who Bayliss recalled being told belonged to "a spooks department or something like that."[19] Defense industry sources have indicated that, in fact, Weir worked for the DIA—the intelligence arm of the MOD. Weir discussed the order with Bayliss, having already discovered from Miller that SRC was behind the project. A further telephone conversation revealed the destination to be Iraq. Weir later told the TISC that the information gathered from these conversations "did not establish that the tubes had a military purpose" and so the order was cleared.[20]

Accepting the fact that at this point Weir did not identify a military purpose for what appeared to be a "giant pea-shooter" destined for Iraq is crucial to understanding the conclusion of the TISC that the export of the supergun components went ahead only because it slipped through the regulatory net as the result of a breakdown in communication due to excessive compartmentalization. However, such acceptance is problematic. Even though Weir, officially described as a metallurgist, apparently failed to identify a huge gun from the specifications supplied, he was filmed personally advising on the dismantling of Baby Babylon itself in Iraq after the Gulf War as part of the U.N. inspection team.[21] Furthermore, for Weir to have noted the potential significance of the order and yet for no further visible action to have been taken would have been consistent with later policy after the fall of 1989, when the British government has conceded that it was aware of and was monitoring the project but did nothing openly to indicate this.

In July Forgemasters was informed that no export license would be necessary for its order. On 17 August Somers telexed the DTI asking for an urgent response by 19 August to a further SRC request for an additional five tubes for Iraq. Somers included the metallurgical composition and referred to the

Table 4.1

The British Contribution to the Supergun

Company	Materials Arrived in Iraq	Quantity	Date of Arrival	Remarks
Forgemasters Engineering Ltd.	Forged tubes of 1,000mm diameter	44	(7) on 5.18.89 (7) on 8.27.89 (4) on 11.2.89 (11) on 1.7.90 (7) on 12.1.89 (8) on 3.3.90	8 tubes blocked
	Studs M56	1,434	9.16.90	
	Tie rod	4	4.10.91	
Walter Somers	Forged tubes 350mm diameter	6	(1) on 8.5.89 (1) on 2.13.90 (1) on 4.2.90 (1) on 4.9.90 (1) on 4.11.90 (1) on 4.14.90	Not used and in good condition, the 7th blocked
	Forged tubes 350 mm diameter	5	(3) on 3.8.89 (2) on 4.10.89	Assembled at Hymreen
	Pivot ring	2	(1) on 2.29.90 (1) on 4.9.90	Assembled
	Standard parts for (350) mm	2 sets	4.14.90	
	Studs M50 with nuts (350) mm	50	4.14.90	
	Buffers (for 350 mm)	2	11.1.89	Assembled at Hymreen
Destec	Wear ring and control ring	1 set	12.1.89	Assembled at Hymreen
	Wear ring and control ring	(2) set	1.15.90	
	Seal ring 350mm diameter	6	3.26.89	Assembled at Hymreen, 2 of them damaged
Hadland	Still video camera	5	3.27.90	
	Objective lens	5	3.27.90	
	Spark light source	5	3.27.90	
	Spark source power supply	5	3.27.90	
	Optical detector	5	3.27.90	
	Trigger interface unit	1	3.27.90	

(continued)

Table 4.1 (continued)				
Company	Materials Arrived in Iraq	Quantity	Date of Arrival	Remarks
	Controller	1	3.27.90	
	Mounting hardware	1	3.27.90	
	Inter connection cable		3.27.90	
	Retro reflective screen	5	3.27.90	
	Alignment wire ring		3.27.90	
	Alignment bracket		3.27.90	

Source: Official Inspection Report (UNSCOM 8) Annex U.[22]

approval given to Forgemasters in July. The enquiry was handled by the same two DTI officials who dealt with the Forgemasters enquiry—one from ELU, one from IMM.[23] Again, the request was treated as a routine civil order, referred to IMM rather than the MOD, and judged to require no license. Somers was informed by telephone on 18 August.

Somers had begun work on what would become Baby Babylon in June 1988. Throughout the latter half of 1988 and the whole of 1989, Forgemasters worked on its £7 million contract, manufacturing a total of fifty-two steel tube sections, while Iraqi technicians visited the plant in Sheffield to oversee progress. Somers completed delivery by March 1990, the tubing being transported from Manchester Airport by an Iraqi air force Ilyushin-76 cargo aircraft, flying directly to Mosul.[24] By this time, Forgemasters had exported forty-four of the fifty-two sections.

However, even as Forgemasters had manufactured and sent the first of the supergun barrels, Bull was nowhere near solving the problems inherent in designing the projectile—the Martlet IV—that would be fired out of it. As the Iraqis increased the pressure on Bull to produce results, Bull began to offer his expertise in other areas to divert Iraqi attention from the problems with the supergun project. It was now, during the summer of 1989, that Bull offered to develop a 350mm gun based on Baby Babylon technology but capable of being elevated and traversed—in other words, a long-range gun with a solely military application. The Iraqis accepted. It was also around this time that Bull agreed to help with the Al-Abid, Iraq's three-stage satellite rocket program, which was first tested on 5 December 1989 at the Al-Anbar Space Research Base.

Although the testing of the Al-Abid was hardly an unqualified success—the second and third stages of the rocket failed to separate as intended—it served to deepen the West's emerging concern, also generated by the military exhibition earlier in the year, that it had gone too far in supporting postwar Iraq and in facilitating its military programs by turning a blind eye or applying the most benign explanation possible to its procurement activities. Iraq's postwar military ambition had not been a part of the original "family of nations" calculation, but openly blocking it would have damaged this long-term strategy and jeopardized the considerable investment already made in Iraq. Now, however, it was obvious that Iraq was close to perfecting ballistic missile technology, which would represent an unwelcome escalation of military competition in the Middle East and which Israel was unlikely to view tolerantly. Bull further involved himself in this program in the aftermath of the December 1989 test by offering to liaise with his Chinese contacts to see if they would be willing to sell Iraq a third-stage rocket to replace what Bull considered to be the inferior and flawed Brazilian design employed by Iraq. The Chinese refused.

How much were the companies involved in Project Babylon aware of the real purpose of the contracts? Given ICI's conclusions, and the transparent difference between what they were being asked to produce and standard petrochemical requirements, did they really believe the cover story that they were manufacturing petrochemical piping? During 1989 and early 1990, Peter Morrison and Alan Clark, both ministers of state at the DTI, and Bryan Kerrison of the DTI's Manufacturing Technology Division visited Forgemasters and were all shown the tubes being manufactured. The management at Forgemasters made a conscious decision to do this. The manufacture of the tubes was also the subject of a film commissioned by Bull and used by Forgemasters as a promotional video for the company. Peter Birtles, managing director of Forgemasters Engineering Ltd, the subsidiary producing the tubes, told the TISC that he and his colleagues were aware from the outset that SRC was a defense company but had accepted Cowley's explanation that they were seeking to diversify.

For his part, the immediate reaction of Philip Wright of Forgemasters to the "revelation" about the tubes' true purpose seems a little exaggerated and designed to deflect responsibility onto the DTI. He told reporters: "If this thing is part of a gun then we, the DTI and many other people, have been victims of the biggest con job in the history of arms manufacture. It sounds to me like something out of a sci-fi fantasy. I do not believe it is part of an enormous gun. We have done everything above board, legitimately and with full clearance from the DTI."[25]

What he didn't say was that, according to Cowley, Forgemasters also tendered for the breech mechanism for the 1,000mm gun but lost out on the contract, which was awarded to Societa delle Fucine in Italy (on the basis of the price it quoted). Clearly, there is no requirement for a breech in petrochemical piping. Customs officers also suspected that Forgemasters and Somers knew what they were building. By and large, however, the TISC lacked the technical expertise to ask the kind of questions that could have determined this.

Another unexplored avenue involved the links between Forgemasters and other European contractors on Project Babylon, especially the Swiss steel company, Von Roll, which manufactured recoil cylinders, drum housing, and pivot gun sections for the project.[26] It was reported that senior engineers from Von Roll visited Special Melted Products, a Forgemasters subsidiary, in January 1989, while an official from this subsidiary reciprocated the following month. Werner Gartmann, a technical manager at Von Roll, and Garston Marz, the company's commercial manager, visited the subsidiary in March 1989 and discussed the possibility of a contract to supply steel nuts and bolts to hold the barrel sections together, as well as the possible manufacture of steel liners.[27] Antonio Perez, the manager of the Swiss company Uldry Trading, also attended this meeting, which was pivotal in coordinating several trans-European supergun contracts.

Furthermore, during 1989 Forgemasters provided the Italian company, Societa delle Fucine, with design information relating to the manufacture of yokes. Somers also had contact with the Italian company, providing it with information on how the tubes it was manufacturing would be fitted to the breech mechanisms.[28] Despite this evidence that the companies involved knew they were not constructing petrochemical equipment, the TISC accepted their accounts of their involvement at face value.[29]

◆ Satellite Launcher or Long-Range Gun?

What was the Iraqi interest in Project Babylon? And what was Project Babylon intended to produce—a satellite launcher or a long-range artillery weapon? This question has generated much debate and has attracted a great deal of speculation since 1990, not all of it particularly well informed. One person who was clearly in a position to know was Chris Cowley, the project manager from 1988 to 1989. He told the TISC:

> For a number of years prior to securing the contract to build Project Babylon Dr Bull had marketed the concept of using large guns as a low cost means of launching payloads into space. SRC's sales brochures carried illustrations of the concept and mentioned the HARP programme. Saddam Hussein willingly paid the insignificant price Dr Bull required for Project Babylon. He would have designed Babylon for free, so consuming was his belief in the use of gun launched space probes.[30]

No one who has read Bull's privately published book about Project HARP and its evolution out of earlier long-range gun projects can be in any doubt that Bull's initial aim in the supergun project was not military but to prove finally what he had maintained all along: that satellites could be successfully launched from big guns.[31] In his book, Bull wrote that "the HARP Project had no direct relation with the Paris Gun Project. While the Paris Gun was a military weapon, the HARP project was dedicated solely to the application of modern technology to gun launched systems for the purpose of non-military oriented high altitude and space research."[32]

Furthermore, Bull acknowledged that the Paris Guns, even in the early years of the twentieth century, had a "military value [that] was negligible."[33] Given this, the archaic nature of big guns as a strategic weapon in the latter years of the century would hardly have been lost on Bull. However, his book also illustrates both the military and satellite-launching capabilities of big guns, and the fact that one grew out of the other. The question really is, while still at war with Iran, did Saddam willingly pay the price of Bull's project because he wanted an updated HARP program, or because he wanted an updated Paris Gun?

Robert Turp, an arms dealer who knew Bull and had served in MI10 (a branch of military intelligence) during World War II, is one person to have noted the similarities between Project Babylon and the Nazi V-3 long-range gun intended to bomb London 95 miles away, which was discovered near Calais toward the end of the war. Bull himself knew of the V-3, the barrel of which was 150m long and, like the supergun, made in sections.[34]

Alternatively, Iraq's interest in Project Babylon has been explained in terms of the prestige that would accrue to the first Arab state to launch a satellite. However, at this stage of the Iran-Iraq War, this explanation seems less credible than straight interest in Bull's military know-how. Indeed, it should not be forgotten that Bull's original contact with Baghdad was over the design and production of a range of long-range artillery, essentially 155mm and 210mm. While Bull may have been flattered that Saddam was interested in his "supergun" (and from this perspective the name is something of a misnomer), from an Iraqi perspective, giving him the freedom to make it would cement the link with Bull and secure his expertise in long-range artillery when it was sorely needed in the context of developments in the war. The War of the Cities had just proved the value of long-range artillery, and moreover, Bull and SRC had just been negotiating with the Iranians. Perhaps Saddam reasoned that if anything came of the gun, then the technology used to launch a payload hundreds of miles into space could be applied to launch a different kind of payload on a scaled-down version toward an enemy hundreds of miles away on the ground, be that Iran or Israel. Hence, at one and the same time, the supergun both is and is not the symbol of Iraq's military ambition that it became in the aftermath of its seizure and the Gulf War. As Cowley surmised: "By pampering [sic] to Dr. Bull's obsession Saddam Hussein gained the considerable abilities of a deluded egoist in the pursuit of glory. Access to SRC provided Iraq with important military technology. Project Babylon was an irrelevance in military terms."[35] At the TISC, when Jim Cousins, MP put it to Cowley that "the whole of Project Babylon [was] a piece of deception by the Iraqis to obtain access through it to this design team and the sophisticated artillery weapons that it was engaged with," Cowley conceded that "there may well be some truth in what you are saying."[36]

This view is supported by Cowley's further observations. He describes visiting SAAD 16 with Bull, Tony Slack of SRC, and Hussein Kamel and discussing the progress being made on the supergun project. When the discussion turned to the kind of payloads that Babylon would be able to launch, Kamel said: "I personally do not care if you launch a box of dates . . . You can put a palm tree up there, as far as I am concerned."[37] While Cowley and Bull took this to mean that it was merely the fact of being the first Arab state to launch a satellite that interested Iraq, it could equally have indicated that Bull's real value to Iraq was not in Project Babylon but in the artillery and related projects he was pursuing in parallel.

Furthermore, Brigadier Azzawi was put in charge of all SRC projects in Iraq: the 155mm, 210mm, and related projects and Project Babylon. Clearly for the Iraqis, Project Babylon, which was based at Mosul, was being treated as a military program. The MOD's Nicholas Bevan linked the program with Iraq's interest in nuclear weapons, explaining that quite clearly the Iraqis were aiming for a military nuclear capability, a nuclear weapon capability. They were not very far down the track towards solving the problems of how to deliver such a capability. They were quite well down the track towards actually being able to manufacture a device, but the problem of delivering that device is quite a different one and technically a very difficult one to crack.[38]

The assessment of the military division of the DRA (Defence Research Agency, formerly RARDE—Royal Armament Research and Development Establishment), was that Iraq would not have possessed the capability to design a nuclear warhead that would fit the size and weight constraints of the 1,000mm gun. It examined the barrels of all the SRC long-range guns designed for Iraq and concluded that all of them could have been used as long-range weapons. It concluded that the 1,000mm gun could have been used as either a satellite launcher or as a long-range artillery weapon, noting: "Use as a satellite launcher would have required very large multi-stage, rocket-powered projectiles and specially designed, 'hardened' satellites capable of withstanding the high acceleration force associated with gun launch." However, the DRA acknowledged the logic of Chris Cowley's argument that the accuracy of the fixed-position guns would have been limited in the absence of a guidance system and would have been enormously vulnerable: "the fixed position of the [1,000mm] gun would have limited its operational flexibility and increased its vulnerability to counter attack: its rate of fire would also have been very slow (perhaps not more than two shots a day)."[39] In fact, given the problems over recoil, cooling down, and reloading, two shots is an optimistic assessment, and certainly not one that could have been maintained for long. For his part Rolf Ekeus, who headed the U.N. Special Commission established through U.N. Security Council Resolution 687 to investigate Iraq's arsenal of weapons, commented "that the Commission's first estimate [was] that this gun would not be accurate enough to deliver conventional weapons and that it may have a relationship to Iraq's chemical, biological and nuclear weapons programs." This was also the conclusion of the DRA report.[40] But as Cowley pointed out, "it would have been, in Bull's opinion and my opinion, a dinosaur in terms of a military weapon. A weapon of this type would be so vulnerable and it had such a miserable payload in terms of military HE."[41] Furthermore, he argued: "If you are building the synopsis that it is possible to use and the intent was to arm Babylon's projectile with a nuclear weapon, then it makes much more sense from a military point of view to put it on any one of several hundred Scud missiles and drag it up to the border."[42]

The "dual-use" nature of the supergun, and confirmation that a satellite launcher was what Drs. Bull and Cowley were aiming to provide, notwith-standing the possibility that Iraq's real intentions could ultimately have been different, came from a technical expert at the MOD, John Coleman. When asked, "Is it your technical assessment . . . that Babylon would indeed have been capable of launching a satellite into space?" he answered, "Yes."[43]

The U.N. inspection team that found Baby Babylon at Jabal Hamrayn, a site about 110 miles north of Baghdad (and which counted Bill Weir amongst its number), reported:

> This gun was built for Research & Development and for getting data for a better design of the 1000mm gun. There was also a plan for the future to build a missile, launchable with this gun. Because of technical problems the Iraqis cancelled the plan. An additional intention was, to have very long range artillery in fixed sites with ranges of several hundred kilometres.

In addition, the team found twelve tons of propellant for the 350mm gun at the Al QaQa plant and the forty-four supergun tubes, that is, the compo-nents for two 1,000mm guns at the Iskandariyah site, as well as Baby Babylon, a steel breech for the 350mm gun, hydraulic shock-absorber cylinders for the 1,000mm gun, a steel base for the 1,000mm gun, and six tubes for a 350mm military gun that had not been constructed. Each 1,000mm gun would have comprised twenty-six sections of barrel. One would have been constructed at an incline, and one horizontally for testing purposes. The Iraqis had not been able to construct either, however, because the wall thickness of the barrels gradually increased toward the base. For reasons of economy of scale, Forge-masters had manufactured each set of two barrels of identical thickness at the same time, so that the eight barrels belatedly seized by the United Kingdom authorities at Teesport were four from each gun, and four pairs with an iden-tical wall thickness. The TISC concluded that Bull and Cowley:

> may have believed at the start of their work for Iraq that they were working on a successor to the HARP project to launch a satellite into space. The one set of tubes which was assembled (350mm by 52mm) was used first as a horizontal test bed for ballistic tests. But after Mr Cowley left SRC, the same tubes were then set up on the side of a mountain and test fired as a gun, albeit without realistic military payloads. The project continued with the uninterrupted involvement of other SRC staff. At the same time SRC and Dr Bull were designing 115mm and 210mm military guns for Iraq.

It is clear from what the Iraqis told the United Nations that they saw the five gun project (two 1000mm by 156mm, one 350mm by 52mm and two 350mm by 30mm) as a single project with military applications.[44]

Reference to this latter gun reflected the fact that, after Cowley left in May 1989, SRC extended the range of its work on long-range artillery, probably at the urging of the Iraqis, in order to keep Babylon on track. Cowley's successor, Tony Slack, produced a design proposal dated January 1990 for a 600mm military gun that, unlike those Cowley was involved in designing for Project Babylon, could be traversed and elevated. The proposal was to produce fifty of these to be strung out across the Iran-Iraq border.[45] The proposal was contained in a *Draft Technical Proposal for a 600mm LRSB System*, Feb. 1990 (by P. J. Bottomley and A. D. Slack). It would be capable of firing a projectile over 300 miles, or a rocket-assisted projectile over 400 miles.

This report also revealed that under Slack, Project Babylon had now evolved into a three-phase long-range artillery project. Phase I of what was now being called Project LRSB was described as having been the development and manufacture of Babylon, the 350mm "model" (Baby Babylon), and the propellant for these systems. By way of introduction, the report says:

In the 1960s the HARP 16″ smoothbore guns demonstrated the possibility of firing sabotted projectiles to extremely long ranges or high altitudes. In the light of this work, and given modern developments in high-strength lightweight materials, the LRSB programme *set out to develop a 1000mm launcher capable of accurate bombardment of distant targets*. When in service, this launcher will fire a 1500kg projectile, containing 600kg of explosive, to ranges in excess of 700km. [my emphasis]

The report also commented on developments on the 350mm military gun (now being termed Phase II) and suggested that the Iraqis accepted that the 1,000mm system would have a limited utility as a military gun:

A parallel programme has taken the 350mm smoothbore originally designed as a model test facility for the 1000, and developed an elevating/traversing mount. . . . This launcher should be capable of firing a 75kg projectile containing 14kg of HE to 450km. Whilst more versatile in application than the 1000 system, which is fixed in elevation and azimuth, this system has the drawback of limited lethality, given the small HE charge.[46]

Hence the need for Phase III. The 600mm gun represented the answer to the 350mm problem of "limited lethality." It would be capable of delivering an increased payload (estimated at 100kg of HE) to a target within a 650km radius, putting Tehran comfortably within range. During the last year of his life, Bull recorded all of his telephone calls. In one, Tony Slack referred to the 600mm system and the Iraqis: "They're really enthusiastic, especially about the S-600s. I told Azzawi they could be located on the Iran/Iraq border and cover the whole range of Iranian cities. They loved that."[47] The report estimated that the program could be completed in two years.[48]

For his part, Cowley did not come across the terms Phase I and Phase II while with SRC. Until he left in May 1989, Babylon was the project to construct a satellite launcher (the 1,000mm gun) and a "model" (the 350mm gun) on which to conduct tests. Neither could be elevated or traversed. However, Phase II, which had begun only after Cowley left, involved converting the 350mm model into a "service system, by using a shorter barrel on a mount capable of elevating and traversing." Phase II, then, produced the 350mm military guns with a 30m barrel length. Phase III involved the design and manufacture of a 600mm artillery system of 60m barrel length that could be elevated from 0 to 55 degrees and would fire between 35 and 55 degrees. There is little doubt that Cowley's successor, Tony Slack, was heavily involved in a military program.

The 20th Monthly Report on the program that had begun as Babylon,

---

Table 4.2

SRC Gun Projects for Iraq: Key Specifications

	G-45	Al Fao	Baby Babylon	Babylon	Military Gun	Military Gun
Caliber (mm)	155	210	350	1,000	350	600
Barrel Length (meters)	7	8	52	156	30	60
Number of component tubes	1	1	5	26	3	some tubes 7–15m
Maximum range (km)	30–40	45–60	390	630	350	430
Maximum payload (kg)	7–9	n/k	15	500	15	116
Traverse and elevation	Yes	Yes	No	No	Yes	Yes
Flanges and bolts	No	No	Yes	Yes	Yes	Yes
Mobile	Yes	Yes	No	No	Yes	Yes

Source: Adapted from TISC: HC-86, p. xxiii.[49]
Note: These figures are DRA and not SRC estimates. The data for the 600mm gun are, however, drawn from the SRC proposal. With regard to the 1,000 mm [super]gun's maximum payload, this is a broad DRA estimate. The Iraqi estimate was 408 kg.

dated January 1990, reported that horizontal test firings being conducted on Baby Babylon would be completed around 20 February 1990: "After this the tubes will be disassembled, inspected, and shipped to the inclined site." The gun was to be assembled there at the end of February for test firings in March 1990, the month in which Bull was murdered. The report also stated that a further two sets of tubes had been manufactured by Walter Somers for what by early 1990 was obviously a project with a military application. The first of these sets had left the Halesowen factory by road on 16 January, while the second was due to be transported by road on 16 February.

This report also indicated that a number of components that had not been required for Project Babylon but suggested a military application had now been ordered by SRC for use with these two sets of new barrels. For example, the Swiss company Von Roll was manufacturing a tube slide, due to be completed on 28 February 1990. It was also manufacturing a breech mechanism and the drum housing and pivot drum. An order for an elevating arm, tension link, and traversing rail had been split between the Spanish company, Athos, and Walter Somers. In addition, the composition of propellant charge required for these smaller guns had been calculated and, following the explosion at Kaulille in Belgium,[50] was now being secured via a Yugoslavian company. This would be Iraq's source until the Al QaQa plant was ready to produce propellant for the entire range of Bull's Iraqi guns inside Iraq itself.

The 21st Monthly Report, dated February 1990, showed that the Iraqis were pressing the SRC team to begin test firings from an inclined rather than horizontal position: "Brigadier Azzawi and Mr Slack agreed that it was most desirable to begin firing from the inclined site at the earliest possible date." Again, there were indications of the military nature of the 350mm project: "Walter Somers reports that the second set of tubes is now complete and ready for shipping. . . . In the coming month, the following components will be completed in Europe: cradle; recoil cylinders; tubes slide bearing; breech; hydraulics; elevating arm; tension link; traversing rail; pivot drum." The first of the 350mm firings from an inclined position was scheduled for 20 March 1990—just two days before the murder of Gerald Bull. Baby Babylon had now become a fixed-position prototype for a 350mm military gun that could be elevated.

This report also suggests that the end-use for the 1,000mm gun was by now clearly military. It noted that a new projectile was being prepared (the S46), which would have a "maraging steel fuselage . . . and will carry approximately 500kg of HE to a range of 700km. The principal difference between the two projectiles is that the S31 [the previous S-1000 projectile] was configured for tail control, whilst the S46, like the S44, will be canard-controlled." This report was signed by Tony Slack and C. Kossioris and dated 14 March—just one week before Bull's murder.

These developments explain why the Iraqi government told the U.N. Special Commission charged with investigating the Iraqi procurement network and overseeing the destruction of its nonconventional weapons that the intent behind Project Babylon was to develop long-range artillery in fixed positions, and why it did not even mention the idea of launching satellites. They may also explain the murder of Gerald Bull. If the key to understanding Bull's long-range gun program lies in his book and whether he was designing what was described in the first half (long-range artillery) or in the second (a satellite launcher), the answer on this evidence seems to be that Bull was designing both. Whether the Iraqis would have sought to use Babylon as a gun or satellite launcher is, however, clarified by their replies to the U.N. Commission questionnaire. The following is an excerpt from the U.N. inspectors' questions to Iraq and the answers.

Q: What was the intent of the superguns? How many guns of all sizes (calibres) were to be built? When and where were the superguns expected to become operational? Were guns of other calibres considered for the project?

A: 1. The intent was to have long range (few hundred kms) artilleries of fixed types positions.

2. Number of guns decided to be built:
2 of calibre 1,000mm
2 of calibre 350mm, 30m long
1 of calibre 350mm, 52.5m long

3. All the guns were under development and no fixed date was set for operation.

4. There was an idea to study the feasibility of having a gun of 600mm calibre.

Q: What countries provided components, parts, propellant, or instrumentation for the project?

A: Supplying countries are:
England, Belgium, Spain, Italy, Switzerland, Austria, USSR.

Q: What were the planned maximum and minimum ranges for the 1,000mm system? How many tubes were required for a single gun?

A: The maximum desired preliminary designed range was 760km.
(26) tubes are required for each 1,000mm gun.

Q: Was a mobile or transportable version of the 350-mm gun ever developed?

A: There was no mobile version ever developed of the 350mm gun.[51]

◆ "Discovery"

From March 1990 onwards, the Iraqi procurement program of which Project Babylon was a central part began to attract the kind of attention it had sought to avoid through its modus operandi. On 10 March, British journalist Farzad Bazoft was sentenced to death after being found guilty of spying. Five days later he was executed. It is indicative of Iraq's importance (from the end of the Iran-Iraq War its strategic importance was increasingly being taken for granted, while its commercial potential came to the fore) that after Bazoft's execution, the only steps that Britain took were to recall the British ambassador temporarily and send home six Iraqis attending MOD courses in the United Kingdom. The government's room for maneuver was severely limited. It could not react so strongly as to risk exclusion from the rewards of the postwar reconstruction and military industrialization for which it had positioned itself. Hence, the views of FCO Minister William Waldegrave, recorded in a memo of 6 October 1989:

> I doubt if there is any future market of such a scale anywhere where the UK is potentially so well-placed—if we play our diplomatic hand correctly—nor can I think of any major market where the importance of diplomacy is so great on our commercial position. We must not allow it to go to the French, Germans, Japanese, Koreans etc. . . . A few more Bazofts or another bout of internal repression would make this more difficult.

Then, on 22 March, Dr. Gerald Bull was murdered outside his Brussels flat.[52] As far as his former colleagues are concerned, his murder was never seriously investigated, as to do so would have revealed much of the Belgian political involvement in arms sales to Iraq and the endemic corruption of Belgian political life, which has since been hinted at through the circumstances surrounding the July 1991 murder of former Belgian Deputy Prime Minister Andre Cools and the related cash-for-helicopters case of the "three Guys," which has come back to haunt former NATO Secretary-General Willy Claes and a number of his former Belgian cabinet colleagues.[53]

As David Halevy, an intelligence analyst, told *Timewatch:* "The execution of Gerry Bull was definitely not a lone assassination but a state execution of an enemy of the state."[54] Attention centered on Mossad, and although there are other possibilities (for example, that through George Wong—whom Bull spoke with often in the last year of his life—Bull himself was providing far too much information on Iraqi weapons programs), the rumor in the U.K.

JIC was that Mossad had carried out the execution.[55] Indeed, there are parallels between the killing of Bull and that of Fathi Shqaqi, the leader of Islamic Jihad, in Malta in October 1995.[56] If one accepts that the Israelis killed Bull, then it seems to have been because he had moved away from the earlier projects for which he had secured the tacit consent of the United States, Israel, and the United Kingdom.[57] Bull had involved himself in Project Bird, firing tests on Project 839—the 600mm gun program—begun under the supervision of SRC's Dr. Jim Chan, and was offering to help out on the Iraqi SCUD modernization program. Were there other areas in which Bull had also become involved? Were the Iraqis dangling the carrot of pulling the plug on the supergun if he didn't go along with them?

Mossad had certainly been active across Europe in trying to frustrate Iraq's nuclear ambitions, and a hit on Bull would have been consistent with earlier efforts. From the late 1970s, a clandestine subplot of Iraq's procurement program was being played out across Europe and elsewhere, as Israeli agents tried to sabotage Iraqi efforts. In April 1979, France's initial attempt to export two nuclear reactor cores for the Osirak program failed when an explosion destroyed the cores as they awaited collection from the town of Seyne-sur-Mer. Although a hitherto unknown environmental group (Groupe des ecologistes français) claimed responsibility, this had been the work of Mossad. After this, Mossad had continued to operate in Europe with the same aim. On 13 June 1980, Yahia al-Meshed, an Egyptian physicist who was working on the Iraqi nuclear program, had his throat slit while he slept in his room at the Hotel Méridien. A prostitute who had been used in the operation was killed the following month.[58]

In addition, Ari Ben-Menashe, an intelligence operative working out of the Israeli Prime Minister's Office, has written of his role in frustrating Iraqi arms procurement efforts while facilitating those of Iran.[59] Although Ben-Menashe has a tendency to embellish, to the point of including meetings with prominent individuals that it seems highly unlikely could have occurred, there is no reason to doubt the central thrust of his account.[60]

Bull's murder was followed by an inflammatory speech by Saddam Hussein to Iraqi army commanders, broadcast by Radio Baghdad on 2 April, in which he boasted of Iraqi possession of a binary chemical weapon and threatened to "make the fire eat up half of Israel." He told his military audience:

The West is deluding itself if it imagines it can protect Israel if Israel comes and strikes at some metal industry factory of ours. By God, we will devour half of Israel by fire if it tries to do anything against Iraq . . .

[Foreign agents] used to come every day to ask us, "Don't you want enriched uranium to make an atomic bomb?" We used to say, "Leave us alone, keep your evil away from us and take your bags with you . . ." We do not need an atomic bomb, because we have sophisticated binary chemical weapons.[61]

The speech, which referred to Bull's murder, suggests three things: first, that Saddam considered Mossad responsible for Bull's death; second, the importance of Bull to Saddam's plans and his consequent frustration at his killing; and, third, given the reference to fire eating up half of Israel at the same time as talking of Bull, that Iraq's intended end-product from Bull's work was a range of long-range artillery capable of delivering chemical weapons— an updated Paris Gun rather than HARP. Saddam's references in the speech to foreign conspiracies and Western enemies seeking to prevent Iraq from achieving strategic parity with Israel need to be understood in the context of Bull's murder.

In response to the speech, the United States sent a demarche to be delivered to Saddam by Ambassador April Glaspie, which warned that "Iraqi actions in recent weeks and months have caused a sharp deterioration in US-Iraqi relations. Iraq will be on a collision course with the US if it continues to engage in actions that threaten the stability of the region, undermine global arms efforts and flout US laws."[62] The final, dawning realization that the "family of nations" strategy was not working and that instead of building up a responsible regional ally, the United States and its Western partners had created a monster bent on acting independently is implicit in this; the rest of the demarche is almost a plea in the face of this realization:

Iraq is now a major regional power and should act in the responsible way such a role requires. At a time when the US and the Soviet Union are methodically divesting themselves of weapons of mass destruction, Iraq's threats to use these systems have become a major impediment to the kind of relationship with the United States that Iraq says it wants.

Your government must take some concrete steps particularly in areas involving human rights and illegal procurement activities to address these concerns and act to reduce tensions. Without such measures on your part what little support that is left in the US for Iraq may further erode.[63]

Shortly afterward, the supergun was seized.[64] On 6 April 1990, following a further telephone call from Sir Hal Miller to the MOD on behalf of Walter Somers, an ELU official contacted the company to discuss an order from Iraq's Ministry of Industries (i.e., a direct order, not channeled through SRC) for three metal fabrications (an elevating arm, tension link, and rail). In response, Somers faxed drawings to the ELU, which were passed on to the MOD for assessment. This was the last British involvement in supergun contracts. On 10 April, Customs and Excise officials raided Teesport docks, seizing, conveniently enough, the final consignment of piping for the supergun. In the aftermath of the raid, sixteen directors and executives from Somers and Forgemasters were questioned by the British authorities. As a result, Chris Cowley and Peter Mitchell, who had become managing director of Somers in 1989, were arrested and charged with "being knowingly concerned in the attempted illegal exportation of equipment with intent to evade a prohibition in force by virtue of the Export of Goods (Control) Order 1987/89."[65] Subsequently, Customs officers prepared charges against eleven people connected with the project. Other components were seized in Spain, Italy, West Germany, and Greece. When Paul Ashwell was arrested in Greece transporting £221,000 worth of slide tube assembly manufactured by Forgemasters Engineering Ltd, he was not transporting parts for the supergun (the original Project Babylon). He was transporting a component of a military gun, part of Project 839 (Phase II).[66]

On 18 April, Nicholas Ridley, the secretary of state for trade and industry, stood up in the House of Commons to announce that the government had only "recently become aware in general terms of an Iraqi project to develop a long-range gun."[67] However, subsequent revelations suggest that this was far from the truth[68] and that, rather than acting promptly when belatedly alerted to what was going on, the British government had a much more detailed knowledge of Project Babylon, possibly even going back to its inception.

One of the most obvious questions that Ridley's statement begged was how Customs came to be aware of the existence of Project Babylon and the role of Forgemasters in it at such a fortuitous time—just as the last consignment was above to leave Teesport docks. Was this the result of a tip-off by the intelligence services? If so, then this would suggest that they had been monitoring the operation for some time previously. Initially, Customs denied any intelligence link, and first reports stated that "Customs was keen to quash reports that the consignment was unearthed after a tip off from the security services."[69] Two days later, however, it was being reported that senior officers "had been tipped off by the security services that a large weapon built by a British company, was about to be shipped, illegally, to Iraq; 'intelligence' pointed them to Teesport."[70] Senior Customs officials subsequently confirmed that they acted on a tip-off from the intelligence services.[71] Just when did the British government first become aware of the project, and how much did they know about Iraqi arms procurement in general? It was a question that former directors of British munitions manufacturer Astra Holdings were able to shed light on, in so doing exposing much of the murky nature of the international arms trade.

N O T E S

1 On the extent of the CIA's involvement in Angola, see John Stockwell: *In Search of Enemies*, London, Andre Deutsch, 1978.
2 William Lowther: *Arms and the Man*, London, Macmillan, 1991, p. 141.
3 Cited in the *Washington Post*, 2.10.91.
4 Figures are taken from W. Lowther: *Arms and the Man*, p. 122.
5 Perhaps the best detailed account of Bull's connection with South Africa can be found in James Adams: *Bull's Eye: The Assassination and Life of Supergun Inventor Gerald Bull*, New York, Times Books, 1992, chs. 9–11. For an overview of South African strategies, see Michael Brzoska: Arming South Africa in the Shadow of the U.N. Arms Embargo, *Defense Analysis*, Vol. 7 No. 1 1991, pp. 21–38.
6 See below and chapter 6.
7 For an outline of this system and its relationship to the licensing system in the British case, see M. Phythian and W. Little: Administering Britain's Arms Trade, pp. 259–277.
8 J. Adams: *Bull's Eye*, p. 209.
9 Interview with Chris Cowley, 2.23.95.
10 Asked later how many Bull-designed guns were used in the Iran-Iraq War, Michel Bull said: "We know there's a hundred South African guns in the Middle East. Our thoughts were originally that these went to Iran. Subsequently, that seems to be wrong and they have gone to Iraq, which would make the total in Iraq about three hundred. . . . My guess is that the Iraqis got about two hundred from Austria and about a hundred from South Africa." Quoted in Dale Grant: *Wilderness of Mirrors: The Life of Gerald Bull*, Scarborough, Ontario, Prentice-Hall Canada, 1991, pp. 184–185. However, this ignores the fact that Voest Alpine sold its version of the Bull gun to both sides. Lowther estimates: "Five or six years into the war, Iran had about 350 of Bull's guns, while Iraq was thought to have 400." Lowther, *Arms and the Man*, p. 170. The 1988–89 edition of *The Military Balance* estimated that Iraq had 100 G-5s and 200 GHN-45s, while it stated that Iran reportedly had both but put no figures on them. This accords with Michel Bull's estimate for Iraq.
11 In February 1991, the U.S. State Department put out a press release on Bull that included a number of less than frank answers. The press release posed the question: "Did the Department of State allow Gerald Bull to ship artillery shells to South Africa, Iraq and China?" The answer minimized the extent of SRC involvement in China, was evasive over Iraq, and maintained the fiction that Bull had attempted to arm South Africa as a freelance operation: "Bull exported 155 millimeter artillery shells to South Africa without US permission. He was prosecuted, convicted and jailed for this violation of munitions export regulations. "Bull, and companies associated with Bull, were also informed at the beginning of the Iran-Iraq War that the export of munitions to Iraq or Iran would not be permitted. The Depart-

ment of State has not approved any exports of equipment or technology by Bull or companies associated with Bull to Iraq.

"The export of some technical data on the manufacture of artillery to China was approved by the Department as part of our larger policy of military co-operation with China which was in effect throughout the 1980s."

12 On the use of the Al-Hussein during the War of the Cities, see W. Seth Carus and Joseph S. Bermudez: Iraq's Al-Husayn Missile Programme, Parts I & II, *Jane's Soviet Intelligence Review*, May 1990 and June 1990; and Joseph S. Bermudez: Iraqi Missile Operations During "Desert Storm," *Jane's Soviet Intelligence Review*, March 1991, pp. 132–135. Of the 189 fired during the War of the Cities, 135 were fired at Tehran, 23 at Qom, 22 at Isfahan, 4 at Tabriz, 3 at Shiraz, and 2 at Karaj.

13 TISC: *Exports to Iraq:* Evidence of Christopher Cowley, HC-86-iv, EQ31, p. 189. (Henceforth, the evidence published as part of the TISC investigation will be referred to in endnotes by the appropriate reference numbers, e.g., in the case of oral testimony; TISC: HC-86-iv, p. . . . , and in the case of written submissions; TISC: HC-86-xiv, EQ80, etc. The report, *Exports to Iraq: Project Babylon and Long Range Guns* (HC-86), was published on 13 March 1992.)

14 In his evidence to the TISC, Cowley says it was Azzawi who used the petrochemical cover story. TISC: HC-86-iv, EQ31, p. 205.

15 Minutes of Meeting Held with SRC on Friday 17 June 1988.

16 TISC: HC-86, p. xxxviii.

17 *Hansard*, 4.18.90, col. 1430.

18 Quoted in the *Financial Times*, 12.4.91.

19 Ibid.

20 TISC: HC-86, p. xv.

21 Horizon Special: *Hide and Seek in Iraq*, BBC2, 8.23.92.

22 Published in TISC: HC-86-ix, pp. 323–324.

23 They were Draper (ELU), and Jacobs (IMM). TISC: HC-86, p. xvi.

24 The authorities initially denied that any such aircraft had landed at Manchester, but it had been photographed there by an aircraft enthusiast. See Chris Cowley: *Guns, Lies and Spies*, pp. 189–190.

25 *Independent on Sunday*, 4.15.90.

26 TISC: HC-86, p. xxv.

27 *Observer*, 1.12.92.

28 Ibid.

29 TISC: HC-86, p. xliii

30 TISC: HC-86-iv, EQ31, pp. 191–192.

31 G. V. Bull and C. H. Murphy: Paris Kanonen—*The Paris Guns (Wilhelmgeschutze) and Project HARP: The Application of Major Calibre Guns to Atmospheric and Space Research*, Herford, Verlag E. S. Mittler & Sohn GmbH, 1988. The Paris Guns had been used by the German army in World War I to bombard Paris from distances in excess of 60 miles.

32 Bull and Murphy: *The Paris Guns*, p. 146.

33 Ibid., p. 234.

34 *Timewatch:* The Man Who Made the Supergun, BBC2, 2.12.92.

35 TISC: HC-86-iv, EQ31, p. 192.

36 TISC: HC-86-iv, p. 221.

37 Ibid., p. 226.

38 TISC: HC-86-vi & vii, p. 263.

39 Ibid., pp. 278–279.

40 TISC: HC-86-vi & vii, EQ65.

41 TISC: HC-86-iv, p. 215.
42 Ibid., p. 229.
43 Ibid., p. 265.
44 TISC: HC-86, p. xlii.
45 TISC: HC-86-iv, p. 217.
46 P. J. Bottomley and A. D. Slack: Draft Technical Proposal for a 600mm LRSB System, February 1990, p. 6.
47 C. Cowley: *Guns, Lies and Spies*, p. 250.
48 The schedule for the 600mm gun programme was to be as follows:
Aug–Sept. 1990—Ballistic range firing programme for the glide and rocket-assisted projectiles.
Nov. 1990—Static motor tests for the rocket assisted projectile.
Dec. 1990–Jan. 1991—Placing orders for the major manufacturing items of the system.
Throughout 1991—Monitoring of supplier performance, design queries, raw material procurement, etc.
Feb–March 1991—Test firing of differing sabot configurations from S350 system.
July 1991 onward—Delivery of components commences.
Dec. 1991—Horizontal system ready for testing.
Dec. 1991–Jan. 1992—Charge development firings from horizontal system.
Jan–Feb 1992—Horizontal testing of glide and rocket-assisted projectiles.
Feb–April 1992—Shoot to range from elevating/traversing system with both glide and rocket-assisted projectiles.
April 1992—Final reporting.
49 See also TISC: HC-86-vi & vii, p. 277.
50 See chapters 5 and 6.
51 Taken from TISC: HC-86-ix, EQ49 (UNSCOM 8, Annex N).
52 There are a number of theories concerning Bull's death, despite the initial acceptance that it was the work of Mossad. See K. Timmerman: *The Death Lobby*, pp. 376–377; J. Adams: *Bull's Eye*, pp. 266–273. Ben-Menashe claims that Bull was killed "by the Israelis" (see *Profits of War*, p. 309), but he has told British defense industry sources that this was at the request of British Intelligence. The incident is also considered in detail by Chris Cowley; *Guns, Lies and Spies*, passim. Former Mossad agent Victor Ostrovsky has also provided an account of Bull's death at the hands of Mossad, although Ostrovsky had left Mossad by this time, so it is difficult to see where he could have got his information other than from the press.
53 The case of the "three Guys" is linked to the murder of Cools on 18 July 1991 as he left a flat in Liège with a companion, Marie-Hélène Joiret. It revolves around the Belgian army's 1983 decision to acquire a new helicopter fleet. From the beginning until the eve of the decision in favor of Italian manufacturer Agusta, army experts were recommending a French Aerospatiale model (Squirrel) or the German MBB Bk117 and were not even seriously considering the eventual winner, the Agusta A109. Yet Agusta won the contract. After investigations into the background to the deal were launched in the wake of Cools's death, a string of leading Belgian politicians were charged with corruption: Etienne Mange (Socialist Party treasurer); Luc Wallyn (former party secretary); Johan Delanghe (former private secretary to Willy Claes); Guy Mathot (former regional minister); and Guy Coeme (former defence minister). In addition, Georges Cywie (the Belgian representative of Agusta) and a Brussels lawyer, Alfons Puelinckx, were also charged. Prior to Claes's resignation from NATO, the affair also claimed Frank Vandenbroucke, the Belgian foreign minister, who resigned in the wake of admitting that he had asked that money secretly given to the Flemish Socialist Party by Agusta be burned so as to avoid its discovery. On 7 March 1995, a Belgian TV documentary implicated former Belgian air force chief, General Jacques Lefebvre, in the affair.

Shortly after it ended, Lefebvre checked into the Hotel Mayfair in Brussels and killed himself by taking an overdose of barbiturates. The affair continues to be investigated by Véronique Ancia. (In addition to Mathot and Coeme, the third of the "three Guys" is Guy Spitaels, a prominent Socialist Party figure.) *Sunday Times*, 3.26.95. *Independent*, 3.23.95.

54 *Timewatch:* The Man Who Made the Supergun.

55 Interview with Robin Robison, 3.27.95.

56 See the *Guardian*, 10.30.95.

57 See chapter 6.

58 See Claire Hoy and Victor Ostrovsky: *By Way of Deception: An Insider's Devastating Exposé of the Mossad*, London, Arrow, 1991, pp. 1–28.

59 Ari Ben-Menashe: *Profits of War: Inside the Secret U.S.-Israeli Arms Network*, New York, Sheridan Square Press, 1992.

60 To take the most unlikely of several: Ben-Menashe claims that in 1983 Mark Thatcher, son of the British prime minister, introduced Gerald Bull to a South African intelligence officer who put him in touch with ARMSCOR and that Bull was subsequently arrested for illegally shipping arms to Iraq, spending six months in prison. In reality, Bull served just four months and was released from prison in 1981—a full two years before Ben-Menashe says Mark Thatcher made the introductions that later led to his arrest! See Ben-Menashe, p. 257.

61 Quoted in John Simpson: *From the House of War*, p. 68.

62 Quoted in B. W. Jentleson: *With Friends like These*, p. 156.

63 Ibid., pp. 156–157.

64 It has been suggested that the Israelis "were able to block the transfer of key parts of the barrels for the supergun by informing European governments of the details of the Project"— John Sigler: Pax Americana in the Gulf: Old Reflexes and Assumptions Revisited, *International Journal* XLIX, Spring 1994, p. 283. However, this seems little more than supposition, as knowledge of the project was clearly not confined to the Israelis.

65 TISC: HC-86, p. xix.

66 The consignee was Ministry of Industry, PC/2, Project 839, Baghdad, Iraq. On 15 August 1989, Somers had sent out a second set of three tubes (each 1,000mm long, but 800mm, 750mm, and 400mm in diameter) for Project 839.

67 *Hansard*, 4.18.90, col. 1427.

68 Alan Clark subsequently told the TISC that Ridley's assertion "was an exaggeration." See TISC: HC-86, p. xxxviii.

69 *Independent*, 4.13.90.

70 *Independent on Sunday*, 4.15.90.

71 Unattributable briefing, Harmsworth House, October 1992.

The Strange Case of Astra Holdings plc

The question of who in government knew what and when came to life with the disclosures by Gerald James and Christopher Gumbley, formerly chairman and managing director of ambitious British munitions manufacturer Astra Holdings plc. In September 1989 Astra had purchased the Belgian munitions company PRB from Gechem. It was to be the final, and ultimately fatal, purchase in an expansion strategy that had seen Astra grow from a small pyrotechnics base to a company with a broad global presence.[1] In little over six months after completing the purchase James, Gumbley, and the entire Astra board (with the exception of the intelligence-linked Stephan Kock) had been removed. The investigations carried out by James and Gumbley in an attempt to explain the misfortune that overtook Astra after buying PRB have shed much light on the reality of the international arms trade, in which dealing with conduits, using false end-user certificates, and paying off civil servants and/or politicians to secure orders or get them through to their intended destinations are a way of life. In this world, few state boundaries are impermeable, and end-user certificates are a commodity to be bought in order to circumvent the regulatory system, not the embodiment of it. It is a world in which the billions involved in arms deals are viewed as a supplementary source of income for both private individuals and political parties, in Europe as well as the Third World. This is the world that Astra entered on buying BMARC and, in particular, PRB.

◆ Development of the Astra Group

Astra was a small company with sixty employees and an annual turnover of less than £1 million when it was taken over in June 1981 by the James and Gumbley management team. By the time they were forced out of the company in 1990, Astra was the United Kingdom's second-largest manufacturer

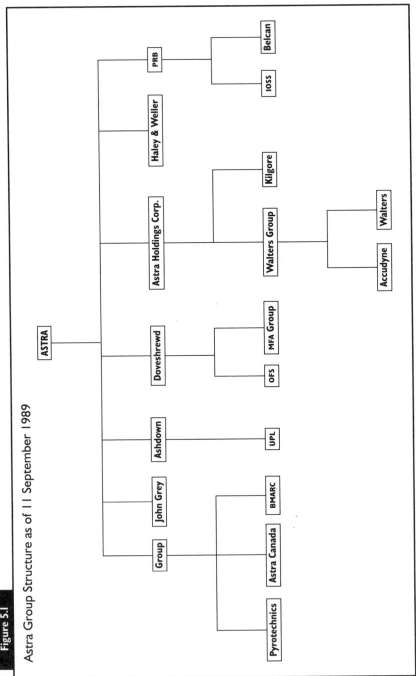

Figure 5.1

Astra Group Structure as of 11 September 1989

Source: DTI: *Astra Holdings plc: Investigation Under Section 431 (2) (i) of the Companies Act 1985*, Report by Colin Percy Farquharson Rimer, QC and John White, FCA, Appendix III.

of ammunition and guns[3] after RO. The group's order book was in excess of £230 million, and it employed around 2,100 people.[4]

The James and Gumbley team built Astra out of the ashes of the Brocks Fireworks Company. During World War II, Brocks had turned briefly to military production, only to revert to fireworks manufacture after the war. In 1979 John Anderson and James were finance and export consultants to Brocks, just as the Brock family was selling its stake. At the same time, Brocks received an order from Nigeria for military pyrotechnics, and this and subsequent orders in the military field transformed the company by opening up new military export opportunities beyond the static fireworks market. However, disagreements over the future direction of the company ensued between a traditionalist wing that wanted the company to concentrate on fireworks production and a group of modernizers, led by James, who saw that profitability lay in expanding the military side of the business. At the end of 1980 the core of the Brocks management team, including Chris Gumbley, walked out, and James and Anderson's consultancy was terminated.

Meanwhile, James had been asked to find a purchaser for Astra Fireworks, and the former Brocks people expressed an interest. In June 1981 the team completed the buyout and Astra Holdings Ltd was formed with the financial backing of the Industrial and Commercial Finance Corporation, later to become 3*i*. Gerald James became chairman, Chris Gumbley production director, and John Anderson director and secretary.

The new company quickly secured 05-24 status (Defence Manufacturing Standard) allowing it to manufacture to U.K. defense standards and later 05-21 status allowing it to carry out research and development work. Early on, it was hit by the loss of substantial orders from Malaysia, following the "Buy British Last" campaign that resulted from Mrs. Thatcher's early handling of bilateral relations with the Southeast Asian state. By this time, it had become apparent to James and Gumbley that North America represented an ideal area for expansion. In October 1985 Astra purchased a Canadian site (representing the cheapest route into North America), from where it began operating as Astra Canada. A further site was purchased and developed in Canada the following year, and orders were secured from Canada and the DOD. Around the same time, Astra was approached by Tom Morrice, a former Canadian army major, to take over Gerald Bull's Highwater site, which straddled the United States–Canadian border.

Further acquisitions were made. In August 1986 Astra purchased Francis Sumner plc. In the same year it also acquired MFA International, a company in the electronics and security field. The owner of MFA, Roy Ricks, was fired after the takeover and went on to become closely involved in the Iraqi procurement network through Meed International. In a further significant addition, Astra acquired Unwin International and related companies in October 1986. This group of companies had been owned by Richard Unwin, who had been closely involved in the supply of Brocks military products to Nigeria and the Middle East. It was at this time that Unwin recommended Stephan Kock to Astra as a nonexecutive director.

The Astra management still regarded the United States as a prime area for expansion, and from August 1986 to January 1987, Astra received considerable support at a very high level from within the DOD and from the Rock Island and Piccatinny arsenals. Astra was even offered the opportunity of running a major "Go Co." It also approached Accudyne—a fuse company based in Janesville, Wisconsin—for a license to manufacture the 81mm mortar proximity fuse, M732. Accudyne was owned by Ed Walters, who during the discussions that ultimately led to the acquisition of the Walters Group[5] (comprising E. Walters, Inc. and Accudyne Corp.) revealed to Gerald James that one of his main customers was International Signal and Control (ISC), for which they had manufactured fuse parts. This relationship later came to assume a much greater significance. Astra purchased the Walters Group for US$33 million in April 1987.

In the fall of 1987, while still negotiating the purchase of BMARC in the United Kingdom, Astra made a further U.S. acquisition, the Kilgore Corporation. Kilgore manufactured a wide range of pyrotechnics, was involved in the most sophisticated military areas, and was at the time the largest supplier of IR decoy flares to the U.S. Navy and the U.S. Air Force.

◆ **BMARC and the Challenge to RO**

During 1987, various sources around the British government suggested that Astra should look to compete with RO in the domestic ammunition market. At the time, RO was under criticism from within the MOD over pricing, technical problems, and slow delivery. It was to be sold in 1987, and Astra was prepared to make a bid, backed by its new bankers, the Midland and Hong Kong banks. However, Astra experienced great difficulty in obtaining the prospectus documents from N. M. Rothschild in order to make a bid. It took the political intervention of three MPs—Astra's local MP, Jonathan Aitken; Gerald Howarth, MP; and Sir Anthony Kershaw, MP (the latter two consultants inherited from Unwin)—for Astra to get the relevant documents. Moreover, by the time it got them, just days before the deadline, it was too late to make a considered bid. By contrast, the government's favored bidder, BAE, had had the documents for over eight weeks by this stage.[6] RO was duly sold to BAE in April 1987, with only BAE and one other British defense manufacturer, GKN, bidding for it.

However, this did not mark the end of Astra's attempts to enter the U.K. domestic ammunition market. As James told the TISC investigation into the supergun and exports to Iraq: "Because of encouragement from the Ministry of Defence including that from John Bourn who was a senior MOD civil servant[7] responsible for the sale of Royal Ordnance . . . Astra continued to look for ways it could realistically enter the United Kingdom ammunition market."[8] These attempts came to focus on the purchase of the U.K.-based BMARC[9] from its Swiss parent company Oerlikon Buhrle. BMARC had been founded in 1937 as a joint venture between the Ministry of Supply and the racing car manufacturer, Hispano Suiza. After 1945, the company made naval guns for export to the Middle and Far East, and during the late 1950s, Harold Macmillan helped it win a £100 million contract to establish the West German army.[10] Oerlikon Buhrle took over the company in 1971.[11]

BMARC had a number of attractions for Astra. It had a large precision engineering plant in Grantham and a 750-acre filling plant in Faldingworth, which also housed one of the best armament- and munitions-testing facilities in Europe. At its Grantham plant, it produced a range of guns—from 125mm to 40mm—naval turrets, land and air weapons, ammunition casings, fuses, and pyrotechnics. At the Faldingworth plant, it produced magazines for explosives and raw materials, and boasted loading plants, pyrotechnic and storage facilities as well as a modern indoor range to 40mm. Gerald James summarized its appeal thus:

The United Kingdom was a cheap base for manufacture due to low labour costs and a low base exchange rate and also due to the fact that the United Kingdom is one of the easiest countries to obtain export licences for arms sales provided the necessary procedures and formalities are followed. As a result of these considerations Oerlikon entered into a very substantial capital expenditure programme. The factory at Grantham was updated and mechanised to a very high standard and the filling and high explosive facility was moved to Faldingworth from Grantham. Faldingworth was a former wartime Lancaster bomber base which had subsequently been upgraded into a nuclear weapon storage facility for nearby Scampton. As a result Faldingworth was a site with huge storage and other facilities, with complete security and with a clear 700 acres. The scope for upgrading the site was obvious. With its size, huge quantities of finished ammunition and explosive raw materials could be stored. Oerlikon upgraded these facilities with twelve new explosive magazines, new filling and process buildings and engineering facilities, passive stores and the most modern indoor firing range (up to 40 millimetres) in Europe if not in the world.[12]

With these facilities, BMARC represented an ideal platform from which Astra could launch a challenge to RO's dominance of the domestic market. Astra made an anonymous approach through Peat Marwick Mitchell, which resulted in a meeting between James, Gumbley, and Michael Funk of Oerlikon during the 1987 Paris air show. At the time, Oerlikon was considering an offer from BAE for the whole group, and so progress was slow, especially during the summer of 1987. Then, at the Royal Naval Equipment Exhibition (RNEE) in Portsmouth in September 1987, Peter Levene, head of the Defence Procurement Division, "went out of his way to visit the Astra stand," where he discussed the domestic ammunition market situation with both James and Gumbley. According to James, "Levene stated that the Ministry of Defence wanted a competitor to Royal Ordnance and that unless Astra came forward there would be no effective competition . . . Levene said categorically that if Astra was competitive it could very quickly acquire up to 40 per cent of the total market (estimated to be worth at least £500m per year) and thereafter all would be open to competition." At the same time, Levene made it clear that this would require a substantial investment on Astra's part, and when told of the proposal to purchase BMARC, he "gave considerable encouragement to this move" and "considerable pressure was put upon Oerlikon to get on with the deal."[13] Astra completed the purchase of BMARC in April 1988.[14] The new management did not seek to remove the entire senior management of BMARC, although most of the Swiss employees left soon after the takeover, leaving Major-General Donald Isles, a former senior procurement officer at the MOD and director of munitions, British Defence Staff, Washington, in a dominant position—even in relation to Bill McNaught, the new Astra appointee as managing director. Gumbley, however, had wanted to let Isles go. The Astra management had been told by Colin Wagstaffe, an Astra (and former RO) employee with good links to the MOD, that while they were negotiating to buy the company, Isles had been trying to block their purchase and had even taken soundings from other companies who might buy it rather than Astra. However, when Gumbley floated the idea of removing Isles, nonexecutive director Kock intervened on his behalf. Isles stayed.

◆ Astra and EPREP

Astra now began to lobby hard to obtain a slice of the RO-dominated domestic market. Astra was asked by Levene for prices for 155mm, 120mm, 105mm, 76mm, 81mm (mortar), 61mm (mortar), 51mm (mortar), and 4.5″ naval ammunition. The prices it quoted were lower than those quoted by RO and, according to James, were used as a basis for further negotiations with RO. It was against this background that in May 1988 James and Gumbley learned from a contact in the MOD (Brian Peet) of the existence of the secret Explosives, Propellants, and Related End Products (EPREP) agreement (its terms were subject to the Official Secrets Act), between the government on the one hand and BAe/RO on the other. This guaranteed RO 80 percent of the larger-caliber orders for the MOD until 31 March 1993, and also allowed it to compete for the remaining 20 percent.[15] In an environment in which all other areas of procurement were open to vigorous competition in order to achieve the best price, this agreement was a curious anomaly. It did, however, address concerns about job security that Labour Party spokespeople gave voice to (although presumably they had foreign rather than domestic competition in mind). James telephoned Levene, who repeated his earlier assurances about the possibilities of competition, but when James challenged him over the existence of the EPREP agreement: "Levene became most angry and denied the existence of any such agreement. In his anger he asked for a name of an informant in the MOD . . . James gave Peet's name and still there were angry denials."[16]

James summed up the situation thus:

> Astra had been led on and misled by the Ministry of Defence. Although a part of the Ministry of Defence was favourable to Astra and very concerned that there should be competition, Astra was induced by the key procurement executive to invest heavily when it was known by certain Ministers and key personnel (although apparently not by Levene) that a five year monopoly had already secretly been granted.[17]

To try to rectify this situation, Gumbley began to work with a firm of lobbyists, Decision Makers, to expose and overturn EPREP:

> This appeared to infuriate [Mrs.] Thatcher and [Alan] Clark, who was by then MOD Procurement Minister. Both corresponded with Gumbley and Thatcher wrote a letter now in the hands of Gumbley's lawyers which he received three days after

his initial arrest. While it could be interpreted in various ways the letter basically said "You will understand the Government's point now."[18]

Following the removal of James and Gumbley in 1990, the new Astra management ceased to employ Decision Makers or lobby against EPREP and instead employed a firm of private detectives, Carratu, to investigate the activities of the former management.[19]

◆ Road to Ruin—The Purchase of PRB

The lesson that the Astra management drew from the experience was not that competition against RO for domestic contracts was futile but that by developing its overseas base and using its U.S. and Canadian connections, Astra could transcend dependence on the domestic market and at the same time position itself better to win domestic contracts from RO. Therefore, when Astra was steered toward the Belgian munitions manufacturer PRB, it seemed the ideal vehicle through which to further its ambitions in this direction.

PRB could trace its origins back to the Napoleonic Wars. Poudreries de Belgique was founded in 1778 by Jean François Cooppal, and PRB emerged following the merger of several companies in related fields. Whereas prior to World War II, PRB had primarily been involved in industrial explosives, after 1945 it became heavily involved in ammunition production under the Marshall Plan. Once these orders began to subside, and given the limited domestic requirements of the Belgian armed forces, PRB had to look principally to the export market to survive. This remained the case at the time of the Astra purchase; its health was based on the success of its export performance, which in the recent past had been based on sales to Iraq. These contracts dried up, however, with the end of the Iran-Iraq War, as the international arms market once more contracted. PRB now found export markets harder to secure, so much so that it had to agree to pay excessive commissions to secure contracts. According to one source, for example, PRB went so far as to pay a £5 million commission to secure a £16 million deal with Thailand.

The company owned five large plants in Belgium. The Balen plant loaded, assembled, and packed high explosives, artillery shells, and tank ammunition and stored phosphorus. The Kaulille plant produced propellant for heavy, medium, and small caliber arms, rocket motors, and charge bags. The Clermont plant produced ball powder, combustible cartridge cases, and initiation and fuse devices. The Matagne plant produced grenades, mines, fuses, pyrotechnics, and artillery up to 155mm in range. The large Mechelen forging plant had the capacity to manufacture shells and cartridge cases, as well as metal motor vehicle components.[20]

Prior to its sale to Astra, PRB's ultimate parent company was Société Générale de Belgique (SGB), Belgium's largest industrial concern, with investments ranging right across the Belgian economy. By the end of the 1980s, SGB boasted between 1,300 and 1,400 subsidiaries. A significant proportion of these investments were in mining and could be traced back to Belgium's colonial presence in Africa. SGB owned a majority stake in Gechem, which in turn owned PRB. Jean Duronsoy was chief executive of Gechem, while Hervé de Carmoy, formerly a senior executive in the Midland Bank's defense finance operation, was appointed chairman. In 1988 there had been a takeover battle over SGB involving Carlo Benedetti, an Italian financier. Although opposed by SGB's management, led by the well-connected Count Etienne Davignon, Benedetti acquired a 50 percent stake, while Banque Indo Suez took a 25 percent stake and installed Hervé de Carmoy as chief executive.

Astra was first steered toward PRB by Paine Webber, Astra's merchant bankers, in the summer of 1988, shortly after the EPREP dispute. It was an attractive proposition for a number of reasons. First, the purchase of PRB would be consistent with the arguments of Peter Levene and the MOD that "defence companies take an interest in Europe with 1992[21] in mind and also because joint projects would provide more competitive and efficient working particularly within NATO where there are common standards and systems."[22]

Second, PRB was well equipped and produced an impressive range of equipment, with a caliber range of 76mm to 155mm. Its product range included "certain classic developments which were in advance of Royal Ordnance and much closer to likely future requirements such as base bleed ammunition, combustible cartridge case technology, ball powder propellants, rocket motors, Eastern bloc technology." The purchase of PRB also opened up a new range of customers and contracts to Astra, although in the event not with the anticipated benefits. Furthermore, PRB possessed plants that "could not have been produced or built in modern times together with licences for under £500 million. It had been created over many years and in normal circumstances would not have been sold by SGB had it not been for the Benedetti bid for SGB."[23]

In sum, to Astra PRB represented an opportunity to strike back at RO by broadening its geographical presence, range of products, and—it was to be hoped—clients. It gave Astra the ability to manufacture a wide range of ammunition, some of which, like base-bleed ammunition, was based on Gerald

Bull's designs and tended to be more advanced than the corresponding RO product. Finally, with bases in the United States, United Kingdom, and continental Europe, Astra would legitimately be able to overcome the political, national, and technological problems that companies faced throughout the arms industry.

At the time that Astra showed an interest in PRB, it was the only interested party to know that PRB was for sale in its entirety. There was also interest expressed in individual parts of PRB from, for example, Cementation, the subsidiary of Trafalgar House involved in the Pergau Dam scandal for which Mark Thatcher had acted as a consultant on deals in the Middle East in the 1980s. Another interested party was Gerald Bull, eager to purchase at least part of PRB through SRC on behalf of the Iraqi government.

Bull's connections to PRB stretched back to the early 1970s and had been maintained throughout the 1980s, when he had dealt with PRB in order to take full advantage of the ease with which arms and military equipment could be transported from Belgium to Jordan for onward transmission to Iraq with the assistance of the Belgian government.[24] Bull had approached Gechem in early 1989 with an offer to buy the assets of PRB for a "token sum," or through some kind of management contract option.[25] The company would benefit because SRC would provide a series of contracts for countries such as China, Pakistan, Jordan, and Iraq. All that Gechem had to do in return was to ensure that the Belgian government would issue export licenses for these sales. At the same time, Bull also saw PRB as a potentially vulnerable company:

> The first concern which I have is the status of the Belgian company. It is a legally organised Belgian entity . . . operating under Belgian law. However it is not integrated into Belgian economic and industrial life. While employing a number of Belgian citizens, it can be regarded with some justification, as simply a group of foreigners using the country for commercial co-ordinating purposes. This leaves it vulnerable to whimsical attack by anyone who wishes to raise issues with the Belgian Government.[26]

The corollary of this, Bull wrote, was that

> it is essential that our major clients have confidence that we will not be subjected to harassment. Among these is the government of Iraq. Suggestions that they should consider procurement from Belgian sources have been opposed on the basis that Belgium refuses export licences to them. The Iraqis make the point that France, Spain, Italy, Yugoslavia etc. openly grant export licences for items to date refused by the Belgians. Their position is that they do not wish to be part of any devious

transhipping, even if technically legal, but still against the Government's policy. Mr Jourdain and the Belgian Charge d'Affaires have dismissed this aspect in a meeting I arranged and attended with Dr Saadi Al Amir . . . in Baghdad. . . . Confirmation of a defined list of items which will be granted Belgian export licences is a critical issue in relation to PRB business.[27]

Not everyone will recognize the sentiments in favor of open delivery that Bull here ascribes to the Iraqis. In making this bid, he was particularly interested in PRB's Kaulille plant, the source of propellant for Project Babylon, rather than in PRB as a whole. His proposal required that it remain Belgian-controlled, ostensibly to avoid the vulnerabilities he had already outlined but also to avoid the kind of openness he claimed the Iraqis were committed to. In reality, Bull's interest in Kaulille was directed toward ensuring a secure supply of propellant. It was a well-known fact in the defense industry that PRB had experienced some difficulty of late, and Bull was anxious that it should not be sold off to a company hostile to Iraq and thus jeopardize supply. For example, he seems to have been almost paranoid about the possibility of Israeli interests securing control of PRB.

On the basis of SGB/Gechem's presentation of PRB's situation, the Astra team regarded the agreed sale price of £21 million as representing good value. Bull himself had been prepared to pay £38 million for a 51 percent holding in PRB, and Astra got 100 percent for just over 50 percent of that bid. So why did SGB/Gechem spurn the higher offer from Bull for just 51 percent of PRB, in favor of a substantially lower offer for the entire company? The answer seems to be that there were political and intelligence considerations at work that overrode commercial instinct and acted to block a purchase on behalf of Iraq.

Negotiations with Astra over the purchase of PRB had begun in September 1988 but moved along slowly into the spring of 1989. By the end of May 1989, pressure was being exerted on the Astra team to complete the paperwork quickly. For example, Sir John Cuckney of 3*i*, Astra's largest shareholder, telephoned James twice asking why Astra was not making faster progress. Sandy Walker, a 3*i* manager, also pressured James in response to pressure put on him by Cuckney.[28] James says that he

found it strange that Sir John should get so involved personally in one of 3*i*'s investments. It was explained that Cuckney was being pressured by Hervé de Carmoy the SGB Chief Executive and Chairman of Gechem who was previously head of the Midland Bank's special trade and defence department. Cuckney and de Carmoy were colleagues at Midland Bank where Cuckney had been Deputy Chairman.[29]

3*i*'s enthusiasm for the purchase grew, James says, after it was made aware that Wafic Said's Saudi Investment and Finance Corporation (SIFCORP) was willing to finance it. Someone else who became enthusiastic was nonexecutive director Stephan Kock. According to James,

> he was so keen that the PRB deal should proceed that he stayed up in the all night meetings, something he did not do with the Walters or BMARC acquisitions. When repeated difficulties were raised by Bank of Nova Scotia[30] Kock telephoned the [agent general] of Nova Scotia late at night to put pressure on the bank. Nobody has ever explained how Kock had these contacts and influences. . . . Kock was desperate for the PRB deal to go through when he knew Cuckney and Carmoy were involved and wished the deal to go through. Previously he had written a memorandum pointing out the dangers of doing business in Belgium.[31]

Gechem did not want Astra to have access to current PRB contracts until after it had purchased PRB, citing reasons of commercial confidentiality. While not particularly unusual in the armaments field, in this case one of the reasons seemed to be that a number of PRB's customers were known conduits for Iraq, and with the end of the Iran-Iraq War, the orders no longer existed. But Gechem did agree that Stoy Hayward, Astra's auditors, could have access. Throughout the negotiations, Gechem was keen to keep a tight rein, rather than allow the PRB management to take the lead. The PRB contract was signed on 17 July 1989 and the acquisition completed on 11 September 1989, finally giving Astra access to leading technology in several areas, including access to the work of Gerald Bull.

◆ Astra, PRB, and Iraq

Having completed the purchase of PRB, James was almost immediately made aware that it was fulfilling contracts for Iraq. He met with PRB's Cardinael and Glibert, who "produced a list of contracts and pointed to a contract with Jordan and made it quite clear that that contract was for Iraq and was for [the propellant for] a very large gun."[32] What James had just been told was that PRB was covertly supplying the propellant for Gerald Bull's Iraqi supergun program.

It was internal PRB contract number E5397, signed on 17 November 1988 between PRB and the Royal Jordanian Armed Forces, having been negotiated by PRB's Jourdain and Binek.[33] It covered both the System 350 and System

1,000 propellants.[34] Jourdain had also arranged for the Belgian air force to fly the initial consignment of 350mm propellant out of Belgium, disguised as a consignment of chocolates, on a C-130 cargo aircraft direct to Amman on 16 June 1989.[35] Meanwhile, the order for the supergun itself had still to be completed, having been slowed by delays in receiving the specifications.

Payment, which was to be made via a letter of credit drawn on the Central Bank of Jordan, was covered by the Belgian equivalent of the ECGD, the Office National de Ducroire. In addition, PRB paid out commissions on the contract to two front companies. The first of these was called the Bilder Trading Company Ltd., widely rumored in the defense industry to be a channel for the king of Jordan; indeed, in a recorded telephone conversation, Gerald Bull at one point asked if Astra, having taken over PRB, knew about the PRB front companies, commenting: "Well, if Astra finds out which Arab is behind Bilder, then the shit will certainly hit the fan. We'll never keep it quiet."[36] This commission was for 5.26 percent of the contract value (account no. 657-809-404V). The second commission, paid to the Gerofin Investment Corporation,[37] was 11.77 percent, a relatively large commission considering that a standard commission would be around 5 percent and that this was not a particularly large contract by arms sales standards. Payments were to be made to the Union Bank of Switzerland, Geneva (account no. 42131860N). Both accounts were controlled by Belgian employees of PRB.[38]

Having been confronted with some of this information, James asked for a list to be compiled detailing all current PRB contracts that used suspected and known conduit countries. This, one of the few Astra-related documents to escape seizure by MOD police during 1990, is reproduced in table 5.1.

Documents prepared by PRB for Astra at the time of the takeover, intended to show an impressive range of markets for their military products for the period 1982–87 and 1988–90, suggest that an even higher proportion of PRB's military contracts may well have been what are termed in the industry "joker" contracts, that is, contracts for equipment that was intended to be channeled to Iraq or Iran through conduits. For example, in its 1982–87 listing, it cites the sale of 155mm propelling charge to Brazil, a well-known conduit for Iran, but no associated projectiles. It cites sales of 155mm ammunition to Jordan and Saudi Arabia and Kuwait—all well-known routes through which Iraq was supplied—and to Morocco, which on paper imported an overwhelming amount of 155mm ammunition for the twelve 155mm guns it is listed as having at the end of the Iran-Iraq War. From these documents Bahrain emerges, surprisingly, as the purchaser of an impressive array of ammunition, as does the United Arab Emirates. France, Germany, Spain, Swe-

Table 5.1

PRB Contracts Using Conduits as of 25 October 1989

Country	Product	Remarks
Jordan (1)	High-energy propellant	Project Babylon: Phase I (end-user Iraq) PRB Contract No. 5397 signed Feb 1989 Product M8M high-energy propellant:
Quantity		235 tons Value scheduled for delivery by 31 March 1990, £1.96 million Order routed from Jordan to PRB via SRC (Dr. Bull) Delivery presently suspended due to technical difficulties Belgian government export license approved
Jordan (2)	Propellant powder	Project Babylon: Phase II (end-user Iraq-SNPE) Sales prospect for large quantity propellant Value £5.5 million Scheduled visit by J. L. Jourdain in November 1989 to begin negotiations with contract signature, January 1990 Partial delivery by October 1990 PRB anticipates export license approval for Iraq will be sanctioned by Belgian government early 1990
Jordan	130mm LR/BB ammunition	PRB forecast sale of 130mm LR/BB by 31 March 1989 Value £11 million Quantity 20,000 rounds
Zambia	Internal security pyrotechnics	While no evidence exists, suggested that pyros are for use by anti-Cuban forces in Angola
Austria	Propellant	Destination Saudi via industrial offset with NORICOM
France	Propellant	Destination Morocco via industrial offset with Luchaire, which provided credit package for PRB products
Spain	155mm components	Destination Pakistan via industrial offset
United States	Propellant powder	Destination Taiwan via OBW/PRB/Astra
Singapore	155mm propellants and CCC	Contract due February 1990 Destination Taiwan
Saudi	Demolition charge mines	No supporting evidence; may be transshipped to Iraq

Source: TISC: HC-86-xii, pp. 413–414. The format has been modified here.[19]

den and the United Kingdom were all capable of producing items cited as being exported from PRB to those countries. The 1988–90 listing shows Austria, another well-known route, as a destination for 155mm and 130mm base-bleed ammunition.[40] In addition, it shows Jordan, Kuwait, Saudi Arabia, and even Qatar—all well-known conduits—ordering 155mm ammunition. At the end of the Iran-Iraq War, Qatar had just six 155mm guns.

James was also made aware of just how heavily involved PRB was in the propellant cartel in conversations he had in 1989 with Pinaud, the managing director of the French arms firm Luchaire, another European manufacturer close to the cartel. James had gone to see Pinaud with a view to "head-hunting" him for PRB. However, Pinaud began talking to James: "he assumed that I knew far more about the European cartel and Iraq than I did and began speaking to me about events which he obviously believed I already knew about. He told me about the depth of PRB's involvement in the supply of equipment to the Middle East war which was on a scale far greater than I had ever suspected."[41]

This meeting helped to confirm for James details about the cartel's modus operandi, rumors of which were rife in the defense industry, and PRB's precise role within it:

> Membership was on the basis of being a large, recognised, supplier who could be trusted to be discreet. The companies involved all had long associations with various Governments and usually had Military Intelligence connections. When Astra bought PRB we bought into the propellant cartel. Employees of PRB attended the cartel meetings. . . . My personal knowledge of the propellant cartel is that meetings were held regularly where a three month "slice" of production was allocated in rotation to the various manufacturers. This was because the Iran/Iraq war effort was consuming phenomenally high levels of propellant and if any one company gained a major part of the contract it would necessarily draw potentially unwelcome attention to itself. The distribution around the members of the cartel of a specific period of production ensured that no one assumed a higher profile than anyone else in relation to the manufacture of propellant. Because of the quantities involved it could only really be used in a major war effort. . . . It is said . . . that Iraq used £1m worth of propellant per day.[42]

Having been confronted with these revelations, James began to compile his own lists of Astra contracts destined for Iraq and Iran, but routed through conduits. It soon became obvious that PRB was not the only subsidiary Astra had recently purchased that was involved in this illicit trade. Indeed, this seemed to be standard practice in the industry. Largely, James was able to compile these lists by applying a simple formula that any licensing body should have been able to apply, namely, that the ostensible recipients did not possess weapons systems that required the type of ammunition being ordered, or at least not enough of them to justify the quantity being ordered. For example, Thailand had few 155mm weapons, and even more obviously, Jordan had no supergun. James informed the Scott Inquiry that in some cases the inconsistencies were so glaring that "the fact that Iran and Iraq were the actual recipients was discussed at Board meetings. There was no secret whatsoever made of this. No one felt that what was being done was in any way illicit."[43]

◆ Liaison with the Ministry of Defence and British Intelligence

The new owners decided to inform the MOD about the suspicious Jordanian contract that had been pointed out to them, even though this would clearly cast doubt on the future of a contract of vital importance to PRB, given its financial position. They decided on this course on the basis of a warning they received from Roger Harding at the RNEE at Portsmouth, the same month they completed the purchase of PRB. Harding was then deputy head of the Defence Export Services Organisation (DESO), the arms sales branch of the British government. James and Gumbley had first met him at a defense exhibition in Las Vegas back in 1983, and he had subsequently helped Astra to establish itself rapidly in the United States. At the RNEE, Harding warned that if anything suspicious emerged from the PRB order book, the MOD should be notified. This would suggest that within the MOD there was by this time, at the very least, a suspicion that Jordan was being used as a conduit to get military equipment to Baghdad, and even that Bull was involved, given his links to PRB. It could also mean that the MOD was aware of the existence and activities of the propellant cartel, and that PRB was a member of it. As the MOD's Nicholas Bevan subsequently explained to the TISC, the advice was given "against the background of the known involvement of continental European munitions firms in the export of armaments to Iran and Iraq."[44] For his part James did not think they "would have got such a strong warning unless there was some knowledge of it."[45] If it had not been reported, Astra could have been the subject of the show trial of the century. It was now involved in arming Iraq and Iran from three countries, two continents, and via a wide range of conduits.

Gumbley therefore got in touch with Bob Primrose at DESO, and a number of meetings were held in London, beginning in October 1989, between James and Gumbley and "intelligence people" from "another department," one of whom James identified as "Holdness."[46] He subsequently recalled:

> In October 1989 Mr Holdness came to see me at my office. I had never met Mr Holdness before this. He gave me two telephone numbers at which I could contact him, one MOD and the other FCO. . . . The feeling that I got from his questioning was that he did not want to know the detail of the contract but was more interested in learning how widespread was the knowledge of the use of Jordan.[47]

At these meetings, James and Gumbley passed on details of the joker contracts they had inherited and handed over evidence showing that Bull was behind the propellant order, which referred specifically to Project Babylon.[48] The officials were very interested to find out what the Astra management knew of the use of Jordan, particularly in view of the fact that the report on PRB joker contracts, which the management shared with the officials, concluded that PRB had "reliable information that ordnance hardware has been cast in the United Kingdom, machined by Royal Ordnance and exported with UK approval to the Kingdom of Jordan for Iraq."[49] They maintained their liaison with the intelligence community throughout October and November 1989 and found that certain individuals within it were "extremely well-informed" about Project Babylon.

Astra's position at this time was a difficult one. Although technically in breach of British arms export restrictions, the actions of its Belgian subsidiary were technically beyond the jurisdiction of British Customs and Excise. Furthermore, the contract had been signed before the Astra takeover, when PRB was owned by Gechem. Bearing these and reasons of its own in mind, MI6 "gave its blessing to the second batch of propellant."[50] MI6 told James "to let the trial order for £3 million of propellant go through. It was quite clear it was for military purposes."[51] Certainly, the legal situation was not clear-cut, because PRB could not be subject to the Howe Guidelines. Indeed, this flexibility had been at the heart of Astra's expansion strategy across the United Kingdom, the United States, and Europe. As James told the TISC: "I am not quite clear that it was illegal in Belgium. It was a Belgian company. The Belgian Air Force were flying the propellant to Jordan for transmission to Iraq. Obviously, I do not think they regarded it as illegal."[52]

As a consequence of reporting this contract to the MOD and intelligence services, Astra lost propellant contracts with Iraq worth £12 million, £20 million, and £3 million,[53] while the MOD did not offer any substituting work as a form of compensation, as the Astra management had reasoned they would.

Despite the advice they were given to continue with the contract, on 3 November Astra's John Sellens instructed PRB "to cease deliveries of propellants to Jordan forthwith." This led Glibert to write a confidential memo arguing that loss of the contract would lead to further unemployment at Kaulille, as well as to the blacklisting of PRB and, probably, Astra, and warning of "possible peripheral damaging effects on neighbouring markets for both PRB and ASTRA, *since the origin of the decision will be clearly identified. This will contribute to the rumor about who is 'behind ASTRA.'*"[54] This latter comment referred to the speculation within the defense industry about who Astra's ultimate owners were, that is, on whose behalf the institutional shareholders were holding shares.

Between October 1989 and February 1990, James spent much time at the PRB plants in Belgium. There he saw Iraqi personnel undergoing training at Kaulille (the major propellant plant in Belgium) and at Matagne, where Iraqis were testing propellants and artillery pieces. He also came across evidence suggesting that the British government's supposed neutrality in the Iran-Iraq War had, at one level, been little more than a pretense, and that IMS—an arms-length arms sales operation—together with RO, had been involved in getting ammunition to Iraq via PRB at the height of the conflict. The evidence indicated

just how close had been the connection between PRB, IMS and Royal Ordnance over a number of years. In particular I discovered documentation disclosing contracts between PRB and IMS for the provision of ammunition (mainly 155mm) to Iraq in 1984, 1985 and 1986. . . . PRB had been contracted by them to carry out the manufacturing side of contracts entered into by IMS and Iraq. . . . The equipment manufactured by PRB on IMS contracts with Iraq included . . . metal casing for shells, propellants, fuzes and sometimes complete rounds.[55]

These observations were consistent with the rumors circulating in the defense industry that the British government used IMS to buy ammunition from PRB to meet the needs of countries, such as Iraq, that Britain was not politically able to supply directly. Having IMS buy from PRB, and having the material exported from Belgium, provided arms-length deniability, as of course did the nature of IMS itself. On 21 December 1989, the British Embassy in Belgium asked the Belgian government via a demarche to get PRB's export license for the Jordanian propellant contract revoked, and Belgian intelligence was asked to investigate further.[56] The need for this had already been removed in practice on 5 December 1989 when, by coincidence, an as yet unexplained explosion occurred at PRB's Kaulille plant, permanently halting production of the propellant and further contributing to Astra's decline.[57] SRC then switched the order for the propellant to Yugoslavia.

Given these contacts with the MOD and the intelligence services, it would seem logical to assume that British government ministers had been made aware of Project Babylon by this time. However Nicholas Bevan, undersecretary at the MOD,[58] told the TISC that ministers had not been informed of any of this, not even of the existence of contracts ostensibly for Jordan that were in reality destined for Iraq. He told the TISC that this decision was taken by Roger Harding and that "the Foreign Office decided that it was not necessary to inform Ministers before contacting the Belgian Government."[59] Unfortunately, neither Harding nor Primrose was available to give evidence to the TISC as, by coincidence, both had retired and therefore, the MOD explained, no longer had access to the relevant papers.[60] Gerald James said he thought it "inconceivable" that the information passed on by Astra to Harding had not been referred to higher levels of government. Labour TISC member Doug Hoyle agreed, saying it was "inconceivable that civil servants would not have informed Ministers at the highest level."[61]

When this liaison with the intelligence services was first revealed on the television program *This Week* in May 1990, it immediately called into question Nicholas Ridley's assertion that the government had only recently become aware, in general terms, of the supergun program.[62] It also lent further credence to early reports that "far from being a secret, the supergun plan was common gossip in European defence and political circles long before the first barrel section was seized at Teesport on April 10."[63]

◆ BMARC

While James and Gumbley's experience with PRB made it clear that a series of networks was operating to supply Iraq and Iran with a range of military equipment and ammunition, it was becoming clear that another recent acquisition, BMARC, was also heavily involved in the same networks.

Perhaps the clearest expression of BMARC's involvement came from the secret order book whose existence James and Gumbley discovered. Although the Gumbley and James team had bought BMARC, in a sense they never felt they had full knowledge of everything that was being produced there. There is a hint of this situation in certain of the BMARC board minutes. For example, on 2 November 1988, "The Chairman expressed concern that the BMARC board had not been appraised of certain matters and specified; the contract for 35mm ammunition to be supplied to China; the agreement concerning armaments production between Oerlikon and Breda." Indeed, it seemed that types of ammunition were being produced that neither Gumbley nor James could account for. Their attempts to discover what these products were met with limited success. As James recalled for the Scott Inquiry: "At BMARC I discovered that a secret order book was being kept. . . . I discovered on visits to BMARC's facility at Faldingworth that booster pellets were being produced and stored which were not relevant to any known order."[64] He explained further:

> [My] first knowledge of this secret order book [came] during a telephone conversation with Gumbley when he told me about it. Subsequently I had further conversations in the office about it. As far as I know it was kept at BMARC's facility at Grantham. The only people I can say with certainty who had access to its contents were Isles, Avery, McNaught and Kock.[65]

To investigate further, James began making early morning visits to the plant to try to find out what was going on and "tried on one or two occasions to secretly monitor operations, and while this was very difficult my suspicions were greatly increased."[66] These visits revealed that the apparent wastage rates were far greater than those officially recorded, deepening his suspicions. These were not allayed when, faced with new orders secured by Gumbley, the BMARC management said they did not have the capacity to fulfill them as they were working flat out, despite officially having a relatively light workload. James shared his concerns with Gumbley, who said he also knew something was wrong at BMARC:

> After I was told about the existence of this book, I challenged McNaught and Avery. They both denied its existence. I therefore made enquiries to discover it. At that time I was also making enquiries into the activities of Kock and the use to which BMARC was being put. However I was dismissed before those enquiries were completed and before I ever physically located the book. . . . Its existence however is undoubted because at Board meetings lists of current and prospective contracts were always circulated. These lists did not include contracts which I later discovered to be current. . . . Additionally I have been told by Jane Renton a journalist then with the *Observer* that Sellens remarked to her at the Portsmouth Royal Naval Equipment Exhibition in 1989 that Gumbley and I were unaware of some of the larger orders going through Astra.[67]

Elsewhere, he wrote:

> In October, November, December 1989 it became increasingly clear to me that
> the group was being used for covert operations on a massive scale. The large size
> and remote locations of some of our explosive sites would have made this compara-
> tively easy particularly where staff we inherited had a continuous role predating
> our involvement and where prior warnings of visits was usual.[68]

Gumbley also refers to the situation at BMARC in a court application to have
Astra documents returned to him:

> I believe that my arrest and untimely removal from Astra was deliberately engi-
> neered to remove me from the company at a critical time and to deflect attention
> away from other matters . . . the management team at BMARC were operating a web
> of deception and were involved in a number of clandestine activities without the
> knowledge of the main Astra Board, including a covert management buy-out, [and]
> the operation of a secondary and secret order book (involving supplying items to
> Iraq and Iran and selling a range of Israeli-manufactured aircraft bombs). The
> BMARC management team were responsible for the implementation of a conspiracy
> to remove both myself and Mr James and subsequently the rest of the Astra Hold-
> ings executive board.[69]

A further suspicious order going through BMARC was one to supply booster
pellets for artillery fuses for Jordan, clearly intended for onward transmission
to Iraq. James and Gumbley knew nothing of this while in charge of Astra; it
did not appear in the official order book and thus did not come up for discussion at main board meetings. However, a few weeks after the supergun seizure, and at a time of heightened media interest in Britain's role in arming
Iraq, Bill McNaught of BMARC (by now Astra Defence Systems Ltd) wrote to
Bob Primrose at DESO:

> I have recently examined in some detail a small contract currently held by Astra
> Defence Systems to produce booster pellets for artillery fuzes for Jordan. Astra's
> customer is Ordnance Technologies Ltd (ORDTEC) of Twyford, Reading. The con-
> tract is for the supply of 300,000 M739 fuze booster pellets between March and
> July of this year. . . . My suspicions have been aroused because I have found a letter
> on our file indicating that the main contractor for this project is SRC Engineering
> of Geneva. . . . I should also add that from the documentation you will see that the
> consignee address is the Al Fao Organisation c/o The Jordanian Armed Forces.[70]

By this time, Astra had manufactured 25,000 pellets, which were to be matched with fuse components sent from Rexon in the United States and then shipped to Jordan for onward transmission to Iraq. At the front of the Rexon documentation was printed: INSTRUCTION LABELS TO BE REMOVED BEFORE THE CONSIGNMENT LEAVES.

In July 1995 John Reed, editor of *Defence Industry Digest*, wrote to Gumbley recalling a meeting with McNaught in July 1991, at which he was allegedly told: "You have to understand that we blew the whistle on the Astra management, Gerald James and Chris Gumbley, because we did not like the direction in which they were taking the company." Reed asked if this meant that it was the BMARC management that had approached the MOD with the "evidence" about Gumbley (see below), and McNaught "replied in the affirmative. This latter question was put to him in several different ways and on each occasion his reply was the same."[71]

Astra was also involved through BMARC in an attempt to sell 35mm ammunition to Cyprus, which is another recognized conduit for prohibited destinations like Iraq and Iran. Indeed, Chris Cowley has commented on coming across a warehouse in Amman, Jordan, in 1989 containing crates and pallets of shells and ammunition marked for shipment to Cyprus (and Egypt) as well as Jordan itself.[72] In the event Astra did not secure the order, not because permission to export would not have been obtained and the order would not have been won but rather because General Donald Isles objected, citing the terms of the license agreement with Oerlikon. However, James is adamant that Oerlikon had always made it clear that with consultation, sales outside the license agreement would be permitted, so long as they were in the commercial interests of both companies.

BMARC's biggest contract after the Astra purchase was called LISI (Licensed for Singapore), a contract initiated by Oerlikon Buhrle prior to the Astra takeover, to supply medium caliber armaments—ammunition, weapons, and tooling—to Singapore. Inside the defense industry, it was an open secret that Singapore was a favored transshipment point from where arms could easily be diverted. It was an open secret at BMARC that LISI was intended for Iran. The project was run by General Isles from a special, dedicated office at the Grantham plant. While LISI was just one case among several that James highlighted in which Astra found itself arming Iraq and Iran through its newly acquired subsidiaries, it was also the one that would return to cause the most embarrassment to the government, and to one serving Cabinet minister in particular.

◆ Other Covert Arms Sales Involving Astra

Astra also became involved in Saudi efforts to reroute arms to Iraq. In December 1989, after purchasing PRB, James was invited to Saudi Arabia to meet with Prince Mishari, a half-brother of King Fahd, to discuss PRB's business with the kingdom. Jonathan Aitken tried to dissuade James from meeting Mishari, on the grounds that he apparently shot the British consul in 1953, but John Sellens, Astra's director of Group Sales and Marketing, and James made the trip in December 1989 anyhow. During their negotiations, the Astra team was made aware that if Astra was prepared to pay commissions, Prince Mishari could be "helpful" to it.[73] Furthermore:

> Both Prince Mishari and his advisor admitted openly during the course of conversations that military equipment received into Saudi Arabia was rerouted to Iraq. The Prince spoke openly about British financing for this trade. In particular he wished to discuss a helicopter contract entered into between the Saudi Government and Westland UTC for the supply of 100 Black Hawk helicopters for which Astra was going to supply the weaponry. . . . It was quite obvious from those discussions that Saudi [Arabia] had no use for the entire consignment of 100 helicopters and a number of them were to go to Iraq. As he put it: "We have neighbours who can use this sort of equipment." Without specifying it was quite clear from the context of the conversation that the neighbour he referred to was Iraq. The helicopters would be built under licence in the UK by Westland and then weaponised by Astra and exported to Saudi Arabia as part of the Al Yamamah deal. Because this was a government-to-government contract, it did not require an end-user certificate. In addition to discussing helicopter contracts we also spent some time in discussion of the Bull 155 [mm] project nominally for Saudi but which was being rerouted to Iraq.[74]

Again, Prince Mishari and his advisers made it quite clear that this was being passed on to Iraq—a fact subsequently confirmed by PRB staff like Glibert, Cardinael, and Jourdain.[75] This latter diversion of 155mm equipment was later confirmed to James by General Last of the MOD, who confirmed it was a part of the Al Yamamah arms package.

In addition, Oerlikon had managed to export the Skyguard anti-aircraft system to Iraq during the Iran-Iraq War from BMARC without contravening the Howe Guidelines.[76] However, in the Middle East BMARC's only official exports of the Skyguard were to Jordan, Saudi Arabia, Kuwait, and the United Arab Emirates, any (or, indeed, all) of whom could have passed it on to Iraq. The Skyguard was visible in operation in Baghdad during the Gulf War, and despite its not having been officially sold to Iraq, Iraqis were trained in its use at BMARC's Faldingworth site. As regards Iraq maintaining a supply of ammunition for it, in 1988 BMARC secured an order to supply Skyguard ammunition to Cyprus. Cyprus did not have the Skyguard gun.

With regard to Kuwait, BMARC was involved in negotiations for a contract to supply cannon ammunition and guns as a way, they hoped, of breaking into the lucrative Kuwaiti arms market. However, Kuwait did not have a use for the quantity or type of equipment involved, suggesting that it too was intended to be passed on to Iraq—a suggestion seemingly confirmed when, with the end of the Iran-Iraq War, Kuwait lost all interest in the contract. The deal never went ahead.

With regard to the United Arab Emirates, Astra negotiated with ISC Ferranti over a contract to fill the American Paveway bomb, despite the fact that the tiny country did not have sufficiently powerful aircraft to carry such equipment. Iraq, of course, did. Gerald James recalled:

> Astra under my chairmanship was asked by Ferranti to fill a large stand off bomb for Abu Dhabi. It was clear that this weapon was not for Abu Dhabi as that country had no aircraft capable of carrying it. This weapon was to be filled for Ferranti's ISC subsidiary in the United Kingdom and was an ISC weapon. It is what is termed a "Paveway" bomb and could not have been exported without US and United Kingdom Government approval. Clearly Ferranti had such approval. The Paveway had a nuclear version but we were asked to quote for filling the H.E. version. Although Astra would have filled these weapons at its Faldingworth plant—a BMARC plant—the price quoted by Astra although very competitive, was still too high for Ferranti who decided to have the weapon filled by a small relatively unknown company "Explosives Developments Ltd."[77]

In addition, both before its purchase by Astra and after, its U.S. subsidiary Accudyne was being used by James Guerin's ISC to supply fuses shipped out to South Africa, from where they were passed on to Iraq.

◆ Astra and the 1989 Baghdad International Military Exhibition

Astra also had a strange experience at the 1989 Baghdad International Military Exhibition, where it was one of seventeen British organizations exhibiting,[78] 25 percent of whose costs to attend were met by the DTI. In the exhibition brochure, each exhibiting company had a page that described its product range and provided an address and contact number. All were printed correctly except Astra's. John Pike, then of BMARC, commented after the exhibition that he could not understand why Astra had not received a single enquiry from it.[79] Scrutiny of the brochure provided the answer. The address and telex number given for Astra (Brooklands Road, Weybridge, Surrey, KTB 0SJ, England, TLX 27111) were those of BAE, Astra's competitor in the ammunition market through its ownership of RO. However, this had not simply been mistranscribed, as BAE's given address in the brochure was that of its London headquarters. James considers that enquiries were channeled through BAE because Astra managers were not fully aware of their newly acquired subsidiaries' involvement in exporting to Iraq and Iran, and so were prevented from receiving enquiries that could have alerted them to the situation.[80] These could have covered three types of export. The first was items, like Project LISI, that went through conduits to Iran and Iraq. The second was those "which were made by ICI, SNPE, PRB, Nobel Germany, Nobel Sweden, Muiden Chemie, where our premises were used as storage/assembly and transit areas. This applied for others over and above the propellant cartel like BAE."[81] The third was those secretly manufactured at BMARC, evidence of which James came across when he and Gumbley discovered the existence of the secret order book.

◆ Collapse

The purchase of PRB brought with it not just the difficulties of the Jordanian order and a host of joker contracts but also the problem that with the cancellation of the Jordanian contract without any form of compensation and the end of the Iran-Iraq War, a company that had been experiencing difficulties of late was now facing a definite slump, at least in the immediate future. When it paid £21 million for PRB in 1989, Astra had been assured it would make a BFr150 million (£2.3 million) profit that year. However, it later emerged that these projections had been based on 1988 figures from the Iran-Iraq War era rather than on the (lower) 1989 postwar figures.[82] After the purchase had taken place, Duronsoy wrote to James to inform him that the "profits were not on target." James began to negotiate a compensation package with SGB and Gechem. While he was doing this, in December 1989 Gumbley approached him and suggested he stand down as chairman. By this time, Astra's financial position had been further undermined by the Kaulille explosion, which took its huge press out of commission. Notwithstanding this,

James claims that at the end of 1989, Astra still had an order book worth £340 million:

> . . . what should be always remembered is that we were advised for our own personal protection to report the supergun propellant contract. That contract alone was worth £35 million. We took £35 million out of one year by reporting it—remember we reported this bloody thing in September originally. We were told not to do anything, and then we were told to carry on with it. But we lost £35 million worth of turnover certainly in the period to March, which we would have otherwise had. And thereafter we would have lost, on the basis of what was projected, £50 million worth of turnover per annum. Well, you can't just take that sort of money out of a company's turnover and expect it to produce good results—it's not physically possible. And PRB wasn't going to have a too brilliant a year in the year that we bought it anyway—we knew that, but to take out £35 million worth of turnover, and not get any offer of . . . any replacement from the MOD, who really by that time had decided they wanted to shut down, was a disaster. But we did it because we were advised to do it. We were told we would be in trouble, and we fully expected that we would be given other work, which we never were.[83]

This was the second of three attempts that would be made to remove James as chairman. In interviews with the DTI inspectors called in to investigate Astra, Stephan Kock admitted to being involved in all of them.[84] The plan was that Kock would become chairman for a limited period. John Anderson, Astra's secretary, told the DTI inspectors that he "got a phone call from Mr Kock stating that the Prudential wanted to remove Mr James as the chairman and . . . I think even Mr Kock put forward his name as interim chairman. . . . I think Mr Kock said he would stand in for a year. He was willing to do that and I think he wanted me to support him for a year." Although this attempt to remove James fell through, in March 1990 a further attempt was made, apparently with the backing of the main institutional shareholders, 3*i* and Prudential. This time it succeeded. James resigned as a director the following month. When Kock told the DTI inspectors of his involvement in all three attempts to remove Gerald James, he told them that he finally secured his removal by issuing an ultimatum: "[I]f he had not resigned on the Friday, my understanding was the Bank of Boston, especially, would have pulled the plug on the company." He later elaborated:

> I said [to Gumbley] Look, I have had enough. I am giving you until 2.15 this afternoon. . . . If you have not thrown him off by 2.15 I will go to the Midland

Bank and I will bring back a letter from the head of corporate finance withdrawing their support. I will also go to the Stock Exchange and give them my resignation and by Tuesday this company will not be trading.[85]

Prior to this, Kock said he had approached Roy Barber "with a view to becoming a non-executive director, then to become Chairman as soon as we could shift James."[86]

At the same time, Gumbley was forced to resign over a bribery allegation. Effectively, the two guiding forces behind the company's development, and the two people investigating irregularities throughout the group—particularly in relation to BMARC and PRB—concerning the supply of arms to Iraq and Iran were removed within days of each other. Roy Barber became chairman, seemingly at the insistence of 3i, and by April 1990 only Stephan Kock remained from the original Astra board. Thereupon, the negotiations that James had been conducting with SGB over compensation were adversely affected, and whereas James had been negotiating for a figure in the region of £30 million, the new board settled for just £3 million. The new management also called in the DTI to investigate what had happened—the first time in history that a company initiated a DTI inquiry into its own affairs. Following the removal of James and Gumbley, Astra's subsidiaries were sold off to members of the propellant cartel. Although nonmembers of the cartel showed an interest in buying various parts, none was successful in doing so. Ed Walters of Walters Group was interested in BMARC, for example, but received no reply to his offers, which were higher than that accepted from RO, to whom it was sold. PRB was sold to GIAT for just £3 million, although there had been offers for its Clermont plant alone for £8 million from nonmembers of the cartel. Although Astra was completely shut down by 1992, the Astra Interim Report for the six months to 30 September 1991 shows that Astra had returned an operating profit of £63,000 after the PRB dislocations had been absorbed. Chairman Roy Barber's message to the shareholders had been upbeat: "[W]e are encouraged by the continuing improvements in the operating efficiency and cost structure of the manufacturing units, which indicates that the improvement in operating profit will continue into 1992 and beyond."[87] Nevertheless, once the old board had been removed, the new Astra board failed to win a single new order, despite the outbreak of war in the Gulf, up to the appointment of a receiver in February 1992—just days before James gave evidence to the TISC.

♦ **Arrests**

Gumbley fell foul of the MOD police and was subsequently sentenced to nine months in prison on a charge of bribing Dennis Stowe, a civil servant at the MOD's Directory of Light Weapons, allegedly buying him an secondhand BMW car worth £12,500 and a holiday in Florida "as an inducement or reward for assisting in the obtaining of a contract with the MOD"—a charge hotly disputed by Gumbley and James. In the event, Gumbley served four and a half months of the sentence.[88] He later filed for bankruptcy over monies owed to Trowers and Hamlins, the lawyers who represented him in the case. Unknown to him, they were also retained by Stephan Kock as Astra's lawyers.[89] Kock was a client during 1989 and 1990 when Mr. A. G. S. Barstow, a partner and, like Kock, a former member of the Special Air Service (SAS), acted for him. Kock kept his use of Trowers and Hamlins secret from the rest of the Astra board until he had to reveal it at a board meeting on 4 December 1990 because the company's fees had to be settled. Indeed, Trowers and Hamlins were recommended to Gumbley by Kock. After Gumbley was obliged to find new legal representation because of his financial situation, his counsel, Mr. Ian Goldsworthy, advised Gumbley that he should consider a claim against Trowers and Hamlins over their advice to him, including the recommendation that he should resign his position at Astra.[90]

Gumbley's was just one of a series of arrests that members of the Astra board were subsequently exposed to. The most outlandish and irregular was that of John Anderson. Following Gumbley's arrest, Anderson was showing prospective purchasers around his house in Fort William, Scotland, when he was arrested in front of them and taken away:

> They bounced him out of the house, drove him at high speed to Glasgow Airport, put him on a plane between two other officers and flew him down to Gatwick. They took him from the plane in a police car which drove at high speed allegedly to Ramsgate for some reason. . . . On the way they had quite a serious accident which shook up everybody quite a lot. As a result of that, they allowed him to spend the night with a friend and asked him to answer a few questions the following day at the Ministry of Defence establishment at Earls Court. Then they gave him an air ticket and let him go home.[91]

Anderson suffered whiplash injuries in the 70mph car crash from which he had to be freed by ambulance men. On arriving at Maidstone Police Station the police officer accompanying Anderson asked that he not be booked in, but the desk sergeant refused, insisting on doing everything "by the book."[92] Although given a plane ticket back to Glasgow, on arrival at Glasgow Airport he was still 100 miles away from his home with no apparent way of getting there. After Anderson was arrested, three other Astra executives—Sellens, Miller, and Hollingsworth—were also arrested. Gumbley was the only one of those arrested ever to be charged with an offense, although even in his case, the basis of the offense shifted three times. He was questioned twice in March 1990, when the basis of his detention shifted from possession of a copy of the secret EPREP agreement to possession of an MOD telephone directory. Eventually, in April 1990, Gumbley was charged with bribing an MOD official, although he was questioned more about his meeting with Gerald Bull (see below) than about this apparent offense. Conveniently, on the day the super-gun barrel sections were seized, Gumbley was being held in custody. He resigned on 11 March 1990. Just four days later, Roy Barber brought in Anthony McCann to replace him. This board then demanded the resignations of Anderson, Miller, and Martin Guest. They refused, but all were forced out by April.[93]

After he had been charged, Gumbley was released on bail and, to his surprise, contacted by Gerald Bull. Bull told Gumbley that he had been set up because of the investigations into Astra that he and James had undertaken following the purchases of BMARC and PRB. He suggested that Gumbley travel to Brussels on 22 March, so that he (Bull) could meet him and offer him some help with his case. Hence, nine days after being charged under the 1906 Prevention of Corruption Act, Gumbley met for a full day with Gerald Bull. The commissions on the Saudi–United Kingdom Al Yamamah deals, about which Bull had informed James when they met in secret in November 1989, were one of the main topics of conversation. Bull gave them both information about "bribes and commissions that had been paid to UK and Belgian officials on British arms sales, particularly in relation to sales to Middle Eastern countries like Iraq and Saudi Arabia. He told us that some of these payments had been made through SGB (PRB's ultimate parent company) and Fabrique Nationale (PRB's sister company) as conduits."[94] Bull explained to Gumbley that because of the huge sums involved in arms deals, they were seen as a source of income for private individuals and political parties in Britain, continental Europe, and elsewhere. Another topic was the way in which RO ammunition was being routed through PRB to Iraq via Jordan, in contravention of the Howe Guidelines. Bull told Gumbley that because of what he had discovered during a trip to the Far East to investigate certain PRB contracts, which were notionally intended for well-known conduit countries like Thailand and

Singapore but were then transshipped to Iran and Iraq, he had become a threat to those running these operations, and so had been set up. Bull advised Gumbley not to go back to England but to get someone to put the evidence and documents he had collected in a safe place for him. Bull would get some money to help with Gumbley's immediate expenses. He should stay in Brussels for the time being, and Bull would help him expose the involvement of high-ranking individuals. Thinking that Bull was being a little paranoid, Gumbley thanked him for his help and agreed to return to meet again after the weekend. Gumbley left Bull in the late afternoon to begin his return journey to England. As soon as he got back to his car, he called James on his car phone. James recalled:

> . . . the last time I had a really open conversation with Gumbley was when he rang me up in a state of high excitement just after he had left Bull when he got back to his car phone, which was obviously being listened to anyway, saying "we're going to sort these bastards out, we'll be able to nail all of them now. We'll get sGB first, and it'll drag the British Government out and everybody else, and we'll fucking well teach them a lesson or two," and "Bull's going to put up all the money." I mean, he said that over the phone! He started off by saying "I bet you'll never guess who I've been to see," I said it straight away, I didn't need any prompting, I said "I know who you've been to see," and he was surprised by that, and I said "well, I'm not totally stupid and I've been doing my own research and investigation and I got there a lot earlier than you did." I said, "I didn't go to the Far East, but I certainly went to the Middle East and Saudi and I discovered enough there, and that's why Kock was trying to have me removed back in December."[95]

Hours later, Bull was dead. And as soon as Gumbley arrived back in Britain, he was rearrested.

Gumbley was asked by the TISC about his meeting with Bull. He told them that Bull "informed me my demise at that particular time had been engineered to remove me from Astra and he was willing to provide evidence and proof of that." Pressed further, he said: "He did say my arrest by the Ministry of Defence Police was an engineered manoeuvre.[96] . . . He said it was carried out to discredit me and to cause me to have to resign from Astra." When asked who Bull thought was behind this, Gumbley replied: "He suggested it was the British Government with Société Générale."[97]

◆ Stephan Adolph Kock

When James came to look for answers to the question of what had gone on at Astra, he found his inquiries focusing increasingly on the activities of nonexecutive director Stephan Kock, on whom he had begun to keep a dossier while chairman of Astra. One of the shadowier figures to emerge from the often shady world of defense financing, Kock has been referred to in a number of newspaper stories since the collapse of Astra, and he has even been the subject of a lead story on *Channel 4 News*.[98] More recently he has also been the subject of a series of parliamentary questions. Despite this interest, relatively little is known about him, and those who worked with Kock at the Midland Bank and Astra say he was vague about his background.

He was born in May 1927 and is a naturalized British subject,[99] claiming to have emigrated from Holland in 1944 to what was then Southern Rhodesia.[100] A résumé produced by the Midland Bank's Defence Equipment Finance Department, where Kock was a consultant/adviser for several years, provides the single most complete account of his career. It reads:

> Having served with the Royal Air Force, he spent some years in civil aviation. Subsequently he carried out specialised duties for the British government in various parts of the world, including as Political Secretary to the Rhodesian Prime Minister in the early sixties during the period of constitutional change.
>
> He had further military service abroad in the intelligence corps as an infantry officer. He also saw service for some years in the Special Air Service regiment. Following his retirement from the army he was for a period International Director for a major international Dutch mining and manufacturing group and subsequently again as International Director for the Shell Oil company. He is at present a nonexecutive director of a public company in the manufacturing sector.[101]

A main plank of Kock's résumé is his service in the SAS. During 1951–52 an entirely Rhodesian squadron of the SAS, C Squadron, was formed by "hard-drinking, hard-fighting idealist" Mad Mike Calvert from a pool of 1,000 Rhodesian volunteers.[102] This was part of a buildup of force levels in response to the Malayan insurgency. It would seem likely that Kock's SAS service was with C Squadron, which served in Malaya alongside A, B, and D Squadrons. Indeed, a 1991 *Financial Times* profile described him as "a one time officer in the Rhodesian Special Air Service Regiment and personal adviser to Sir Edgar Whitehead, former Rhodesian prime minister."[103] This background and the contacts made would have provided the basis for Kock's subsequent work. The experience in Malaya would also go some way toward explaining what qualified Kock to act in so prominent a way on the Malaysian arms deal at the center of the Pergau Dam scandal,[104] one element of which involved the construction of a special forces' base at Mersing.

From 1958 until December 1962, according to his Midland résumé, he served as political secretary to Sir Edgar Whitehead, prime minister of Rhodesia. A second long-term connection, that with the Midland Bank, could also date from this time. As his résumé notes, it was during Whitehead's premiership that Walter Monckton, then chairman of the Midland Bank, headed the advisory commission that undertook a review of the Rhodesian Constitution. The period from 1962 to 1967 constitutes something of a gray area, although Kock was apparently still based in Rhodesia. For instance, in 1978 Kock gave evidence to the Bingham Inquiry on Rhodesia, and in its report he is described as having been "National Accounts Advisor to BP Rhodesia" in 1965.[105] However, according to the Midland résumé cited above, Kock saw further "military service abroad" during this period. He also told the TISC that he "was a military intelligence officer in Rhodesia," a role that would also seem to date from this period.[106]

There is an apparent contradiction in his résumé with regard to the late 1960s. In 1967 his oil connections were strengthened when he became a director of Billiton, a subsidiary of Shell based in The Hague—a position he held until 1973.[107] While his résumé states that he took up the position with Billiton following his retirement from the army, an internal Astra newsletter seemingly adds a further dimension to his career: "Following his military career, *he carried out special assignments for the Foreign Office*"; this type of formulation is usually employed to indicate involvement with MI6.[108]

In 1973 Kock became a nonexecutive director of Biddle Holdings, and in June 1984 the Midland Bank took him on as a part-time consultant/adviser to the Bank's Defence Equipment Finance Department (DEFD), "a team of specialists with banking, military and industrial experience who can provide dedicated assistance to the defence industry,"[109] housed within the Midland Bank Group International Trade Services (MBGITS). The establishment of the DEFD was the outcome of the Midland Bank's bid to involve itself in the lucrative and secure world of arms finance. Perhaps having so many senior executives with an intelligence background made Midland more aware than most banks of the rewards and limited risk involved, due to ECGD underwriting. Hence, it established a department intended to deal solely with the financing of arms deals from within its MBGITS department. The DEFD was established with the aim of challenging the position of banks like Morgan Grenfell in the arms-financing field. It was staffed by a collection of former intelligence, SAS, and military personnel—including the Arabic-speaking Stephan Kock—who were expected to target specific contracts. The section operated in a semiclandestine manner from its inception until its closure in

1990. Its existence was kept secret from most employees, it did not figure in the company accounts, and hence its estimated loss of £75 million was hidden from its shareholders.[110] Its history illustrates the nature of the arms sales process at this level.

Kock joined Astra as a nonexecutive director in October 1986 while working in the DEFD, after being recommended by the manager of the Maidstone branch of the Midland Bank "as being a man connected with the very top levels of Government and influence re the arms trade."[111] At around the same time, Kock was also being recommended by Richard Unwin as a useful nonexecutive director, after Astra had taken over Unwin's group.

While at Astra, Kock left other directors in no doubt as to his connections. The *Financial Times* profile noted how "on several occasions Mr Kock has boasted of his close connections with Mrs Thatcher. He told colleagues he was one of the few people trusted with the number of her private telephone when she lived at Number Ten."[112] Former directors have also recalled Kock's boasting of the various figures he knew, ranging from Ian Smith in Rhodesia to Margaret Thatcher to John Bourn. Elsewhere, he has been recalled as "talking reasonably plausibly to fellow diners about being on speaking terms with King Hussein of Jordan" at a reception at the 1988 British Army Equipment Exhibition.

Meanwhile, for a nonexecutive director, Kock was highly active in certain areas and apparently involved himself in areas of Astra's business without the knowledge of either James or Gumbley. For instance, in September 1989 he traveled to Belgium to visit the PRB plant at Kaulille without their knowledge. It was upon returning from this trip that he claimed to have contacted the security services and informed them of an "unusual propellant." However, this level of activity did not extend to the United States. When Astra acquired the U.S. Walters Group in 1987, Kock wanted to go and inspect it but, according to former directors of Astra, was unable to do so as he was refused a U.S. visa. According to Gerald James, he never visited any of Astra's U.S. acquisitions.

Kock was called to give evidence to the TISC investigating the supergun and exports to Iraq, largely on the basis of his claim to have tipped off the intelligence services about the existence of PRB's propellant contract with Jordan. When his Midland résumé was read out to him he was asked if he had ever "been part of the British intelligence services," he replied: "I have never been an officer in MI6 as it has been alleged," telling them instead, "I was a military intelligence officer in Rhodesia."[113] In its report, the TISC settled for describing him as "a non-executive director of Astra with military intelligence experience."[114]

During his trip to Kaulille and discovery of the "unusual propellant," Kock told the TISC that on his return he immediately "reported the fact of the matter and discussed it with my colleagues who were more qualified than I was. . . ."[115] However, he was forced to concede that he did not inform the Astra board. Neither did he inform the board of his decision to inform the "security services." The manner in which he claimed to have done so revealed a further familiarity with the intelligence community. He was asked by the TISC: "When you say you reported it to the Security Services that is exactly what you mean, you do not mean [to] a member of the MOD's team or to somebody in the DTI, you are quite clear it was to the Security Services it was reported?" Kock explained: "Initially I did it by telephone, a very brief discussion on, I think, the Monday following 20th September [1989]. Then the first time I could get down was 11th October when I had a meeting. I did speak, of course, later to the Ministry of Defence people *and I know quite a lot of them well.*"[116] This independence of spirit on the part of a nonexecutive director led Dr. Keith Hampson, MP, to seek further clarification:

KH: Did you actually report this directly to the intelligence services without consulting or informing the chairman of the company or chief executive of the company?

SK: Yes, I did, Sir.

KH: You did?

SK: Yes.

KH: You actually went straight to Dr Pike and Major General Donald Isles?

SK: Yes.

KH: You did not first go to the chairman of the company?

SK: No, I did not.

KH: Is this the normal approach of a non-executive director, would you not normally consult with the chairman?

SK: It depends whether he needs to be consulted.

KH: Quite an interesting thought.[117]

This was also picked up on later by Stan Crowther, MP, when he asked:

SC: You have these telephone numbers in your diary, do you? Not many people are familiar about how to contact MI5 or MI6. Mr James and Mr Gumbley had to get on to the Ministry of Defence who then sent people from MI6 to speak to them. How do you come to be so involved?

SK: I spent a lifetime—
SC: —involved—
SK: I have never been a member of MI5 or MI6.
SC: I am not talking about being a member.
SK: If I find anything which I consider to be contrary to the interests of this country I will report.
SC: . . . The question is how do we report it? How do we get in touch with them? You certainly know how to get in touch with them all the time, do you not?
SK: I know how to get in touch with some of them, yes.[118]

When he was interviewed by the DTI inspectors, Kock was even more forthcoming, perhaps because the transcripts were not going to be made public; in fact this is the first time any have been cited outside the report. In that knowledge those involved could be more forthright:

Q: Your visit to the security services to report information you had been given by the Kaulille manager, was that accompanied by anyone else? Did you go with anyone else?
A: No; I had the deputy head of MI5 come to see me at 6, St. James's Place . . . I can, in fact, get the member of the security services I spoke to give you a ring if you like.[119]

Former JIC official Robin Robison says that Kock had strong links to the intelligence world, so much so that he was known as a figure on the fringes of the JIC and even attended JIC social functions. Robison described him as being "probably someone who was useful."[120] James was also told by Robison "that Kock frequently attended the JIC offices and had access to the MOD at a high level." In his memoirs Chris Cowley recalls a conversation with Gerald Bull at the time Bull was considering purchasing PRB:

I could remember Bull mentioning him [Kock] to me as long ago as 1988 . . . I had discussed the Astra bid [for PRB] with Bull and been shown a number of papers which Bull had somehow got hold of . . . But among them was a list of those present at talks between Astra and PRB, held in November 1988:
"What's Kock doing at this meeting?" he wanted to know.
"Who's Kock?"
"He's a Yarpie—a Rhodesian. He works for the Midland Bank arms department, but he's also part of MI5 like Cuckney."[121]

The TISC also heard a tape recording of a telephone conversation made by Campbell Dunford, formerly of the Midland and Moscow Narodny Banks, between himself and Kock. In it Kock tells Dunford that, regarding Astra: "I am in command. There is no question about that. I am in command *because of all the various people who have taken an interest in Astra.*" When asked what he meant by that and who the "various people who have taken an interest in Astra" were, Kock told the TISC that he had merely "tried to convey to him I had the influence necessary to influence the appointment of another director" and that "all the major shareholders and banks were concerned at the situation and that is what I meant."[122]

One theme that was central to Kock's testimony was his consistent opposition to the purchase of PRB by Astra. It was important for Kock to seek to establish this because subsequent events, culminating in what he termed the "revolution,"[123] left Kock as the only board member who had been in place at the time of the PRB purchase, by virtue of the fact that he was untarnished by having supported it at any point. Indeed, when asked by the TISC why he was the "only director left on the board," Kock told them: "I remained on the board because there was no reason for me to resign."[124] TISC Chairman Kenneth Warren (like Kock, a member of the Special Forces Club) read Kock a section of Gerald James's evidence: "Mr Kock was desperate for the PRB deal to go through when he knew [Sir John] Cuckney and [Comte Hervé de] Carmoy were involved and wished the deal to go through." Kock replied: "That is a fabrication, Mr Chairman."[125] However, in a note added to his evidence, Chris Gumbley stated: "I must also add that Mr Kock did ring me early in the morning once before the PRB purchase and demanded that we got a move on with the purchase. He told me that he had been talking to Mr De Carmoy of SGB. Mr Kock asked for my assurance that we were proceeding with the PRB purchase with all speed."[126] Hervé de Carmoy had, of course, been the head of MBGITS while Kock was there.[127] Kock's claim that he was consistently opposed to the purchase is also contested by other former Astra directors and by a former senior official at the Midland Bank, all of whom have recalled his support for it. In his evidence to the TISC, Gumbley said: "Mr Kock advised at the beginning of the difficulties of Belgium and he was not 100 per cent for the move forward. His position changed and he became very much in favour of the acquisition."[128] In fact, the acquisition could only go ahead in the final analysis because Kock intervened to telephone the agent general for the Nova Scotia government to get him to secure the Bank of Nova Scotia's support for the deal. According to Kock, James "made great efforts not to keep me informed of the PRB affair and there were many, many arguments because I was not kept informed."[129] This main theme of Kock's evidence to the DTI inspectors is also contested by James and another former member of the Astra board.

When the new management at Astra called for a DTI inquiry into the company (a move hardly likely to invigorate a then rapidly declining share price), the DTI inspectors had to reconcile these two sets of recollections on this most important issue. Kock told the inspectors that he "remained opposed to the PRB acquisition and that at some stage [he] had a long and heated argument with Mr James about it."[130] However, the inspectors conceded that James, Gumbley, Miller, Guest, and Anderson (almost the entire board of directors apart from Kock) recalled that Kock moved from his earlier opposition and "became positively in favour of the acquisition." Notwithstanding this, their report effectively accepts Kock's version of events. It states:

> Mr James and Mr Gumbley told us of further specific incidents which they said illustrated Mr Kock's positive support for the acquisition. *We do not consider it necessary to detail these* . . . Mr Kock was insistent to us that he was throughout opposed to the acquisition, and when in due course we come to consider the roles played by each of the directors in connection with the acquisition *we shall assess Mr Kock's role on the basis that he was so opposed.*[131]

The DTI report criticized the former Astra directors for going ahead with the purchase of PRB, but the DTI initiated disqualification proceedings (under the 1986 Company Directors' Disqualification Act)[132] against only six of the directors "in the public interest." The one person not pursued was Stephan Kock.

When Gumbley was asked by the TISC if he could explain "why Mr Kock was the only board member to stay after you [i.e. the old board] were all removed," he replied: "I suppose they had to keep somebody and he has stated he was probably involved in removing me at one stage and I assume that applied to the rest of the board."[133] Kock told the TISC:

> It was in my opinion, time for [James] to retire. That was the first one and then Mr Gumbley resigned himself, he was not pushed by me. He resigned for reasons of which you are aware. The new chairman then got the board resolution passed which I seconded which suspended the rest of the directors and the rest of the directors subsequently resigned leaving me the only previous director there.[134]

However, James is convinced that it was the knowledge he and Gumbley gained as a result of their investigation into the use of Astra in covert arms supplies, principally to Iraq and through the Far East, that led Kock to engineer his and Gumbley's removal. According to the *Independent:* "Mr Kock subsequently boasted of playing a key role in the reconstruction of Astra, after he had forced out or, as he described it, 'pressed the button' on three Astra directors."[135] As James recalled:

> I became aware that our company was heavily involved in covert and illegal arms supplies from US, UK and Belgium. In the course of investigations by myself and Gumbley it became clear that Kock became alarmed. Gumbley investigated Far East contracts including a contract for Thailand which PRB had for 155mm equipment. This contract involved £5m commission on [a] £16m contract and was with a company called Lotberi or Lopberi. Lotberi or Lopberi is and was also a project to build a huge special forces complex in Thailand just across the border from Malaysia. This project is complementary to the special forces base in Malaysia which is part of the Malaysian arms deal. . . . My understanding and knowledge is based on direct personal contact with people in our company PRB . . . and also with hearing conversations between Kock and others and to seeing faxes and telexes sent to Thailand by Kock on our office machines.[136]

The *Independent* reported: "What Mr Gumbley threatened to uncover during his few days in Thailand was an arms ring which reputedly spreads from Whitehall to Washington via Belgium and other loosely regulated countries to some of the world's most pernicious regimes, including Saddam Hussein's Iraq."[137] While at Astra, Kock appears to have spent much of his time putting together the arms deal with Malaysia at the center of the Pergau Dam storm. Indeed, his central role in it has been referred to on a number of occasions. The *Financial Times* has described how Mrs. Thatcher's 1988 visit to Malaysia to sign the £1 billion arms deal "was preceded by a team from Midland's defence department led by Mr Stephan Kock, together with Ministry of Defence and other officials and a small delegation from Britain's Special Air Services. The main consortia were bidding for contracts for a proposed special forces base at Mersing, close to Malaysia's East Coast. 'Kock was there to ensure that Midland got a big slice of the action,' said one former official."[138]

In addition, a "former senior executive from Midland Bank" told the *Independent* that Kock (described as "a consultant to Midland who also advised the Government's Joint Intelligence Committee") was the "architect of the different strands" of the Malaysian deal.[139] At around the same time, the *Observer* described him as "an arms adviser, who visited Malaysia with officials from the Ministry of Defence and members of the Special Air Service before 1988, at about the time the Government was discussing aid to the Pergau project."[140] To James, as a result of his investigations, "it became very clear that he was involved in all the Thatcher inspired arms deals."[141] He recalled: "He was much involved with [Richard] Unwin in orchestrating a huge Malaysian arms deal about which we heard a lot almost every week. Unwin was a £75,000 p.a. consultant to Astra but did little for us as he was preoccupied with Malaysia."[142] In January 1994 Kock issued a (brief) statement to *Channel 4 News*, which conceded: "I was involved in the Malaysian Dam project."[143]

But his involvement seems to have been more significant than this was intended to suggest. In his statement for the Foreign Affairs Committee (FAC) investigation into the Pergau Dam scandal, Gerald James highlighted Kock's role in the Malaysian arms deal, observing that

> from the time of Kock's involvement with Astra he was much occupied with Unwin on the Malaysian negotiations . . . and organised a series of events including a Malaysian evening at the Porchester Hall. This was a supper and "knees up" for the Malaysian High Commission and took place in 1987. Both Chris Gumbley and I were invited, although unlike Kock and Unwin, we did not sit at the VIP table.[144]

Moreover, he recalled another incident:

> With Chris Gumbley, I attended a meeting in Midland Bank in July 1988 with Nigel Rudd, a close friend of Kock and Chairman of Williams Holdings . . .
> The meeting with Rudd which took place in Midland Bank's Cannon Street offices, took one hour. When Rudd left, Richard Unwin and various Malaysian military personnel trooped into the office. They included Colonel Harry Adnam and General Yakob or Jacob. There were, I believe, also representatives of the Malaysian High Commission. Kock started talking about the Malaysian arms deal before we had left, quite openly mentioning some very sensitive matters. He said they were having problems with Mahathir's bagman who was an Indian or an Indian Malay or Malay of Indian extraction. Kock also complained about various parties who were being too greedy re kick backs or commissions and suggested certain officials from the UK end had done private deals and were too familiar with the bagman.[145]

Kock told James that "he was personally organising the Malaysia arms deal [and] he would see to it that Astra would at least get 'one or two crumbs off the table'. . ."[146] However, as James notes, this was "something which he in fact never did, in spite of running up large costs from Astra in connection with the deal. Those included items like £150 bills or more for one day's telephone conversations from a hired car and expenses for shuttling up and down from his new home in Scotland."[147]

Kock had been resident in Scotland for a couple of years when, on 15 January 1990, he drove up to two men who were repairing their broken-down van near his Argyll home. Kock brandished a gun and fired a shot into the air over their heads. A *Financial Times* report on the incident quoted police investigating the incident as saying that it was "very delicate," given Kock's intelligence connections and in view of the "big names" who provided references. It further reported that "his solicitor, at the court hearing following the shooting incident said Mr Kock's defence work had left him with an acute concern for his personal safety."[148] He went on to say that Kock's career had been "delicate in both nature and locations."[149] The *Independent* reported: "Police admit privately that their investigations were stymied by protestations on Mr Kock's behalf by the intelligence services."[150] While discharging a firearm in public is a serious offense, he was just fined £650. When questioned about this by the TISC, Kock told them, "I do not carry a gun" and "I never carried a gun."[151] However, a former director of Astra clearly remembers that when Kock used to travel from his home in Scotland by car, he always used to take with him a 9mm Luger pistol in a sports bag, which he did not like to travel without. Kock would, according to the former director, then leave the pistol with the director's secretary. Kock was unable to travel to work on British Midland aircraft as, according to the same former director, he was banned by the airline following an incident with a flight attendant. There also exists a record of an unsavory incident in February 1989 at the Angel and Royal hotel in Grantham, where a drunken Kock threatened an assistant manager, telling him he was Major Kock of the SAS.[152] Perhaps it is these kinds of incidents that help explain why not everyone who worked with Kock was keen to discuss the experience afterward. Take this section of John Anderson's interview with the DTI inspectors, for example:

Q: There seems to have been a good deal of animosity between Mr James and Mr Kock . . . Insofar as Mr Kock had anything to do with the ultimate demise of Mr James, it looks as if he was rooting for Mr James to stand down as chairman?

A: He most certainly was.

Q: Do you consider that he was motivated by what he regarded as being in the best interests of the company or was it something more personal?

A: Unfortunately, I have seen Mr Kock when he has been a bit under the weather, and I have seen results of that in Grantham. There was an incident in Scotland where he shot at people. I was very much aware of that. There have been various other incidents . . .

Q: Granted all that, did you form the view that he was acting in what he regarded as the best interests of the company?

A: Fifty/fifty. There was animosity between him and Mr James. There most certainly was. I mean I do worry about us having had threats on the phone recently. There were quite a few and I wondered about Mr Kock. If this is to be typed up for public exhibit, I would rather that that was not put in. I still value my life.

Other questions have arisen about Kock's testimony, notably the suggestion that Kock was present in Baghdad in November 1988, along with Hervé de Carmoy, negotiating the finance for the supergun propellant contract. David Hellier, a journalist on the *Independent*, had first asked Gerald James if he knew of this back in July 1991. When asked by the TISC if it was true that he had been in Baghdad, Kock said: "That is totally untrue, Mr Chairman. I have not been in Baghdad for over 20 years and that was when I spent an hour at the airport on my way to Bombay. . . . It is a total fabrication . . . I have never been to Baghdad."[153] He had already told this story, albeit in more detail, to the DTI inspectors.[154] However, Chris Cowley has now revealed that he did see Kock in Baghdad, and that Paul Henderson of Matrix Churchill also claims to have seen Kock in Baghdad and to have photographs of him there:

I think [Kock] definitely worked with British intelligence, and he lied to the Select Committee and said that he'd never been to Iraq. He has been to Iraq . . . I'd seen Kock, but the problem is that, I learned that if you make that statement to the Select Committee, somebody will say, "Have you got evidence?" People were actually saying to me at the Select Committee when we were talking in the bar, "Well you said you were with Bull, you say you were in China, you say you were in South America, but do you have any photographs, do you have any written evidence?" Well, I know Kock was in Baghdad—I saw him in Baghdad. He says he wasn't there—what the hell can I do?[155]

When Kock was asked about his intelligence links on *Channel 4 News*, the following exchange took place:

Q: Some people have suggested that you enjoyed a relationship of . . . trust with elements of the Government and that they were happy to see you in these positions because, basically, for the things they were concerned about you'd be prepared to talk to them about them.

A: Of course, I'm an ex-airman, an ex-soldier and I've worked for Her Majesty's Government in various aspects abroad . . .

Q: Intelligence aspects?
A: I'm not going to answer that.[156]

Inquiries into Kock have met with limited success. There have been several attempts in Parliament to pursue the matter. On 22 April 1993, for instance, Allan Rogers, MP asked "what the official duties of Mr Stephen Adolphus Kock have been since 1980." However, when the question appeared in Hansard, the date included was 1990. The reply given was "None."[157] On 28 February 1994, Menzies Campbell, MP asked "on what occasions Mr Stephen Kock has represented Her Majesty's Government in campaigning for defence exports to Oman, Jordan, Indonesia and Thailand." Jonathan Aitken replied: "Mr Stephen Kock has not, on any occasion, been asked to represent Her Majesty's Government on these matters."[158] On the same day, Sir David Steel's question, "On how many occasions and in what capacities [has] Mr. Stephan Kock acted on behalf of Her Majesty's Government in relation to contracts arising out of overseas development since 1988?" received the answer "None."[159]

On 1 July 1994 Michael Meacher, MP asked, "for what reason Stephan Adolph Kock has Special Branch protection; and what other names he uses or has been known by," and on 5 July was informed: "It is not in the public interest to disclose whether any person has received official protection or not. There is no Ministerial responsibility for names by which Mr Kock is known or has been known." Perhaps most revealingly, in answer to a further question by Meacher on 24 May 1994, the government came as close as it yet has to acknowledging Kock's intelligence connections. Meacher asked "what duties Stephan Adolphus Kock has performed for (a) the Prime Minister, (b) the Ministry of Defence, (c) the Foreign and Commonwealth Office, (d) the Department of Trade and Industry and (e) any other Department between 1964 and 1979; and in which countries overseas each of these duties was carried out." The reply was: "Mr Kock performed no official duties for any Government Department during the period 1964–79. It remains the Government's policy not to comment on the contacts which an individual may or may not have had with the security and intelligence agencies."[160]

Although cited as a central figure in the Malaysian arms deal—in the press, on television, and in statements to the FAC and Scott Inquiry—Kock is not mentioned once in the FAC report, nor in the accompanying published evidence. Although a number of the TISC's sessions involved discussion of Kock (the evidence of James, Gumbley, the Midland Bank, and of course Kock himself) he appears only fleetingly in the final report, in connection with his claim to have informed the security services of the "unusual propellant" ahead of Gumbley and James. Yet his claims before the TISC that his role involved no more than that normally expected of a nonexecutive director do not appear consistent with the prominent part he is said to have played in the Malaysian deal and the influence and contacts he apparently had in arranging it. Perhaps revealingly, Gerald James has recorded in a letter to Allan Rogers, MP how, after the FAC report was published, he bumped into Peter Shore, MP, who had chaired the inquiry: "I . . . asked him why Kock had not been interviewed—I said 'why has the main witness not been interviewed?' Shore assumed I meant [Mrs.] Thatcher as he said it was her prerogative as a former Prime Minister . . . I . . . said I meant Kock. To this Shore said 'I know, but that is another level of Government.' "[161]

◆ Investigations

James has given evidence regarding the uses to which Astra was put to the TISC inquiry into the supergun, the FAC inquiry into Pergau, the DTI inquiry into Astra, the Scott Inquiry, and now to the TISC again as it looks at BMARC and arms sales to Iran. His statement to the Scott Inquiry included a color photograph of the lid of a box of 81mm mortar shells, taken inside Iraq during Operation Desert Storm by a serving British officer. Its existence is consistent with the observation of Chris Cowley while resident in Iraq (see below), the only difference being that the artillery boxes observed by Cowley were labeled MOD RO JORDAN, while this one appears to have been exported directly from RO to Iraq, in direct contravention of government policy and contrary to the assurances being given to Parliament by the government at the time. A & S indicates it passed through the Ammunition and Supply division of the MOD. The rest reads MOD RO IRAQ L/C NO 86/1/450. MOD is Ministry of Defence, and RO Royal Ordnance. L/C is Letter of Credit, and the figures indicate the number of the letter of credit (450) and the date, suggesting that the box was part of a consignment shipped in January 1986, during the Iran-Iraq War. When *Business Age* journalist Kevin Cahill showed this photograph to a senior Customs official, he was told: "We have hundreds of photographs, too. We know all about that stuff going direct to Iraq. We have prosecuted no one because we cannot prove that there was an intention to evade the law in relation to military exports."[162]

When Bob Keen of the MOD was quizzed about the photograph by the Scott Inquiry, he replied that the fact that the box was marked "MOD" did

Figure 5.2

Photograph of Box of Mortar Shells Taken Inside Iraq During Operation Desert Storm

Source: Scott Inquiry: Statement of Gerald James, Appendix.[163]

not "imply a UK provenance." However, he did not seek to explain the other markings—above all "RO," which is clearly a reference to Royal Ordnance, or the L/C number.[164] Despite the existence of this photographic evidence, Jonathan Aitken told the House of Commons: "My Department has not carried out an extensive analysis of the origins of all ammunition captured during the Gulf conflict. However, the analysis that has been carried out has produced no evidence to suggest that Iraqi forces used any ammunition of British manufacture."[165]

For his part, during his evidence to the TISC, Gerald James identified a group known as the "Savoy Mafia,"[166] a group of defense-based industrialists and officials who met regularly at the suite of Alan Curtis, chairman of Lotus, at the Savoy Hotel in London and allegedly exerted influence over the course of British arms exports under the Thatcher governments. At the TISC's prompting, James provided a list of those he knew to be associated with it, which included the name of the committee's chairman, Kenneth Warren, and which the committee refused to accept in evidence.[167] James had become involved on the fringes of this group while negotiating the purchase of PRB.

He and Gumbley had first met Curtis through Brigadier John Shrimpton, a colleague of Kock's at the Midland Bank whom James had known in the army, at an Army Air Corps open day at Middle Wallop in July 1988. Between March and May 1989 James met Curtis on several separate occasions at his suite at the Savoy:

> Curtis appeared to have extraordinary pulling power. On two occasions James had to leave an evening meeting because Curtis was entertaining George Younger Minister of Defence, Colin Chandler Head of Defence Sales, Peter Levene Head of Defence Procurement, Sir David Plaistow and senior representatives of British Aerospace and Marconi to dinner in his suite. It was also clear that Curtis had considerable influence with major American contractors like General Dynamics, United Technologies, McDonnell Douglas etc. to whom he introduced James at a high level at the Farnborough Air Show. Curtis also seemed to work closely with a young man called Steve Tipping, a close friend of Mark Thatcher and the best man at his wedding. Curtis also had an entrée to Downing Street where he seemed to visit regularly.[168]

It was Curtis who suggested to James that Wafic Said could be encouraged to take an interest in Astra by an issue of new shares, and subsequently a number of meetings were held between members of the Astra team and a Dr. Idilby, managing director of SIFCORP, who appeared willing to finance the purchase of PRB. It was this willingness, says James, that led to 3*i*'s enthusiastic backing for the takeover.

For its part, the DTI investigation into Astra—which began on 16 August 1990, concluded on 7 April 1993, and cost £2,170,000—was clearly flawed, in that it failed to take account of the context in which Astra was operating. Doing so would have required it to consider the distorting impact of the Iran-Iraq War on the international arms industry, and the contracts Astra subsidiaries were fulfilling for Iraq and Iran through conduits like Singapore. Furthermore, the 540-page report made no mention of the EPREP agreement, the secret existence of which had a critical bearing on BMARC profit projections and made the purchase appear overpriced, as it effectively denied Astra 80 percent of the domestic ammunition market, when the government's policy of promoting competition and the approaches of Peter Levene had led the Astra management to conclude that they would be able to compete for all of it. The narrow focus was spelled out by President of the Board of Trade Ian Lang in 1995:

> The Inspectors did not look at allegations of illegal exports to Iran or elsewhere. The Inspectors' investigation was primarily concerned with circumstances sur-

rounding the acquisition by Astra of a Belgian company PRB in September 1989 and the rights issue made by Astra in that connection. They also considered a number of other matters concerning Astra and its former directors, and also the accounting policies of the group.[169]

James attempted to provide much of this context, but the inspectors chose not to consider it, dismissing it in their Introduction as follows:

> The views volunteered to us by Mr James covered a wide range of subjects, certain of which apparently had little or no direct connection with Astra, and included allegations involving senior UK politicians and civil servants and allegations of illegal arms deals involving foreign governments and government agencies and the security services of the UK and of other countries. . . . We . . . concluded that it was inappropriate for us to embark upon an investigation of these allegations.[170]

In August 1994, Michael Meacher, shadow minister for public services and science, wrote to President of the Board of Trade Michael Heseltine, who instigated disqualification proceedings, to protest that

> the real reason for the MOD's closing down Astra is clearly that the directors found out that subsidiaries the company had purchased, were being used, with the connivance of Government, for the illegal export of armaments to Iraq during the Iran-Iraq war, and MOD and the security services in particular were anxious to remove all trace of their involvement in this illegal trade. . . . It is also, I believe, the real reason why Mr Christopher Gumbley, then chief executive of Astra, was arrested at the same time (on a charge of receiving a bribe) shortly after he returned from Thailand and Malaysia to which he had travelled to investigate why PRB, soon after it had been acquired, had paid out hundreds of millions of pounds in secret commissions.

He concluded by calling the disqualification proceedings a "shabby and sordid political vendetta designed to intimidate and discredit the former Astra directors because of what they have revealed about the secret and illicit arms trade with Iraq and the Government's connivance in it in breach of their own Howe Guidelines."[171]

Support for James's case could also be found among government backbenchers. The influential chairman of the Defence Select Committee, Sir Nicholas Bonsor, wrote in 1993: "I can assure you that I and the Defence Committee will do what we can to secure the future of our national defences and to prevent the re-occurrence of any of the underhand methods of policy-making which clearly led you and your company, together with many others, to disaster."[172]

♦ Project LISI: Arming Iran via Singapore

Confirmation of one of the conduit contracts that Astra had inherited came on Tuesday 13 June 1995, against a background of growing parliamentary interest in the issue. President of the Board of Trade Michael Heseltine announced to the House of Commons that, as Gerald James and John Anderson had consistently claimed,[173] Project LISI "could well" have been bound for Iran.[174]

LISI was the name given to the 1986 £30 million order, which Astra inherited upon taking over BMARC from Oerlikon, to export 140 naval cannon to Singapore. They were exported to a company called Chartered Industries, owned by the Singapore government, for onward transmission to prohibited Iran. BMARC was one of three manufacturers involved in a ruse designed to provide deniability if it was exposed. While BMARC exported the gun parts and machine tools from its Grantham site, Oerlikon's outpost in Sao Paulo, Brazil (an enthusiastic backer of Iran in the war), sent the gun barrels, and Asco in Belgium the gun mounts to Chartered Industries, Singapore. There the guns were assembled and shipped to Pakistan, from where they were taken overland to Iran.

Heseltine suggested that the TISC should look into the matter, saying that the DTI would "be very ready to co-operate if the Trade and Industry Select Committee wished to examine the issues raised by the allegation that Singapore was used as a conduit for arms exported by BMARC to Iran."[175] This unusual offer further strengthened the argument that the official inquiry or select committee inquiry had by this time become the favored device for deferring judgment on a government's actions until interest had subsided.

Apparently, the statement was the outcome of a six-week investigation within the DTI initiated by Heseltine, but the timing and the decision to reveal it so openly in a Commons announcement rather than try to conceal it in a written reply, preferably on a day of newsworthy activity elsewhere (a favorite government tactic)[176] reinforced suspicions that Heseltine's motives might have had something to do with internal Conservative Party politics and his leadership ambitions.[177]

There had been considerable speculation about BMARC prior to this, all of which had made life difficult for the chief secretary to the Treasury, Jonathan

Aitken. He had been a nonexecutive director of BMARC at the time LISI was being discussed at board meetings. Obviously, if he had known of the illegal intent behind it, his position would have been untenable. Aitken had certainly had a colorful career to this point. Born on 30 August 1942, he had been Conservative MP for Thanet since 1974[178] and as such was Astra's local MP.[179] Aitken was well connected in the Middle East. He had served on the board of Al-Bilad (U.K.), a company whose aim was to promote trade with the Middle East and whose activities were underwritten by the Saudi royal family,[180] alongside Prince Khalid and Sheikh Fahad al-Athel, a front man for one of King Fahd's sons, Prince Mohammed bin Fahd.[181] Sheikh Fahad was allegedly one of the agents involved in brokering the Al Yamamah agreement. Indeed, it has been suggested that he was later put to work by Aitken to try to secure contracts for Astra in Saudi Arabia. The BMARC board minutes of 2 November 1988 record: "The agent acting for Mr Aitken pulled off the Vosper contract, is ambitious and is working hard at establishing relationships."[182]

Aitken also made it clear to Gerald James on a number of occasions that he knew Walfic Said personally and that Said too was close to the Saudi royal family, in particular to Prince Sultan, the minister of defense and aviation (and a key figure in the world of Saudi arms procurement) and to his two sons, Princes Khalid and Bandar. Aitken had himself, he told James, "looked after" the two Saudi princes while they studied in the United Kingdom.[183] In addition to these connections, SIFCORP, one of Said's companies, held a significant interest in Aitken's investment company, Aitken Hume International plc. It was on the basis of these connections that Aitken told James in mid-1988 that he could further Astra's interests in Saudi Arabia. In the fall of 1988, at the same time that Astra was negotiating the purchase of PRB from SGB/Gechem, he asked to be put on the Astra board. Instead, James appointed him to the board of the recently purchased BMARC as a nonexecutive director at a salary of £10,000 per year.[184]

Meanwhile, Aitken's climb up the political ladder had stalled, allegedly because he dumped the prime minister's daughter, Carol Thatcher, winning fame as the "man who made Carol cry." He finally made it into the government in April 1992, when John Major appointed him minister of Defence Procurement at the MOD. In so doing, Major sought to use Aitken's links with the Saudi royal family in order to keep the vulnerable Al Yamamah agreement on track. In July 1994 he was promoted to the Cabinet post of chief secretary to the Treasury.

It was while in this position that the LISI affair finally broke out into the open. But Aitken's links to the Middle East meant he had been no stranger to controversy even before this.[185] A *World in Action* television documentary, "Jonathan of Arabia," which explored his links with Saudi Arabia, and in particular with Prince Mohammed bin Fahd, alleged, for example, that Aitken had attempted to procure girls for Saudi visitors to a health farm in Berkshire, where Aitken was a director until 1992. According to a former employee interviewed on the program: "He rang . . . and said was it possible to get any girls for the Arabs? I said, no, I don't know any girls; if you need girls, you bring them up yourself."[186] There had also been a very public dispute with the *Guardian* newspaper about who had paid Aitken's Fr8010.90 hotel bill when he stayed at the Paris Ritz in September 1993.[187] The newspaper alleged that a Saudi businessman, Said Ayas, had paid it on Aitken's behalf, but Aitken denied this and instead produced an account of events so convoluted that it failed to put the *Guardian* story completely to rest. A former secretary did not help his cause by revealing that "Said Ayas always paid the bill, anywhere they went sort of *en masse*. It was the same deal in Cannes, in Paris, in Geneva—a number of rooms would be booked out in the particular hotel, people would come and go, and at the end Said Ayas would pay the bill on Prince Mohammed's behalf."[188]

Hence, the LISI can of worms that Heseltine's statement opened up could only add to a series of scandals that cumulatively risked damaging Aitken's prospects of rising further in the government. On LISI, Heseltine told the House:

I commissioned detailed research into two aspects: first, the intelligence information available to the Government; second, the export licensing history . . .

In 1986, intelligence was obtained that Iran had concluded a contract with Oerlikon for the supply of weaponry and ammunition. The intelligence picture developed in 1987, when it was revealed that naval guns made by Oerlikon had been offered to Iran by a company in Singapore. In July and September 1988, two intelligence reports rounded out the picture by referring to naval guns and ammunition being supplied by Oerlikon through Singapore to Iran. . . . I must emphasise that none of these intelligence reports mentioned BMARC . . .

I now refer to allegations made by the former chairman of Astra, Gerald James. He made allegations about the involvement of BMARC in a project called LISI. According to Mr James's evidence to the Trade and Industry Select Committee, which was looking into exports to Iraq, that was to supply "medium calibre armaments— ammunition, weapons and tooling to Singapore for onward transmission to Iran." These allegations were first drawn to my department's attention in March 1991. . . . Those same allegations were repeated by Mr James in his written evidence to the Trade and Industry Select Committee, and were then passed by my Department to Customs and Excise in November 1991. At that time Customs came to the view that the allegations . . . did not justify initiating a full investigation. . . .

I have had a check done on the number of applications by BMARC in the period 1986 to 1989 that enclosed the full supporting documentation. . . . That showed that 36 per cent of BMARC applications did not enclose the full supporting documentation. . . . I have commissioned a sample survey of military list licence applications over a similar period, which suggests that, on average, 74 per cent of all applications during the same period did not include the full supporting documentation.[189]

Shadow Trade and Industry spokesman Jack Cunningham replied: "The House is entitled to ask what really was going on in the Government at this time when, publicly, we were said to be denying weapons of war to Iran and Iraq but, privately, Ministers were conniving in their supply."[190] Sir David Steel pressed home the point: "Ministers presided over a period when a war was raging between Iran and Iraq, and there was a sudden increase in demands for export licences made to Government Departments in this country for innocent places such as Singapore. Did no one in the Government put two and two together?"[191] And as Nick Harvey, MP asked: "Did it really need expensively gathered intelligence to make clear to Ministers the fairly obvious point that Singapore was hardly a credible destination for any of these items?"[192]

Aitken issued a number of libel writs over the *World in Action* and *Guardian* allegations, which he condemned in a theatrical speech in which he pledged to "fight to cut out the cancer of bent and twisted journalism . . . with the simple sword of truth and the trusty shield of British fair play."[193] His initial position was that, while he was a director of BMARC, he had no recollection of "ever having heard about Project LISI or read about it in company reports,"[194] even though he had been at board meetings where it was discussed and had been circulated with board minutes containing discussion of the LISI contract. He shifted this position slightly later to claim that, although he knew of LISI, he was completely unaware that it was going anywhere other than Singapore:

> . . . I had never been given any indication or information which could suggest that a BMARC contract with Singapore might result in onward shipments of components to Iran. My view of this matter has been supported by all the former directors of the company with the exception of the former chairman, Mr Gerald James. However, Mr James has said publicly that he did not brief me about his alleged knowledge of onward shipments to Iran.[195]

However, Aitken's attempts to line up the BMARC board behind him did not go unchallenged for long. John Anderson told journalists that he agreed with Gerald James—that the real destination of LISI was common knowledge and that Aitken must have known.[196] In addition, so must the government, Anderson argued, as the export of each consignment was approved by the MOD after consultation with the British High Commission in Singapore: "Both parties must have known it was ludicrous to suggest that Singapore needed these guns. There were enough cannon to arm 20 navies of the size of Singapore."[197] Indeed, the 1987–88 edition of *Jane's Fighting Ships* lists the Singapore navy as operating just twelve Swift Class patrol craft, each equipped with one 20mm Oerlikon cannon. "The fact is the Government and the secret services knew all along what we were doing and could have stopped us at any time."[198] In addition, a public relations consultant to Astra, Julian Nettlefold, spoke out to say that it "was such an important part of BMARC's accounts that he must have known about it."[199] Kock took part in a *Channel 4 News* interview at this time to speak up for Aitken, but like Aitken could not remember much about LISI, explaining: "I can't really recall. . . . The name sounds faintly familiar but I can't recall exactly what it was all about, I really can't."[200] Anderson also noted how this new openness on the part of the government appeared to be a complete reversal of the previous policy of trying to keep himself and Gerald James quiet: "Only five months ago a man identifying himself as Robertson from the MOD police rang to remind me that I had signed the Official Secrets Act. I had been talking to journalists, he said, and I should remember what I had signed."[201]

To illustrate how easy it was to get an export license for suspicious sales to Iran or Iraq during the 1980s, Anderson cited the £4 million order Astra received from Iran in 1988 for "distress rockets for fishing vessels." This order specified flares topped with aluminum chaff, the material used by fighter aircraft to act as a decoy and evade oncoming missiles. His suspicions, which were aroused by this requirement, were then compounded by the high number Iran wanted, and so he showed the license to the MOD to ensure clearance: "But no one showed any interest and we got an export licence without any trouble."[202]

Major General Donald Isles, the man responsible for the contract within BMARC, also insisted that the government was fully aware of Project LISI.[203] He had stated: "There was the odd rumour the guns were going to Iran" but maintained: "As far as we were concerned, they were going to Singapore, that is all there is to it."[204] William Miller, a fellow director, stated: "There were rumours about the guns going to Iran."[205] He also recalled that the board was "informed by Donald Isles [that] everything had been approved and cleared by the Government. The board did not need to go further . . . I certainly knew about it probably being shipped to Iran."[206]

Meanwhile, Jonathan Aitken's bid to distance himself from knowledge of LISI was undermined by the fact that he had clearly attended more meetings of BMARC than he had confessed to doing. Documents released to Gerald James showed that while Aitken claimed to have attended three meetings (2 November 1988, 28 February 1989, and 25 April 1989), he had in fact attended a further two (26 July 1989 and 3 October 1989), but only after the name BMARC had been changed to Astra Defence Systems. In a statement issued to the *Times* on 29 March 1995, Aitken had stated: "I only attended three board meetings of BMARC as a non-executive director between August 1988 and 1990. Had I ever been told about anything that might have contravened the guidelines on arms sales I would have most certainly not have agreed to it."

At the two meetings that Aitken did not initially acknowledge, two further interesting projects were discussed. The first of these, Diana, was a project to supply guns and ammunition to Thailand; the second was to supply Chile with 126 GAMs of the same type being supplied through LISI (i.e., GAM BO 1 light naval guns), despite the fact that Chile had no use for so many of them, having a surface fleet of just thirty-one vessels at the time the order was placed.[207]

Aitken's already weak grip on his Cabinet position was fatally undermined when a public relations adviser, Patrick Robertson, inadvertently faxed his confidential advice to Aitken to someone else's fax machine, from where it was passed on to a national newspaper. The fax referred to a meeting between the two the day after the Heseltine statement. It revealed Aitken's fear that "one more bad story will break the camel's back" and that further bad press was imminent, as a competition was under way between rival Sunday tabloids to run Aitken sex-scandal stories in the wake of the *World in Action* revelations, something Aitken was aware of. The fax from Robertson said:

> The simple truth is that *we do not know* if there is going to be a story on Sunday. I was informed this afternoon by an excellent source who is close to a certain Sunday tabloid, that at least 3 papers were sniffing around. But they have no evidence of anything, it is only Wednesday and anything could happen between now and Saturday. . . .
>
> If the objective is to stop the tabloids from running a nasty story against you on Sunday there is only one way to do it: you would need to talk to the other person involved. Nothing else will work.[208]

As John Major moved to preempt any attempt to challenge his position as party leader in July 1995 by calling a leadership election, Aitken announced that he would resign at the Cabinet reshuffle that would follow it in order to pursue "legal battles with my adversaries in the media . . . I need to give my full commitment to fighting my current and possible future libel actions. I also wish to give my full co-operation to the Trade and Industry Select Committee's inquiry into BMARC."[209] This reference to possible future libel actions looked somewhat prescient when the *Sunday Mirror* won the tabloid race to be first with an Aitken sex story, on consecutive weeks running an account titled "My Sex Fling with Aitken" about how in December 1980, while his wife was recovering from giving birth to twins, he began an affair with a prostitute lasting more than two years.[210] Subsequently, Aitken issued a further statement, this time to his local newspaper, *Kent Today*, saying: "I deeply regret the embarrassment and anguish caused by the *Sunday Mirror* story to my family, my friends and constituents. The article contains many falsehoods relating to alleged details, clues and conversations. However, the central allegation is true. I did have a brief affair with this woman 15 years ago."[211]

Michael Heseltine's explanation of why the LISI contract was allowed to go ahead—that there had been a widespread failure in the DTI to check export licenses during the Iran-Iraq War—flatly contradicted yet another of the main planks of the Howe Guidelines (point iv), namely, that the government "should continue to scrutinise rigorously all applications for export licences for the supply of defence equipment to Iran and Iraq." Effectively, what Heseltine had offered, for the third time at least in illicit arms sales to Iraq/Iran sagas, was the breakdown in communications/compartmentalization defense—one that seems to preclude any minister bearing responsibility. Rather than immediately agree to Heseltine's offer to launch an inquiry into LISI, the TISC initially held back, seeking reassurances that it would have access to the information unearthed in Heseltine's internal DTI investigation and that it would have the kind of access denied it during the 1991–92 investigation into the supergun saga. For example, it demanded clear undertakings that it would have access to classified Whitehall and MI6 reports, which normally fall outside its remit. In addition, it wanted a free hand in deciding which ministers and officials could be questioned, so as to avoid any repetition of the supergun imbroglio.

That the TISC should have taken the unusual step of demanding explicit assurances before agreeing to investigate arms sales to Iran or Iraq again was an indication of the damage done to its reputation by the 1991–92 investigation. Nevertheless, on 27 June 1995 the TISC announced that it had received the necessary assurances from Michael Heseltine at a private meeting and would be investigating the BMARC affair. The assurances fell into four categories: cooperation over supply of information from ministers and named civil servants; from Customs and Excise; and from the intelligence services. However, as Jim Cousins, MP, a member of the TISC at the time of the supergun investigation, noted during the BMARC debate: "The issue of Iran and Iraq is not some marginal matter. . . . It is one of the great secrets of the 1980s, and it will, sadly, take far more . . . than a Select Committee inquiry to get to the bottom of these very murky affairs."[212] Moreover, he observed: "The Select Committee will face the puzzle of understanding why, if the Government did not know about arms sales to Iran, a wholly owned Government company, International Military Services Ltd., had an office in Iran that was open throughout the entire period of the first Gulf war."[213]

This was the environment in which a further surprise development occurred. Like the unexpected intervention of Heseltine, it served to heap further credibility on the story of James and Anderson. On 17 June, Tony Comben, a deputy chief constable of the MOD police (MDP), issued a statement saying that a number of Astra files relevant to the BMARC affair had been "accidentally" overlooked when his forces moved to new headquarters in 1994, and noting further: "It is deeply regretted that the recently discovered documents were not discovered earlier, and that Ministers were inadvertently and wrongly advised to tell Parliament that all the documents in the possession of the MDP had been returned. It is also much regretted that Sir Richard Scott's inquiry was inadvertently misled over this." These "50 or so documents"[214]—an estimate that soon increased to around 100[215]—were part of the estimated one million Astra papers, contained in 1,600 boxes, which were seized in 1990. While the MDP attempted to dismiss the oversight as incompetence, Labour MP Stephen Byers said that it had "all the signs of a conspiracy at the heart of government." Gerald James said he suspected that "they were hiding these documents and they were forced to disgorge them out of fear." Commenting on the coincidence of timing in their discovery and parallel developments in the BMARC affair, Brian Wilson, MP said: "It is astonishing beyond the bounds of belief that these documents should suddenly come up at this juncture."[216] Indeed, especially as Stephen Byers had raised a parliamentary question due to be answered on the Monday (the press release was made at 5:00 PM on the Saturday) by Defence Secretary Malcolm Rifkind, asking what documents had been retained by the MDP following their 1990 raid on BMARC offices.[217] This development also meant that some previous parliamentary answers on the subject had been false. Stephen Byers noted: "At the time all the documents should have been handed over by the MOD police one of their political masters was Jonathan Aitken and perhaps their non-disclosure at the time was an attempt to save his political embarrassment."[218] The Scott Inquiry immediately asked for copies of these documents. Christopher Muttukumaru, the secretary to the inquiry, told the MDP that it was "a very unwelcome development. Every time new papers are found, the inquiry has to read them to see if they are relevant. If they are relevant, draft sections of the report have to be rewritten. It is an unnecessary waste of time at this late stage."[219]

The "discovery" of LISI by the DTI prompted a review of all license applications for Singapore during the late 1980s. Among other things, this inevitably uncovered some of the under-the-counter activities of RO. As Roger Freeman told Dale Campbell-Savours, MP in the House: "Following the statement . . . on BMARC, departments have, as a prudent measure, started to research some associated areas of defence exports to Singapore." In a further answer to Llew Smith, MP, he revealed that RO and the mysterious Allivane International were both exporters to Singapore during this period. The availability of this information to then Defence Procurement Minister Freeman seemed to contradict a written answer given in January 1994 by Jonathan Aitken to Llew Smith, when he said that the MOD held no information about the sale of artillery shells by RO to Chartered Chemical Industries of Singapore. Freeman was forced to concede the inaccuracy of that answer, telling Smith: "In the course of recent researches it has come to light that Singapore Technologies [the parent company of Chartered Chemical Industries] was, on occasion, a consignee of exports from Royal Ordnance." He also confirmed that it had been the consignee of exports from Allivane.[220]

Freeman's acknowledgment seemed to rest, yet again, on the fortuitous discovery of further documents that were unavailable as late as January 1994. Perhaps this was because they touched on the operations of the propellant cartel to which both RO and Allivane, not to mention BMARC and PRB, either belonged or were close, in addition to arming both sides in the Iran-Iraq War. Allivane went bust in 1988, but a source described as close to it told one newspaper: "Singapore was a sophisticated false end-user. You could send components out there and they were able to assemble them and then forward them on." The report went on: "Former employees of Allivane say the Government was aware of their illegal trade and actively assisted them with the transport and purchase of components. Senior civil servants at the MOD, claim Allivane sources, were involved in regular briefings."[221]

One suggestion that this may indeed have been the case involved the export of mortar bombs. One of Allivane's exports was the AM52A3 fuse, which is used in mortar bombs. Although Singapore does not employ that fuse itself, Iran did. In 1987, 20,000 were exported from Britain in one shipment alone.[222]

The strange case of Astra Holdings, then, illustrates many facets of the Iraqgate affair. It sheds light on the involvement of politicians with major arms companies, reveals something of the role played by banks and financial institutions, hints at the corruption that exists in the contemporary arms trade, and suggests that the way in which the blanket invocation of national security is used to justify the secrecy surrounding these activities is no longer, in a post–cold war environment, particularly convincing. Whistleblowers are rare in the arms trade. By virtue of his former position as chairman of an emerging and important international arms manufacturer, Gerald James has become, since his engineered removal, the most important and high-level whistleblower ever to emerge from the arms world in Britain. His position allowed him to observe firsthand the realities of the contemporary arms trade. It also made him one of several people able to comment on the role of intelligence agencies in Iraqgate and find out who knew what and when.

NOTES

1 In addition to selling to the U.K. Ministry of Defence and the U.S. Department of Defense, at its height Astra also dealt with states such as Saudi Arabia, Kuwait, Abu Dhabi, Dubai, Jordan, Egypt, Kenya, Zimbabwe, Zambia, Indonesia, Taiwan, Singapore, Malaysia, Brunei, India, Pakistan, China, and Thailand.

2 All holdings are 100 percent. The diagram is a simplified one.

3 In terms of orders.

4 Thomas F. Dooley v. United Technologies Corp, Declaration of Gerald James, pp. 1–3. The order book figure would have been at least £100 million higher if PRB's books had been consolidated with Astra's, and the number of employees would have been around 4,000 had PRB personnel been included.

5 The purchase was completed in May 1987 at a cost of around US$35 million. See G. R. James in TISC: HC-86-x, EQ15, p. 339.

6 TISC: HC-86-xii, p. 340.

7 Now the comptroller and auditor general.

8 TISC: Minutes of Evidence, 2.19.92, p. 340.

9 James has since made it clear that Astra would not have considered such a move if it had known of the EPREP Agreement at the time (see below).

10 *Guardian*, 6.20.95.

11 *Guardian*, 6.14.95. Under Astra its name was changed to Astra Defence Systems Ltd., but

it reverted to the name BMARC in April 1991 after James and Gumbley were ousted, before being sold off to RO in April 1992.

12 TISC: HC-86-xii, p. 340.

13 TISC: HC-86-x, p. 341. In addition to Levene, James states that Levene's assistants, Brigadier Peter Landry and Stephen French, also encouraged Astra to become a competitor to RO.

14 In December 1987, a deal was reached whereby Astra agreed to pay £3 million for a manufacturing agreement whereby it would have the right to manufacture on the Faldingworth site for five years while taking out an option for a nominal sum to complete the acquisition of BMARC by 30 April 1988. This Astra subsequently did, at a cost of £63 million, including associated loans.

15 "The Explosives, Propellants and Related End Products (EPREP) Agreement between the Ministry of Defence and Royal Ordnance plc . . . was signed on 28 July 1988. Under EPREP, the Ministry of Defence had to purchase 80% of its requirements for certain natures of ammunition and explosives from Royal Ordnance during the five year period from 1 April 1988 to 31 March 1993.
"The Agreement was part of the arrangements for the sale of the Royal Ordnance Factories to British Aerospace. The guarantee of a core workload over the five year period assisted in establishing the newly privatised company as an efficient competitor and provided a guaranteed source of supply to the Ministry of Defence during what would otherwise have been a period of instability.
"The value of the orders placed with Royal Ordnance under the EPREP Agreement was £560M and covered over 40 types of ammunition." Answer from Defence Procurement Minister Roger Freeman, *Hansard*, 6.22.95.

16 On EPREP, see also *Hansard*, 6.28.88, col. 231w; *Hansard*, 7.27.88, cols. 351–352w. See also the then secretary of state for defense's statement on the sale of RO to BAE: *Hansard*, 4.2.87, cols. 1238–1245.

17 TISC: HC-86-x, EQ15, p. 345.

18 Ibid., p. 353.

19 *Sunday Correspondent*, 6.17.90.

20 PRB: *The PRB Defence Department of the Gechem Group*, 8.16.88.

21 i.e., the advent of the single European market.

22 TISC: HC-86-x, p. 346.

23 Ibid.

24 To take just one example, in August 1984 PRB had sent a G5 155mm gun and three cases of ammunition (air freighted by the Belgian air force) to Jordan as a demonstration model. Invoice, dated 8.7.84 (Licence No. 49094392).

25 Memo from Gerald Bull to General de Banque: Suggestions for the Future of PRB, 3.8.89, pp. 2–6.

26 "Confidential" letter from Gerald Bull to P. Glibert, 7.6.89.

27 Ibid.

28 Despite this contact with James, and the fact that Cuckney had worked closely with him in the 1970s, when James wrote to Cuckney in April 1993 at the request of Michael Mueller (the lawyer in the U.S. Dooley/Westland-Sikorsky case) asking if Cuckney would meet with Mueller, he received an odd reply. It was a handwritten note that was signed on the back rather than in the space on the front, in which Cuckney wrote that he had only recently been prompted into remembering who James was—something James regarded as a pretense. Cuckney's note said: "It was, incidentally, only recently that I realised we must have met some 23 years ago over the Mersey Dock and Harbour Board situation. I saw a Baring's director the other day who confirmed you were part of the Baring's team." Letter from

John Cuckney to Gerald James, 4.14.93. James's interpretation is contained in a memorandum to the Scott Inquiry dated 9.13.95, p. 2.

29 TISC: HC-86-x, EQ15, p. 348.

30 One of the banks, led by Bank of Boston, that were supporting the purchase of PRB but had taken a cautious line over it.

31 TISC: HC-86-x, EQ15, p. 351.

32 TISC: HC-86, p. xxxii.

33 As well as working for PRB, Binek also worked for SRC as a consultant, and as such had a good knowledge of Project Babylon, as he had been party to all supergun design drawings. PRB was completely unaware of this connection.

34 The delivery schedules were as follows:

System 350	System 1,000
12,000kg—2.20.89.	30,000kg—6.15.89.
6,500kg—3.1.89.	30,000kg—7.15.89.
6,500kg—4.1.89.	60,000kg—8.20.89.
	60,000kg—9.30.89.
	30,000kg—10.30.89.

The System 1,000 schedule was not followed in the event, due to a delay in forwarding the technical specifications. The total value of the contract (Systems 350 and 1,000) was BF 190,225,000.

By the time the 600mm system came to be designed, the explosion at Kaulille had already occurred, and the propellant was being sourced via Yugoslavia.

35 C. Cowley: Letter to A. Kennon, 2.23.92. TISC: EQ94, unpublished evidence.

36 Cited in C. Cowley: *Guns, Lies and Spies*, p. 251.

37 Incorporated in Panama.

38 This was discovered by Chris Cowley; see *Guns, Lies and Spies*, pp. 237–238.

39 The memo also noted that PRB had "reliable information that ordnance hardware has been cast in the UK, machined by RO and exported with UK approval to the Kingdom of Jordan for Iraq."

40 Austria's willingness to act as a front for Iraq and to supply Iraq and Iran with 155mm artillery is discussed further in chapters 2 and 6.

41 Scott Inquiry: Response by Gerald James to supplementary request, pp. 9–10.

42 Ibid., pp. 34–35.

43 Ibid., p. 6.

44 TISC: HC-86-xv, p. 484.

45 TISC: HC-86-x, p. 362.

46 *Guardian*, 5.31.90. See also the *Independent*, 2.6.92. For a comprehensive overview of this process, see TISC: HC-86-x, passim.

47 Scott Inquiry: Statement of Gerald James, pp. 14–15.

48 This was confirmed by Gumbley in his evidence to the TISC: HC-86-xii, pp. 393–395: "We felt that as we had acquired the company in Belgium we wanted to make sure that the contracts that we were going to be involved in were acceptable to the British Government and we wanted to make [Primrose] aware of them to get his opinion." Ibid., p. 395. The Astra approach, and the fact that they reported that they "had heard an allegation that [the propellant was] to be used in a very large artillery piece in Iraq to produce a weapon of strategic range" was confirmed by the MOD. See TISC, HC-86-xv, p. 495. James and Gumbley believed Primrose to be an MI6 or Defence Intelligence Staff (DIS) officer attached to DESO. It appears more likely he was DIS, as the MOD did not subsequently state that he did not work for them, as it did Holdness. See also TISC: HC-xv, EQ85.

49 Quoted in the *Economist*, 5.7.94, p. 31.

50 *Financial Times*, 9.25.91.

51 Quoted in the *Guardian*, 2.6.92.

52 TISC: HC-86-x, p. 358. John Pike told the TISC:
"It is a moot point whether the UK could legally have prevented PRB delivering either the propellant contract or any further like contracts under ASTRA jurisdiction, since as far as the Belgian Government was concerned, the contract paperwork was totally in order to allow delivery from Belgium to Jordan. It would have been an interesting commercial test case. Happily, it never happened." TISC: HC-86-xv, EQ88.

53 TISC: HC-86-x, p. 365.

54 "Confidential" memorandum—P. Glibert to W. McNaught and J. Pike, 11.15.89. My emphasis.

55 Scott Inquiry: Statement of Gerald James, pp. 16–17.

56 *Independent*, 2.20.92.

57 This is discussed in more detail in chapter 6.

58 Bevan was later made secretary to the Speaker in the House of Commons.

59 Quoted in the *Independent*, 2.28.92.

60 "Ministers therefore consider that their appearance before the Committee would be inappropriate and unproductive." TISC, EQ85. Harding subsequently told reporters that he had "strong views" on this version of events but declined to be more specific "for the time being." He did submit a memorandum to the TISC (EQ103) on his role.

61 *Independent*, 2.29.92.

62 It is worth noting that Ridley's reply reveals many of the characteristics of answers to arms sales questions. It is studiously vague, and yet could conceivably be claimed to be consistent with these disclosures. Clearly, however, it was intended to convey the impression that Customs had acted as soon as it had become aware of the nature of Forgemasters' work, although it quickly became apparent that this was not the case.

63 *Guardian*, 5.31.90.

64 Scott Inquiry: Statement of Gerald James, p. 5.

65 Scott Inquiry: Response by Gerald James to supplementary request, p. 7.

66 Letter from Gerald James to Sir Richard Scott, 7.13.95.

67 Scott Inquiry: Response by Gerald James to supplementary request, pp. 7–8.

68 Gerald James: Press statement, background note, 6.17.93.

69 In the matter of Astra Holdings plc and the matter of the Company Directors Disqualification Act 1986: First affidavit of Christopher William Gumbley.

70 "Private and confidential" letter, W. W. McNaught to Bob Primrose, DESO.

71 Letter from John Reed to Chris Gumbley, 7.7.95. Reed went on to say that "the statement by McNaught is central to my belief that there was a gross abuse of power in certain of the government's actions . . ."

72 Scott Inquiry: Statement of Gerald James, pp. 28–29. Scott Inquiry: Statement of Chris Cowley, p. 17.

73 Scott Inquiry: Statement of Gerald James, pp. 28–29.

74 Ibid., pp. 30–31.

75 Scott Inquiry: Response by Gerald James to supplementary request, pp. 21–22.

76 Iran had already purchased an earlier version at the time of the shah.

77 TISC: HC-86-x, EQ15, p. 331.

78 These were Astra Holdings plc; BAE; Defence Manufacturers' Association; Errut Products Ltd; GEC Avionics; Graviner Ltd; Mantech Ltd; Matrix Churchill; Olympus-KMI; Racal Electronics plc; Rapid Metal Developments; Rolls-Royce Ltd; Rotabroach Ltd; SIP Holdings Ltd; Stumech Engineering Ltd; Thorn EMI; and United Scientific Holdings.

79 In an internal BMARC memo of 1.31.92, he writes: "Curiously there was never any follow-up from Iraq."

80 Jane Renton, an *Observer* journalist, was told by John Sellens, head of sales at Astra, at the 1989 RNEE that James and Gumbley "were unaware of some of the large orders going through Astra." Scott Inquiry: Response by Gerald James to supplementary request, p. 8. James told the Scott Inquiry: "The purpose of including the incorrect name and telex number was to disguise these practices and filter repeat orders for equipment never supplied in the first place." Letter from Kevin Robinson to C. Muttukumaru, 6.15.93, p. 3.

81 Letter from Gerald James, 2.9.93.

82 For more detail on this see TISC: HC-86-x, EQ15, pp. 347–351. In the event, it registered a £12 million loss. See also *Sunday Correspondent*, 8.19.90.

83 Interview with Gerald James, London, 3.1.95.

84 The first was made in February 1989, the second in December 1989, and James resigned at the third attempt, on 2 March 1990.

85 DTI: Minutes of Proceedings, Tuesday 12 February 1991: Evidence of Mr Stephan Adolph Kock, pp. 7, 70.

86 DTI: Minutes of Proceedings, Thursday 10 October 1991: Evidence of Mr Stephan Adolph Kock, p. 8.

87 Astra Holdings plc: *Interim Report for the Six Months to 30th September 1991*.

88 See, for example, the *Guardian*, 4.4.90, *Financial Times*, 4.4.90, the *Engineer*, 4.12.90, the *Observer*, 4.15.90.

89 "to provide independent advice during the period of Board room battles with Mr James . . . to catalogue events and evidence to be handed over to S. J. Berwin relative to the DTI inquiry . . ." Astra board minutes, 12.4.90.

90 C. W. Gumbley: Affidavit in Support of an Application to Set Aside a Statutory Demand, pp. 2–4. Advice along these lines, including the suggestion that Gumbley should resign, is contained in two letters dating from March 1990, of which I have copies.

91 TISC: HC-86-x, p. 358.

92 Letter from John Anderson to Charles Kennedy, MP, 7.1.95.

93 The sequence of events is covered by the DTI report: *Astra Holdings plc: Investigation Under Section 431(2)(c) of the Companies Act 1985*, pp. 542–545.

94 Ibid., p. 20.

95 Interview with Gerald James, London, 3.1.95.

96 This has subsequently been confirmed by other sources.

97 TISC: HC-86-xii, p. 398.

98 *Channel 4 News*, 1.28.94.

99 He was registered as a citizen of the United Kingdom and Colonies on 20 March 1969. Letter from the Lord Advocate to Michael Meacher, MP, 9.1.94.

100 TWR Laxton: Memorandum on Stephan Adolf Kock, p. 3. The FAC chose not to publish this or a statement by Gerald James, former chairman of Astra Holdings, on the same subject in the volume of Minutes of Evidence and Appendices that accompanied the FAC's Report (*Public Expenditure: The Pergau Hydro-Electric Project, Malaysia, the Aid and Trade Provision and Related Matters*). However, the FAC decided to "receive" both and consequently they are both lodged in the House of Commons Library and House of Lords Record Office.

101 Midland Bank Group International Trade Services: In Support of Excellence (brochure).

102 See Tony Geraghty: *Who Dares Wins: The Story of the SAS 1950–1992*, 3rd ed., Warner, London, 1993, pp. 333–335.

103 Financial Times, 7.15.91.

104 The Pergau Dam scandal erupted in 1993–94 and revealed the existence of a covert government policy to link arms sales to the provision of overseas aid. It related to a large 1988 defense deal between Britain and Malaysia and, as noted in endnote 100 above, was investigated by the FAC in 1994.

105 TWR Laxton, memorandum, p. 6.
106 TISC: HC-86-xii, p. 409.
107 These are the dates given by TWR Laxton: memorandum, p. 6.
108 Quoted in Chris Cowley: *Guns, Lies and Spies*, p. 227. My emphasis.
109 Midland Bank Group International Trade Services: In Support of Excellence. On its activities and performance, see the *Financial Times*, 7.15.91.
110 Ibid.
111 Statement for Foreign Affairs Committee: Gerald Reaveley James, p. 8.
112 *Financial Times*, 7.15.91.
113 Ibid., pp. 408–409.
114 TISC: HC-86, p. xxxiii. As referred to above, an internal Astra newsletter carried a similar description: "Served in both the Air Force and the Army, including service in military intelligence and special forces. Following his military career he carried out special assignments for the Foreign Office."
115 TISC: HC-86-xii, p. 402.
116 Ibid., p. 407. My emphasis. When pressed as to whether he had passed on his information on the propellant to MI5 or MI6, he asked to be allowed to "answer this in confidence." Ibid., p. 412.
117 Ibid., p. 408. My emphasis.
118 Ibid., p. 412.
119 DTI: Minutes of Proceedings, Thursday 10 October 1991: Evidence of Mr Stephan Adolph Kock, p. 15.
120 Interview with Robin Robison, 3.27.95.
121 Chris Cowley: *Guns, Lies and Spies*, pp. 226–227.
122 TISC: HC-86-xii, p. 404.
123 Ibid., p. 411.
124 Ibid., p. 409.
125 Ibid., p. 403.
126 Ibid., p. 393.
127 DTI: Minutes of Proceedings, Tuesday 12 February 1991: Evidence of Mr Stephan Adolph Kock, p. 29.
128 Ibid.
129 Ibid., p. 411.
130 DTI: Astra Holdings plc: *Investigation Under Section 431(2)(c) of the Companies Act 1985—Report* by Colin Percy Farquharson Rimer, QC and John White, FCA, HMSO, 1993, p. 267.
131 Ibid., pp. 268–269. My emphasis.
132 Letter from Andrew Leithead, assistant Treasury solicitor, to Harry Cohen, MP, 8.8.94.
133 TISC: HC-86-xii, p. 400.
134 Ibid., p. 409.
135 *Independent*, 7.6.91.
136 Gerald R. James: Statement for FAC, pp. 16–18.
137 *Independent*, 7.6.91.
138 *Financial Times*, 7.15.91.
139 *Independent*, 1.26.94. In addition, Campbell Dunford, a former manager with MBGITS, confirmed Kock's role and told Gerald James that he "was asked to set up 'special banking arrangements' for the deal." Gerald R. James: Statement for FAC, p. 28.
140 *Observer*, 1.30.94.
141 Gerald R. James: Statement for FAC, p. 19.
142 Ibid., p. 12.
143 *Channel 4 News*, 1.28.94.

144 Gerald R. James: Statement for FAC, p. 13.
145 Ibid., pp. 23–24.
146 Ibid., p. 19.
147 Ibid., pp. 24–25.
148 *Financial Times*, 7.15.91.
149 *Independent*, 10.11.91.
150 Ibid.
151 TISC: HC-86-xii, p. 410.
152 Report made by Astra Holdings into incident and statement of the assistant manager, 2.21.89.
153 TISC, HC-86-xii, pp. 403–404.
154 Minutes of Proceedings, Thursday 10 October 1991: Evidence of Mr Stephan Adolph Kock, pp. 15–16. The inspectors told Kock that the suggestion that he had been in Baghdad was "based on what I think amounts to something in the nature of double hearsay, at least." p. 15.
155 Interview with Chris Cowley, 2.23.95.
156 *Channel 4 News*, 3.30.95.
157 *Hansard*, 4.22.93, col. 193w. Stephen rather than Stephan was an error contained in the original question draft.
158 *Hansard*, 2.28.94, col. 589w.
159 Ibid., col. 545w.
160 *Hansard*, 5.24.94, col. 102w.
161 Letter dated 8.8.94.
162 Kevin Cahill: What Lord Justice Scott Hasn't Been Told, *Business Age*, Vol. 3 No. 34, July/August 1993, p. 33.
163 The photograph was actually taken by one of James's sons serving in the Gulf inside Iraq to the north of the Saudi border.
164 Letter, R. D. Keen to C. Muttukumaru, 7.28.93.
165 *Hansard*, 11.17.92, cols. 195–196w.
166 James did not introduce the term into the proceedings. This was done by the chairman, Kenneth Warren, who asked of James's knowledge of it. See TISC: HC-86-x, p. 364.
167 The names were reprinted in *Private Eye*, No. 794, 5.22.92, and partially in the *Daily Mirror*, 5.15.92. On 27 February 1992, twenty-eight Labour MPs signed a motion calling for an inquiry into the "so-called Savoy Mafia whose members include Mark Thatcher."
168 TISC: HC-86-x, EQ15, p. 348.
169 Letter, Ian Lang to Jim Cousins, MP, 7.14.95.
170 DTI report, p. 3.
171 Letter, Michael Meacher, MP to Rt. Hon. Michael Heseltine, MP, president of the Board of Trade, 8.22.94.
172 Letter, Sir Nicholas Bonsor to Gerald James, 12.14.93. He later added:
"Undoubtedly, I do not think that Mr James's company was treated properly. It is quite clear that whenever someone in the government hierarchy led him to understand one thing, another person in government did something else . . . there are elements of what happened which are clearly unsatisfactory." *Independent*, 4.22.95.
173 During the debate, Dale Campbell-Savours asked whether Gerald James would:
"now be offered an apology for all the leaking by Government Departments, Ministers and civil servants against him, and for the assassination of his character in the past three years . . . As it was he who stated in 1990 that, when Astra took over BMARC in 1988, he found that it was running a secret order book that was being managed by three other directors of the company, and as everything that has been said today points to the fact that his allega-

tions at that time were true, does he not deserve an apology and should he not receive one." *Hansard*, 6.13.95, col. 603. This was a theme Sir Nicholas Bonsor touched on in the subsequent BMARC debate, saying: "I believe that Mr James has been treated very badly . . . by certain members of the Administration, with or without the Government's knowledge." *Hansard*, 6.19.95, cols. 56–57.

174 *Hansard*, 6.13.95, col. 596. Heseltine's statement is cols. 595–606.

175 *Hansard*, 6.13.95, col. 597.

176 For example, the 1994 Cabinet reshuffle was timed for the same day that the critical FAC report into the Pergau Dam scandal was published.

177 On this line of speculation see, for instance, the *Times*, 6.14.95, the *Independent*, 6.20.95. The *Guardian*, 6.15.95, commented: "He was out of office during the arms-to-Iraq affair in the late 1980s. He is Mr Squeaky Clean . . . if anyone gets hurt it will not be him. But if anyone benefits it probably will be [him]." On 6.20.95, it referred to the "domestic sub-text . . . the implications of the arms export argument for Michael Heseltine's ruthless attempt to supplant John Major this autumn."
Heseltine himself referred to the tactic of concealing information via answers in the debate on BMARC held on 19 June 1995, arguing that he could have used
"a device which all governments have used from time to time in different circumstances, and that is to seek some bland form of words which would have skated over the issues. I didn't try to do that . . . We all know that there are and have been throughout time, answers to questions which do not reveal the whole story. And I could have sought for a form of words which would have had that effect. I was not prepared to do that." *Hansard*, 6.19.95. See also the *Guardian*, 6.20.95. Heseltine admitted that, in the light of his previous statement, a number of parliamentary answers would have to be "revisited" and "modified, adjusted and even changed."

178 For Thanet East until 1983 and, following boundary changes, for Thanet South from June 1983.

179 Astra's registered office was situated in Sandwich.

180 From 1988 to 1991 inclusive, Aitken's entry in the Register of Members' Interests described Al-Bilad as a "subsidiary of foreign parent company which receives payments from contracts with Saudi Arabian royal family interests and government agencies."

181 Al Bilad (UK) Limited, Annual Report 1990.

182 BMARC: Minutes of a Meeting of the Board of Directors, 11.2.88, p. 2.

183 Dooley v. UTC: Declaration of Gerald R. James, p. 10.

184 He was appointed a nonexecutive director of BMARC on 13 September 1988.

185 See the profiles of Aitken in the *Independent*, 7.23.94, and the *Observer*, 7.17.94.

186 *World in Action:* Jonathan of Arabia, ITV, 4.10.95. See also the *Guardian*, 4.10.95.

187 For the original story, see the *Guardian*, 5.10.94.

188 *World in Action*, 4.10.95.

189 *Hansard*, 6.13.95, cols. 595–597.

190 Ibid., col. 598.

191 Ibid., col. 604.

192 Ibid., col. 600.

193 Cited in the *Independent*, 4.11.95.

194 *Independent*, 3.31.95.

195 *Times*, 6.14.95.

196 James later told *Newsnight* that Aitken would have known the real destination of LISI because "it was referred to as ultimately being for Iran in general discussion in the board meeting." *Newsnight*, 3.30.95.

197 *Guardian*, 6.15.95.

198 Ibid.
199 *Independent*, 4.1.95.
200 *Channel 4 News*, 3.30.95.
201 *Guardian*, 6.15.95.
202 *Times*, 6.20.95.
203 *Independent*, 6.16.95.
204 *Independent*, 3.31.95. In a statement prepared for the TISC investigation into BMARC, Isles noted:
   "Subsequently, I believe late in 1987, I was informed that there were rumours on the shop floor to the effect that components being made on the LISI contract were going to Iran. I was fairly relaxed about this because I had not received any information from any department of HMG which might have suggested that anything manufactured by BMARC was ultimately reaching Iran; additionally, there was nothing in the Defence Press to suggest that . . . I did mention these rumours . . . to Oerlikon Sales but was assured . . . that there was no substance in them." Memorandum submitted by Major General D. E. Isles, 9.18.95.
205 *Guardian*, 6.20.95.
206 *Independent*, 3.31.95.
207 *Guardian*, 6.14.95, *Observer*, 7.9.95.
208 Quoted in *Independent on Sunday*, 6.18.95.
209 Aitken's resignation letter, quoted in the *Guardian*, 7.6.95.
210 *Sunday Mirror*, 7.9.95 and 7.16.95.
211 *Times*, 7.13.95.
212 *Hansard*, 6.19.95, col. 65.
213 Ibid.
214 Ibid.
215 *Guardian*, 6.20.95.
216 *Observer*, 6.18.95.
217 *Sunday Telegraph*, 6.18.95.
218 *Guardian*, 6.19.95.
219 Ibid.
220 *Independent*, 7.7.95.
221 Ibid.
222 Ibid. According to sources cited in the article, there were several similar shipments in 1987.

Intelligence Monitoring of the Western Arms Trade with Iraq

The strange case of Astra Holdings strongly suggests that, far from seeking to prevent military goods and technology from reaching Iraq during the 1980s (the course of action suggested by the Howe Guidelines), it had been the policy of at least elements of the British and other Western governments, principally of course the United States, to allow arms to reach Iraq as well as Iran. Central to all of these revelations was the role of the intelligence services. Ministerial statements since that of Nicholas Ridley at the time of the supergun seizure gave the impression that the intelligence services had enjoyed limited success in the difficult job of tracking the Iraqi procurement network. However, the perspective of industrialists and businesspeople caught up in the affair suggests that intelligence monitoring of the network and knowledge of Iraqi activities were more widespread than previously believed.

This view is a reflection of the fact that a number of structural factors relating to the international arms trade render monitoring the flow of arms, while not straightforward, less difficult than some politicians have suggested. These factors would have aided the intelligence community in tracking direct Iraqi arms procurement, but they do not necessarily apply to the dual-use machine tool industry in the same way. Such companies are less likely than mainstream defense companies to be cooperative or to contain government elements, and they are therefore potentially more difficult to monitor. Neither do these factors necessarily apply to the tracking of chemical and other nonconventional weapons procurement; the dual-use nature of selected components or chemicals for these weapons, when ordered in isolation from a number of states, is inherently difficult to track, notwithstanding the existence of the Australia Group which seeks to control the proliferation of biological and chemical weapons components. However, a comparable degree of subterfuge is less easily achieved with conventional arms and technology. Hence, although it is not the intention here to credit the intelligence services

with omniscience they do not possess, in tracking the Iraqi procurement network and the British contribution to it, they were confronted with a number
of favorable structural factors, as well as some inherent difficulties.

Before considering these, it is worth noting that within the regulatory
structure, the DTI, MOD, and FCO are aware of what constitute suspicious exports that may be for an end-use or end-user other than that stated on a
license application. These considerations were neatly summarized for the
benefit of the Scott Inquiry by the FCO's Peter Vereker:

> [W]e would be interested in the company to which the goods were being exported
> abroad, was it a company which was known by the intelligence agencies to have
> been involved in supplying known proliferated countries before? We would be
> interested in the quantities of the goods involved, are they constant, are they in
> line with the stated end use of the product, or are they too great quantities, or do
> they seem to be too sophisticated, the material for the stated end use, does it look
> more like something that could be used to produce a biological agent than some-
> thing which could be used to produce a vaccine? We take account of this sort of
> web of considerations, the country to which it is going, the end use to which it was
> going to be put and the company to which it was being sent.[1]

Similarly, it is worth noting that despite the efforts of some ministers who
testified at the Scott Inquiry to play down the importance of intelligence,
numerous officials attested at the inquiry to the volume that was received
daily. Take, for example, this exchange between the FCO's Simon Sherrington
(a member of the Iran section of the Middle East Desk) and Lord Justice
Scott:

> **Q:** How often did you [see intelligence reports] while you were at your desk? Was
> it a frequent occurrence, irregular or what?
> **A:** The amount of intelligence material passing those desks, both the Iran desk
> and the Iraq desk was very frequent, yes.
> **Q:** Very frequent?
> **A:** Yes.
> **Q:** Daily?
> **A:** Yes, certainly, and large amounts.[2]

Discussing intelligence reports, the FCO's Ian Blackley told Scott that
". . . individual desk officers, *particularly on Iran and Iraq*, were receiving daily
a pile so high of these things. There was a vast amount of intelligence."[3]

While this does not testify to quality of information, it attests to volume and implicitly points to the special attention being paid to these two countries. Of the several structural factors that aid the monitoring of the conventional arms trade, one is the internationalization of the arms trade. Increasingly, weapons tend not to be manufactured entirely in any one country. Rather, there is a marked trend toward international collaboration, with various components being manufactured across several countries. The need to collaborate over production increases the likelihood of an order being brought to the attention of national intelligence services and governments. Furthermore, the necessity for transnational communication provides the raw material of Signals Intelligence (SIGINT) and makes secrecy, even if desired, difficult to guarantee. To take a few representative examples of this process: The Italian Agusta A129 attack helicopter has a Rolls-Royce Gem 2-2 turboshaft engine; the French Aerospatiale AS 332 SuperPuma helicopter has Decca navigation equipment; the Hawk T-Mk1 is armed with U.S. AIM 9L Sidewinder missiles; the Israeli Soltam L155mm SP Gun has a Cummins VT 8 460 Bi Diesel engine; the Israeli Lar-160 multirocket system has a Westinghouse Quickfire radar control system, and so on.

A second factor is that the international arms business, despite the enormous sums involved, involves relatively few people. This makes monitoring, either via embassies or via people within this group acting on behalf of governments, relatively easy. Chris Cowley, one of those formerly involved, has observed:

> The international arms trade is a multi-billion dollar business which, despite its size, is dominated by a relatively small, select group of companies. During my time with SRC I travelled to many countries in connection with the manufacture of arms and arms-related equipment. Wherever I went I always came across the same group of people, including Baghdad.[4]

In Baghdad Cowley recalls discussing SRC's work with staff from the British Embassy while socializing and running with them. There were thirty to forty SRC employees in Baghdad at any given time from mid-1988 on and, according to Cowley, around sixty to seventy Matrix Churchill personnel programming and installing machine tools, so the idea that the whole operation escaped the attention of the embassy is unlikely.

Having embassy staff (particularly defense attachés, whose roles revolve around selling arms and monitoring force levels) or government "representatives" attend military fairs or exhibitions in various parts of the world where equipment, buyers, and sellers are conveniently collected together is a further useful means of monitoring the arms trade. In this respect, the exchange between Menzies Campbell, MP and Nicholas Bevan of the MOD during the TISC hearings into the supergun is instructive:

> **Q:** Do you agree with me that what are sometimes called "arms fairs" or military exhibitions are important sources of intelligence as to what is being sold by whom and who is buying?
>
> **A:** Yes indeed.
>
> **Q:** Is it a matter of custom that representatives, and I deliberately use a general word, of the Ministry of Defence attend arms fairs around the world for the purpose of acquiring the information I have just indicated?
>
> **A:** It would certainly be normal practice for the defence attache or some of his staff in the country concerned to attend an arms fair of that sort . . .
>
> **Q:** Can you tell me did any representatives—and again I use a general word deliberately—of the Ministry of Defence attend the Baghdad Military Exhibition on the 28 April to 2 May of 1989?
>
> **A:** Yes, the defence attache in Baghdad and two of his staff did.
>
> **Q:** As a result of attending the exhibition would it be customary for the attache to send to the Ministry a report of what he had seen and anything of significance which is learned about the possible trade in arms between countries with which or about which the United Kingdom was interested?
>
> **A:** Yes.
>
> **Q:** Do you know if such a report was sent on this occasion to the Ministry of Defence?
>
> **A:** Yes it was.[5]

By way of example, Bevan said that the MOD had received "a very full report" on the Iraqis' SRC-designed 210mm Al Fao gun, which was on display for the first time at the exhibition. The British ambassador also attended this particular exhibition,[6] while Paul Henderson of Matrix Churchill was asked to report back to MI6 on his observations. He subsequently wrote: "I did a lot of intelligence gathering, collecting material from the various exhibits: leaflets on new weapons, brochures on the line of tanks for sale and descriptions of advanced military technology."[7] Furthermore, as mentioned earlier, the MOD's David Hastie was seconded back to his former company, BAE, in order to attend, albeit under instructions to keep a low profile.[8] According to a former official of the JIC, his reports were circulated in intelligence circles.[9] In addition, it would appear that specialist defense journalists have tended to inform the MOD of interesting or suspicious developments in the defense world.

With regard to Baghdad, any probing of British businesspeople that individuals attached to the British Embassy wished to carry out would have been aided by the fact that the Iraqis rounded up almost all foreign businesspeople (most of whom were engaged in military work) in the Al-Rasheed Hotel, so as to be able to keep an eye on them.[10] Elsewhere, former military intelligence officer turned arms dealer Robert Turp recalled that "the supergun project was the talk in all the expatriate bars in Brussels";[11] and Chris Cowley has confirmed that SRC's links with Iraq were openly discussed around Brussels.[12]

As an indication of the methods employed elsewhere to monitor arms-related activities in Baghdad, Chris Cowley has recalled the Mata Hari–like role of a woman attached to the Belgian Embassy named Bernadette. She struck up a relationship with an SRC employee, Graham Ingham, who was involved in Project Babylon: "By listening to their conversations Iraqi intelligence concluded Ingham was openly discussing Project Babylon with an official of the Belgian Government," says Cowley. Cowley believes he was tipped off about Iraqi interest in this relationship by Azzawi so that he could get Ingham out of Iraq. This he did, but only after Ingham went away for a "camping weekend" in Iraq in February 1989 with members of both the U.S. and Belgian embassies. He subsequently became persona non grata and was not allowed to return to Iraq. However, this was not quite the end of the story. As Cowley recalls: "After Ingham's departure from Baghdad, the same lady attempted to establish a similar relationship with Bernard Lasarge. Lasarge was a young Canadian engineer, responsible for much of the design work on the 210mm gun project known as Al Fao. He was warned by Dr Bull to have nothing to do with foreign embassy employees."[13]

A third structural factor aiding the monitoring of the international arms trade is the considerable volume of traffic between government (MPs, former ministers, civil servants, and armed forces personnel) and the defense industry. While this is intended to give defense companies people with access to government, it also gives government people "on the inside" of the defense industry. Over the last decade, more than two thousand MOD civil servants and armed forces personnel have joined British *and foreign* defense companies.[14] In practice, the defense industry and seats on the boards of defense companies are natural resting places for retired or former MPs, civil servants, and military personnel—some of whom, it is fair to assume, will have intelligence backgrounds. However, the activities of the dual-use machine tool industry are not overseen to the same extent, because unlike defense, this is not considered a strategic industry. Furthermore, such companies do not attract the same traffic in former government employees that mainstream arms companies do. They do not need such people to market their goods, as these people would not be able to open doors as lucrative as those in the mainstream arms business. As a consequence, the rewards are nowhere near as attractive, the companies involved being, without exception, smaller companies with smaller turnovers.

Fourth, it also appears that many individuals with an intelligence background have gone to work for major banks and financial institutions, which represent an ideal vantage point from which to monitor the overseas activities of defense companies. In the modern world, no arms deal can go through without the financing first being provided by a bank via a letter of credit. As a former JIC official has observed: "There is no real clear dividing line between the private and the public in that sense . . . I know for a fact that a number of senior people from the intelligence world and from the diplomatic world now work in big merchant banks in senior positions."[15]

With regard to Iraq, for example, there is the case of Stephan Kock, discussed in chapter 5. Gerald James, former chairman of Astra, told the Scott Inquiry he believed Kock to be "an agent of the British Government. He took part in a great many discussions which concerned export of military equipment to Iraq from the Astra group of companies and I do not doubt for a second that he shared his knowledge with others."[16]

Accountants are similarly well placed and could, from their vantage point, provide much useful information on a company's activities as recorded in its order book. As an illustration of the way in which accounting firms can have a considerable involvement in the arms trade, KPMG Peat Marwick acted as auditor to both BNL and BAE/RO, and also produced a project study for SRC concerning its purchase of the old Lear Fan plant in Belfast.

Furthermore, the proposition that end-user certificates are an effective way of policing the international arms trade, and that arms, once exported, find national borders impermeable, is a myth intended for public consumption only. At various times, for a variety of mainly political and strategic reasons, Western states have knowingly used conduits to get military equipment and technology through to prohibited destinations. In the case of Iraqgate, then, it seems difficult to accept that, when a merely rudimentary curiosity (e.g., about ordnance ordered for weapons a state did not possess) would have revealed the conduit function of such countries, the intelligence services remained unaware of the role performed by states such as Jordan. In fact, official documents show that the British government was aware of this and that it was willing to channel equipment through Jordan in the full knowledge that it was destined for Iraq. To be sure, there is an element of deniability built into the government's position, as the furor over Project LISI illustrated, in that it has been U.K. government policy not to monitor officially the end-use to which its military products are put once they leave Britain. By contrast, because of the "dual-use" fallback position, machine tool companies do not generally have to resort to the use of conduits; here the essence of determining end-use rests on an assessment of the size of an order, the prevailing political and military climate in the client state and surrounding region, and the context of other materials being sought by the client. Rather than misrepresenting the end-user, these companies aim to bypass any restrictions by misrepresenting the end-use. Drawing on his experiences, Chris Cowley said of false end-user certificates: "Virtually all South American countries sell them, at rates of commission ranging from 10 per cent to 200 per cent. 'Quickie' end-user certificates are available over the counter in Pakistan or Thailand, while there is a standing joke that Singapore would long since have sunk had it kept all the arms that its nationals had signed for."[17]

Finally, and most important in terms of guaranteeing the active cooperation of the producer sector, there is the nature of the defense industry where, typically, around 90 percent of a (British) company's business will be acquired via the British government. Of the remainder, it is not uncommon for some to be with the U.S. DOD (which shares most of the foreign policy and security objectives of the British government), making British defense companies highly vulnerable to any cancellation of contracts. Defense companies are therefore unlikely to accept contracts counter to the wishes or interests of either government and are always likely to err on the side of caution and seek consent before entering negotiations with any potential client of uncertain suitability. This is of course precisely what James and Gumbley of Astra did after being tipped off about Jordan in September 1989. As James himself has observed, British defense companies "are not going to accept even an attractive contract if it offended those people because they could just kill you stone dead overnight—there's no point in doing that."[18] The nature of defense manufacturing also works in the government's favor here:

what a lot of people don't understand is that [the loss of government contracts] is much more serious to the defence industry than perhaps to other manufacturing industries. You can't convert defence companies to peaceful functions without setting up a totally new operation, and the type of manufacturing in the defence industry is such, the quality standards are so high compared with normal commercial manufacturing, . . . that you can't take ingredients which are designed to manufacture military stuff and translate them into a commercial environment, because commercial things are made cheaply, as cheap as possible . . . So, if they stop your contracts because you had been doing something, to convert your business to something else would be prohibitively expensive.[19]

The compelling power of this consideration is reflected in the fact that the intelligence services were voluntarily given detailed information about company intentions and contracts for Iraq from several independent sources, drawn from those companies involved in selling military equipment and technology to Iraq. These sources are discussed in detail below.

◆ Gerald Bull, Chris Cowley, and SRC

Chris Cowley told the TISC investigating exports to Iraq that MI6 and the U.S. and Israeli governments knew of Project Babylon even before contracts were placed. In addition, he stated that Dr. Bull and his son Michel, an SRC executive, held meetings at the Belgian foreign office while negotiating the contracts with Iraq.[20] Given his experiences over South Africa, Gerald Bull was acutely aware that he needed the approval of certain governments before becoming involved in sensitive destinations like Iraq.[21] Indeed, as we have seen, at the time SRC began its involvement with Iraq, it had just completed a long military project for COCOM-proscribed China, which could not have gone ahead without the blessing of the U.S. and U.K. governments. In this case Bull had used George Wong as a conduit to gain approval. Cowley recalled: "Wong told . . . how MI6 used businessmen as intelligence gathering agents and he made it as plain as he possibly could without actually saying so that he was speaking with firsthand knowledge. In his conversations with me Gerald Bull was in no doubt whatsoever that George Wong worked for MI6."[22] Indeed, one of the reasons for claiming Public Interest Immunity (PII) in the Matrix Churchill trial seems to have been to conceal just how prevalent this practice had been. Cowley expanded on the intelligence role of George Wong for the TISC, in evidence which it chose not to publish:

> During the time I spent in China with SRC I attended a whole series of meetings with Chinese Government officials from the Ministry of Defence. Whenever Dr. Bull attended, George Wong, a director of Rothschild Bank was always present. These meetings did not discuss commercial matters, but were always specifically directed towards the technical needs of the GC 45 Gun Programme. Dr. Bull often spoke of George Wong in terms of him providing a conduit to British Intelligence.

. . . To my knowledge Rothschild's Bank never provided, or became directly involved in providing financial support to SRC.

Bearing this in mind it seems rather strange that Dr. Bull would continue to involve George Wong in the affairs of SRC unless it was for the reasons he always gave, i.e. to keep British Intelligence informed.[23]

Chris Cowley is one of only a few people who, by virtue of holding senior positions in organizations working with Iraq at the time, were in a position to observe the mechanics of the international arms trade at work, including the need for some kind of political approval for certain projects. He described the situation regarding clearance for dealing with Iraq in his statement to the Scott Inquiry:

> He [Bull] told me that before we could begin working in Iraq it was necessary to obtain the consent of three Governments. They were the US, Israel and UK. In March of 1988 Gerald Bull's son, Michael, [*sic*] Luis Palazzio, a Vice-President of SRC and an American lawyer, Chris Olhy went to the State Department to discuss Bull's desire to work in Iraq. I was told that the US Government had consented to Bull taking this on. I was personally involved in discussions in Brussels with Bull and a representative of the Israeli Government following which their consent was given. With regard to the UK Bull told me that he was dealing with George Wong as an intermediary. In the light of my knowledge of George Wong this did not cause me any surprise. I knew that George Wong was heavily involved in military contracts because I had not only been with him in China but I had met him in other parts of the world where he was involved in defence equipment sales. In March 1988 Bull told me that he held a number of discussions with Wong to try to obtain British Government approval to pursue the proposed contracts . . . I was present on two occasions with Bull when he had telephone conversations with George Wong when Bull was pressing him very hard saying that the whole thing was taking too long and that the Iraqis were pushing him . . . It became critical at one point when there was a meeting arranged in Frankfurt with Forgemasters. I did not know whether to attend the meeting or cancel it because Bull had not been given "authority to proceed." Fortunately about 24 hours before the meeting was scheduled to take place . . . Bull phoned me to say he had got permission from the UK Government.[24]

A number of drafts of faxes sent by Chris Cowley from the period May–July 1988 have survived and clearly illustrate this process.[25] An undated fax from early on in this process, which notes that the Midland Bank was willing to finance Project Babylon, concludes: "We are still optimistic on signing contracts for both the 350 and 1000mm systems by mid-July, assuming all necessary approvals granted." One, dated 18 June, reads:

> Please inform Dr Bull Forgemasters have informed me application for licence now forwarded to DTI. Mr Azzawi will have to provide end users certificate which will be impossible to obtain unless approval is obtained from British Government sources. This subject now most urgent and could delay or result in cancellation of project. Suggest Dr Bull contacts me on his return from China tomorrow.

An undated fax to Bull's assistant, Monique Jamine, apparently from late June, says: "Ask Dr Bull, 'what is current situation regarding British Government approval on PC2.' Call me at Hotel Rashid." A further fax, to Azzawi, the Iraqi overseeing SRC's work in Iraq, dated 1 July, states: "The DTI will require an End Users Certificate issued by the Ministry of Industry, Iraq. No attempt should be made to issue this document until Dr Bull has confirmed he has received approval from the UK for this Project." On the same day, a fax to Bull informed him of the urgency of British government approval. Then, in a fax to Azzawi dated 2 July, Cowley notes the last-minute confirmation of which he told the Scott Inquiry: "Last night Dr. Bull confirmed he has received approval from his sources within the British Government to proceed with the manufacture of the 1000mm system [i.e., supergun] using UK manufacturing facilities to produce the tube assembly." The meeting with Forgemasters in Frankfurt thus went ahead between 4 and 7 July.[26]

Hence, it would appear that Bull and SRC had sought clearance to deal with Iraq prior to signing contracts with manufacturers, just as they had sought clearance for other projects and proposed projects (e.g., China, Iran). If this is the case, then a number of intelligence agencies (U.S., U.K., Israeli) were aware of SRC's intentions by June 1988. In terms of British intelligence, SRC had identified the companies manufacturing the barrels, enabling intelligence agencies to monitor the progress of their manufacture—information that proved useful, as the political and strategic climate in the roughly two years between approval and completion of production had changed sufficiently for Customs to be tipped off and so prevent Babylon itself from being assembled. It is also useful to note that the Forgemasters subsidiary that produced the barrels was the only plant in the United Kingdom with the facilities to make barrels to the demanding specifications required for Project Babylon, another factor that would aid the monitoring of the project.

In a memorandum prepared for the TISC investigation, Cowley recalled a further incident:

Dr Bull told me on several occasions about conversations he had with British Government officials concerning Project Babylon. One particular occasion can be clearly recalled in February 1989 when Dr Bull arrived in Baghdad from London. During the flight he had sat next to a man he described as the military attache to the British Embassy in Baghdad. Apparently this person knew the details of all the Iraqi src projects. More impressively he had knowledge of the 350mm model firing programme planned for the following month . . . At that time I had believed only three people knew the actual firing schedule for the 350mm horizontal model. These people being Dr Bull, Azzawi, and myself. I had been reluctant to confirm the actual firing date as I was still awaiting components from W. Somers which were being flown to Iraq from Manchester. I inquired how anybody could know details being made on a daily basis by myself. Some project decisions were made only after telephone conversations between Baghdad and Brussels. Dr Bull suggested "it was probably through gchq monitoring telephone conversations" and I should not concern myself.[27]

There could also have been an agent planted inside src itself. In June 1989, Bull's Swiss bank contacted him to say that it had received an unusual request from the src accounts department: to provide a complete list of all accounts connected with src and ati, together with details of the Bull family's personal accounts. In the event, the bank was suspicious and informed Bull rather than supply the information.[28]

In its report on Project Babylon, the tisc, in assessing Cowley's evidence of intelligence knowledge of the Project, neither dismissed nor endorsed it, restricting itself to stating: "We accept the evidence that Iraq went to great lengths to disguise its real intentions."[29] Elsewhere in its report, however, the committee voted to minimize references to the intelligence services.[30]

mi6 had a final use for Chris Cowley, as they would also have for Paul Henderson. In the fall of 1990, as U.N.-sanctioned forces assembled in the Gulf and prepared to expel Iraq from Kuwait, Cowley was introduced by a Customs officer to a Major Monkbridge, a senior intelligence official who represented mi6 on the jic. Monkbridge asked about saad 16, where Cowley had worked, and if he could identify certain places on a map of Baghdad, and so on. The full significance of his cooperation came home to Cowley as he watched the U.N.-backed assault on Baghdad during the 1991 Gulf War.

◆ **Gerald James, Chris Gumbley, and Astra Holdings plc**

As we have seen, after buying prb, Astra was made aware that it was fulfilling a number of contracts using conduits and that one of these was to supply

Jordan with the propellant for a very large gun.[31] Upon learning that it was intended for Iraq, James and Gumbley informed the intelligence services through the MOD. At this point, two shipments of propellant had been exported to Jordan on board a Belgian air force C-130 cargo aircraft, arranged by SRC in return for a payment of $25,000 in gold. Bob Primrose, a longstanding contact at DESO, arranged a series of meetings between Gumbley and James and MI6 during October and November 1989. At these meetings, James and Gumbley handed over evidence showing that Bull was behind the project and specifically referring to it as Project Babylon.

At these meetings between James and Gumbley and "Holdness" and Primrose, held at the MOD offices in Stuart House, James and Gumbley concluded that Holdness represented MI6.[32] Furthermore, James and Cowley both suspected that Holdness and Monkbridge, who had debriefed Cowley, were one and the same person. Monkbridge certainly did work for MI6, representing it on the JIC, and Nicholas Bevan of the MOD confirmed that Holdness was "not a Ministry of Defence employee," while Trade Minister Tim Sainsbury stated that he was not, "to the best of my knowledge" a DTI employee.[33] In addition, James suspected that Primrose, although attached to DESO, worked for either MI6 or the Defence Intelligence Staff (DIS) because "he told me when he had finished his period of duty at DESO, he was going back to full-time intelligence work. He made no secret whatsoever of this."[34] As a result of these meetings, MI6 gave the go-ahead for Astra to export the next batch of propellant to Jordan, enabling it, for the time being, to continue to monitor the operation. Subsequently, in late November James and Gumbley provided further documentary evidence to the MOD. From this point, Astra rapidly collapsed.

In terms of intelligence surveillance of exports, James has referred to an occasion when Astra was

> exporting decoy flares to Iran, and [John] Anderson handled the shipment, Jonathan Aitken was involved as our MP. We had difficulty getting an export license, Aitken helped us with that. Anderson handled the documentation, he went to the Iranian procurement office in 4 Victoria Street . . . and subsequently . . . after the Astra upheavals Anderson was interviewed by two people who came up from London who said they were Special Branch officers . . . They showed him photographs of himself coming out of the Iranian procurement office, and that was in '86 or sometime.[35]

For his part, Anderson recalls being told by a security vetting officer visiting Astra that he had been filmed entering and leaving the Iranian offices from an old camper van parked outside![36]

◆ Paul Grecian and Ordtec

Ordtec, which emerged out of the ashes of Allivane, was not a major company. In many ways, its actions have more in common with the Matrix Churchill case than companies like SRC or Astra, in that Paul Grecian supplied information to the intelligence services because doing so strengthened the case for Ordtec to continue its export trade. The emphasis in Paul Grecian's intelligence was not on what Ordtec itself was doing but on what else he observed and heard while in Baghdad on Ordtec business.

Nevertheless, Grecian provided a third independent source of intelligence from arms companies. From the mid-1980s, Grecian had been passing information on to the Special Branch. He had known a Detective Constable Steven Wilkinson for a number of years, and when in 1986 Wilkinson joined SO13, Scotland Yard's antiterrorist branch, Grecian began to bring matters of interest to his attention. Later, in 1988, Ordtec was awarded a contract by SRC to manufacture a fuse assembly line for Iraq via Jordan, and in December of that year Grecian flew to Baghdad to discuss the contract with SRC personnel. While there, he learned of Project Babylon.

The fuse assembly line was shipped to Aqaba, Jordan, in October and November 1989. It was then loaded onto trucks and taken overland to Iraq. Meanwhile, Grecian continued to meet with his Special Branch contact, and at one point they both attended a debriefing session with an MI5 and an MI6 officer in a London hotel.[37] They met again, and in Grecian's opinion "they obviously had other sources which were providing them with a considerable amount of intelligence."[38]

Grecian revisited Iraq several times during 1989 and 1990 and, he says, passed on information to the intelligence services throughout this time at six-weekly debriefing sessions:

> In addition to Project Babylon . . . there were regular discussions about various installations in Iraq and the work that they were involved in; those Iraqis that were responsible for procurement in various areas; those directors that were travelling; Iraqi relationships with Cardoen particularly; and the sort of projects that Cardoen were looking to involve themselves in.[39]

This line of questioning was similar to that which Paul Henderson has described, and just like Henderson, Grecian found that his intelligence contacts were not prepared to intervene on his behalf once Customs and Excise became involved. Grecian's contacts with MI6 were subsequently confirmed by Mark Higson, a former official on the FCO's Iraq Desk, who told the *Daily Telegraph:* "Information was known to me and a number of other people very early on that Ordtech [*sic*] was supplying things via Jordan to Iraq, and giving us information about it. The company name appeared in intelligence reports I saw from March 1989 and Paul Grecian's name individually a little later."[40]

Ordtec had represented one of the government's few successes in prosecuting "arms to Iraq" trials. At the Ordtec trial at Reading Crown Court in 1992, the government had been prepared to claim PII, and in the face of this, the Ordtec Four (Grecian plus Stuart Blackledge, Bryan Mason, and Colin Phillips) had decided to plead guilty. All were found guilty of illegally exporting the fuse assembly line and either given a suspended sentence or fined. However, in the wake of the Matrix Churchill debacle, Grecian went public about his work for the intelligence services, and the Ordtec Four launched an appeal against their convictions.

On 7 November 1995, the Court of Appeal, presided over by Lord Taylor, the lord chief justice, overturned the convictions of the Ordtec Four, ruling them "unsafe and unsatisfactory" on the grounds that the accused had been denied a fair trial because the government had determined to withhold documents key to their defense that suggested, as did evidence subsequently heard at the Scott Inquiry, that the government knew of and turned a blind eye to exports to Jordan, even where it was possible that they were then being passed on to Iraq. Lord Taylor ruled that this amounted to a "material irregularity." At the end of the appeal, Robin Cook, the shadow foreign secretary, demanded that those who had claimed PII "not in the public interest but for the convenience of the Conservative party" should resign.[41] In addition to the PII certificates signed by Kenneth Baker (then home secretary), and Peter Lilley (then secretary of state for trade and industry) at the original Ordtec trial in 1992, at the appeal Home Secretary Michael Howard and Douglas Hurd had signed further certificates to continue to deny them access to documents key to their defense, despite the critical attitude of the cotemporaneous Scott Inquiry to the government's use of PII.

Nevertheless, in July 1995 the appellants were finally granted access to hundreds of documents originally denied them; these confirmed the extent of Grecian's liaison with intelligence and clearly showed that officials had sought to play this down at the original trial.[42] The effect of the documents' release was to destroy the government's case. For example, one shows full British government knowledge of Jordan's conduit role. Written by an official at a British Embassy in the Middle East and dated 28 May 1990, it asks: "Are we trying to . . . stop . . . further Jordanian involvement in Iraqi procurement? Have we not turned a blind eye to Jordanian involvement in the past? (The ambassador seems to think that this has been the case.)"

A second memo provided further confirmation of Grecian's role as an informer, warning: "If Ordtec ends up in court [Grecian] may be persuaded to keep quiet about his connection with [the security services] but there is the obvious risk he will try the 'working for British Intelligence' ploy." The memo concluded by showing just how finely balanced were the considerations of justice versus concealment in the FCO over Iraq. It argued that Grecian could be kept quiet by threatening to make him give evidence in the proposed trial of Cowley and Mitchell: "Perhaps this could be turned to our advantage if he could then be put on the stand . . . However, his personal future might be in some doubt if ever publicly identified as the man who blew the gaff. If we were not too squeamish we might use this point to ensure silence."[43]

The judgment was a warm-up for the Scott Inquiry, in that it found that the "interpretation and application of the [Howe] guidelines were more relaxed and lenient towards Iraq than they had previously been"; in other words, the Howe Guidelines *had* been relaxed after August 1988, no matter how hard William Waldegrave and others tried to prove they had not.[44] It also accepted that Jordan's conduit function had been "well known." The outcome also meant that the government had now failed in every single attempt to bring a prosecution over arms to Iraq. In addition to its failure in the Ordtec case,[45] it had failed in relation to Chris Cowley and Peter Mitchell; Ali Daghir and Jeanine Speckman (the so-called "nuclear triggers" case); BSA (where Customs dropped a case due to come to court immediately after Matrix Churchill); Matrix Churchill itself; and Reginald Dunk and Atlantic Commercial (see below), after the Scott Inquiry revealed how officials from the Foreign Office had interfered with the judicial process.

◆ Informants in the Dual-Use Goods Industry

Unlike the conventional arms industry, the machine tool industry is not dependent on the government for orders—rather, its viability is largely dependent on the export market. Commercial common sense dictates that companies will still approach the DTI for a decision on licensability rather than risk incurring production costs for an order they might not be allowed to export upon completion—not to mention to avoid the risk of prosecution. However, the dual-use nature of certain industrial orders means that this does not necessarily entail "full disclosure." Nonetheless, here just as in the arms industry, businesspeople are used by MI5 and MI6 to collect intelligence. As Paul Henderson of Matrix Churchill noted: "Both branches of the intelligence service often use British businessmen to gather information because they have access to places where government officials are not allowed. We can, by nature of our job, ask questions about a wide variety of matters. In short, we have access. We make unlikely spies."[46]

♦ **Walter Somers, David James, and Sir Hal Miller**

"The Government recently became aware in general terms of an Iraqi project to develop a long-range gun based on designs developed by the late Dr. Gerald Bull."[47] No sooner had Nicholas Ridley made this statement to the House of Commons than this official version of events received a setback from backbench Conservative MP Sir Hal Miller, who asked Ridley:

> Since, more than two years ago, I made an offer to his Department, to the Ministry of Defence and, I believe, to a third agency, on behalf of Walter Somers, to withdraw from the contract, to meet the contract and to enable it to be traced, or to carry on with the contract, and as I repeated that offer 12 months later, does my right hon. Friend share my surprise that there can be any question of prosecuting the company for any contravention of regulations or lack of good faith in the matter?[48]

As we have seen, representatives from Walter Somers had met with Chris Cowley from SRC in May 1988, and as a result reached agreement that Somers would manufacture the barrel for a prototype supergun. Somers did not have the facilities to manufacture a barrel of the dimensions requested for the supergun itself (Babylon), and this contract went to Sheffield Forgemasters, formerly part of British Steel.

Somers's suspicions had led the managing director, Rex Bayliss, to contact Sir Hal Miller. Although Miller declined to appear before the TISC, he later told the Scott Inquiry that in June 1988 he had informed an intelligence officer named "Anderson" ("my recollection is it was something like Anderson") who was "extremely well-informed" about the SRC order, and that he had replied: "Frightfully good of you, old boy, this confirms everything we know."[49] Given that at this time knowledge of Project Babylon was limited, unless this information had been picked up via SIGINT, it can only have come via Bull and src's approaches to the British government or briefing at the State Department. Anderson asked Miller how he could get in touch with the company. Miller told the Scott Inquiry that he replied: " 'They are MOD contractors, ring them up yourself.' He said 'I cannot possibly do that, I do not exist.' "[50]

In view of this, it was agreed that Anderson would find someone in the MOD whom Bayliss could contact; this turned out to be Bill Weir. Miller then gave Bayliss Weir's name and telephone number and told him Weir belonged to "a spooks department or something like that."[51] Hence, before construction of the barrels for either gun had begun, Miller had approached two government departments and a "third agency"—a clear reference to the intelligence services—and had put Rex Bayliss in touch with Bill Weir, the metallurgist who worked for DIS.[52] Miller also revealed to the Scott Inquiry that he had passed on Azzawi's name to Anderson, and offered to pass on his aliases, passport numbers, and flight numbers so that his movements could be followed. He also revealed that Peter Mitchell of Somers had subsequently confided in him that "there had been coaching of Somers people by intelligence as to how they should answer questions . . . in the Trade and Industry Select Committee."[53] David James subsequently denied this to the Scott Inquiry.[54]

David James was the chairman of Eagle Trust, which had purchased Somers in 1989, after it had entered into its contracts with Iraq. He told the inquiry that at a board meeting held on 5 January 1990 he was made aware of an outstanding order for piping for Iraq. When he was shown this order, James noticed that the pipes were tapered and asked the managing director, Peter Mitchell, what they were for: "He replied: 'Well it is for a petrochemical plant. That is what we have been told it is for.' I think I said to him: 'It looks extraordinarily odd . . .' He said: 'We do not know any more than we have been told. They are for a petrochemical plant.' " James described how he became suspicious of this explanation and decided to act: "I phoned MI6 and told them what we had got in the factory and asked them whether it was of any interest to them."[55]

The rest of James's testimony has been described as being, "like a Biggles adventure set in the world of John le Carre,"[56] and it certainly raises a number of questions. However, its significance lies partly in the fact that although this account and the reference to the "petrochemical plant" (the original cover story for Project Babylon) served to confuse the piping James saw with Somers's Project Babylon work, this piping could not have been part of Project Babylon. Somers's piping for Baby Babylon had arrived in Iraq early in

1989 and was test-fired there by Chris Cowley in March, almost a year before James says he was shown it in Halesowen. What had in fact attracted James's attention were the barrels for the SRC 350mm military gun—Project 839— which had been placed with Somers after Project Babylon in the summer of 1989. James described this piping as tapering and having "at the thin end . . . what one can only describe as a thumping great muzzle."[57] However, Baby Babylon did not taper; neither did it have a muzzle. It was based on the technology behind the prototype and may well have grown out of Project Babylon, but it was not part of it. This barrel would not have been long enough to launch satellites. Its only application was as a military gun. It represented a clear breach of the guidelines.

◆ Paul Henderson, Mark Gutteridge, and Matrix Churchill

The Matrix Churchill case shows how arms sales can be approved or allowed to continue to a sensitive destination in return for information on that state's holdings or intentions if that state is of concern in terms of proliferation and/ or is relatively closed and information on it is therefore difficult to come by. The same quid pro quo can also be evidenced in SRC's dealings with China in the mid-1980s and, to a lesser extent, with Ordtec.

Unknown to Bull, Cowley, Grecian, Walter Somers, or the Astra board, British intelligence had been in receipt of Human Intelligence (HUMINT) on the Iraqi military procurement operation from a further independent source before any of them had approached British intelligence and sought approval for their work in Iraq, or sought to reveal their involvement in Iraq. From late 1986, Mark Gutteridge of machine tool manufacturer Matrix Churchill was reporting to MI5 on his contacts and observations in Iraq.

From 1973 to 1979, Paul Henderson had passed information on to MI5 about his business trips to Eastern Europe. He would make contact prior to going abroad and on his return set up a meeting at which he would be debriefed. In addition, he was asked to contact MI5 whenever Eastern European customers or prospective buyers were visiting the Matrix Churchill factory. Of course, Henderson was not alone in this: "Over the years it became obvious that they had a number of contacts to gather information and that they used each of us to verify what the others had told them."[58] As time went on, Henderson was pressed by his MI5 controllers (they were changed in 1976) to identify employees of Eastern Bloc countries he had come into contact with who might be "turned." He was later to be asked to provide information on Iraqis for the same reason. After Henderson had left the company in 1978, he was asked by his last MI5 controller to recommend a replacement. He recommended Mark Gutteridge, later to become export sales manager, and another salesperson.

Gutteridge reported back to MI5 during the 1980s. In March 1987 he took a party of Iraqis led by Safa al-Habobi on a tour of the Matrix Churchill plant in Coventry. He told Henderson (who had returned to work for the company in May 1985) that they were interested in munitions products.[59] Henderson later recalled that

> when we first started working on orders with the Iraqis, Mark had told me he was passing the information on to his contact at MI5. He didn't go into how much detail he was sharing, but I gathered he was giving the intelligence people some good information: the types of machines we and other companies were selling to the Iraqis, where they were being installed in Iraq and what they were being used for.[60]

Indeed, the documents the government was obliged to release at the trial of the Matrix Churchill Three—Paul Henderson (former managing director), Peter Allen (former marketing director), and Trevor Abraham (former commercial manager)—revealed that Gutteridge had passed on much valuable information, in which the first reference to the Iraqi arms procurement network was made at a 6 May 1987 meeting. Crucially, at an early stage, Gutteridge was able to provide his MI5 controller, "Ford," with details of arms production at the Hutteen establishment. For example, one crucial early report dated 11 November 1987 read:

> According to a British businessman involved in some of the deals, the Iraqi government has been signing contracts with British, West German, Italian and Swiss firms for the purchase of general purpose heavy machinery for the production of armaments in Iraq . . . The armaments production is to take place in two main factories in Iraq: the Hutteen General Establishment for Mechanical Industries in Iskandaria, and the Nassr General Establishment for Mechanical Industries in Taji, near Basra. Both factories are large by western standards and the annual production targets for the Nassr factory (the smaller of the two) are as follows:
> i) 10,000 122mm missiles per annum
> ii) 150,000 130mm shells p.a.
> iii) 100,000 mortar shells (80mm and 120mm) p.a.
> iv) 300,000 fin stabilised 155mm shells p.a. (similar to those produced by PRB in Belgium).

At the Matrix Churchill trial, Ford recalled how Gutteridge passed on information about the supply of arms-producing technology to Iraq at monthly meetings between 1987 and 1989 and supplied him with drawings of machine tools ordered by Iraq. He also confirmed that MI5 had recommended the approval of export licenses for Matrix Churchill exports to Iraq so that it could continue to monitor the Iraqi procurement program.

In 1988 Gutteridge left the company, and when he in turn was asked to suggest a replacement contact, he recommended Paul Henderson. Less than a month later, "John Balsom" of MI6 contacted Henderson, and the two met for the first time in September 1988.[61] They met again in London in October, when Balsom asked about Chilean arms manufacturer Cardoen, and Gerald Bull and SRC. They met for a third time in January 1989, when Henderson was able to brief Balsom on SRC, having been approached to supply machine tools for a factory designed to manufacture fuses. They met regularly from then on, for example in April 1989, just as Henderson was about to leave for Baghdad to attend the International Military Exhibition, when Balsom asked Henderson to collect intelligence from the exhibition. On his return he met Balsom, handed over the literature he had collected, answered the MI6 man's questions on Cardoen and the French exhibits, and disclosed that he had learned of SRC's intention to acquire the Lear Fan plant in Northern Ireland. A further meeting took place in August 1989, when Henderson agreed to travel to London to meet Balsom's superiors. The two of them met again in London in September 1989. On 22 September Henderson met Balsom and was driven to a safe house in Carlton Gardens, London, where he was introduced to three other men, quizzed about Project 1728 (a SCUD missile modification/upgrade program), and asked to point out on a wall-sized aerial photograph where it was located. He also discussed developments at the Nassr establishment; Cardoen; SRC; and, for the first time, the supergun program.

Henderson continued to pass information to MI6 after this meeting, for example about the production of 122mm and 155mm shells at Al Hutteen, the work going on in Sheds C and D at Nassr on a variety of artillery and rocket programs, and in particular the work being conducted there on Project 144 (a ballistic missile project toward which Matrix Churchill had been asked to contribute). On 5 March 1990 he again met Balsom, this time in London, where a scientist accompanying the MI6 man asked about Project Babylon. He met Balsom immediately before leaving for a frosty visit to post-Teesport Iraq in April 1990, and again on his return. Their final meeting took place on 31 July 1990 in London. By this time Henderson was being asked to delve ever deeper into an Iraqi procurement operation that had clearly got out of hand, and in an increasingly dangerous environment. However, after Customs and Excise officers arrested Henderson on 16 October 1990, he found that Balsom no longer returned his calls. This relationship was the heart of Henderson's defense at the 1992 Old Bailey trial: Far from deceiving the government about the true nature of his relationship with Iraq, he and Gutteridge had put themselves at risk by reporting to MI5 and MI6 on Iraq's military buildup.

Henderson also believed that his and Gutteridge's intelligence was being shared with the United States, writing in his autobiography: "As early as December 1987 information on the Iraqi arms network provided to MI5 by Mark Gutteridge had been passed on to the CIA. Since then there had been a steady sharing of intelligence between the two countries." He also noted that in 1989 Balsom had told him how "MI6 had widened the network that was receiving my information. It had been going to the other ministries; and to the Americans, the CIA."[62]

◆ SIGINT

In addition to these HUMINT sources, British and Western intelligence agencies were, of course, well positioned to monitor arms trade developments via SIGINT. Because SRC was based in Belgium but was operating in Baghdad and was involved elsewhere during the course of its work in Iraq (Germany, France, Britain, etc.), there was a clear need to communicate via telephone and fax. Indeed, SIGINT traditionally forms the bulk of raw intelligence.[63] John Major told the Scott Inquiry that the proportions were roughly two-thirds SIGINT and one-third HUMINT, and this impression has been confirmed by a former JIC official, Robin Robison.[64] Robison was also in a position to confirm the interest of British and other Western intelligence agencies in the international arms trade; when asked to what extent this was regularly monitored by Western intelligence agencies, he replied: "All the time. I mean that, all the time. It was a major piece of interest when I was there, GCHQ was constantly churning out stuff on the arms trade." And when asked if this was all fed into the JIC, he said: "Yes, I am confident of that because of the quantity of it and there was actually an officer whose sole job was to keep an eye on what was known as technological transfers . . . The Middle East was watched constantly, so that when, for example, the Halabja incident happened, we knew within minutes."[65]

This SIGINT would be collected through a global network, at the heart of which lies the 1947 U.K.-U.S.A. Agreement, for many years treated as a national security secret by most of its signatories. It is an agreement involving the United States (the "first party"), through the National Security Agency (NSA), and four "second parties": the United Kingdom (via GCHQ); Australia (via the Australian Defence Signals Directorate [DSD]); Canada (via the Canadian Communications Security Establishment [CSE]); and New Zealand (via its Government Communications Security Bureau [GCSB]). It divides responsibility for monitoring different regions of the globe among the signatories and provides for the sharing of the SIGINT that is produced.[66] As John Major conceded, the bulk of intelligence reaching the JIC is SIGINT from GCHQ and the more important listening outposts, like the soon-to-be-abandoned Little Sai Wan Station in Hong Kong, and (important for targeting the Middle East) the Abut Sovereign Base Area on Cyprus.

However, the agreement did more than just carve up the globe; it institutionalized intelligence links, cooperation, and exchanges among the signatories, creating very close ties over the years. The existence of U.S. SIGINT facilities in the United Kingdom (Menwith Hill), Australia (Pine Gap—the Joint Defence Space Research Facility), and Germany (Bad Aibling)[67] has further cemented these ties. The exchange of personnel has, for instance, resulted in a CIA representative sitting on the U.K. JIC, British representatives working in the NSA, and liaison staff working under diplomatic cover in the relevant embassies. Although there have been fluctuations in this relationship—usually relating to the exposure of spies on both sides—the U.S. intelligence relationship with Britain, although somewhat uneven (Britain is very much the junior partner), has been a central plank of the "special relationship." It has been so important because of the continuing commonality of U.S. and U.K. interests across the world. As one commentator put it: "The two countries often see the world through similar lenses because they share a common language and to some extent a common political culture—or at least a common subscription to basic political values."[68]

Conversely, the absence of such ties explains why other European states remain outside this intelligence-sharing relationship. In particular, French foreign policy has followed far too independent a path for it to be allowed such privileged access to U.S. intelligence. The often different agenda of French foreign policy, especially in the Middle East—for example, the course of French diplomacy during the Desert Shield phase of the conflict in the Gulf—has meant that it cannot be trusted in the same way that Britain can. Indeed, France seems to have been an object of U.S. intelligence operations rather than a partner in them in recent years. Similarly, there is little advantage from a U.S. perspective in freely sharing intelligence with, say, Germany, Italy, or Spain, in that their willingness or ability to reciprocate is limited.

Despite this, several ministers went to some lengths at the Scott Inquiry to deemphasize the significance of intelligence[69] and to indicate that all relevant intelligence was not always passed up through the departmental chain. However, none dwelt at length on the role of the JIC, or the possible usefulness of its "red books." It was very unlikely that these would be mislaid or go unread:

> ordinary departmental records and so on at sort of lower level were more likely to get buried at the bottom of an in-tray. The JIC stuff and Cabinet papers doesn't get buried in an in-tray. It comes in a red box marked "Secret"—you open it, you read it, and you send it back. It is a priority. If it didn't come back within two days we rang up and said "where the hell is it?"[70]

♦ Other Sources

There was also evidence from other sources suggesting that the government was aware of various activities involving British companies and nationals on behalf of Iraq from an early stage, even from their inception. For example, in August 1989 the government, on the advice of the FCO, turned down a bid by SRC for a development grant from the Northern Ireland Industrial Development Board (NIIDB), following its purchase of the former Lear Fan plant in Belfast for £3 million.[71] The purchase had been intended to allow SRC/ATI to produce the carbon fiber required for the nose cones of the Martlet IV projectiles Bull was designing, which would be fired from the supergun.[72] In September 1989 Richard Needham, a junior Northern Ireland minister, wrote to Kevin McNamara, the shadow spokesperson, explaining that the bid was rejected because the FCO believed that SRC intended to use it to manufacture and export missile components: "The Foreign and Commonwealth Office said that Iraq was known to be involved in an advanced ballistic development programme in co-operation with other countries, including Argentina. Composite materials, which the former Lear Fan factory produced, could be used in ballistic missiles and other weapons systems."[73] The FCO subsequently noted that at this time they "were aware that SRC did consultancy work for the defence industry; that directors of SRC, including Dr Bull, were convicted in 1980 in the US of contravening the UN arms embargo by shipping artillery to South Africa; and that there were links between SRC and the Iraqi Government."[74]

In a letter to Philippe Glibert of PRB, Bull told how he and his son, Stephen, had visited Belfast at the invitation of the NIIDB and how subsequently

> the Foreign Office decided to run a press campaign through "leaks" . . . The utter nonsense they spread was beyond belief. A warehouse and scrap equipment becomes the key to UK security etc . . . I addressed a blunt memorandum to the Foreign Office on the whole matter. Through publicity, they were making me a target of terrorist groups. I was advised in a letter of an imminent "accident." The Foreign Office was advised about the curious fact that accidents often happen in series.
>
> After the memo was delivered, the whole matter was dropped from the press. Also we were assured that the action was taken by "a few irresponsible juniors and did not reflect the Foreign Office views of myself, our companies, the past etc."[75]

If nothing else, this clearly suggests that Bull had contacts in, or at least contact with, the British FCO, and that he had received some form of reply from them. Despite the existence of this letter, when asked about Bull's contacts with the FCO, Foreign Office Minister Douglas Hogg told Tam Dalyell, MP: "As far as we have been able to establish, there is no record of any meeting between this Department and Dr Gerald Bull."

◆ Intelligence and the TISC

In attempting to establish just what the various arms of the British government knew about the role of British companies in arming Iraq and when, the gaze of the TISC belatedly fell on the role of the intelligence services. However, a number of witnesses made it clear that they were unwilling to discuss such matters with the committee. When Labour MP Dr. John Gilbert asked the DTI's John Meadway whether the intelligence services had requested the DTI to allow the export of arms to Iraq "for the sake of surveillance," Meadway restricted himself to replying: "It is not the place of a government department to discuss matters of the intelligence service in public."[76]

Customs was of no greater help. Alexander Russell, a Customs commissioner, told the TISC that Customs only became aware of the supergun's existence at the beginning of April 1990, about a week before the Teesport seizure, and that this knowledge was the result of a tip-off from within the interdepartmental "machinery." He refused to locate the source any more precisely, saying he was "constrained from going further and identifying specific parts of the machinery of government"[77]—a clear reference to the intelligence services. This impression was strengthened by further answers indicating that the information had come via an informal tip-off rather than through a formal interdepartmental meeting.[78] In general, Customs' testimony merely frustrated the committee. Controversy about its highly limited nature[79] was fueled by the disclosure that John MacGregor, then leader of the House of Commons, had told Customs officials that they need not answer the committee's questions about the supergun. In addition, the fact that the prosecution of the three Matrix Churchill executives was pending, and that matters relating to the export of machine tools and so on were sub judice, affected the breadth and depth of the Committee's investigations.

Furthermore, there is a case to be made that the DTI, FCO, and MOD sought to mislead the investigation. The DTI produced a lengthy memorandum showing direct exports to Iraq, when in reality, as evidence to the Scott Inquiry subsequently made abundantly clear, it was an open secret within Whitehall that the most sensitive items were being routed through Jordan and also Saudi Arabia, Kuwait, and so on. Even then, witnesses like James and Cowley alerted the TISC to the role of Jordan, although the issue was not pursued. Furthermore, even though new evidence was emerging toward the end of the inquiry concerning the transnational procurement network, the Conservative majority on the committee still insisted that a prearranged nine-day junket to China, Taiwan, and Hong Kong should go ahead in preference to the investigation, thereby giving up ten to fourteen days toward the end of the investigation during which this aspect could have been investigated further.[80]

Although Sir Hal Miller declined to appear before the committee, he had warned, following the arrest of Peter Mitchell of Somers, that he possessed detailed notes of his contacts with Whitehall and, if necessary, would give evidence at Mitchell's trial, which would include the contents of a letter to Mrs. Thatcher. He said that "it was inconceivable that the Government would want his evidence given in open court."[81]

Former associates of Gerald Bull repeatedly claimed that British intelligence knew of the project, that Bull had held talks with British Embassy officials in Baghdad, and that he and Cowley had briefed MI6 back in September 1988.[82] Moreover, in 1992 *U.S. News and World Report* reported: "[U.S.] intelligence sources confirm that US listening posts made more than 1,200 intelligence intercepts of Bull's activities in the years before Iraq's August 1990 invasion of Kuwait."[83]

However, it was Chris Cowley who was best placed to comment on all of this. No one else who gave evidence to the TISC or the Scott Inquiry was closer to Project Babylon, Gerald Bull, their Iraqi customer, and the arrangements made to ensure the project's continuation than Cowley (he was described by the TISC as being "at the heart of a web of deception"). Given his proximity to events until his departure from SRC in May 1989, his ability to provide information unobtainable elsewhere, and his availability to give evidence, it would have been natural for the committee to attach particular importance to his testimony. In practice, the opposite happened. Any of his testimony judged uncorroborated appears not to have been considered, and most of his written evidence was omitted from the published report.

Cowley later told the Scott Inquiry that he would have been able to provide the committee with a wider range of information, had he been asked for it. But unusually, the night before he was due to give evidence, he was contacted in his hotel room by Ken Warren, the TISC chairman, who asked if they could meet that evening, which they did. Warren later defended his actions by saying: "I just did not want him to feel there was any pressure to say things he was not sure of."[84] Warren asked Cowley what he intended to say to the committee the next day. Cowley recalled:

> I went into considerable detail about George Wong and his relationship with Bull and the obtaining of prior permission for the SRC Iraqi projects from the British Government. I described the other projects that SRC were involved in, in addition to Supergun . . . I mentioned the names of companies which were actively engaged in supplying military equipment to Iraq . . . I described how British machine tools were involved in the manufacture of the ammunition used in Iraqi artillery . . . I further mentioned the use of Jordan to transfer British military equipment to Iraq.

However, when he came to give evidence the next day, he was surprised that the questioning avoided these areas: "It focused entirely on Supergun and not on the wider question of military sales to Iraq which I had spoken about at length and in detail with Mr Warren."[85]

Gerald James also considered that he had been pressured before appearing before the committee. He received a telephone call from Astra consultant and MP Gerald Howarth the night before he was due to appear and was told "not to go over the top" in his evidence. Howarth later explained: "I told him not to be too wild because it wouldn't be helpful to him.[86] James has recounted how "late in the evening before I was due to give evidence I was telephoned by Mr Gerald Howarth MP. He told me in the course of the conversation that he was working for Mrs Thatcher. He additionally said that he and others felt it would be in my own interest if I kept a low profile in relation to what I had to say."[87]

When he came to give evidence, Cowley told the committee that, as discussed above, MI6 and other Western intelligence agencies knew of the supergun project before contracts were placed. Furthermore, he claimed that the Midland Bank's MBGITS and Whitehall military sales experts, both with intelligence connections, were represented in Baghdad when Bull negotiated arms deals and so were aware of the relationship between Bull, SRC, and Iraq.[88]

For the Scott Inquiry, Cowley built on his evidence to the TISC and went on to record occasions on which he observed British-made arms in Baghdad, in apparent contravention of the Howe Guidelines. For instance, in August 1988 Cowley visited an artillery range to conduct tests for the supergun project: "During several visits to the firing range I saw pallets marked MOD RO Jordan. There were pallets of shells which measured 4 × 3 × 2 m. Put simply there were thousands of shells on these crates and pallets marked in this way. New supplies arrived constantly brought by lorries with Jordanian civil markings."[89]

At Hutteen, where SRC was involved in a project to design a 155mm shell for the Iraqis, the template that was used was, according to Cowley, a British shell that had arrived from RO via Jordan on pallets marked "Al Fao Jordan." At Hutteen, Azzawi informed Cowley that the ammunition he could see arriving to be fused had come from Britain's RO via PRB in Belgium.[90] Moreover, Cowley records:

> In January 1989 I visited Amman [Jordan] with an Iraqi official . . . to clear the 350mm model Supergun propellant consignment delivered by the Belgium Royal Airforce a few days earlier. The propellant was being stored in a large area secured by the Jordanian army . . . I noted that convoys of lorries were arriving, loading and setting off along the road which ran into Iraq. I noticed among the items stored there crates and pallets of shells marked for shipment to Cyprus and Egypt as well as for shipment directly to Jordan . . . Whilst walking around the warehouses I saw extremely large amounts of weapons and ammunition . . . The source of manufacture was clear from markings on crates and pallets although many were marked for shipment to non-Arab countries. I noted that some of the pallets were marked as originating from MOD RO. The quantities of UK manufactured ammunition would, in my estimation, have been worth several millions of pounds.[91]

The TISC's report avoids any detailed assessment of the evidence of intelligence knowledge and involvement in the arming of Iraq and limits itself to observing that the investigation "raises serious and important questions about the accountability of the intelligence services both to Ministers and to Parliament."[92] This conclusion was the source of some friction within the committee, with some members clearly unhappy about the thrust of the final report, on which the committee members divided along party political lines. Doug Hoyle, MP for one was angry that it barely dealt with the role of the government and intelligence services, arguing that "the fact is the Government knew from the very beginning."[93] He suggested the insertion of a paragraph into the report critical of both:

> It seems hardly credible that a large military project such as Babylon would not have been known to British and other intelligence services. Dr Cowley claimed that at a very early stage he had personally kept the British intelligence service informed about this matter and to his knowledge Dr Bull had been in touch with the US and other intelligence services from the outset. Certainly Gumbley and James of Astra and Kock claimed they approached MOD and security services in September and October 1989, yet no statement was made to the House until April 1990. It is a serious matter that Ministers were not informed that brings into question the accountability of intelligence sources to their responsible Ministers and we leave it to others to decide whether these matters should be considered elsewhere.[94]

However, Chairman Warren used his casting vote to keep this criticism out of the published report. He did this on three other occasions to ensure the passage of amendments that minimized references to the involvement of the intelligence services.[95] Other members also proposed a number of amendments that served to omit references to the intelligence services, thereby lending greater weight to the importance of the formal administrative failure. At a news conference to present the report, described as "sometimes heated," Jim Cousins, MP argued that there was "absolutely no doubt that Parliament was deceived about this matter. Either the intelligence services knew about this from the beginning or they are grossly incompetent and ought to be sacked."[96]

In order to achieve this result, several areas that would have called into question the wisdom of such a narrow focus were left open. The question of why ministers were not informed in autumn 1989, it having been established that people within government definitely knew of the project then, was not fully explored; neither was Cowley's evidence on British intelligence or the role of George Wong. The circumstances surrounding the dropping of charges against Cowley were left open, as were those surrounding the mysterious explosion at PRB's Kaulille plant. Furthermore, the evidence that Forgemasters and Somers were knowingly involved in a trans-European procurement network was not followed up. Finally, investigation of areas that involved alleged intelligence activity was hampered by the nonappearance of witnesses (Hal Miller, George Wong, Roger Harding, Bob Primrose, "Holdness"), the sending of the wrong witnesses, and the stubborn refusal of government witnesses to say what they knew (DTI, Customs and Excise, attorney general, MOD, FCO).

On 15 November 1990, charges of illegally exporting British-made arms were dropped against both Cowley and Mitchell. In Mitchell's case, insufficient evidence was cited, whereas in Cowley's it was considered "inappropriate" to proceed against him alone, even though Cowley himself admitted he had a prima facie case to answer.[97] Attorney General Sir Patrick Mayhew was somewhat reticent in explaining this decision when he appeared before the TISC and would go no further than asserting that evidence regarding the dropping of charges should not be "paraded in public." In addition, he "endorsed the intention of [Customs and Excise] not to disclose evidence that had been revealed to them in the course of their investigations," which could have shed light on the episode.[98] Hence, no convincing explanation has ever been offered of why Chris Cowley should not have been prosecuted, other than fear of embarrassment. After all, his position was very different from that of Peter Mitchell. Whereas Mitchell was accepting orders and, supposedly, accepting the presentation of those orders made by SRC, Cowley was actually placing the orders. At a meeting between the attorney general and customs officials to discuss the prosecutions, a minute records the attorney general as noting: "Counsel were clear that . . . *with the exception of Mr Cowley*, prosecutions would fail by a substantial margin."[99] At the same meeting, Sir Brian Unwin, then chairman of Customs and Excise, is recorded as saying that on the the basis of the evidence and report submitted to him, he had "no doubts as to the guilt of the respective defendants"[100] even though they had yet to come to court, let alone be convicted!

◆ From Monitoring to Manipulation?

As outlined above, the entire Iraqgate episode needs to be seen against the background of a concerted operation to back Iraq during the Iran-Iraq War and thereafter in its rearmament so that it could "contain" Iran from within the "family of nations." Having allowed and participated in the arming of

Iraq, Western policy toward Iraq began to shift toward the end of 1989. This shift may be attributed partly to Iraq's mounting difficulties in paying for arms, but the more likely explanation is Saddam's ambition for Iraq and the unwelcome direction in which Iraqi interest was clearly beginning to point: nonconventional technology.

As long as Iraq's concern had been conventional arms, meeting this demand had been consistent with Western interests. However, from 1989 there is evidence of growing British and Western anxiety. At the Matrix Churchill trial, Alan Clark remarked that by 1989 concern "had started to shift towards Iraq's nuclear and chemical capability, and this rather pedestrian technology [i.e. conventional arms and technology] was no longer a matter of very great concern to us."[101] This was also the central concern of Henderson's MI6 controller. At their first meeting he "started to discuss how keen the government were to keep an eye on the Iraqis. With the Iran-Iraq war just ended, Whitehall was worried that Saddam Hussein might turn his resources to more destructive weapons: nuclear warheads, missiles, and chemical and biological devices."[102]

At a later meeting he told Henderson: "We're not really interested in conventional armaments."[103] It has been suggested by defense industry sources that the 1990 Ali Daghir capacitors "sting" operation was set up to signal this concern and to draw attention to this change of direction.[104] Furthermore, by late 1989 there was evidence that Iraq's intended end-use for Project Babylon was somewhat different from that envisaged in Bull's earlier HARP work, and that the technology involved could eventually be harnessed for direct military purposes—through Project 839, for instance. Furthermore, the Iraqis were beginning to involve Bull in missile design work as the price for continuing with his personal priority, Project Babylon.

Such developments seem to have strained the tacit alliance between the United States, Britain, and Israel, which seems to have needed to be in place for the covert arming of Iraq to go ahead. Such developments potentially affected Israeli security. Hence, Western intelligence was required to move by late 1989 to early 1990 from monitoring the procurement operation to manipulating it. Given its approval and knowledge of this trade, the option of taking remedial action through the conventional route of Customs and the courts was not the first choice of the intelligence services, as their involvement could be exposed in court. Cases where no rules had been broken but action had to be taken—as with Astra, for example—would have been even more problematic. Hence, other steps were taken to terminate Iraqi interest in this area.

On 5 December 1989, following Astra's contacts with the intelligence services to inform them of the "Jordanian" propellant contract, there was an explosion inside the press that manufactured the propellant at the Kaulille plant in Belgium (referred to by Gerald Bull as the "so-called accident"). The plant was quite remote and, although fenced, quite difficult to police effectively. The explosion happened during a tea break when no one was at the press, so there were no injuries. This had been one of only two or three presses in existence that were able to produce propellant to the specifications required for Babylon. Did this represent an effort to sabotage Project Babylon, given the direction in which the Iraqis were now looking to apply its technology? The answer to this question seems to rest on whether the propellant was stable, or whether it was unstable and could have combusted and itself caused the explosion. John Pike of PRB suggested to the TISC that this was the case, and that the likely cause was an "air bubble in the propellant dough."[105] However, according to Chris Cowley's evidence: "The Supergun propellant charge was extremely stable, it was even difficult to burn with a match."[106] He has also recalled his time working for the firm Henry Wigan in Hereford, where SAS soldiers would visit the factory as part of their training to learn how to disable such equipment.[107] Cowley is convinced that the explosion was an act of sabotage. He points out that if the propellant really was so unstable, it would have set off multiple explosions. Yet, although there were 12 metric tons of propellant in the press at the time of the explosion, it didn't all go off. The explosion at Kaulille was small, but given its location, it made the press inoperable. Are we to believe, then, that just a little of the propellant in the press went off—just enough to damage the column and prevent further production?

When giving evidence to the TISC, Gerald James was pressed by Chairman Kenneth Warren, who suggested that the propellant "would probably be in an unstable condition anyway, would it not?" and told James: "I know you are not a technical man . . . You were dealing with material which could be recognized to be unstable?"[108] However, Belgian anti-terrorist police determined the explosion to be sabotage, as did Astra's loss adjustors, Harris and Partners. James himself insists that "it was non-volatile material, the only way that thing could have blown up was if someone had put an explosive charge to it."[109] Conveniently, the final MOD and intelligence contact with Astra occurred just prior to the explosion, on 23 November.

From the accounts of businesspeople involved, the intelligence services evidently received intelligence on Iraqi arms procurement and British involvement in it from several sources. With one exception, the accounts discussed (those of Chris Cowley, Gerald James, Chris Gumbley, Paul Henderson, Mark Gutteridge, Paul Grecian, and Sir Hal Miller) are consistent. They recall evidence of intelligence knowledge from other sources, similar lines of interest and questioning, and possibly even the involvement of the same intelligence officers. The exception is the account of David James, although he is describing contact that began after most of the above ended. In addition, other structural factors would have worked to aid the monitoring of the international arms trade. Taken together, these allowed British and other intelligence agencies to monitor at least the parameters of the Iraqi military procurement operation following the Iran-Iraq War and to pull the plug when it clearly began to exceed the bounds of the desirable.

Nevertheless, the modus operandi of the intelligence services in this episode raises questions about accountability that the application of PII was intended to conceal. These questions relate to the demise of major companies after they had purchased companies apparently involved in an illegal arms-trading network: the demise of Astra after its purchases of BMARC, the Walters Group, and particularly PRB, and of Ferranti following its purchase of James Guerin's intelligence-connected ISC.[110] Further questions relate to the consequences of such a heavy reliance on businesspeople and industrialists in such circumstances, when the agencies are not prepared to intervene on their behalf if they are arrested, nor make it sufficiently clear in advance that their cooperation offers no protection against prosecution (which would certainly have made spying less attractive to this group). This was one of the issues raised by Balsom. Following Paul Henderson's arrest, he noted: "This case shows again the dangers of us concentrating our anti-proliferation efforts on British businessmen who often end up getting into trouble." The question remains, however, whether the issue of accountability is as central with regard to overseas intelligence operations—where national security is more clearly at issue, and where many would argue that the ends justify the means—as it is to the domestic activities of MI5, where national security seems to be in the eye of the beholder. After all, the operation to frustrate the Iraqi nonconventional weapons procurement effort was not without success, but because of the Western approach to Iraq and the Middle East during the 1980s that made it necessary, neither was it without cost.

NOTES

1 Scott Inquiry—Day 16: Evidence of Peter Vereker, p. 7.
2 Scott Inquiry—Day 40: Evidence of Simon Sherrington, p. 68.
3 Scott Inquiry—Day 20: Evidence of Ian Blackley, p. 99. My emphasis.
4 Scott Inquiry: Statement of Chris Cowley, p. 3.
5 TISC: HC-86-vi & vii, p. 259.
6 TISC: HC-86-viii, p. 281. John Goulden of the FCO said: "The Embassy did send a report back on what they saw at that fair, because arms fairs are a very important source of military intelligence and we encourage our Attaches *and other people* to produce such reports." Ibid. My emphasis.
7 Paul Henderson: *The Unlikely Spy: An Autobiography*, London, Bloomsbury, 1993, p. 149.
8 Scott Inquiry—Day 50: Evidence of Alan Clark, pp. 112–121.
9 Interview with Robin Robison, 3.27.95.
10 Scott Inquiry: Statement of Chris Cowley, pp. 4–5.
11 *Guardian*, 3.7.92.
12 Interview with Chris Cowley, Bristol, 2.23.95.
13 Letter from Chris Cowley to A. Kennon, 2.19.92, TISC: EQ94. Unpublished evidence.
14 *Guardian*, 1.25.95.
15 Interview with Robin Robison, London, 3.27.95.
16 Scott Inquiry: Statement of Gerald James, p. 19.
17 Chris Cowley: *Guns, Lies and Spies*, pp. 109–110.
18 Interview with Gerald James, 3.1.95.
19 Ibid.
20 TISC: HC-86-iv, EQ31, p. 191.
21 In addition, at a later date, the Saudi government was another made aware of the supergun program—it approved an Iraqi request to test-fire the gun, whose 1,000 km range meant that the Martlet 1 projectile would land in Saudi Arabia.
22 Scott Inquiry: Statement of Chris Cowley, p. 9.
23 Letter from Chris Cowley to Andrew Kennon, clerk to the TISC, 2.19.92. Unpublished evidence.
24 Scott Inquiry: Statement of Chris Cowley, pp. 10–11. With regard to U.S. clearance, as discussed elsewhere in this volume, it was Cowley's understanding that this was given at an SRC–State Department meeting in March 1988 where "a number of projects were discussed. One became known as the Al Fao, the 210mm self-propelled gun, the derivative of the GC45, the 155mm gun, certain ballistics programmes, and a continuation of Project HARP which subsequently . . . became Project Babylon." TISC: HC-86-iv, p. 208.
25 The process was that Chris Cowley would draft out a fax on SRC stationery and then Monique Jamine would type it up and return the draft to him. The originals were seized from the SRC office in Brussels by the Belgian police after Bull's murder.
26 See chapter 4.
27 TISC: HC-86-iv, EQ31, p. 190.
28 Cited in W. Lowther: *Arms and the Man*, p. 243.
29 TISC: HC-86, p. xlv.
30 For instance, it voted against including an explicit reference to Cowley's faxes (TISC: HC-86, p. lx) and against inserting a sentence after that quoted above which said: "It would be surprising if such a wide range of activities had not come to the attention of the intelligence services. If it did not this suggests unacceptable failures on behalf of the intelligence services." Ibid., p. lxvi.

31 It was not necessary to have any further details about Project Babylon to make this assertion. The size of the gun could be calculated from the size of the propellant ordered.

32 The MOD went some way toward confirming this at the time of the TISC inquiry. It submitted a memorandum dated 17 February 1992 (TISC: HC-86-xv, EQ85), which in part stated: "Mr Holdness is not, and never has been, an employee of the Ministry of Defence."

33 Robin Robison confirmed that Monkbridge attended JIC as a representative of MI6. On Holdness, see Pike, TISC: HC-86-xv, EQ88, the MOD memorandum, TISC: HC-86-xv, EQ85, and ibid., p. 494. Menzies Campbell had pressed Bevan: "You said he was not an employee of the MOD, but that was not an answer to [the] question. [It] asked was he known to the MOD," to which Bevan replied: "I cannot make any further comment."

34 Scott Inquiry: Statement of Gerald James, p. 15.

35 Interview with Gerald James, London, 3.1.95.

36 Letter from John Anderson, 8.23.95.

37 A Special Branch witness statement prepared for his 1992 trial confirmed that Grecian met with the Special Branch to pass on information about Project Babylon and that "on 21st December 1989 GRECIAN was introduced to the appropriate authorities who had an interest in the matters." *Dispatches*, Grecian Tragedy, Channel 4, 5.5.93. See also the *Daily Telegraph*, 7.31.95. The basis of his conviction was that although MI6 acknowledged the intelligence he had provided, this provision began only after the completion of the contracts with Iraq over which he was being prosecuted.

38 *Dispatches*: Grecian Tragedy.

39 Ibid.

40 *Daily Telegraph*, 7.31.95.

41 *Financial Times*, 11.8.95.

42 For a good summary of the appeal, see Patrick Fitzgerald: Ordtec Verdict Shames Government, *New Statesman and Society*, 10.10.95, p. 7, and the *Daily Telegraph* and the *Independent*, 11.8.95.

43 *Sunday Times*, 9.17.95. See also the *Times*, 9.18.95.

44 See chapter 3.

45 There is a final part to the Grecian saga. In December 1995, Grecian was arrested by Interpol agents as he landed in Johannesburg, South Africa, for a holiday with his South African fiancée. New Jersey–based U.S. prosecutors had requested Grecian's arrest and extradition, as he was wanted in the United States on charges of fraud, perjury, and conspiracy to sell weapons components to Iraq. A South African magistrate refused to grant bail, because Grecian's links with MI5 made him a "flight risk." *Independent*, 12.23.95.

46 Paul Henderson: *The Unlikely Spy*, pp. 24–25.

47 *Hansard*, 4.18.90, col. 1427.

48 Ibid., col. 1430.

49 Scott Inquiry: Day 8—Evidence of Sir Hall Miller, p. 10.

50 Ibid., p. 11.

51 *Financial Times*, 12.4.91.

52 This was confirmed by former JIC official Robin Robison. Interview, 3.27.95. The TISC hearings, held with Weir in camera, went some way to confirming this. TISC member Menzies Campbell began one question to him with the preamble: "But you are in a part of the Ministry of Defence, and I do not want you to tell me too much about it, which is highly specialised, which is not simply a place to which applications come for consideration. I guess you do a whole range of work in which you initiate action rather than respond to pieces of paper which are sent to your desk." TISC: HC-86-vi & vii, p. 269.

53 Scott Inquiry—Day 8: Evidence of Sir Hal Miller, p. 27. See also pp. 37–38.

54 Scott Inquiry—Day 15: Evidence of David James, p. 63. He said that it was "a matter of

undebated acceptance that there would be no answer given on any subject of intelligence." Ibid., p. 67.

55 Scott Inquiry: Day 15—Evidence of David James, p. 16. However, his TISC evidence is characterized by a reluctance to admit to any such contact, despite what he and Sir Hal Miller later told the Scott Inquiry. TISC: HC-86-ii, pp. 134–135.

56 Richard Norton-Taylor: *Truth Is a Difficult Concept: Inside the Scott Inquiry*, London, 4th Estate, 1995, p. 123.

57 TISC: HC-86-ii, p. 125. "If you went to the Tower of London or any museum you would see an identical piece of metal stuck on the end of anything which is a cannon to the naked eye . . . it was indistinguishable from any cannon from any period of warfare." Ibid.

58 Paul Henderson: *The Unlikely Spy*, p. 29.

59 By this time Matrix Churchill already exported machines intended for munitions production to the United States, France, Belgium, Pakistan, India, and Egypt. Ibid., p. 77.

60 Ibid., p. 93.

61 For whatever reason, in a report dated 10.31.90, Balsom says that, "my contact with him only began in May 1989."

62 Ibid., pp. 172, 185.

63 For one example of a document sent from the Iraqi military attaché in London to Baghdad, and intercepted by the United States as long ago as 1979, see the *Independent on Sunday*, 9.30.90. This document was one of thousands captured and later published by the Iranian government, following the storming of the U.S. Embassy in Tehran.

64 Interview with Robin Robison, 3.27.95.

65 Ibid.

66 On the U.K.–U.S.A. Agreement, see Jeffrey T. Richelson: *The U.S. Intelligence Community*, Boulder, Westview, 3rd ed. 1995, ch. 12. However, in 1985, in retaliation for its antinuclear stance, New Zealand was cut out of much of this intelligence-sharing arrangement by the Reagan administration. In 1994 the Clinton administration restored the status quo ante.

67 Germany is one of several "third parties" to the agreement. In practice, their access to intelligence gleaned by the first and second parties is more limited.

68 Ken Matthews: *The Gulf Conflict and International Relations*, London, Routledge, 1993, p. 85.

69 A good summary of this is contained in Richard Norton-Taylor: *Truth Is a Difficult Concept*, pp. 99–109. The activities of the intelligence services were certainly of interest to the Scott team. The inquiry heard oral testimony from thirteen members of the "security services," including serving and retired MI6 officers. Press release, 12.13.94.

70 Interview with R. Robison.

71 It had previously been valued at only £650,000. On the Lear Fan episode, see James Adams: *Bull's Eye*, pp. 232–241; and William Lowther: *Arms and the Man*, pp. 236–240. Bull set up a new company to handle the Lear Fan purchase: SRC Composites. This was owned by a Belfast holding company, Canira Technical Corporation, which in turn was half-owned by SRC and TDG. "Canira" was an amalgam of "Canada" and "Iraq." See *Flight International*, 9.9.89 and 9.16.89. See also the *Financial Times*, 9.25.89.

72 Chris Cowley has suggested that the purchase may also have been driven by a need to consider how best to lighten the weight of the 600mm military gun that Bull was working on toward the end of his life, and that Iraq's SCUD and Condor II missile programs could have used the technology. *Guns, Lies and Spies*, pp. 204–205.

73 Quoted in A. Darwish and G. Alexander: *Unholy Babylon*, p. 191. See also TISC: HC-86, p. xxxv.

74 Ibid., p. xxxv. An FCO document of 8 August 1989 summarized FCO Minister William Waldegrave's views on the proposed purchase thus: "He has commented that there is far more danger to HMG in a scandal based on reports

that, while we keep a high moral tone about the Germans and others, we have Iraqis based in Northern Ireland in an MTCR technology. He is afraid that the damage to Northern Irish jobs pales into insignificance and believes that HMG must (a) refuse the grant (b) brief as openly as possible, and (c) take far more vigorous action to press for legal controls, even if that means legislation which would enable us to refuse such a purchase."
Scott Inquiry—Day 26: Evidence of William Waldegrave, pp. 15–16.

75 Letter from Gerald Bull to Philippe Glibert, 10.31.89. *Hansard*, 11.29.93, col. 278.

76 Quoted in the *Independent*, 11.27.91.

77 TISC: HC-86-xi, 1.29.92, p. 305.

78 See, for example, ibid., p. 307, q. 2151.

79 At one point, committee member Dr. Keith Hampson was driven to exclaim to the four Customs witnesses: "I am sorry, the gentleman on your right is always whispering 'do not answer,' I wish he would keep his mouth shut and not influence the answers." TISC: Minutes of evidence 1.29.92, pp. 319–320.

80 A motion by Liberal Democrat MP Menzies Campbell that the trip be canceled, backed by Labour MPs Jim Cousins and Doug Hoyle, was defeated by those Conservative MPs and Labour MP John Gilbert taking the trip. See the *Guardian*, 2.27.92.

81 *Guardian*, 1.16.92. The TISC report criticizes Miller over his refusal to appear. TISC: HC-86, p. xli.

82 *Guardian*, 1.16.92.

83 *U.S. News*, 11.2.92.

84 *Independent*, 2.24.92. Cowley's version of the meeting is contained in his statement to the Scott Inquiry, pp. 13–15.

85 Scott Inquiry: Statement of Chris Cowley, pp. 12–15.

86 In the corridor, as James left after giving testimony, Howarth told him: "You know you're in very grave danger, Gerald, of becoming paranoid about all this." *Observer*, 3.22.92.

87 Scott Inquiry: Statement of Gerald James, p. 3.

88 *Independent*, 1.16.92.

89 Scott Inquiry: Statement of Christopher Cowley, p. 16.

90 Ibid.

91 Ibid., p. 17. Cowley assumed this to be part of the Jordanian defense package then being purchased from Britain. Ibid., p. 28.

92 TISC: HC-86, p. lxvii.

93 Quoted in the *Guardian*, 3.14.92.

94 TISC: HC-86, p. lxvii.

95 Warren was knighted in 1993 and subsequently proved very sensitive to any criticism of his role during this inquiry. Following one letter from him to *Private Eye* (1.28.94.), fellow TISC members Jim Cousins and Doug Hoyle wrote to the magazine to set the record straight:
"Poor old Sir Ken Warren, our beloved ex-chairman, must be suffering from amnesia. Has he forgotten all the votes that took place on the amendments put forward by Labour and Liberal Democrat members of the trade and industry select committee, which were voted upon on party lines and very often defeated on the casting vote of himself as chairman?
"Has he forgotten the evidence from officials and ministers to the supergun inquiry, which, day by day, the Scott inquiry shows to be untrue?
"Has he forgotten that he met one key witness the night before he gave evidence, for a quiet chat?
"Has he forgotten the Labour amendment which said 'it seems hardly credible that a large military project such as Babylon . . . would not have been known to British and other intelligence services . . .' Ken Warren used his casting vote against that one, too.
Arise sir Ken, but the real honours lie elsewhere." *Private Eye*, 2.11.94, p. 15.

96 *Financial Times*, 3.17.92.

97 *Independent*, 1.16.92. On the same day the charges were dropped, the affair had apparently been discussed in Cabinet. See the *Independent*, 11.16.90. See also the *Times*, 11.16.90.

98 *Guardian*, 2.27.92, and TISC: HC-86, p. xli.

99 Scott Inquiry—Day 85: Evidence of Sir Brian Unwin, p. 23. My emphasis.

100 Ibid., pp. 25–26.

101 Quoted in David Leigh: *Betrayed: The Real Story of the Matrix Churchill Trial*, London, Bloomsbury, 1993, pp. 210–211.

102 Paul Henderson: *The Unlikely Spy*, p. 139.

103 Ibid., p. 141.

104 In 1991 Ali Daghir and Jeanine Speckman of Euromac were convicted of attempting to illegally export electrical capacitors to Iraq, supposedly for use in the Iraqi nuclear weapons program. Their conviction was later overturned on the grounds that the trial judge had misdirected the jury.

105 TISC: HC-86-xv, p. 498. On Pike's evidence to the TISC, see Gerald James: Letter to A. Kennon, 3.31.92, which should be available in the House of Lords Record Office along with other evidence to the TISC that it chose not to publish.

106 Letter from Chris Cowley to Andrew Kennon, clerk to the TISC, 2.23.92. Unpublished evidence.

107 Chris Cowley: *Guns, Lies and Spies*, pp. 220–221.

108 TISC: HC-86-x, p. 361.

109 Interview with Gerald James, London, 3.1.95. The blast was first reported in the U.K. press by Jane Renton of the *Observer* in April 1990, following the murder of Bull and seizure of sections of the supergun. Her article noted:

"The blast at PRB occurred during the afternoon when most of the workforce was on official break. A number of windows were shattered and a building was severely damaged, but no casualties were reported. The incident, shrouded in secrecy, has given rise to rumours that the factory was deliberately sabotaged by British or possibly Israeli secret agents alerted to the 'Babylon' connection. Roy Barber, who took over as Astra's chairman last month, confirmed reports of the explosion, but denied that the blast was the work of saboteurs: 'I would not read anything sinister into this,' he said. Barber claimed that such explosions occurred occasionally in munitions factories where high explosives are stored. He did not elaborate on the incident. However, one senior gunnery expert contacted by the *Observer* challenged this perspective. 'Munitions factory explosions are exceedingly rare. If explosions occurred the factories would be closed down because no one would dare work there,' he said."

110 For an overview, see Michael Meacher: Bomb Proof, *New Statesman and Society*, 10.14.94, pp. 18–19. On ISC's CIA connections see, for example, the *Independent on Sunday*, 6.16.91.

Matrix Churchill, Dual-Use Exports, and Government Knowledge

While the Astra and supergun dimensions highlight the British involvement in supplying Iraq with arms, albeit largely through conduits, the Matrix Churchill affair exposed the important contribution made by dual-use equipment to the arming of Iraq. At the same time, it illustrated the increased importance of arms-manufacturing technology in an arms market where, either overtly or covertly, Third World states are attempting to establish their own indigenous arms industries that will ultimately end their reliance on outside suppliers.

Customs' misplaced determination to prosecute the three Matrix Churchill executives (Henderson, Abrahams, and Allen)[1] resulted in an Old Bailey trial exposing a level of government knowledge about the British role in arming Iraq that had previously been concealed. The company was one of a number of manufacturers of dual-use equipment that were the principal beneficiaries of the approach to Iran and Iraq enshrined in the Howe Guidelines. However, this governmental beneficence, toward machine tool manufacturers in particular, came to an abrupt end with the Iraqi invasion of Kuwait. At the same time, its extent became a source of embarrassment to the government, something it was keen to downplay or even deny.

Although not the only machine tool manufacturers involved in selling arms-manufacturing equipment to Iraq, Matrix Churchill came to assume a symbolic importance because of its Iraqi ownership and the revelations about the government's knowledge that emerged when the attempt to apply PII failed. Other companies—such as Colchester Lathes, BSA Tools, and Wickman Bennett—all sold machine tools to Iraq during the same period. In 1992, prior to the Matrix Churchill trial, Wickman Bennett and Contractors 600 (part of Colchester Lathes) were each fined between £30,000 and £50,000 in out-of-court settlements, the terms of which prevented them from making any comment on the cases.[2] The BSA Tools case was due in court after that of Matrix Churchill, but in light of events there the case was dropped.

◆ Involvement

Coventry-based Matrix Churchill was originally owned by the TI Group and was known as TI Machine Tools Ltd. In March 1987 an Iraqi delegation led by Safa al-Habobi—the director general of the Nassr plant and a senior figure in Iraqi Intelligence—visited the company.[3] It was a visit that had been arranged by Anees Wadi and Roy Ricks of Meed International,[4] both of whom seemed to Paul Henderson to have intelligence connections[5] (one with British and one with Iraqi Intelligence). As noted above, Henderson and the company were made aware from this first visit that the Iraqis were interested in machine tools to produce armaments.[6] In May 1987 the company secured its first contracts with Iraq, for 150 machines worth £18.9 million, the largest component of which was a contract worth £11.5 million for machines to produce 155mm shells at the Hutteen plant. The remaining contracts were for machines to produce 122mm shells and the so-called ABC contract. At the same time, TI was looking to offload the loss-making TI Machine Tools, so when Wadi told Mark Gutteridge that the Iraqis were looking to buy a machine tool manufacturer, it was suggested they consider TI. To this end, in July 1987 Henderson and Gutteridge flew to Iraq to give a sales presentation at the Nassr plant. It was shortly after this that Gutteridge confided in Henderson that he was passing on the details of their Iraqi contracts and orders to his MI5 contact.

In October 1987 the loss-making company was sold by TI to the Iraqi front company Technology Development Group through its subsidiary, TMG Engineering Ltd.[7] At the time of the sale to the Iraqis, the deputy director of TI was Sir John Cuckney, a former MI5 officer and chairman of IMS.[8] The purchase also bought the Iraqis the company's U.S. sales and service subsidiary based in Cleveland, Ohio, which the new Iraqi owners began to operate as a front for purchasing U.S. technology for Iraq. Following its sale, the company, now renamed Matrix Churchill, secured a number of further orders for machine tools from Iraq, immediately making Iraq its largest customer and transforming it from a loss-making into a thriving concern, which in 1990 employed 600 people and made a £2.5 million profit.[9]

From the time of the sale until the Iraqi invasion of Kuwait, Iraq and Cardoen of Chile were by far Matrix Churchill's most important customers. However, as the U.N. inspection team that toured postwar Iraq discovered, they were far from being Iraq's most significant supplier of machine tools. As the British government knew at the time, German and Swiss companies such as Gildemeister, SHW, Schaublin, and Oerlikon were very much at the forefront of Iraq's machine tool acquisition program. Nevertheless, David Kay, a senior figure in the postwar U.N. inspection of Iraq's weapons programs, has said that Matrix Churchill machine tools were found to have been used in a wide range of Iraqi weapons programs—in the production of conventional armaments; shells for the range of Bull-designed guns; missiles (including the SCUD); and gas centrifuges for the Iraqi nuclear weapons program.[10]

Was the sale of Matrix Churchill a means of monitoring the Iraqi procurement operation, just as allowing the manufacture of the supergun barrels to go ahead seems to have been? Paul Henderson commented: "There is no doubt in my mind that the business was sold to the Iraqis so that we could monitor them."[11] MI5 already had an agent, Mark Gutteridge, operating in the company at the time. Furthermore, Gutteridge did provide just the kind of intelligence that the sale may have been designed to facilitate. In November 1987, for example, his MI5 controller, "Ford," wrote that Gutteridge "has been able to provide details of the Iraqi contracts with UK companies for general purpose machine tools. Source is in no doubt that all these tools will be used in Iraq for the production of armaments."

However, after the sale had gone through, it became apparent that the export license application for the set of three Iraqi contracts already signed, on which the machines were described as having a "general engineering" rather than armaments production end-use, was being held up by the DTI—ironically, because of the high quality of Gutteridge's intelligence about their real end-use. In January 1988 Matrix Churchill learned that its export licenses (along with those of other machine tool manufacturers dealing with Iraq) were to be revoked. This development led to an infamous meeting between representatives of the Machine Tools Technologies Association and DTI Minister Alan Clark on 20 January.

According to Henderson, Clark said: "I know what the machines are being used for. You know what the machines are being used for," and advised those present to submit license applications stressing their civilian rather than military applications. The association's minute of the meeting records his advice:

> The intended use of the machines should be couched in such a manner as to emphasise the peaceful aspect to which they will be put . . . Applications should stress the record of general engineering usage of machine tools supplied in the past . . . The application should be supported by voluminous material. The application should be biased technically. The application should be made as soon as possible.
> . . . If the political overtones of the Iran-Iraq conflict change and if the United States becomes more supportive of one side than at present, then the current order may change.[12]

The following month the DTI told Matrix Churchill that the export of thirteen CNC 750-series machines to Hutteen did not even require an export license.

By 1988 Matrix Churchill was becoming more deeply involved with Iraq, and in that year it entered into a technology transfer agreement under which Iraq would ultimately be able to manufacture its own 2 and 3 series CNC machines at the Nassr plant, moving the country closer to self-sufficiency. This contract, the company's fifth with Iraq, involved training Iraqi engineers at the Coventry plant. It was also the first of its Iraqi contracts to be financed by the Atlanta branch of BNL, following a visit to Coventry by Paul von Wedel. A couple of months after this, the Matrix Churchill plant had a further significant visitor, Dr. Carlos Cardoen.

Cardoen explained that his company was involved in an armaments project for Iraq for which it required a significant number of machines, and for which Cardoen was being paid in oil. He asked Matrix Churchill to quote on a turnkey project to manufacture artillery fuses in Iraq. The company submitted a quote for twenty-four 2 series and twenty-four 3 series CNC machines, and in July 1988 Henderson flew to Miami to meet with Cardoen. The company's quote was reluctantly accepted by Cardoen, but only after the intervention of the Iraqis. However, approval of the necessary export licenses for this deal would prove even more difficult than winning the contract. At around the same time, Matrix Churchill entered into the ABA contract with Iraq for machine tools to be installed at the Nassr plant for use in the Iraqi missile program (again, financed by BNL), which required eight CNC machines.

It was at this point that Gutteridge, who had been keeping MI5 informed about the company's dealings with Iraq, left the company and Henderson reactivated his old intelligence role. When Henderson began to meet with his MI6 contact, "Balsom," he was left in no doubt as to where MI6's interests lay. He was debriefed about Cardoen, SRC, and Gerald Bull and told: "We're not really interested in conventional armaments. Find out all you can about Bull and SRC and any other projects they might be working on. They are a very important link."[13] As discussed earlier, when Henderson attended the Baghdad military fair in April 1989, he was asked to collect intelligence: "There was no mistaking the military nature of the fair. Almost every other stand displayed strictly military hardware: artillery, machine-guns, rifles, radar, field radios, and models of tanks and fighter aircraft. British Aerospace had a model of a Hawk trainer at its stand; the real plane was sitting at Baghdad's airport."[14]

At an August 1989 meeting with Balsom, Henderson again raised the on-going problem of the delay in issuing the export licenses for the lucrative Cardoen contract. He was told that the delay was due to the opposition of the FCO and was given the name of an FCO contact, Rob Young, whom he agreed to meet on the same day that he agreed to the wide-ranging debriefing session at an MI6 safehouse in London. In fact, this session was so extensive as to suggest that MI6 for its part was ready to agree to refuse to issue the licenses because the intelligence from within Matrix Churchill had clearly shown that its machines were being used in Iraq's nonconventional arms pro-grams. While selling machines that contributed to Iraq's conventional arms capability was no problem and could be allowed to continue so as to retain the intelligence source and monitor Iraq's nonconventional initiatives (the area Henderson was asked to concentrate on), it was nonconventional arms development to which they were hoping the intelligence would alert them. Ironically, instead of providing intelligence with warnings of these develop-ments, MI6's source was now a major contributor to the Iraqi nonconven-tional weapons program. Hence, it seems, the decision was made to get everything possible out of Henderson in one long session and then cut him loose. At the end of the session, Balsom told him it might "be some time before [they] spoke again."[15] If the Matrix Churchill applications were to be approved in the future, it would not be because of an insistence on the part of the intelligence services. Rather, it would depend on the outcome of an ongoing battle in Whitehall between the FCO on the one hand and the DTI and MOD on the other.

After meeting with Young to pursue approval of the outstanding license applications, Henderson went to a meeting later in the month with a DTI minister, Lord Trefgarne—a meeting that was to cause Henderson much dis-comfort at the Scott Inquiry. Although he had apparently passed on informa-tion to Balsom about the real end-use of the Cardoen contract, he admitted in his autobiography to misleading Trefgarne: "I acknowledged that the ma-chines had commercial and military uses. I also knew the intelligence services had informed all of the Ministers about the real use of the machines. So I stressed the Iraqi plans for automotive projects such as the Daimler-Benz and General Motors plants. And the loss of jobs if the licences were refused."[16]

From this meeting, Trefgarne argued for release of the licenses at a 1 No-vember meeting with Clark and Waldegrave, and they were duly issued. This was not the final export license difficulty that Matrix Churchill would face. The final part of the ABA contract was still being held up, and it was still awaiting a license when the unholy Bazoft-Bull-supergun trinity altered the climate of bilateral relations. However, despite the increasingly frenetic government activity as it became clear that Customs and Excise was preparing to investigate Matrix Churchill, the DTI's Mike Coolican told Henderson on 1 August 1990 that all outstanding Matrix Churchill licenses had been approved. As Paul Henderson recalled for BBC's *Panorama:*

> On the 1st of August I actually telephoned Michael Coolican at the Department of Trade and Industry regarding a number of licences that were outstanding both for Matrix Churchill and other companies, and during that conversation he informed me that all the licences had now been cleared except for five machines which were to be imported from the USA.[17]

There was no problem. But there was. The next day Iraq invaded Kuwait.

◆ Trial

The legal process that was to culminate in the Old Bailey trial began with the arrest of Henderson, Allen, and Abraham on 16 October 1990.[18] But the question remains, why did the government allow this case to come to court in the first place? The answer seems to be that although Customs officials were latterly aware of Henderson's intelligence connections, they were determined to prosecute this breach of the law. They were perhaps especially motivated because the government had failed to go ahead with the prosecutions of Mitchell and Cowley in the supergun case, although Customs had what it considered to be a strong chance of a conviction, particularly in the case of Chris Cowley. Customs had undertaken to alert the DTI before deciding on any prosecution in the Matrix Churchill case but failed to do so, infuriating the DTI but "equaling the score" over the supergun.

When the Matrix Churchill case finally came to trial, four ministers—Michael Heseltine, Malcolm Rifkind, Kenneth Clarke, and Tristan Garel-Jones—signed PII certificates to prevent disclosure of government documents that the defense argued were central to its case. The case had a number of parallels with the Ordtec case, and here the Ordtec formula was being repeated. The crucial difference between the two cases, however, was to be that in one the judge accepted the government's argument, whereas in the other, he rejected a large part of it. Even after the trial and the revelations it contained, Garel-Jones seemed to argue that the documents should not have been revealed, telling the Scott Inquiry that "the fact that those documents have become public knowledge has, in my view, been injurious to the public interest."[19] In the event, Judge Smedley refused to grant PII, but only after Henderson's counsel, Geoffrey Robertson, had revealed his defense in advance and after Alan Moses, counsel for the prosecution[20] (Customs and Excise) had told the judge: "These documents do not assist in any way the defence."[21]

The secrecy that the government sought to apply to the trial extended to its proceedings. Those who attended the public gallery to view the trial reported that, unusually, identification had to be produced to gain entry, and the names of those entering were, on occasion, taken. In addition, the FULL sign was displayed outside the gallery on a number of occasions when there were very few people inside.[22]

The case itself concerned two contracts. The first was the Cardoen contract, the second the ABA missile contract. A number of uncertainties hang over Customs' preparation of the case, heightened by the fact that Moses was shown crucial Cabinet Office papers relating to the case only three days before the trial was due to begin and that Alan Clark for one, a key prosecution witness, did not even know which batch of machine tools was the subject of the prosecution and was not forewarned of the likely defense argument of prior government knowledge.[23] In addition, there were government fears about Clark's likely performance as a prosecution witness based on what Sir Michael Quinlan, permanent secretary at the MOD, described as Clark's "occasionally idiosyncratic behaviour." Nevertheless, no one sought to intervene and interfere with Customs' much-vaunted independence. The trial went ahead.

The prosecution's case was that Henderson, Allen, and Abraham had deceived the DTI by not informing them of the true nature of the machines being exported, that "they were involved in the pretence that they were for the production of certain civilian items," but that this was merely a way of "getting round the ban on export."[24] But this was precisely what the Howe Guidelines encouraged, what Alan Clark as trade minister had personally encouraged Henderson to do, and what the relevant government departments—except, apparently, Customs and Excise—had known all along they were doing and allowed them to continue doing. Furthermore, Henderson had openly admitted in the *Financial Times* in September 1989 that Matrix Churchill machines exported to Iraq were making components for conventional arms.[25]

Gutteridge agreed to testify to his intelligence work on behalf of Henderson at the trial, and their respective intelligence contacts were called to give evidence, although on behalf of the prosecution. This was to be the first time that serving intelligence officers had given evidence in a court of law, and a makeshift screen was erected to protect their identities. They were referred to throughout the trial as Officer A and Officer B. Officer A was Henderson's MI6 contact "John Balsom," and Officer B was Gutteridge's MI5 contact "Michael Ford."

Ford recounted how Gutteridge regularly passed on information about the supply of arms-producing technology to Iraq and even supplied him with drawings of machine tools ordered by Iraq. They had met monthly between 1987 and 1989, he said, to discuss the Iraqi situation. He told the court that MI5 had recommended that ministers approve export licenses for Matrix Churchill exports so that further intelligence could be collected from Gutteridge. In a report dated 6 May 1987, Ford recorded, "Gutteridge told me of . . . dealings with a London-based Iraqi company. This company is buying milling machines specifically tooled up for arms production." After a further meeting three months later, he noted that Gutteridge "outlined his understanding of the Iraqi arms production in Hutteen and Nassr. Provided details of contracts signed by the Iraqis with companies in UK and West Europe."[26] From this we can date firm government knowledge of the Iraqi procurement network and its use of front companies in Britain and Europe to mid-1987—well before the government had previously been prepared to admit to, but consistent with the claims of SRC employees like Cowley and even the evidence of Sir Hal Miller.

Balsom recounted how he met with Henderson some twenty times before August 1990. Between 1989 and 1990, Henderson had visited Iraq eight times, and so was in an excellent position to provide up-to-date intelligence on those nonconventional armaments areas in which MI6 was particularly interested: Iraqi missile development, nuclear and chemical facilities, SRC and Project Babylon, and even the personal lives of the Iraqi arms procurers. His testimony revealed the extent to which British arms sales to Iraq were permitted in order to maintain this flow of information before the Howe Guidelines were relaxed, regardless of the legality of the situation.

However, at the same time that one arm of government was invoking the national interest and urging Henderson to continue to pursue a course of action that was clearly dangerous (and at one point involved him in identifying Iraqis who might be "turned" by British intelligence) as well as illegal, another was preparing to visit the company to ensure that it was not breaching the Howe Guidelines. The problem for Henderson was that his actions were contravening the guidelines, and therefore Customs had the power to prosecute. The fact that Customs was unaware of the use to which MI5 and MI6 were putting the intelligence gleaned from Matrix Churchill's involvement was immaterial. As Balsom admitted in court, MI6's priority was to gather intelligence, regardless of whether those it worked with broke the law or adhered to it. Conversely, it was the job of the DTI and Customs to formulate and enforce the regulations. On this basis, acting illegally in order to gather intelligence information in the national interest was no guarantee of immunity from prosecution. Then again, it would be wrong to suggest that Matrix Churchill was acting illegally solely to satisfy intelligence. For the Coventry-based company, passing on intelligence secured its continued access to the Iraqi market, without which, as subsequent events showed, it would be in severe financial difficulty. Thus, Henderson did not volunteer information on areas of his company's dealings about which Balsom displayed no knowledge. For example, he said nothing about the contract to supply Cardoen with fuse-making technology, which was one of the breaches of export regulations with which he was charged.

The trial testimonies of DTI officials and intelligence officers had damaged the prosecution's case, and that of Alan Clark further undermined it. Under cross-examination by Robertson, Clark admitted approving and lobbying on behalf of the supply of equipment in apparent contravention of the Howe Guidelines, which he considered, "elastic . . . tiresome and intrusive." When cross-examined about his advice to exporters at the infamous Machine Tools Technologies Association meeting, at which he was considered to have given a "nod and a wink" to machine tool exports to Iraq, Clark justified all the Whitehall fears about his suitability as a witness, telling Robertson that his advice had been

> AC: a matter of Whitehall cosmetics to keep the record ambiguous . . . It's our old friend, being economical.
> GR: With the truth?
> AC: With the actualité. There was nothing misleading or dishonest in making a formal introduction that Iraq was using the current orders for general engineering purposes. What I didn't say was their use for munitions. It would not have been appropriate at a meeting of this kind to widen from the stilted and rather formal language that I used.[27]

He went on to say that he shared intelligence concerns over Iraq's nuclear and chemical warfare capabilities but was not concerned about the more "pedestrian technology" and found in practice that "by bending and stretching [the guidelines] we could get the best results." Nevertheless, he accepted that certain equipment being exported was "over the edge" of the guidelines.[28] After two days of the key prosecution witness's testimony, the Matrix Churchill trial was adjourned, and the prosecutions dropped.[29]

◆ The Documents: The British Government and Exports to Iraq

The documents released to the defense when the attempt to claim PII failed reveal much about the application of the Howe Guidelines and U.K. government knowledge of the Iraqi procurement program. However, this information did not come just from Henderson and Gutteridge. In addition, intelligence on Iraq was routinely pooled by the U.S., Israeli, Italian, and British intelligence communities; and according to statements from the U.S. House of Representatives, these services were under instruction from national politicians not to intervene in the procurement operation but merely to monitor its progress.

Gutteridge's early intelligence was collected in an August 1987 MI6 document, *Iraq: The Procurement of Machinery for Armaments Production,*[30] delivered to the DTI on 30 November 1987 and circulated to the MOD and FCO. This formed the basis of a widely circulated warning memo from Alan Barrett of the MOD dated 25 January 1988. Noting the approval of licenses for the export of machine tools by Matrix Churchill, BSA Tools Ltd, and Wickman Bennett, it went on to reveal:

> We have obtained intelligence, thought by the DIS to be reliable, that the lathes are to go to set up munitions factories to produce missiles and shells in large quantities. Had this information been available at the time the licence applications were considered, the MODWG would have advised the IDC that the military assessment was that the use of the lathes for this purpose would constitute a significant enhancement in Iraq's capability to prolong the conflict with Iran.

After the usual litany of justifications for their export to be interpreted as compatible with the guidelines, the memo concluded: "The intelligence community recommends against revoking the licences as they fear for the safety of their source, and they also believe that far more important information could cease to become available as a result."[31]

One day after this was written, a letter dated 22 January was received by the FCO from a Matrix Churchill employee. This warned that the company was selling Iraq machines to make armaments, and provided collateral for the intelligence whose use MI6 would not sanction in denying any Matrix Churchill applications because of concern for its source. It said: "These machines are going to be used to machine shell cases. Hundreds were destroyed last week after being machined as test pieces. We are also helping to set up a company in Baghdad which will produce CNC machines from kits."[32]

A further document, *Iraqi Long Range Projectile*, dated 27 October 1989, notes: "Henderson gave us the attached blueprints. This could have a range of 1,200 km: it could be connected with the Space Research Corporation's involvement with long-range artillery research." A further document from late 1989 (again, based on information from Henderson) refers to the opening of a unit at the Nassr plant that "would be capable of producing high-quality barrels of the sort used in Project Babylon, Iraq's long-range gun plan."

As well as providing evidence of government knowledge of the Iraqi procurement program, the documents also revealed the efforts to achieve the broadest possible interpretation of the Howe Guidelines. An FCO paper of 9 September 1988, approved by the Inter-Departmental Committee (IDC), and headed *Implications of a Ceasefire for Defence Sales to Iran and Iraq*, said:

> As part of our analysis of the implications of peace in the Gulf, we have been considering our policy for defence sales to Iran and Iraq . . . officials recommend that we should retain the present guidelines on defence sales over the next six months but at the same time exploit their inbuilt flexibility to relax restrictions in line with progress towards a peace settlement. This would allow us to release a number of categories currently deferred, notably dual use equipment and give favourable consideration to military training.[33]

It did warn, however, that Britain needed to be "sensitive to concerns of our best customer in the Middle East: Saudi Arabia." This marked the first de facto change (i.e., loosening) of the guidelines. However, questions of presentation and political embarrassment meant that the foreign secretary, Sir Geoffrey Howe, did not want to make any announcement of this change. An FCO note explained:

> He is reluctant to put this paper forward and thereby to initiate a process whereby it will become known that our line on arms sales to Iraq has relaxed while the Kurds/chemical warfare question is still hanging over us . . . he feels that it could look very cynical if, so soon after expressing outrage over the Iraqi treatment of the Kurds, we were to adopt a more flexible approach on arms sales.[34]

This loosening was soon being applied. For example, on 22 September 1988, at an IDC meeting, MOD representatives argued that supplying mortar-locating radar "would not enhance Iraq's military capability" on the basis that "Iraq already had large numbers of such equipment supplied by the UK."[35]

The documents show how the IDC continued to approve arms sales to Iraq up until the invasion of Kuwait. In October 1988 the IDC recommended approval of a license for the export of spare parts for armored recovery vehicles. On 1 December it approved licensing "for demonstration" for the Marconi Quickfire artillery fire control system. On the same day it also approved six shotguns and shotgun cartridges. The recorded justification indicates an awareness that in effect the guidelines were being breached, noting "that they *could be allowed to fall outside the scope* of the guidelines, particularly now that the Secretary of State has spoken of a more flexible interpretation of the guidelines."[36] This reflects the DTI's desire to secure a relaxation or outright removal of the guidelines as soon as possible after the cease-fire, so as to leave British exporters best placed to exploit the postwar Iraqi market. In a letter from Clark to Waldegrave copied to Mrs. Thatcher and dated 4 November 1988, Clark noted that a number of license applications were being held up:

> Para 2 of the official note enclosed with Geoffrey Howe's of 31 August suggested: "We can use discretion within the ministerial guidelines to adopt a phased approach to borderline cases, relaxing control on a growing number of categories as peace takes hold." It would in my view be entirely consistent with this policy to issue without further delay the licences mentioned above. Not to do so will harm the efforts of British companies to re-establish themselves in both markets and deny them industrially valuable orders. Our international competitors are not so inhibited.[37]

On 30 November, Clark complained to Waldegrave: "It seems . . . not only illogical but unnecessarily restrictive to continue to allow ourselves to be restrained by guidelines when the original raison d'être has now been removed" and argued that only goods featured on the COCOM-proscribed munitions list should be opposed. Waldegrave replied that "the continuing uncertainty about the prospects of an earlier peace settlement will require us to adopt a rather more cautious approach than the one you propose." He suggested that Clark, Trefgarne, and Waldegrave should meet to discuss the situation.[38]

In a briefing note for that meeting prepared for Lord Trefgarne by Alan Barrett, Trefgarne is advised that Clark is pushing to have the outstanding Matrix Churchill licenses approved. It reads (in part):

Matrix Churchill lathes. 16.5 million worth to Iraq. Intelligence sources indicated that the lathes were to be used for making shells and missiles . . . The Prime Minister agreed that, in order to protect the intelligence source, the licences already granted should not be revoked. The current applications for supply of complete lathes and in kit form have been held up while we have tried, unsuccessfully, to obtain collateral for the intelligence which we could use without jeopardising the original source. We . . . were about to recommend releasing these applications, but intelligence is now available, we believe, but have not yet seen, suggesting more disturbing news of the lathes. This case needs to go back to the Prime Minister before we could recommend approving the current applications.[39]

Despite this warning, Trefgarne, Clark, and Waldegrave met on 21 December 1988 to discuss revising the guidelines and proposed the change that became the new point iii). A letter summarizing what was agreed at the meeting from Waldegrave's private secretary suggests that at the time what occured was seen as a change:

The Ministers agreed at the meeting that the ceasefire in the Iran-Iraq War had changed the circumstances which the Guidelines had been drawn up to meet, and Mr Clark argued it was becoming increasingly difficult to justify the Guidelines for British firms. The Ministers agreed, after discussion, that it would now be right to consider modifying them, while preserving our flexibility to interpret the restraints on supplying defence equipment to Iran and Iraq on a case-by-case basis.

Ministers agreed to consider the revised attached guidelines, which were circulated at the meeting. The aim of the revised wording would be to reflect the various concerns of departments, to provide a line which would be publicly defensible and give us additional flexibility over the supply of certain kinds of equipment, while retaining the Government's ability to decide on the export of individual items according to changing circumstances.[40]

This revision was then sent to the British Embassy in Washington, an indication of how closely the United States and United Kingdom cooperated over the issue of Iran and Iraq in the 1980s, and to Gulf embassies for reaction. The reply from the Saudi Embassy was hardly enthusiastic, warning that the United Kingdom would be unwise to "outpace the policy of other defence suppliers." An FCO brief summing up the response noted that "the change in policy would not be welcome in Saudi Arabia, where the rearming of either Iran or Iraq would be viewed with some dismay."[41] The reply from Washington recommended that any announcement of the change be delayed so that the incoming Bush administration could first be briefed. These reactions in effect discouraged the planned announcement of the change. While subsequent parliamentary answers deployed a different wording that could be taken as hinting at a change, they nevertheless continued to say that the original guidelines were being enforced. This was now clearly not the case. The revision was implemented but not announced. To this end, on 10 January 1989 Clark wrote to Waldegrave:

> Neither we, nor I, believe the MOD feel that . . . an announcement is either necessary or desirable. Any such announcement would trigger a significant number of enquiries from the UK defence industry and the press, as well as interested third parties in the Gulf. With so many conflicting interests, any change would be likely to upset someone. We would, therefore, favour implementation of a more liberal policy without any public announcement.[42]

The third party in the Gulf that Britain was most anxious not to upset was clearly Saudi Arabia. As Lord Trefgarne told the Scott Inquiry, while the Saudis "were very concerned about the rise in fundamentalism in Iran, which might have had an effect upon their own situation in their country, they were also concerned about the rising military strength of Iraq."[43] But at this particular juncture these concerns were also part trade. Saudi Arabia had just signed up for the Al Yamamah II arms deal, the richest arms deal in British history. However, the deal was in the form of a "memorandum of understanding," meaning that contracts for the material Saudi Arabia had indicated its intention to buy would be signed at various points over the next decade or so, as the Saudi economy allowed, rather than all at once. This gave Saudi Arabia a certain leverage over British foreign policy in the Gulf by making the British arms export industry very vulnerable to cancellations or fluctuations in Saudi requirements.

Waldegrave accepted the new guideline iii), being

> content for [the government] to implement a more liberal policy on defence sales without any public announcement on the subject. However, there remains the possibility that [Howe] will be asked a direct question about our policy either in the House or by foreign governments. We would propose to answer along the following lines: "The Guidelines on the export of defence equipment to Iran and Iraq are being kept under constant review, and are applied in the light of the ceasefire and developments in the peace negotiations."

Clark replied, saying he was "pleased with [Waldegrave's] agreement to implement a more liberal policy without any public announcement."

Meanwhile, a strong warning that the three junior ministers would not have been aware of came from the DIA. Headed *Iraq Machine Tools for Various Facilities*, it warned:

> We understand that, with the outbreak of "peace" that DTI have returned to the fray in regard of the outstanding ELAS [Export Licence Applications] for these machines, especially the Matrix Churchill machines. I understand that one of their arguments is that previous licences have been granted and they feel that Matrix Churchill are being disadvantaged. . . .
>
> Both the consignees [Hutteen and Nassr] are armaments production facilities, which would serve to make Iraq self-sufficient. As any soldier will tell you, artillery is a very potent component of the battle and is often the decisive factor in defeating the enemy. Any facility that makes them self-sufficient and precludes the use of hard currency reserves for purchase in a market where sanctions or market price may restrict the quantity must be assessed as a significant enhancement.
>
> Despite a source problem it is our view that this offers Iraq a significant enhancement . . . and Defence Intelligence will oppose vigorously any shipment of the machine tools to these two establishments in particular and to any others that we know are armament production facilities.[44]

However, on 6 January 1989 an internal MI6 note struck a different, contradictory chord, that seemingly supported continued export:

> We discussed at the REU [Restricted Enforcement Unit] meeting the control of exports of machine tools to Iraq. . . . A decision on whether to relax export controls on machine tools to Iraq has been deferred pending our advice as to how this would affect the future of Matrix Churchill. We told the REU that the security of our source was now best maintained if reasonable exports of machine tools by Matrix Churchill were allowed to continue. We also drew attention to the recent expansion of activities in the procurement network into the nuclear proliferation field and the importance this plays on maintaining access to the general activities of the network. We suggested that the criteria for denying exports of machine tools to Iraq should be the same as for other proliferating countries. These are clearly set out in the EGCOS [Export of Goods Control Orders] and apply only to sophisticated CNC multi-access tools, well above the specification of those presently supplied by Matrix Churchill.[45]

The situation as of February 1989 was summed up in a Foreign Office briefing for Waldegrave:

> IDC has had reservations about allowing the export of Matrix Churchill equipment since before the ceasefire. Export of this general purpose equipment is not prohib-

ited under the ministerial [Howe] guidelines and in 1987 export licences for Matrix Churchill were approved. However, the Security Services subsequently obtained intelligence information which revealed that Matrix Churchill had been taken over by Iraqi shareholders. Our information suggested that the Iraqis intended to use the company to supply machinery for the new armament and munitions factories of the NASSR and Hutteen state establishments headed by Dr Habobi. . . . We recommended that, in fact, no licensable equipment should be cleared for export by Matrix Churchill to Iraq. However, no outright ban could be issued as this would compromise the intelligence source for which we have no collateral. A temporary compromise was reached in practice by deferring the application.[46]

Hence, officials were left in a position where they could not take advantage of the intelligence they had received and act on it immediately to stop the export of the Matrix Churchill machines, as this would expose the intelligence source. Most of those outside MI6 seem to have assumed that this was a high-ranking Iraqi who was putting himself at risk by informing on Saddam's weapons programs and would be compromised if the machines were stopped. The intelligence was an interesting window on this aspect of the procurement network but was of limited use because it could not be used for the purpose for which it was originally obtained—an impasse that Waldegrave called "a constant problem of intelligence over the years."[47]

In any case, there remained the explicit intelligence distinction, and implicit FCO and MOD distinction, between the flow of equipment that was known to be going to make *conventional* arms—necessary for Iraq to pose as an effective counterweight to the more heavily populated Iran and maintain stability in the region—and equipment that could be used in *nonconventional* weapons programs. Despite a growing anxiety about Iraq's commitment to the latter, there was little consideration that the machine tools were going to do anything but the former, and while knowledge of this could throw them outside the guidelines, continued export would be consistent with foreign policy aims. Furthermore, Iraq had given states like Britain, which required a cover for presentational reasons, the perfect alibi by combining military production with a modest amount of industrial production at the same sites—a duality that seems to have paralyzed the FCO in the face of vigorous DTI and even MOD opposition, and also provided a convenient pretext for continued U.S. exports.

However, this alibi was seemingly put at risk by a report from a businessman who visited the Nassr plant in March 1989. A report on his observations noted:

Businessman described the following facilities:

(a) A foundry built by German firm. He was not allowed inside but, from pictures outside, the quantity of steel tubing being delivered, he assessed the foundry was producing shell and missile casings. There was no evidence that any explosives or propellant were being handled;

(b) A huge heavy casting facility was under construction which included cranes. . . . Businessman commented that the facilities were suitable for casting tank turrets etc;

(c) A forge was under construction, which included 14 metre-deep heat treatment pit. Businessman was in no doubt from machinery being explored that forge was for production of gun barrels[48]

This was clear evidence that after the cease-fire, when advocates of the machine tool trade were arguing that Iraq was seeking to rebuild its industrial infrastructure, it was in fact involved in munitions manufacture at one of the plants to which the Matrix Churchill machines were being exported. Yet even this level of evidence proved insufficient to block the export of machine tools, because it still did not rule out the *possibility* that the Matrix Churchill machines were going to be used on purely civilian work inside the plant. However, it did swing the *probability* firmly in favor of solely military usage. As Waldegrave told the Scott Inquiry when confronted with this evidence: "I would consider that was clear evidence that Nassr is still involved in munitions and armament manufacture. It does not *prove* that it did not have other functions as well."[49]

Nassr was to be identified in further intelligence reports as being at the center of Iraq's armaments program. For instance, a detailed fourteen-page MI6 report of 5 September 1989 talked of Iraq negotiating with "at least 15 countries for the supply of missiles, liquid rocket fuels, freshly manufactured components, machinery production tools, production lines, technical assistance, training [etc.] . . . These negotiations were connected to Project 1728, a large missile project headed by Dr Safa [al Habobi] of the Nassr State Establishment." Again, this was not sufficient to rule out the *possibility* that the Matrix Churchill machines had a civilian use, but in a situation in which missile production was being planned—the gray area joining conventional to nonconventional weapons technology—and the United Kingdom was a signatory to the Missile Technology Control Regime, informed suspicion and likelihood should sensibly have taken the place of the need for unimpeachable certainty.

In a statement to the Scott Inquiry, "Mr. J" of MI6 gave the intelligence overview of the Matrix Churchill applications. This analysis was not entirely consistent with some of the advice that had apparently emanated from intelligence sources earlier in the affair, and in addition it directly contradicted some of the arguments in favor of export that the DTI had attempted to apply to the machine tools:

> Although these machines were not defence equipment per se . . . they were to be used in armament production facilities and they represented a significant enhancement of the military capability which could prolong or exacerbate the Iran-Iraq conflict. This apparently contravened the Guidelines in force at the time. By being able to either replace or augment her existing arms suppliers, Iraq would no longer be entirely dependent on external suppliers. Nor would it need to use hard currency to purchase armaments on either the open or black markets. Consequently, Iraq would be able to prosecute the war with Iran with minimal external interference. This would undermine UN and western efforts to terminate or control the conflict. I have no reason to change this assessment following the ceasefire in 1988, given the nature of the Iraqi regime.[50]

On 1 March 1989, Iran issued its *fatwah* (death decree) condemning to death the British writer Salman Rushdie over his treatment of the Koran and the Prophet Muhammad in his 1988 novel *The Satanic Verses*. This produced another shift in the guidelines. From this point, a more relaxed interpretation of the guidelines was to be used toward Iraq, along the lines being discussed from December 1988, but there would be a more hard-line approach toward Iran, more in keeping with the original formulation. This formula was agreed by the three junior ministers on 24 April 1989. Despite increasing disquiet about Iraq's nonconventional weapons intentions as evidence mounted throughout 1989, culminating in the 5 December 1989 "space launch,"[51] this remained the de facto position until the execution of Farzad Bazoft on 15 March 1990 brought about a stricter interpretation for Iraq as well, although it was not strict enough to deter the continued export of machine tools to Iraqi weapons establishments.

Because the further tilt toward Iraq as a result of the *fatwah* could still be reconciled with the latitude inherent in the guidelines, it was again decided that this did not in fact amount to a change of policy, and hence there was no need for it to be announced. According to the IDC:

> The guidelines had been drawn up, and were kept under review in the light of the conflict, and, now, the ceasefire. The possibility of imposing a Defence Sales em-

bargo against Iran in retaliation for its action over Rushdie was a matter for the Cabinet Office Committee, and the IDC should not preempt any decision.

However, the IDC agreed that, in the present uncertain circumstances, the more flexible implementation of the guidelines, which ministers had decided to take since the ceasefire, would no longer be appropriate for Iran. The exact nature of the new guidelines for Iran would have to be agreed once it was known where the downward spiral in bilateral relations began to level out . . .

The IDC agreed that we should not penalise Iraq for the crisis with Iran and so should continue to use more flexible interpretation with the Iraqi applications. *We had already used differing interpretations for the two countries during the conflict and the 1985 guidelines were sufficiently broad to cover this.*[52]

Waldegrave had agreed that this was sensible, writing to Trefgarne and Clark on 28 March:

> I see no reason to change this flexible approach for applications to export defence-related equipment to Iraq. Nor should we at this stage change the Guidelines themselves [*sic*], for example, to limit or prevent the supply of defence-related equipment to Iran . . . I therefore propose we should now revert to the stricter implementation of the present Guidelines as applied to Iran along the lines which we operated before Iran accepted [U.N.] Resolution 598.[53]

He reaffirmed this in a letter of 27 April, which followed the 24 April meeting of the three, saying that "we should continue to interpret the Guidelines more flexibly in respect of Iraq as we have done in practice since the end of last year, but . . . we should revert to a stricter interpretation for Iran along the lines operated before the ceasefire."[54]

Despite this recognition within the administrative apparatus that different criteria were being applied to Iran and Iraq, answers to parliamentary questions and inquiries continued to be met by the fiction that an impartial approach rooted in the original 1985 guidelines was being followed. For example, on 3 May 1989 Waldegrave wrote to John Patten, MP: "The government have not changed their policy on defence sales to Iraq or Iran. These are governed by the strict application of guidelines which prevent the supply of lethal equipment, or equipment which could significantly enhance the capability of either side to resume hostilities."[55] This was clearly untrue.

According to an MOD official, writing in August 1989 to advocate a liberalization of the military training offered to Iraqis but not to Iranians (in keeping with the way in which the guidelines were then being applied):

It was decided to alter the confidential interpretation, rather than the published equipment guidelines themselves, in order to avoid publicity which, apart from attracting domestic political criticism, might also have given misleading encouragement to industry and caused alarm in the Gulf states. Although I am effectively recommending quite different training policies for each country, there would again be distinct political and military advantages in considering these as differing interpretations of a single set of guidelines, especially if these are derived from their equipment counterparts.[56]

Mark Higson, a former first secretary on the FCO's Iraq desk in 1989, had a clearer interpretation of the government's approach to trading with Iraq at this time, arguing:

It was simply a matter of us not telling the truth, of knowingly not telling the truth to the public and parliament.

The policy was bent and we concealed that policy. There were a small number of people in the Department of Trade, the Foreign Office and the Ministry of Defence who were conniving in the export of these things. They were turning a blind eye. It was well known that these machines were going to make shells.

By mid-1989, the FCO was beginning to distance itself further from the enthusiasm apparent in the DTI and MOD for continued export, on the grounds that the intelligence being provided by Henderson was of diminishing value (perhaps a reflection that his access was not as good as that of Mark Gutteridge), and the exports were clearly going to installations involved in nuclear and chemical and biological warfare (CBW) programs. It was not in British or Western interests for them to be used in any such programs. On 24 August 1989, a senior official at the FCO's Middle East Desk sent William Waldegrave a briefing note recommending that applications for Matrix Churchill equipment be refused, as they could

enhance Iraq's ability to rebuild its military capacity, in particular, by allowing it to manufacture artillery rockets. We know from secret sources that Matrix Churchill has supplied equipment to Iraq's munitions factories . . . this is in contravention of our policy on defence sales to Iran and Iraq. In addition the lathes could be used to produce components for a nuclear explosive device. . . . Intelligence have now agreed . . . that it would be possible to draw selectively on information should it be necessary in order to justify a refusal.[57]

As a result, Waldegrave returned to the fray in what had been an unequal battle of wills. He wrote to Lord Trefgarne (who had swapped roles with

Alan Clark to become trade minister, while Clark had moved to the MOD), copied to Clark, on 6 September 1989. He again argued that the Matrix Churchill license applications should be refused:

> You will already be aware of our concerns about Matrix Churchill, which was taken over as part of a procurement network for the Iraqi nuclear, CBW and missile programmes. We know, originally from secret sources, that contrary to the assurances of the manufacturer, its high technology machine tools have been shipped to the major Iraqi munitions establishments.
>
> We have approved the company's applications in the past, but only because of the need to protect these sources. I now understand, however, that we could draw selectively on information from secret sources should that become necessary in order to justify a refusal. Our concerns can only be reinforced by the activities of the Iraqi procurement network, about which the Prime Minister expressed concern in April. The Learfan issue in July demonstrated the lengths to which the Iraqis are prepared to go in order to obtain sensitive technology and materials and the consequent need to undermine their procurement activities.[58]

But Trefgarne's reply rejected these concerns, arguing:

> The continuing ceasefire has necessitated reconsideration of the operation of the ministerial guidelines and weakened to the point of extinction any case for prohibiting exports of general purpose industrial equipment for fear that it might be put to military use . . .
>
> I see no grounds for jeopardising Matrix Churchill's prospects by refusing licences to export the equipment to Iraq. Quite apart from the commercial damage to the company and the risk to employment, frustration of these orders could well affect the prospects in Iraq of other British machinery manufacturers and of exporters generally.[59]

Meanwhile, within the DTI, the same preoccupation with being able to reconcile exports with the narrow concerns of the guidelines rather than wider issues of security and national interest was rendered transparent in a "secret" memo from Tony Steadman of the ELU to Eric Beston, a senior DTI official. This concerned how the DTI should respond to Waldegrave's letter of 6 September, recommending the refusal of the four current license applications from Matrix Churchill. The memo began by noting that previous Matrix Churchill machine tool exports had gone to Nassr and Hutteen, both of which were military establishments. Regarding compatibility of export with the (by now revised) guidelines, he said:

The ceasefire has been in place for over a year. In December 1988 Ministers agreed on a more flexible interpretation of the guidelines to reflect a more relaxed approach to the less sensitive items such as civil aircraft, spares and machine tools. Though the need to protect intelligence sources was a factor in approving the company's licences last February, the fact that the lathes could be used for munitions manufacture was regarded as less of a concern in the light of the cease fire, in that the machines would not, under the more relaxed interpretation of the Guidelines, be of direct and significant assistance in the conduct of offensive operations in breach of the cease fire.

No firm evidence has been offered that Matrix Churchill machines have been used to further Iraq's nuclear programme. The February approvals took account of the fact that a refusal of the licences would not prevent Iraq developing a nuclear weapon. *Though the company is largely Iraqi-owned and Mr Safa al-Habobi, a director, is Head of Nassr and known to have an interest in acquiring nuclear technology, this is not in itself evidence of Matrix Churchill's involvement in that programme.*[60]

Clearly, it is difficult to see what the DTI *would* have regarded as firm evidence, given this mood. The guidelines were flawed in many ways, but a major flaw was the assumption in favor of sale unless a compelling reason not to sell was apparent, which created a situation whereby absolute proof rather than exposed risk was the criterion for denying any export. The memo went on to argue that a refusal would damage wider commercial interests: "Coming hard on the heels of the decision on the Hawk Trainer Project, a refusal will be regarded by Iraq as provocative and this could affect our export effort generally to that market. . . . Equivalent products could easily be sourced from other competitor countries, such as Switzerland, Germany, Italy and Japan."[61]

Trefgarne adopted the same line at the Scott Inquiry, arguing that even had it been known conclusively that the machines were going to be used in conventional armaments production, this use could still have been compatible with the guidelines, as long as it did not represent a "significant enhancement" of Iraqi capability. For Trefgarne, the question seemed to come down to one of quantity: "If it was going to make one round a week, that would not have been a significant enhancement, clearly. If it was going to make 100 rounds a minute, it might be."[62]

Meanwhile, further intelligence on Matrix Churchill—this time on its links with Cardoen—was coming through GCHQ. A detailed report, dated 13 October 1989, was circulated to all relevant departments (FCO, MOD, DTI, Customs). Titled *Chile-Iraq Military Trade: Chilean Arms Firm to Turn Over Munitions Factory to Iraqi Government*, it said:

The Chilean arms firm Industrias Cardoen in late September 1989 was preparing to turn at least part of a large munitions factory and associated workers' camps it has been constructing in Iraq over to the Iraqi Government. The factory, called the Nahrawan plant, was built by Cardoen under contract with the Al Fao General Establishment. It is designed and equipped for the manufacture of bomb and rocket fuses, including types 904 and 905 (bomb nose and proximity fuses respectively) and fuses for the Soviet design BM-21 rocket. A plant for assembly and manufacture of cluster bombs is also associated with the same contract.[63]

The report went on to say that a British firm was supplying machine tools to manufacture fuses but did not name it. After a significant delay, inquiries to GCHQ revealed that the company was Matrix Churchill. At the same time, however, the FCO seemed to be in receipt of contradictory evidence from the intelligence services, which caused the FCO's Simon Sherrington to note: "The arguments remain finely balanced. . . . Our friends [i.e., MI6] have since said that they believe that the lathes may not, at any rate initially, be used for the direct manufacture of munitions or for nuclear applications. They are inclined to believe statements by Habobi, Head of NASSR and Hutteen State Establishment, that his organisation is now dedicated solely to post-war reconstruction of Iraq."[64] Crucially, when he wrote this, Sherrington had not seen the GCHQ memo of 13 October.

This DTI/MOD–FCO statelmate continued until Waldegrave, Trefgarne, and Alan Clark met in the House of Lords on 1 November 1989. Prior to this meeting, Trefgarne was given a briefing stating that the DTI did "not consider FCO's strategic concerns outweigh the commercial importance of these exports. Iraq is third best market for machine tools" and that the "fact that Matrix Churchill is virtually Iraqi-owned by an organisation known to be procuring nuclear technology is not sufficient to refuse these applications." An FCO minute of the meeting itself shows that Waldegrave argued that the intelligence being provided by Henderson was no longer of sufficient importance to justify allowing the supply of further machine tools. Trefgarne and Clark pressed for the continuation of the trade. Waldegrave was therefore unable to secure acceptance of the FCO position, and the meeting ended with his accepting the DTI position on the understanding that any ensuing "presentational problems"—for example, questions in Parliament or stories in the media—would be handled by the DTI. Trefgarne agreed to this.

Waldegrave's private secretary's summary of the meeting's conclusions stated: "We agreed that we should continue to interpret the guidelines more flexibly in respect of Iraq, as we have done in practice since the end of last year; but that we should revert to a stricter interpretation for Iran, along the guidelines which operated before the ceasefire."[65]

In March 1990 Trefgarne sought to use this understanding as the basis for approving the export of further equipment, arguing that neither the Daghir nuclear capacitors sting nor the December 1989 rocket "launch" was sufficient grounds for refusal of a license. The execution of Bazoft and the exposure of the supergun program had no apparent effect on the DTI and MOD's joint enthusiasm for the continuation of the trade. A briefing note written for Trefgarne by Tony Steadman on 28 March 1990, in spite of the pace of events at this time, pulled the arguments for granting the outstanding Matrix Churchill licenses (for Cardoen) together:

> . . . the decision to approve [the licenses] last November was made against the background of Iraq's known involvement in arms manufacture and the acquisition of CW, nuclear explosives technology and ballistic missile development.
>
> Nonetheless, it was considered right to allow exports of machine tools which are generally used for peaceful purposes . . .
>
> The launch by Iraq of a ballistic missile does not seem to be a reason to reverse our policy, given our previous knowledge that the Iraqis had such a development programme. In any event, it is difficult to see how a refusal at this stage would have any significant impact, given that they are presumably so well advanced.

However, these events served to reinforce the FCO's concerns, which were duly passed on to Trefgarne by Waldegrave in a letter of 30 May:

> It is a difficult time in our bilateral relationship with the Iraqis following the execution of Farzad Bazoft and recent revelations about their illegal procurement activity in the UK and elsewhere . . . The nuclear capacitors and supergun problems have . . . generated a very high level of interest in parliament and the media in the supply of high tech equipment to Iraq. Matrix Churchill's links with Iraq and involvement in the Iraqi procurement network are well-known. In the present circumstances I believe the government would be strongly criticised if we allowed the export of machine tools which could be used on the supergun or related projects, particularly given Matrix Churchill's links with SRC. We would with some justification, be accused of being inconsistent if not irresponsible.[66]

Despite this, the DTI and MOD resisted Waldegrave's proposal that current applications be reassessed in three months "when the interest generated by the supergun may have subsided." Waldegrave wrote again on 19 June, arguing the rational line that informed suspicion and likelihood, given the developing climate, should be sufficient to block export of the outstanding machines:

> Although we have no incontrovertible proof that the equipment in question will be used in arms manufacture, the overall intelligence picture suggests it might well. If, as seems likely, there are further revelations about indigenous Iraqi arms manufacture and Matrix Churchill are again implicated, we would entirely justifiably in my view be sharply criticised for approving such licences. We cannot argue that we had not been adequately warned.[67]

Prior to the Bazoft execution in March 1990, Alan Clark was circulating a note arguing that "the evenhanded approach has long been anachronistic—and, in my view, its merit was always doubtful. Now that hostilities are at their lowest ebb they are ever likely to reach between two such implacably mutually antagonistic countries, I believe the sole criteria for determining our export policy to both Iran and Iraq should be commercial interests and national security."[68] Notwithstanding the fact that a tilt in any case existed, this reflected Clark's view that Iran was the real enemy, and that British and Western interests were best served by unambiguously aligning with Iraq. The following day, 9 March, the MOD's Nicholas Bevan wrote:

> At present most Gulf states, especially Saudi Arabia, see Iran as a greater threat to their interest in security, but fear of Iraq's external ambitions, for example in Kuwait, should not be underestimated . . . Iran is, for various reasons, a lost cause to us for the foreseeable future, but Iraq has the material and human resources to continue to be a major regional affair. There is a case for moving gradually to less restrictive export policies on these grounds.[69]

This upbeat assessment went no further, because a week after it was written, Farzad Bazoft was executed.

◆ Panic

Six weeks before the invasion of Kuwait, the trade and industry secretary, Nicholas Ridley, was alerted by the DTI's Mike Coolican to Customs' interest in Matrix Churchill. In view of the government's intimate knowledge of and involvement in the case, as outlined above, Coolican sent him the following distress signal:

Customs have prima facie evidence that current machine tools exports from Matrix Churchill and other UK companies under licence are being routed via Chile to Iraq for arms manufacture.

Evidence was available in 1987 to the same effect, but to protect sources ministers took a decision to let the exports go ahead.

Customs now have absolute evidence of the fact that Matrix Churchill . . . knew about the real end-use of all these machine tools and thus made false descriptions to us and Customs. An investigation will clearly bring all these to light.

The dirty washing liable to emerge from the action proposed by Customs & Excise will add to the problems posed by the [super]gun. For the DTI the timing is extraordinarily embarrassing given recent correspondence between ourselves, MOD and FCO.[70]

Concerned that Customs was determined to exercise its theoretical independence and was about to expose Matrix Churchill, and with it Government complicity in the arming of Iraq, Ridley wrote to Prime Minister Thatcher. The previous day, Ridley's private secretary, Martin Stanley, had written to his counterpart in Customs about a planned visit to the Matrix Churchill plant in Coventry. His letter referred to earlier assurances that Customs would inform the DTI in advance of any visit, which would give his department "the opportunity to object." Stanley complained: "You assured me that the visit would be used for factfinding only, and no action would be taken as a result without consulting ministers."[71]

Ridley's follow-up letter to Mrs. Thatcher suggests something approaching desperation, and further suggests that Customs was acting independently of the governmental machinery implicated in the affair. It was certainly the only arm of government that considered the Howe Guidelines as anything other than a means of assuaging parliamentary and public opinion and allowing the Government to do as it pleased first and reconcile its actions with an interpretation of the guidelines second. Ridley wrote:

Any action following that visit is likely to worsen relations with Iraq. . . . Relations are of course already strained. Following our action to intercept shipments of parts of the big gun and the nuclear triggers, the Iraqi Ministry of Industry and Military Manufacturing, which accounts for around 60 per cent of Iraqi industrial procurement, announced that trade with the UK was under review. . . . I wrote to the Iraqi minister to assure him of our wish for normal commercial relations with Iraq. . . . The Iraqi minister's response was not reassuring. . . . The minister is the President's son-in-law and a member of the inner circle of the regime. . . .

I can see no prospect of any improvement in the position while investigations into possible breaches of export controls continue. On the contrary, I see a considerable risk of further deterioration from which only our competitors can benefit since we have no evidence that they take as restrictive a view as we do.[72]

Clearly, this statement was couched in language designed to appeal to Mrs. Thatcher, as would the revelation that the ECGD's exposure in Iraq amounted to £1 billion (US$1.5 trillion), and that because of this an Iraqi default would "clearly be extremely serious for ECGD and would have implications for PSBR [Public Sector Borrowing Requirement]." The letter concluded by asking for a meeting to consider "a thorough review of our policy in this area which would take into account the policy and political arguments in favour of export controls, the commercial consequences for British industry and the financial risks for ECGD of continuing friction in our relations with Iraq."

As a result of Ridley's appeal, a meeting, chaired by Foreign Secretary Douglas Hurd, was called by Mrs. Thatcher for 19 July 1990 to resolve the problem. However, Ridley was no longer in a position to attend it, having been forced to resign five days earlier over off-the-cuff anti-German remarks made toward the end of an interview with *Spectator* magazine. At this point, only a few politicians and civil servants were aware of the shift in policy toward Iraq, which had only been agreed in an informal manner and never codified. This was to be the function of the meeting chaired by Hurd. The MOD argued for "no special export controls" on either Iran or Iraq, that is, the outright abolition of the guidelines or any similar codified restrictions. It noted that the government's guidelines had "lost whatever relevance they might have had now that there has been a cease fire for over two years." If it could not secure this, the MOD's fallback position was a continued prohibition on "lethal" weapons:

> If Ministers will not wear complete removal of the guidelines, we could revert to the original and simpler formula that "lethal" equipment would not be exported to either Iran or Iraq. This would be a measure of liberalisation and therefore more welcome than retaining the full guidelines. The retention of even this measure of control, however, is irrelevant and hurtful to [the government's] commercial interests for the same reasons but not to the same extent as the retention of the full guidelines.[73]

For the MOD, however, defining "lethal" in the strictest way, as items capable of killing,[74] meant that weapons platforms were excluded from the definition. This would exclude aircraft, possibly reopening an export opportunity for the Hawk, and would have resulted in such a liberal definition that little other than missiles and nonconventional technology would have been excluded. The meeting agreed to the relaxation of the guidelines along the lines sought by the MOD, which had been the de facto position for some time anyhow. A source present told the *Independent* that the implementation of the guidelines between December 1988 and July 1990 was "little more than notional in terms of stuff at the margin" and characterized the purpose of the meeting as merely to legitimize previous practice.[75]

In effect, this formalization of the relaxation marked the culmination of a long Whitehall dispute between the FCO on the one hand and the DTI and MOD on the other, largely conducted after the cease-fire. Those who attended the meeting insisted that Parliament this time would have been informed of the changes approved, but that the wording still had to be agreed when Parliament rose for the summer on 26 July.[76] Two weeks later, Iraq invaded Kuwait.

NOTES

1 The names and addresses of all three featured in a U.S. government Office of Foreign Assets Control listing of "Individuals and Organizations Determined to be Specially Designated Nationals of the Government of Iraq" (taken from 7.1.92 version). Also included were people like Saddam's son, Uday; Safa al-Habobi; Ali Daghir; and Roy Ricks.

2 *Independent*, 11.19.92.

3 British intelligence either already knew or were soon apprised of Habobi's position and intelligence connections. During 1988, an internal Whitehall debate was conducted over whether or not to grant him permission to enter the United Kingdom. Initially, in May 1988, the FCO and the Home Office (from where the home secretary would ultimately approve or deny entry) warned against allowing entry on the grounds that there was "sufficient evidence to suggest that the purpose of Dr Habobi's visit to the UK is to assist in the procurement of equipment for the Iraqi munitions industry." Later, the FCO changed its mind and Habobi was allowed entry, but his movements were monitored by MI5. For the relevant documents, see: Scott Inquiry—Day 19: Evidence of Sir David Miers, pp. 81–88.

4 Wadi was one of thirty-one Iraqis ordered out of Britain in September 1990. On his involvement, see the profile by Tim Kelsey in the *Independent on Sunday*, 9.23.90.

5 Henderson reflected in his autobiography: "I always suspected Ricks had something to do with British Intelligence, but I never knew it for a fact." P. Henderson: *The Unlikely Spy*, p. 81. Ricks later teamed up with a former director of GCHQ, Sir Brian Tovey (1978–83) as managing director and chairman respectively of IES Group plc. See *Private Eye*, 1.27.95, p. 27.

6 P. Henderson: *The Unlikely Spy*, p. 77.

7 According to Henderson, the initials TMG were arbitrary, and did not stand for anything in particular.

8 The revelation of Cuckney's intelligence links was made by Peter Wright in *Spycatcher*. He

recalled that in MI5: "The training program was the responsibility of a tough, no-nonsense officer named John Cuckney . . . He made it clear that MI5 operated on the basis of the 11th Commandment—'Thou shalt not get caught.' " Peter Wright: *Spycatcher: The Candid Autobiography of a Senior Intelligence Officer*, New York, Viking, 1987, p. 31.

9 *Financial Times*, 10.19.90. The value of British machine tool exports to Iraq as a whole also increased markedly at this time. Prior to 1986 there had been no direct sales. In 1986 £1.1 million worth were exported, in 1986 £2.9 million, and in 1988 £31.5 million. *Financial Times*, 9.13.89.

10 Also involved here in similar capacities were companies such as Schaublin AG and Bonaventure of Switzerland; Zayer of Spain, Innocenti of Italy, and Friedrich Deckel, Neue Magdegurger, and Lurgi of West Germany.

11 Quoted in John Sweeney: *Trading with the Enemy*, p. 39.

12 P. Henderson: *The Unlikely Spy*, p. 117.

13 Ibid., p. 141.

14 Ibid., p. 148.

15 Ibid., p. 167. This view is further borne out by the content of Waldegrave's letter of 6 September 1989, outlined below.

16 Ibid., p. 169.

17 *Panorama:* UK Ltd—The Arming of Iraq, BBC1, 11.23.92.

18 They were charged with two charges of "being knowingly concerned in the exportation of machines and parts for Industries Cardoen between 20 July 1988 and August 9 1990, and for ABA Project Nassr Enterprises for Mechanical Industries, Iraq, contrary to the Export of Goods (Control) Orders of 1987 and 1989" and two charges of "being knowingly concerned in the attempted exportation of the equipment with attempt to evade prohibition under the export control orders," charges all three denied.

19 Scott Inquiry—Day 68: Evidence of Tristan Garel-Jones, p. 29. Later he added: "The reason I regard the public disclosure of these documents as injurious to the public interest is because it has, I think, implanted in the minds of ordinary citizens that public servants are in some way engaged in a conspiracy with Ministers to see if they can sort of slip arms to Iraq when no one is looking or something. It is absurd." Ibid., p. 51. It may have sounded absurd to Garel-Jones, but it was disconcertingly close to the truth in some respects.

20 Moses had then recently prosecuted the Daghir nuclear capacitors case for Customs.

21 Quoted in David Leigh: *Betrayed: The Real Story of the Matrix Churchill Trial*, London, Bloomsbury, 1993, p. 74. Based on Richard Norton-Taylor's trial notes, this is the most detailed account of the trial itself.

22 Indeed, until the end of the trial, the whole issue aroused little general interest. For example, the BBC did not cover the trial until it was over, and neither did the *Times*. On the secrecy surrounding the trial see, for instance, the experiences of Gerald James and Tim Laxton, recounted in D. Leigh: *Betrayed*, pp. 126–127.

23 See Scott Inquiry—Day 51: Evidence of Alan Clark, pp. 91, 85.

24 See D. Leigh: *Betrayed*, ch. 6.

25 *Financial Times*, 9.8.89.

26 *Sunday Times*, 11.15.92.

27 An account of the cross-examination can be found in D. Leigh: *Betrayed*, ch. 11. Clark told the Scott Inquiry: "I had to indulge in a fiction, and invite them to participate in a fiction" and that the "meeting had to be governed by a tacit assumption that tools which were capable of more than one use were, in fact, going to be devoted to civilian use." Scott Inquiry—Day 50: Evidence of Alan Clark, p. 84, and Day 51, p. 92.

28 *Guardian*, 11.5.92, *Daily Telegraph*, 11.5.92.

29 The government subsequently sought to explain the collapse of the trial in terms of Clark's testimony rather than the revelations contained in the documents it had attempted to conceal. For example, John Major told the House of Commons: "In any case, the prosecution in the Matrix Churchill trial failed not because of the disclosure of documents but because of the change of evidence of a key witness." *Hansard*, 2.4.93, col. 472.

30 See chapter 6.

31 *Machine Tools for Iraq*—Memorandum from Alan Barrett, MOD, 1.25.88.

32 Scott Inquiry—Day 19: Evidence of Sir David Miers, p. 69.

33 Scott Inquiry—Day 26: Evidence of William Waldegrave, p. 48.

34 Scott Inquiry—Day 18: Evidence of Sir David Miers, p. 111.

35 *Financial Times*, 11.12.92.

36 Ibid. My emphasis.

37 *Financial Times*, 11.11.92.

38 Scott Inquiry—Day 26: Evidence of William Waldegrave, pp. 74–77.

39 Scott Inquiry—Day 81: Evidence of Lord Trefgarne, pp. 168–169.

40 Ibid., pp. 78–79. See also Day 26: Evidence of William Waldegrave, pp. 97–102.

41 Scott Inquiry—Day 26: Evidence of William Waldegrave, p. 158.

42 Scott Inquiry—Day 81: Evidence of Lord Trefgarne, p. 91.

43 Ibid., p. 160.

44 Scott Inquiry—Day 22: Evidence of David Gore-Booth, pp. 32–34, and Day 30: Evidence of William Waldegrave, pp. 6–7.

45 Scott Inquiry—Day 27: Evidence of William Waldegrave, pp. 3–4.

46 Scott Inquiry—Day 30: Evidence of William Waldegrave, pp. 20–21.

47 Ibid., p. 41.

48 Ibid., pp. 64–65.

49 Ibid., p. 65. My emphasis.

50 Scott Inquiry—Day 37: Evidence of Alan Barrett, pp. 101–102.

51 At a 13 December 1989 IDC meeting, the FCO MED: "made the point at the meeting that the launching of the Iraqi space vehicle and the fact that this demonstrated a far more sophisticated capability in Iraq than we had imagined would certainly incline us to be very wary about Iraqi procurement activities. MOD agreed this was a fact which was of considerable concern to them." Scott Inquiry—Day 30: Evidence of William Waldegrave, pp. 158–159.

52 Quoted in Scott Inquiry—Day 17: Evidence of Mark Higson, pp. 41–42. My emphasis.

53 Scott Inquiry—Day 37: Evidence of Alan Barrett, p. 20.

54 Ibid., p. 48.

55 Scott Inquiry—Day 21: Evidence of David Gore-Booth, p. 133.

56 Briefing note from Mr. Preston, MOD, 8.11.89. Cited in Scott Inquiry—Day 17: Evidence of Mark Higson, pp. 94–95.

57 Scott Inquiry—Day 30: Evidence of William Waldegrave, pp. 81–82.

58 Letter from William Waldegrave, MP, FCO, to Lord Trefgarne, DTI, 6 September 1989. This reference to the need to "undermine their procurement activities" has generally been overlooked, but is significant in relation to subsequent events. This letter was written in September 1989. In December the Astra (PRB) Kaulille plant was the scene of an explosion; in March 1990 the capacitors sting occurred, and Bull was murdered; and in April the supergun barrels were seized as the last sections were about to be delivered.

59 Letter from Lord Trefgarne to William Waldegrave, 10.5.89. In a briefing note for this reply, Eric Beston had argued that export of the outstanding machines would be consistent with the Howe Guidelines, because some had already been shipped to Iraq, so "we would not, therefore, be giving the Iraqis a capability they do not already have." Scott Inquiry—Day 82: Evidence of Lord Trefgarne, p. 54.

60 *Matrix Churchill Ltd: Export Licence Applications for Iraq*—"Secret" memorandum from Tony Steadman to Eric Beston, 25 September 1989. My emphasis. In an 8 July 1988 memo, the FCO argued "that we should allow Dr Habobi to enter the UK, but ensure that no licensable equipment could be exported which could be used in munitions manufacturing by means of close monitoring of his activities by the agencies." Scott Inquiry—Day 22: Evidence of David Gore-Booth, p. 59.

61 Memo: Steadman to Beston, 9.25.89.

62 Scott Inquiry—Day 82: Evidence of Lord Trefgarne, p. 61.

63 Scott Inquiry—Day 30: Evidence of William Waldegrave, p. 74.

64 Scott Inquiry—Day 40: Evidence of Simon Sherrington, pp. 48–49. Sherrington could not remember how he had come by this new (and inconsistent) intelligence assessment, and although he realized it was contrary to previous assessments, he does not seem to have followed this up. Ibid., p. 56.

65 *Financial Times*, 11.12.92.

66 Letter from William Waldegrave to Lord Trefgarne, 5.30.90.

67 Letter from William Waldegrave to Lord Trefgarne, 6.19.90.

68 Scott Inquiry—Day 56: Evidence of Nicholas Bevan, p. 38.

69 Ibid., pp. 39–40.

70 Memo: Coolican to Ridley, 6.14.90.

71 *Guardian*, 11.11.92.

72 Ibid.

73 "Confidential" speaking brief for Min (DP).

74 As per definition given in *Hansard*, 5.2.90, col. 602.

75 *Independent*, 11.18.92.

76 However, this does raise the question subsequently put by Robin Cook, MP: "if the meeting at Cabinet level decided that the House of Commons should be told, when Ministers were repeatedly asked questions during the next two years, not a single reference was made either to the meeting in 1990 . . . or to the changes in the guidelines in 1988 or the many decisions in between that represented a weakening of those guidelines to the point of extinction. If it was decided in July 1990 to tell Parliament, why was there a failure to do so in the subsequent two years?" *Hansard*, 11.23.92, col. 642.

The Scott Inquiry

The revelations of the Matrix Churchill trial showed not only that the British government had connived in the breach of its own guidelines with regard to the arming of Iraq but that to keep this information from the electorate, ministers had been prepared to conceal key documents and allow those businesspeople involved to go to prison by denying them confirmation of their defense that "the government knew." The government's response was to establish the Scott Inquiry. Its terms of reference were announced by John Major on 10 November 1992:

> Having examined the facts in relation to the export from the United Kingdom of defence equipment and dual use goods to Iraq between December 1984 and August 1990 and the decisions reached on the export licence applications for such goods and the basis for them, to report on whether the relevant Departments, Agencies, and responsible Ministers operated in accordance with the policies of Her Majesty's Government; to examine and report on decisions taken by the prosecuting authority and by those signing public interest immunity certificates in R v Henderson and any other similar cases that he considers relevant to the issues of the inquiry; and to make recommendations.[1]

There was something of a precedent for this kind of inquiry. In 1935 a Royal Commission on the Private Manufacture of and Trade in Armaments had been established following a public outcry over the role of the "merchants of death" in encouraging and perpetuating conflicts by arming competing sides. It had been critical of government policy but was largely ignored by government. By 1992, the technology had changed, but the principles involved seemed in many ways remarkably similar. As the inquiry progressed, so too did government attitudes toward it.

By the end of 1995, the Scott Inquiry had been at work for over three years. By the time of its last public session, in September 1994, it had received written evidence from over 250 witnesses, sat in public session for over 430 hours and in closed session for around sixty hours, and gathered over 200,000 pages of documents. Sixty-one witnesses had been heard in eighty-seven days of public hearings, and a further twenty-one in closed sessions.[2]

Although the decisions that gave rise to the foreign policy failure termed "Iraqgate" related to the sale of arms to both Iran and Iraq during and after their war, the Scott Inquiry would examine only Iraq—the issue that had given rise to the trial of the Matrix Churchill Three. However, by looking at Iraq but not Iran, the inquiry was going to run the risk of isolating its subject from the context in which its procurement network operated. Ultimately, it would have to consider certain issues relevant to Iran (although it continued to decline various offers of information on related regional intrigues, such as details of Mark Thatcher's Swiss bank account, for example), for the fundamental reason that the Howe Guidelines, the flawed nature of which had contributed to the need for this inquiry in the first place, addressed both Iran and Iraq, though in practice not equally. However, at the inquiry's outset, when it was thought that a report could be published relatively quickly, bringing Iran within its terms of reference was ruled out as a time-consuming and unnecessary extension. In retrospect, this can be seen to have been a mistake. The terms of reference were further clarified at a press conference to mark the beginning of the inquiry. Lord Justice Scott said that he would be required to examine:

i) the statutory basis whereby the Government has power to control the export of goods from this country to foreign countries;

ii) the licensing procedures whereby the Government exercises its statutory power of control;

iii) the publicly declared policy of the Government towards exports to Iran and Iraq over the period 1984 to August 1990;

iv) the particular procedures put in place by the Government in order to implement its policy to control exports to Iraq and Iran;

v) the manner in which the procedures in question worked, the basis upon which decisions to grant or refuse licences were in fact taken and whether the decisions taken were consistent with Government policy as publicly declared;

vi) to the extent that arms and arms related material may have reached Iraq from the United Kingdom otherwise than via the licensing system, whether there was any participation or acquiescence in that process on the part of Government or any Government Ministers, officials or agencies;

vii) the procedures for enforcement of the statutory controls, including prosecution for alleged offences;

Table 8.1

Witnesses Questioned in Public Session by the Scott Inquiry

Day of Inquiry	Date	Name of Witness
Day 1	4 May 1993	Sir Richard Luce (formerly minister of state, FCO)
		Mr. Day, FCO
Day 2	5 May 1993	Mr. Hart, ECGD
		Mr. Bryars, ECGD
Day 3	10 May 1993	Mr. Sandars, MOD
Day 4	11 May 1993	Lt. Col. Glazebrook, MOD
Day 5	12 May 1993	Lt. Col. Glazebrook
Day 6	17 May 1993	Sir Adam Butler (formerly minister for defence procurement)
Day 7	19 May 1993	Mr. Channon (formerly secretary of state for trade and industry)
Day 8	24 May 1993	Sir Hal Miller, MP
Day 9	27 May 1993	Sir Patrick Mayhew (formerly attorney general)
Day 10	11 June 1993	Mr. Collins, FCO
Day 11	15 June 1993	Sir Stephen Egerton, FCO
Day 12	21 June 1993	Lt. Col. Glazebrook
Day 13	22 June 1993	Lt. Col. Glazebrook
Day 14	28 June 1993	Mr. Patey, FCO
Day 15	30 June 1993	Mr. James, Eagle Trust plc
		Mr. Fellgett, HM Treasury
Day 16	7 July 1993	Mr. Vereker, FCO
Day 17	15 July 1993	Mr. Higson (formerly FCO)
Day 18	19 July 1993	Sir David Miers, FCO
Day 19	20 July 1993	Sir David Miers
Day 20	27 July 1993	Mr. Blackley, FCO
Day 21	13 September 1993	Mr. Gore-Booth, FCO
Day 22	14 September 1993	Mr. Gore-Booth
Day 23	15 September 1993	Mr. Young, FCO
Day 24	20 September 1993	Mr. Renton (formerly minister of state, FCO)
Day 25	21 September 1993	Mr. Mellor (formerly minister of state, FCO)
Day 26	22 September 1993	Mr. Waldegrave (formerly minister of state, FCO)
Day 27	23 September 1993	Mr. Waldegrave
Day 28	6 October 1993	Mr. McDonald, MOD
Day 29	7 October 1993	Mr. McDonald
Day 30	12 October 1993	Mr. Waldegrave
Day 31	19 October 1993	Mr. Fuller, FCO
Day 32	20 October 1993	Mr. Lamport, FCO

(continued)

Table 8.1 (continued)

Day of Inquiry	Date	Name of Witness
Day 33	25 October 1993	Mr. Haswell, FCO
Day 34	26 October 1993	Mr. McDonald
Day 35	28 October 1993	Mr. McDonald
Day 36	1 November 1993	Mr. Barrett, MOD
Day 37	2 November 1993	Mr. Barrett
Day 38	3 November 1993	Mr. Barrett
Day 39	4 November 1993	Mr. Barrett
Day 40	8 November 1993	Mr. Sherrington, FCO
Day 41	22 November 1993	Mr. Beston, DTI
Day 42	23 November 1993	Mr. Beston
Day 43	24 November 1993	Mr. Beston
Day 44	25 November 1993	Mr. Beston
Day 45	26 November 1993	Mr. Beston
Day 46	30 November 1993	Mr. Steadman, DTI
Day 47	1 December 1993	Mr. Steadman
Day 48	8 December 1993	Baroness Thatcher (formerly prime minister)
Day 49	13 December 1993	Mr. Clark (formerly minister for defence procurement and minister for trade)
Day 50	14 December 1993	Mr. Clark
Day 51	15 December 1993	Mr. Clark
Day 52	17 December 1993	Mr. Beston
Day 53	11 January 1994	Mr. Baker (formerly home secretary)
Day 54	12 January 1994	Lord Howe (formerly foreign secretary)
Day 55	17 January 1994	Mr. Major, prime minister
Day 56	21 January 1994	Mr. Bevan, Cabinet Office
Day 57	25 January 1994	Mr. Hurd, foreign secretary
Day 58	26 January 1994	Mr. Petter, DTI
Day 59	28 January 1994	Mr. Coolican, DTI
Day 60	2 February 1994	Mr. Collins, QC (Ordtec trial—Evidence taken in private)
Day 61	3 February 1994	Mr. Steadman
Day 62	9 February 1994	Sir Robin Butler, Cabinet secretary
Day 63	10 February 1994	Sir Robin Butler
Day 64	17 February 1994	Mr. Leithead, Treasury solicitor
Day 65	21 February 1994	Mr. Clarke (formerly home secretary)
Day 66	22 February 1994	Mr. Rifkind, secretary of state for defence
Day 67	23 February 1994	Mr. Lilley (formerly secretary of state for trade and industry)
Day 68	24 February 1994	Mr. Garel-Jones (formerly minister of state, FCO)
Day 69	28 February 1994	Mr. Heseltine, president of the Board of Trade
Day 70	2 March 1994	Mr. Hosker, Treasury solicitor

(continued)

Table 8.1 (continued)		
Day of Inquiry	**Date**	**Name of Witness**
Day 71	3 March 1994	Mr. Hosker
Day 72	9 March 1994	Mr. Wiltshire, Customs and Excise
Day 73	10 March 1994	Mr. Wiltshire
Day 74	11 March 1994	Mr. Andrew, Customs and Excise
Day 75	17 March 1994	Miss Bolt, Customs and Excise
Day 76	18 March 1994	Miss Bolt
Day 77	21 March 1994	Mr. Moses, leading counsel, Matrix Churchill prosecution
Day 78	22 March 1994	Mr. Moses
Day 79	24 March 1994	Sir Nicholas Lyell, attorney general
Day 80	25 March 1994	Sir Nicholas Lyell
Day 81	29 March 1994	Lord Trefgarne (formerly minister of state, MOD, DTI)
Day 82	30 March 1994	Lord Trefgarne
Day 83	4 May 1994	Mr. Tweddle, Customs and Excise
Day 84	6 May 1994	Mr. Russell, Customs and Excise
Day 85	9 May 1994	Sir Brian Unwin (formerly chairman, Customs and Excise)
Day 86	10 May 1994	Mrs. Strachan, Customs and Excise
Day 87	12 May 1994	Mr. Biker, Customs and Excise
Day 88	7 July 1994	Mr. Henderson (formerly managing director, Matrix Churchill)

viii) the prosecutions, of which the Matrix Churchill prosecution is one, brought in respect of traffic to Iraq;

ix) the use of PII certificates in connection with those prosecutions.[3]

Subsequently, as Scott explained to John Major, as a result of evidence submitted by businesspeople and industrialists involved, it also "proved necessary . . . to inquire into the use of third countries as diversionary routes for the export of lethal equipment from this country to Iraq."[4] This part of the inquiry came, in practice, to focus on the role of Jordan and British government knowledge of its conduit function.

The team Scott assembled was led by Presiley Baxendale, counsel to the inquiry, whose quietly effective style of questioning dominated the public sessions, and Christopher Muttukamaru, secretary to the inquiry. Each witness was sent a comprehensive request for detailed background information and specific questions the inquiry wished to have answered. The longest questionnaire, running to 172 pages, was sent to Alan Moses, QC. The inquiry established a principle that it would hear as much evidence as possible in public, with witnesses being given advance notice of the areas about which they were likely to be questioned.[5] Sir Robin Butler, the Cabinet secretary, wrote to ask Scott to restrict the amount of evidence heard in open session, suggesting, "you should direct that hearings go into closed session when in your view disclosure in public would be damaging to the public interest." Scott firmly rejected this approach:

> The test which I intend to apply in order to decide whether a hearing should be in closed session is whether the public disclosure of the documents or information in question would cause serious injury to the interests of the nation . . . I shall not direct that hearings be held in closed session unless I feel able to conclude that the public interest in an open hearing is outweighed by the public interest in protecting from disclosure in public the documents or information in question.[6]

◆ Issues

Export Licensing Procedure

In part, the Matrix Churchill and Ordtec elements of the Iraqgate scandal in Britain were rooted in an export culture that extended to arms and is characterized by a proclivity to sell unless there are concrete reasons for not doing so.[7] Lord Trefgarne told the inquiry: "When considering ELAs for Iran and Iraq, both at the MOD and DTI, I would approach the application on the basis that it should be granted, unless there was firm evidence to the contrary. At the MOD, my principal concerns were the threat to British forces and the Government's international treaty obligations."[8]

Where objections were raised, he went on, these would often be for "presentational reasons," which can only refer to the nature of the recipient regime and likely public and parliamentary reaction to such a sale. Even where there were suspicions about the real end-use of dual-use equipment, as opposed to the stated end-use, ministers (and the MOD Working Group)[9] erred on the side of approval. In the Matrix Churchill case, for example, intelligence sources inside the company had openly admitted the real purpose of the machines and had provided drawings. In addition, it was acknowledged that the plants they were going to were involved in military production. But still this was not enough. Lord Trefgarne agreed

> that there was evidence that these machines were going to Hutteen or Nassr, which were involved, *inter alia*, in weapons manufacture, but it was not clear that these

machines were going to be used exclusively, or even at all, for weapons manufacture and, unless we had reasonable evidence, more than the mere circumstantial evidence of their destination, we were not entitled to assume that they would be used for weapons manufacture.[10]

Really? That this approach was evident throughout the administrative system was confirmed by Lt. Col. Glazebrook, who told the inquiry:

> Nassr Enterprises was a very large state-owned organisation that produced munitions. It also produced a limited amount of civil goods and consequently whenever its name came up in discussion [at the MOD Working Group] Regional Marketing used to emphasise that we could not prove that this particular machine was going to be used for military goods, because we had to accept that its factories also produced civil goods.[11]

Alan Barrett seemed to suggest to the inquiry that the Matrix Churchill machines could, at the time, have justifiably been considered by Whitehall to be needed, "to make weapons or umbrella stands" (at Nassr) because of which there were "no suspicions." Scott told him: "This is what I do not understand. Here is Iraq spending . . . between 30 and 45 million [pounds] . . . on a large number of machine tools . . . Was there no suspicion that they were going to be used for military purposes? It almost begs belief." He went on: "If [the civil servants involved] did think about it, then I find it very, very difficult to follow the thought processes that led to a conclusion that you have expressed here, that they had satisfied themselves that the lathes were for civilian items, not destined for military end use."[12]

Hence, instead of erring on the side of caution when a buildup of complementary evidence pointed in the same direction, Whitehall continued to exercise its tendency toward export, the blocking of a sale requiring a degree of evidence so firm as to be unattainable. Barrett told the inquiry that to satisfy the DTI that the machine tool exports should not go ahead, those advocating refusal would have to have been "absolutely certain" that the lathes were going to be used for a military purpose. Scott asked: "Why should 'absolutely certain,' which is a criterion as rigorous as one can find, be the right criterion? Absolute certainty is absent in most forms of inquiry. Why should absolute certainty have been requisite in this case?"[13] The wrong question was being put to the wrong department. Instead of the DTI demanding of other departments how they could be certain the machines would be used to manufacture arms, the DTI should have been asked by other departments how it could be absolutely certain they would not, and this should have been the criterion that determined permissibility of exports to sensitive destinations like Iraq.

In part this situation arose out of a set of differing perceptions of the degree of influence enjoyed by departments involved in the regulatory structure. Technically, the DTI issues export licenses, and as such only asks the MOD and FCO for nonbinding advice to help it reach a decision on licensability. However, Alan Clark for one clearly thought that the FCO was the most influential department in this process, by virtue of the fact that if it objected to a particular export and chose to pursue its objection through the system to the highest level (the Cabinet) then its case would be advocated by a far more senior minister (the foreign secretary) than would the argument in favor of export. The FCO, however, did not view itself in so powerful a light vis-à-vis the DTI and felt it needed to present a watertight case against export to the DTI, as the license-issuing body, to have a chance of influencing the outcome, especially when the relevant DTI minister was a vigorous believer in minimizing trade restrictions, as was Alan Clark, for example. The MOD was divided between regulators and sellers (DESO), and with regard to exports to Iran and Iraq, as Glazebrook testified, clearly tended to favor export. Thus in practice the MOD tended to side with the DTI against the FCO, as in the Matrix Churchill case.

However, even when the time came that the DTI tacitly had to accept that the machine tools had a military application, they did not stop using the guidelines to frame fresh, disingenuous, arguments in favor of sale. The cornerstone of this practice was the DTI argument that even if the goods did have a military end-use, this would not represent a "significant enhancement" of Iraqi capabilities, because it merely meant substituting indigenous for imported Soviet weaponry. This was, at best, a facile argument—one characterized by Baxendale as "pretty useless"—which deliberately ignored the fact that self-sufficiency would obviate Iraq's need to import and use hard currency.[14] Even where witnesses accepted the advantages of self-sufficiency over importing, they still cited the "significant enhancement" clause as a consideration. Hence, William Patey of the FCO:

> You could argue that their capability was enhanced. It is a question of whether it is significantly enhanced. Clearly it is easier . . . for them to make their own munitions than it is to import them, but at the end of the day they have the same munitions, so they do not have any more munitions to fire than they would have had otherwise . . .[15]

But once a state develops an indigenous capacity, it is impossible to guarantee what quantities will be produced, and given the capacities of Nassr and Hutteen, Patey's argument seems both ill-conceived and ill-informed.

Answers to Parliamentary Questions

Another area the inquiry explored at length was the question of when, if ever, it is right for ministers to seek to mislead Parliament—either by withholding information or not providing as full an answer as possible to a parliamentary question. In theory, the answer seems straightforward. *Questions of Procedure for Ministers* says that it is ". . . the duty [of a Minister] to give Parliament and the public as full information as possible about the policy decisions and actions of the Government and not to deceive or mislead Parliament or the public." However, for a number of senior civil servants appearing before the inquiry, the matter was not so easily resolved, and the issue produced lengthy exchanges characterized by distinguished semantic jousting. For David Gore-Booth, for example, parliamentary questions "should be answered so as to give the maximum degree of satisfaction possible to the questioner," and these answers "might be half the picture" because "half a picture can be accurate."[16] In addition, he went on to protest: "You cannot base foreign policy on telling everybody everything. It would not work."[17]

Intelligence

One obvious theme for the Scott Inquiry was that intelligence warnings were not circulated to all those involved in the decision-making process who needed to be apprised of them, when they needed to be apprised of them. Lord Trefgarne, on the basis of his evidence to the Scott Inquiry, was blissfully unaware of intelligence on Matrix Churchill. Alan Clark admitted to having access to intelligence but also seems to have been unaware of much of the context within which he was encouraging trade. At one point in the inquiry, an exasperated Lord Justice Scott opined that "one has to wonder whether the arrangements for the disseminating of information are all that they should be."[18] However, this element provides only partial answers to the machine tool dimension of Iraqgate and does not provide answers to the SRC and Astra elements of the affair.

Nevertheless, it may well account for Paul Henderson's uncomfortable time at the inquiry. Henderson finally gave oral evidence in open session on 7 July 1994, the last such witness. He had asked to give evidence to the inquiry after hearing the evidence of Lord Trefgarne concerning a meeting between the two on 26 September 1989 over outstanding Matrix Churchill license applications.[19] Trefgarne told the inquiry that Henderson had presented the machines in question as being for general engineering purposes, principally for the production of automotive components.[20] This information implied that Henderson had, as Customs claimed, misled the government concerning the end-use of the machines being exported. However, as Henderson noted, the intelligence services knew the reality, and he had been almost frank with Rob Young of the FCO earlier that month in saying that he could not "guarantee" that the machines would not be used in armaments production.

Notwithstanding this, Trefgarne clearly had not been party to the information Henderson shared with intelligence on the reality. He was taking his cue from what Henderson told him. His account of the meeting seemed to be backed up by a briefing note sent by Henderson prior to this meeting, which treated arms as the fourth of five general applications for the machines, and the automotive industry as the first:

Matrix Churchill targets as its key markets:
a) the automotive industry and appropriate subcontractors;
b) the oil industry;
c) aerospace industry and associated subcontractors;
d) the defence industry; and
e) the general engineering industry.[21]

Henderson denied that Trefgarne's account was accurate, just as he had in his statement to the inquiry, saying that no specific licenses were discussed at the meeting. However, a DTI note of the meeting recorded Trefgarne asking about the intended end-use of the machines: "Mr Henderson said the order comprised four machines worth [£]6 million . . . They would be used for general engineering purposes, principally for production of automotive components. He understood they would be used for civil production only. During the war with Iran, the factories in question had produced munitions but were now reverting to civil production."[22]

John Noseworthy of the Machine Tools Technology Association attended the meeting alongside Henderson, and his note of the meeting also confirmed Trefgarne's rather than Henderson's account: "Lord Trefgarne then asked what was the intended use of these machines. Mr Henderson replied that they were intended for industrial use at two factories, which had been previously involved in the war effort. They now had new manufacturing licences from Ford etc. and were seeking to build an automotive manufacturing industry."[23]

Henderson's difficulties were compounded by the transcript of his trial, in which Geoffrey Robertson put to Eric Beston of the DTI, who had also been present at this meeting, an account of it that seemed to show Henderson suggesting an automotive end-use. Although the purpose of the meeting was to get licenses then being held up released, Henderson insisted that the main thrust of the meeting was future trade with Iraq and not the individual licenses themselves. The final account of the meeting with Lord Trefgarne came from Henderson's own autobiography, *The Unlikely Spy*, which ironically also supported Trefgarne's account. This evidence presented Henderson with some difficulty, leading him to explain that "the book basically is not a verbatim record of the meeting" and that it was written by a ghost writer who had combined elements of prior communications with the DTI with what occurred at the meeting. From Henderson's point of view, the session had been a difficult one, and it badly damaged his credibility.

Conduits: Jordan and the Vereker "Gap"

Initially, the Scott Inquiry team had not expected to have to look at the role of conduits in any particular depth. However, as the team members gradually became aware of the scale on which diversions had occurred, they added this area to those they were already investigating. One consistent theme of British government statements and protestations when it came to the arming of Iraq was that, unlike other countries, Britain had not in fact sold arms to Iraq and hence did not appear on listings of those states that were major suppliers. This claim was similar to that deployed by the Bush administration in the United States. While both were superficially true, neither claim stood up to rigorous scrutiny. In the case of Britain, there were two explanations of how it armed Iraq without appearing to do so. The first was the trade in machine tools—exporting the means for Iraq to produce its own weapons. The second was the diversion of arms through Jordan and other conduits. With regard to Jordan, through a series of parliamentary questions, Jim Cousins, MP managed to unearth the fact that in the 1980s, exports to Jordan under the general category "arms and ammunition for military purposes" were valued at £581.5 million—over thirty times the figure (just £18.5 million) for the 1970s. Notwithstanding the Jordanian defense package, the United Kingdom armed Iraq through Jordan.

Scott was initially alerted to the role of Jordan in particular through the written statements of Chris Cowley and Gerald James. Brief questioning of early witnesses toward the ends of their sessions seemed to confirm that Jordan had been widely used. Lt. Col. Glazebrook, who had already given evidence over two days, was even recalled for a further two days' questioning, specifically on Jordan. As the inquiry progressed, it became clear that the lead that Cowley and James had given on Jordan had emerged as a central area of the investigation. In addition to their evidence, James Edmiston, another British businessman who had visited Aqaba, also told of seeing boxes of arms and ammunition from Britain, the United States, Germany, Spain, Italy, the Netherlands, Belgium, Switzerland, and Austria stacked up at the port.[24] Not that Jordan was the only neighboring state to act as a conduit or transshipment point. The inquiry also heard evidence on Saudi Arabia and Kuwait, and about the general attitude of other Gulf states to the practice. For instance, Sir Stephen Egerton, a former ambassador to Saudi Arabia, described reports of the use of "a small military port of Jedda called Al Quadima [which] was occasionally used for transhipment of heavy equipment in transit to Iraq" and that "Al Quadima was in a restricted military zone, very difficult to get to. You were warned off the road if you got anywhere near and you were not allowed to follow anything coming out of it."[25] But it was Jordan that became the focus of the inquiry's concern over conduits. Britain's historical relationship with Jordan, its contemporary geopolitical significance, and the importance of not undermining King Hussein's position were all important factors in encouraging it to turn a blind eye to Jordan's conduit role and to mute any criticism of it.

It became apparent at the Scott Inquiry that Jordan's role had been an open secret throughout the government but that because of these countervailing concerns, and British policy toward Iraq, little of consequence had been done about it. During the war with Iran, the Jordanian port of Aqaba was a favored route through which goods Iraq was otherwise prohibited from acquiring could be received. So extensive was this trade that Iraq had a whole section of the port to itself. It was fenced off from the rest of the port and known as the Iraq Ports Authority. As long ago as 1975, it was revealed at the Scott Inquiry, an intelligence requirement was set up over the use of Jordanian facilities for the transshipment of goods to Iraq.[26] Sir David Miers told the inquiry that "in general, in the Foreign Office, we were quite, how shall I say, concerned, alert, or aware of the possibility that other countries, particularly Jordan, might be used as a diversionary destination" and that the FCO was aware of what Presiley Baxendale called "problems with Jordan" even prior to 1983.[27]

Even so, the British Embassy in Jordan was not, according to Miers, instructed to investigate the use of Jordan as a diversionary route. Ian Blackley said that the FCO was "aware that Jordan, Kuwait and Saudi Arabia were being used as transhipment ports for goods destined for Iraq."[28] The FCO's Simon Fuller, in his written statement to the inquiry, conceded that there was "a general knowledge that Aqaba was a major route for the supply of military equipment" and that "Jordan was a strong and consistent supporter of the Iraqi war effort against Iran."[29] This support even extended to the upgrading of the road from Aqaba into the equivalent of a four-lane highway to cope with the volume of traffic coming from Iraq to pick up military and other supplies. The inquiry was also given MI6 reports indicating clear knowledge of Jordan's role. For example, one dated 14 March 1986 gave details of Jordan passing on goods to Iraq, and another dated 12 November 1986 spoke more generally of abuse of the end-use certificate system by several Arab states in favor of Iraq.

In July 1990, a memo was circulated (the so-called Iraq Note) prior to the Cabinet Committee meeting called to consider dismantling the Howe Guidelines. This alerted its recipients as follows: "It appears that Iraq systematically uses Jordan as a cover for her procurement activities almost certainly with the connivance of senior figures in the Jordanian administration." However, despite the existence of such evidence, even after the invasion of Kuwait, a consignment of 5,000 RO shells, part of the Jordanian defense package, was shipped from Hull on 14 September 1990 aboard the *Tara* to Aqaba and on to Iraq, where U.S., British, and U.N. troops would have to face them in the coming conflict.[30]

Former FCO official Mark Higson told the inquiry that "it was long suspected amongst FCO officials that Jordan was being used as an arms conduit. Indeed, even during my time in the British Embassy in Kuwait [March 1983– July 1986] we knew Jordan through Aqaba was being used for imports of hardware from the UK, which was then going on to Iraq." He was asked what this knowledge was of: "[T]he port of Aqaba [is used] quite openly because it is very convenient, and as we know there is a . . . convenient motorway . . . There is the false end user certificates and there is procuring ostensibly for your own use, when really it is for someone else's use." And to which of these was Higson referring? His answer: "All three of those, to be honest." But Higson also revealed that FCO knowledge of conduits was even wider than this, explaining that during the time he was attached to the British Embassy in Kuwait, "there were two main ways of getting things into Iraq and one was Aqaba and the other was the port of Kuwait" and that "we knew that false end user certificates were part of the Iraqi procurement network."[31] In his statement to the Scott Inquiry, Alan Clark conceded: "It is certainly true that a lot of illicit traffic was going through Jordan at this time."[32] Within

Whitehall, the battle between those eager to promote arms and those arguing that evidence existed that should be met by a refusal to sell was a very uneven one.

One of those who performed the latter role in an environment relatively unsympathetic to notions of export restraint was the MOD's Lt. Col. Glazebrook. His job was to argue for restraint on the MOD Working Group on Iran and Iraq. Counterarguments would come from DESO, and the outcome would be passed up to the IDC, where it would represent the official MOD view on each case presented to it. As early as 1984, Glazebrook was aware that both Jordan and Egypt were acting as conduits for Iraq. With regard to Egypt, for example, he found evidence suggesting that Egypt was passing on 122mm missile casings to Iraq. These were of Soviet design and capable of being fitted with a chemical warhead. He presented his evidence to the MOD Working Group, only to have it rejected. However, after the Gulf War, the U.N. inspection team found this very type of missile in Iraq fitted with "nerve agent warheads."[33] During the Iran-Iraq War, however, it was made clear to Glazebrook that there was no prospect of the guidelines being extended to cover known diversionary routes like Jordan—they were to be applied only to Iran and Iraq:

> It was impressed upon us several times that although we were controlling sales to Iran and Iraq it was no part of our job to interfere with legitimate trade to other countries, and therefore, especially in the case of Jordan, knowing there was strong evidence they were diverting to Iraq, one was concerned that they had just enough and the right sort of things for their own use and not enough for their own use and to pass over to Iraq in addition.[34]

However, the regulatory machinery made this job more difficult by rejecting a license only when confronted with incontrovertible proof—as we have seen, neither informed suspicion or likelihood was sufficient reason to refuse a license application. This is not to say that there were not a number of finely balanced cases. For example, in March 1985 an application by Jordan for Chieftain tank spares was discussed. The Jordanians had a genuine use for the spares but could also have been fronting for Iraq, which had captured a number of Iranian Chieftain tanks (150, according to the MOD)[35] during the Iran-Iraq War. Where there could be no distinction between genuine need and diversionary intent, as in this case, the license was approved. However, other cases were more clear-cut.

According to Glazebrook:

End user certificates are not terribly reliable assurances that the person concerned will keep [the arms] for his own use and will not pass them on to a third party. There have been a number of proven instances where false end user certificates have been produced by various countries for various reasons and, consequently, it is really a question of what are you gaining by going to the trouble of asking for an end use certificate? My personal view is the only use is that after supply is taken . . . if you find that it has been diverted to somebody else, then you can use it as a justification for refusing any further supplies, but it is too late by then to actually stop the initial supply going to the wrong destination.[36]

Neither did it really matter who had supposedly signed the certificates, that is, who was guaranteeing that they would not be passed on to a third party: "You really could not tell. . . . You had a signature block and it gave the name and it gave the appointment to the person there, but I had no means of checking, for example, whether it was a genuine signature or not."[37] From Alan Clark's perspective "false end user information had almost the status of a commercial practice in the Middle East."[38]

To take a good example of this, in July 1986 Glazebrook was asked to consider an application that listed the Austrian MOD as the end-user for 40,000 rounds of RO High Explosive Squash Head ammunition destined for Jordan. The application was from an Austrian company for the export of the components, which would be assembled as complete shells in Austria and then sent on to Jordan. In the event, this was turned down because of Austria's known role in arming Iran and Iraq. In addition, there were several suspicious circumstances:

That particular ammunition only fitted the British tank gun. The British tank gun was only in service in about six countries in the world. Austria was not one of those countries. What was being suggested was that Royal Ordnance . . . should send the components out to Austria where they would be assembled into the complete shell. Now that meant that the company in Austria had to set up a manufacturing line to do this assembly. It had to train its people to do the assembling on the manufacturing line. This takes time and money. This means that the price of the ammunition has to be increased to pay for it.

If it really was going to Jordan, the Jordanians did have the 120 millimetre tank gun. They could have bought the ammunition directly from Royal Ordnance in the UK and it would have been cheaper for them to have done that. It did not make sense for them to take a more expensive route to buying this ammunition. Finally, [there was] the offer that the end user certificate would be furnished by the Austrian MOD, where we knew they were not supplying the Austrian MOD, because they did not have any guns to fit this ammunition.[39]

Another case that came before Glazebrook was the Ordtec application in early 1989 to ship an entire assembly line for the production of artillery fuses (a contract worth £500,000 to Ordtec) to Aqaba on behalf of SRC, with the consignee listed as "Chief of Staff GHQ Jordan Armed Forces" and certified "for the sole use of the Jordan Armed Forces." Again, Glazebrook was rightly suspicious:

> It did not make financial sense. You need one fuse for each artillery shell. Artillery shells are exceedingly expensive things and therefore the numbers that you use in peace time for training are very limited. When you buy shells in the outset, you buy them complete with fuses normally, and therefore, for a small country like Jordan to set up a special production line and train the staff on it to produce fuses for the sort of quantities that they would be likely to use on training, did not make financial sense.[40]

To put this further into perspective, this assembly line was designed to produce around 300,000 fuses a year (i.e., enough for 300,000 artillery shells). At the time, the Jordanians had about 450 guns capable of firing shells containing this type of fuse. Glazebrook told the Scott Inquiry that on the British Army scale of training, 160 shells were fired from each gun per year, so if Jordan had a requirement of around, say, 72,000 fuses, this would have seemed reasonable, although even this would have been expensive for a small country like Jordan, putting the cost of this level of training at around £20 million per year. However, this production line was capable of producing over four times this volume each year. Nevertheless, this order, and a subsequent Ordtec application for booster pellets, again for SRC, was approved in the regulatory machinery. In the event, Ordtec went into liquidation before it could complete delivery of the assembly line (which was intended to be passed on from Aqaba to Baghdad), and so Iraq was never able to produce fuses with it.

Further evidence of knowledge of Jordan's role came from the IDC. On 11 August 1988, the IDC had considered the case of "Chieftain armoured recovery vehicles. MOD asked the IDC for their views on the question of spares for the Chieftain armed recovery vehicles for Iraq. Iraq has asked Jordan to front for them." This suggestion had been put to the head of DESO in July 1988 by Jordanian Field Marshal Bin Shaker during a visit to Jordan. Bin Shaker had said that when King Hussein had visited Iraq the previous week, he had been asked to supply the Iraqis with British military equipment. Miers told the Scott Inquiry that there was a possibility that King Hussein "might have thought that we were prepared to connive at Jordan acquiring things and then sending them on to Iraq" and that "this suggestion that they could feel that they could volunteer the Iraqis are . . . to use them as a front, suggested that they were wishing to draw us into a connivance that we could send things to Iraq via Jordan."[41] Nor was he alone in recognizing this danger. The jovial David Mellor told the inquiry how he "knew that all the rest of the Arabs wanted Saddam to win [the war with Iran], and of course knew that he was being provisionally supplied through continguous countries, Kuwait and Jordan."[42] A further IDC meeting on 19 October noted that supply had, in any case, been approved direct to Iraq: "These parts were linked to the Jordan deal but would be supplied direct to Iraq as they were automotive parts only, and not armour or lethal equipment."[43]

However, within the FCO there was a strong "Jordan lobby" that may have worked to prevent a wider dissemination of the knowledge of Jordan's role. David Gore-Booth accepted that there was a "hands-off Jordan" feeling in the FCO, explaining that "the Anglo-Jordanian relationship is one that is very fundamental to both countries."[44] The FCO's Charles Haswell told the Scott Inquiry: "A stable Jordan is a crucial western interest."[45] Waldegrave agreed: "Jordan is absolutely crucial, the King of Jordan is an absolutely crucial ally and ally for good sense in the Middle East."[46] When Mrs. Thatcher was asked by the inquiry if she was "aware of concerns about Jordan being used as a diversionary route for equipment to get to Iraq," she replied:

I cannot tell you that. I know that in August 1990, after the invasion, the information was put to me, because the King of Jordan was coming to see me, that it was known that Jordan diverted goods to Iraq. This is extremely serious and was totally unacceptable, the more so because we had a very good and friendly relationship with King Hussein.

Evidence was put to me that I thought was horrifying, and it appeared that certificates saying that the weapons supplied to Jordan were for Jordan and not to be diverted had been signed quite high up, very high up in the army.

. . . I tackled him about . . . this evidence that goods which had been supplied to Jordan in good faith . . . were, in fact, being diverted. He was very, very taken aback indeed. I do not know whether he knew or he did not. . . . The stability of Jordan was very important . . . [but] . . . there was a possibility that this rather remarkable country and this very, very courageous king, who never flinched from physical danger, might be destabilised. That would not have done British interests any good at all, nor would it have done countries in the Gulf any good at all. . . . To destabilise Jordan would have been a very, very serious matter indeed. So we took the course of doing as much as we could and seeking what for the King was [an] unusual . . . personal assurance.[47]

In a similar vein, Sir Stephen Egerton told how:

We all very much admired the way King Hussein had maintained his position, in spite of all the difficulties over the Palestine dispute, for more than 40 years, and we were always disposed to help him. The only time we fell out, really, was when he supported Saddam Hussein so unexpectedly in relation to Kuwait, but he maintained he had to do that to maintain his internal position . . . However, recently, of course, he has fallen out with Saddam and he is back . . .[48]

Alan Clark, on the other hand, thought that with Jordan

you were getting into this collision between security considerations, or intelligence considerations, and trading advantage. I had never fully understood the level of trust that was proposed in Jordan, which seemed to me to override a purely objective assessment of what was happening, but I would assume there were wider political and diplomatic considerations that came into this . . . It may have been involved with American policy and the complexities of relations with Israel.[49]

For his part, Sir David Miers illustrated how the Thatcher government's wider arms sales drive acted to limit foreign policy options in the region and may have constrained officials from wanting to draw close attention to Jordan's role:

At this time . . . we were actually mounting a very large defence sales campaign in Jordan. We were trying to sell them things rather than to stop them getting things, and this was something that was being carried on at the highest level . . . the Ministry of Defence, indeed the whole British Government from Ministers down was trying to conduct a sales campaign in Jordan to sell military equipment.[50]

Furthermore, he explained: "We also wanted to try to sell them the Tornado and so it was a very important export market for us, both commercially and also politically."[51] Consequently, anything that could have embarrassed Jordan, or King Hussein personally, could also have resulted in the scaling down or cancellation of the package and the loss of the Jordanian arms market to the French or another competitor. This alone seems to have been considered a good enough reason to turn a blind eye to the rerouting of conventional arms shipments to Iraq. Married to the desire to see the Iran-Iraq War end in a stalemate, and the need to get arms to Iraq to ensure this outcome, this explains the charmed life Jordan led as a conduit right up to August 1990.

Indicative of the existence of this Jordan lobby is the story of the Vereker "gap." Peter Vereker gave evidence to the Scott Inquiry as head of the FCO's Arms Control and Disarmament Department. Although, as Vereker conceded, it was widely known within Whitehall by 1991 that Jordan had acted as a conduit for Iraq, when in that year the government came to compile a list of sensitive destinations, which would henceforth be subject to closer scrutiny, Jordan was successfully excluded.

Douglas Hogg, MP had written to Tim Sainsbury, then minister for trade, in October 1991 to urge Jordan's inclusion, saying: "I see a strong case for including countries like Jordan whose governments actively connive in proliferation or diversionary activities."[52] Evidence that Jordan knowingly played such a role, and even that it had continued to do so after the Iraqi invasion of Kuwait, had come from DIS and other intelligence agencies.[53]

Despite this, the FCO's area desk network began a rearguard action to have Jordan excluded. It was argued that regardless of whether Jordan was a known diversionary route—as the information received from both British and French intelligence indicated—and was being used as such with the knowledge of the Jordanian government, it should not be included because of the potential damage it would inflict on bilateral relations. One of those leading this action was Charles Haswell.[54] For example, during the process of drafting the list of suspect end-users, an FCO official described a meeting as follows:

The problem of diversion was discussed. It was agreed that countries should be included for diversionary reasons only when there was Government knowledge of or support for connivance and diversionary activities.

Jordan was firmly assessed as about the only country falling into that category. Mr Haswell has challenged this assessment and has argued that the inclusion of Jordan would be politically damaging to our bilateral relations.[55]

Hence, when the list was completed and sent to the prime minister on 26 November 1991, Jordan had been hastily removed. The letter that accompanied the list said that "the identification of countries of concern will make a significant contribution to strengthening our present control system," and yet for diplomatic reasons this control was being undermined by Jordan's exclusion. On an A–Z list of suspect destinations, the entry for "J" had simply been whited out. This exclusion produced one of the Scott Inquiry's classic exchanges. The list was shown to Vereker and it was pointed out by Presiley Baxendale that if you look at [page] 64, there is a gap, is there not?

PV: Yes.

PB: Where Jordan should be. You can see it is alphabetical. It looks rather as though someone has just snowpaked it out, or it has just gone, has it not?

PV: That is a gap.

LJS: The gap is the omission of Jordan? That is plain, is it not?

PV: It seems likely. I do not know.

PB: It is obvious. If you have an alphabetical list and there is a gap at J.

PV: I am going through my mind if there are some other Js.

LJS: Mr Vereker, are you seriously telling me that your response to the question, whether the gap shows that Jordan has been removed is only that that seems likely?

PV: I do not know the answer, but I think it is very likely.

LJS: It is certain, is it not?

PV: I had not even noticed the gap before.

PB: You had not noticed? You mean you had not noticed that Jordan was not on it, or you mean you had not noticed that there was a gap?

PV: Of course I know Jordan was not on it. I had not noticed the gap.

PB: I keep thinking of [other] countries beginning with a J and I can only think of Jersey . . . at the top of this handwriting, there is some handwriting. It says: "Mr Haswell, Jordan has disappeared, well done."[56]

Although the Cabinet Office subsequently ruled that Jordan should be included, the list had already been printed without Jordan's inclusion. Despite this, the FCO approved the following answer to any parliamentary questions concerning Jordan's relationship to the list: "The inclusion of Jordan on the list was considered by FCO and MOD officials, but on balance it was decided it should not be."[57] This was clearly a misrepresentation of what had actually occurred. Jordan had been identified as a destination of concern but had been deliberately removed from the list.

Some time later, giving evidence to the Scott Inquiry, Haswell was asked by Lord Justice Scott whether, given his knowledge of the Jordanian government, widespread use of the country as a conduit for illegal exports to Iraq would have been possible without the government's knowledge. His response: "Ultimately, no."[58]

The Dunk Case

Sir David Gore-Booth's evidence also considered the case of Reginald Dunk, of Atlantic Commercial, and the Sterling Guns Affair. In November 1985 Dunk and a business partner, Alexander Schlesinger, pleaded guilty to illegally exporting 200 submachine guns with a Jordanian end-use certificate signed by a major general in the Jordanian Army but intended for onward transmission to Iraq. They were each fined £20,000.[59] However, documents released to the inquiry showed that they pleaded guilty only following the highly improper intervention of the Foreign Office.

Dunk and Schlesinger had approached officials from both the Jordanian and Iraqi Embassies in London to appear as defense witnesses when their case was brought to trial. The officials had agreed to do this. They would argue that the guns had been passed on to Iraq as a "gift" from Jordan and that Dunk and his associates had therefore not acted illegally. This is precisely what FCO officials sent to the embassies in question had been told. The FCO then set about dissuading the embassies from allowing their staff to appear, thereby denying the defendants their defense. The process was captured in a Foreign Office memo read out at the Scott Inquiry:

> You asked for copies of my officers' reports concerning their visits to the Iraqi and Jordanian embassies. These are enclosed. You will see that, given time, the two embassies have put their heads together and produced a united front with a story that is neither credible nor supported by the documentary and oral evidence we now possess.
>
> My only concern is the possible effect this story may have in future criminal proceedings should the defence lawyers decide to obtain the agreement of Embassy personnel to appear as witnesses. It may be prudent for us to confront the Ambassadors with the contradictory evidence in our possession before such an eventuality becomes fact, in the hope that this will deter them from taking a potentially embarrassing course of action.[60]

When Presiley Baxendale asked Miers whether he thought this proposed course of action was "a proper thing for the Foreign Office to be involved in doing," Miers seemed uncertain but conceded, "it is rather a curious procedure."[61] Following the FCO intervention, the embassy staff did not appear as witnesses, leaving the defendants with no option but to change their plea.

Subsequently, Dunk and Schlesinger used this newly available information about governmental interference in the judicial process as the basis of an appeal. There, Lord Taylor told the Court of Appeal: "The machinations in this case to prevent witnesses for the defence being available coupled with the non-disclosure of what had been done, constituted such an interference with the justice process as to amount to an abuse of it."[62]

British and Western policy toward Jordan appeared to have paid dividends when, in August 1995, Jordan granted refuge to the rump of Saddam's family, including Hussein Kamel, following their flight from Iraq. This step was followed on 23 August by a televised speech by King Hussein highly critical of Saddam, which met with the approval of the U.S. State Department and British Foreign Office. The former described it as "a dramatic shift in policy. It's a clear and public signal that the king has indeed made a strategic shift in his alliances. His speech is as close as you can get to an apology to Kuwait and Saudi Arabia for his position during the Gulf War."[63] The CIA was reportedly unwilling to give MI6 access to the high-profile refugees,[64] but, in any case, the men decided to return to Iraq in February 1996, apparently after being offered a pardon. Both Hussein Kamel and his brother Saddam Kamel were executed almost immediately upon arriving back in Baghdad.

◆ Delays in Publication

The inquiry took over three years to produce a report it had originally intended to produce within one, before the end of 1993. An indication of the main cause of these delays, and of Lord Justice Scott's early frustration at Whitehall foot dragging, is contained in a progress report from Scott to John Major in July 1993:

> [D]elays in obtaining some documents have had the consequence of hindering the efficiency of the questioning of witnesses. Some witnesses may have to be recalled to give further evidence (one already has). In addition the process of formulating the questions to be dealt with by witnesses in their written evidence has been made much more burdensome and time consuming by the piecemeal manner in which documents have been forthcoming than would otherwise have been the case.[65]

As Scott approached the end of the inquiry and was in a position to send out draft sections of his report to those criticized in it, he found himself further delayed by a fresh flood of previously undisclosed documents. Christopher Muttukumaru told Stephen Byers, MP that in response to Scott's draft, the inquiry received "69 replies and more than 1,500 pages of comments and underlying documents, most of which we had not previously seen." Byers, quite reasonably, interpreted this as another delaying tactic.[66]

In explaining a further last-minute delay, Muttukumaru went into more detail, citing several reasons. First, Whitehall was still dragging its feet in responding to sections of the first draft of the report that the inquiry had sent

out. Second, the process of Whitehall foot dragging had led some departments to submit papers late, in some cases after the relevant sections of the
report had already been sent out for comment. Significantly, this was particularly the case with papers relating to Astra:

> We have read the papers that Coopers and Lybrand have sent us and we have
> examined others at their offices. We have also asked for more papers held by the
> Government. This is all part of the process of inquiry, no more, no less. If there is
> anything to follow up, we will of course do so but we will not say any more about
> their content until the Report is published.[67]

Third, the inquiry had been alerted to new issues as it proceeded, for example, the alleged use of the United Arab Emirates as a diversionary route
for Precision Guided Missiles to Iraq.

♦ Access to Documents

There is no way of knowing how many documents the Scott Inquiry did not
get to see, or what they would have revealed. Those that Scott was given
were often given late in the day and contributed to the slow progress of the
inquiry. In an article in *Business Age* in 1993, Kevin Cahill suggested that
some types of document would not be seen because they had been destroyed:

> Many documents relating to the invoicing and payment for ammunition supplied
> direct to Iraq from government stocks were deliberately destroyed when Interna-
> tional Military Sales was wound up two years ago.
>   As part of a massive clean-out operation just before the [1992] general election,
> sources in Whitehall say that further records relating to the captured arms and
> ammunition were shredded in February and March 1992.[68]

This latter comment seems to refer to a shredding operation known as
Snow White that destroyed a large number of files, many of which referred
to arms sales to Iraq and their financing.

♦ Criticisms of Scott Inquiry from Politicians and Whitehall

The inquiry faced numerous criticisms from within Whitehall, with Lord
Howe, the man after whom the infamously flawed guidelines came to be

named, leading the way. He outlined his complaints when appearing before the inquiry, and at the end of an article in the *Times* critical of the inquiry's procedures, he claimed:

> I raise none of these points on my own behalf. I do so not least because I feel some moral obligation towards the many public servants for whom I once had ministerial responsibility. "You spoke for all of us," one witness has written to me, "who have had to undergo humiliation, even degradation, for doing our duty in good faith and—in fact if not in the fiction which passes for it these days—with honour and a reasonable degree of success." We should not be surprised by this reaction on the part of many, who feel that their case has so far been heard only in their own replies to the inevitably hostile-seeming cross-examination. If the enquiry is already being seen in this way by some who have appeared before it, its report will need to be remarkably detached if it is to be seen to achieve justice for all concerned.[69]

Sir Robin Butler concluded the first day of his oral evidence to the inquiry by reading a prepared statement that, to many observers, included a coded attack on the inquiry (despite Butler's protestations to the contrary) as well as the media. It referred to

> the grossly distorted and prejudicial allegations in the media about the role of Government and individuals. . . . While I make no criticism or complaint about the Inquiry's procedures, the absence of the restraints on comment about the course of proceedings which would apply if this was a court of law, has permitted wild allegations and pre-judging of issues in media reports. . . . I repeat that I neither make nor imply any criticisms of the procedures of this Inquiry, but I register my concern and my confidence on behalf of the civil servants involved that the Inquiry will in due course put the record straight and undo, in so far as it is in its power, the damage which has been unfairly done to our system of Government, to the reputation of the Civil Service and to individuals.[70]

Typical of the whispering campaign against the inquiry, in June 1995 the *Financial Times* quoted a "former Tory minister" as saying: "Sir Richard has been living in a world of his own . . . It is a tragedy that the conduct of this inquiry has been shaped in such a way. It could have taken much less time and cost much less." The same report observed: "Some senior members of the government have alleged that Sir Richard and his counsel Ms Presiley Baxendale QC have been distracted by outside work from finishing the report expeditiously."[71]

As publication neared, so the whispering campaign intensified. At the end of October 1995, Sir Richard Luce, the inquiry's first witness back in May 1993, launched a public defense of his role in the columns of the *Sunday Telegraph*. He criticized the inquiry's procedures and the amount of time it had taken, commenting: "There is something very wrong both in the timescale and the way it has developed."[72] The following month, Michael Heseltine, by now deputy prime minister, told the BBC that the government could reject the findings contained in the Scott Report, telling David Frost: "We certainly have every right to do that if we should be so minded." He explained: "It must be a matter of judgement in the light of the conclusions and of the evidence. You can't say whatever comes out of it we will sign up to in advance. But what you can say is here is somebody who has seen all the evidence and will publish his conclusions, then there will be a proper debate."[73]

Even Prime Minister John Major was unwilling to endorse fully the work of the inquiry in advance of the publication of the report, and he replied to a letter from Robin Cook, MP asking "for an assurance that you have complete confidence in Sir Richard, and the procedures his inquiry has followed" by saying: "The Government is aware that some witnesses have expressed concern about some aspects of the procedures and have made representations to the Inquiry. It is for Sir Richard to determine how to respond to these concerns. The Government does not expect to reach a view on Sir Richard's Inquiry until it has been completed."[74]

As publication of the report neared, Geoffrey Howe returned to the attack. In a long and scathing article in the *Spectator*, during which Howe spoke of Scott's "tenacious enthusiasm for his own views," and his "marathon contest with reality," he delivered a kind of alternative Scott Report. At its heart was the notion that no minister or official was responsible for any errors of British policy, and that if Scott dared to suggest this, then his report should be ignored. On the attorney general, Sir Nicholas Lyell, for example, Howe wrote that "neither the Attorney-General nor anyone else should be condemned for their conduct—nor even unduly troubled by such idiosyncratic conclusions." It was the crudest form of damage control.[75]

◆ Cost

The need for the Scott Inquiry represents one of many costs to the British taxpayer of a barely restricted arms export policy conducted by the Thatcher governments during the 1980s. These costs were not immediately apparent at that time but are now being felt. For example, in addition to the Scott Inquiry, there is also, of course, the cost of the Pergau Dam illegality. In July 1995 it was revealed in a parliamentary answer that at least eighteen civil servants were involved in combating criticism of ministers by the Scott Inquiry, with five Whitehall departments maintaining units to deal with Scott-related issues. The cost of their operation was put at £1.7 million.[76] This sum was in addition to the cost of the inquiry. Parliamentary answers revealed that the "Scott units" were established in November 1992, at the same time that the inquiry itself was set up. The largest was that operated by Customs and Excise, where six staff were employed, at a cost of £612,000, exclusively to provide backup for the seventeen Customs officials who gave evidence to the inquiry. The next largest Scott unit was situated in the Cabinet Office, with five officials costing £400,000, followed by the FCO, with three at £164,027, followed by the DTI, with two at £247,000, and the MOD, also with two at £190,000.[77] Furthermore, the Treasury spent over £90,800 providing evidence. The total cost of the inquiry recorded by July 1995 was £1,703,827. This also covered the costs of the inquiry team itself, including twelve lawyers and administrative staff, and the interviewing of over 250 witnesses.[78] By the end of 1995, this cost had risen to an estimated £2.5 million. To this cost must be added that to the taxpayer resulting from the Dunk and Ordtec appeal cases, the costs of the original trials, the cost of the DTI investigation into Astra, the cost of private lawyers employed by civil servants and ministers under fire at the inquiry and paid out of public funds,[79] and any compensation claims that arise in the wake of the Scott Report.

◆ **Assessment**

At the beginning of this book, the question of what we mean by the term "Iraqgate" was posed, and something of the range of victims of the illicit arming of Iraq was highlighted. But not all the players in this drama were victims. On the industrial side, the victims were comparatively small companies fulfilling orders consistent with the requirements of British and Western foreign policy toward Iraq and Iran, especially while the two states were at war with each other. Reginald Dunk and Atlantic Commercial, Walter Somers, Matrix Churchill, Ordtec, and even Astra—which seems to have manufactured and stored much illicit equipment on behalf of the bigger players—represent the level at which Customs sought to intervene. Of these, Astra was the only big company. Even then, Astra's was the challenge of a relative newcomer to the established arms industry, run by outsiders and as such ultimately expendable. But what about the big players? What about RO, untouched despite the evidence that its ammunition was exported directly to Iraq as well as via Jordan during the Iran-Iraq War? What about the other major British weapons contractors who armed Iraq, albeit through conduits like Jordan and Saudi Arabia, and escaped prosecution?

There were no victims at a higher level in a different sense either. The British arms trade with the rest of the world does not involve just the arms companies themselves. It has become institutionalized and an important, albeit unpublicized, way of making money for banks, financial institutions, and professional firms. The major banks that were heavily involved in financing the British arms trade with Iraq all seem to have escaped the attentions of the Scott Inquiry. No private companies have been asked to account for their activities. Their roles in financing the arming of Iraq have effectively gone unchallenged. The corollary of this situation is that pivotal City figures, some of whose involvement in Iraqgate touches on several different segments of the whole, have not been investigated, nor asked to account for their involvement, either by the TISC or the Scott Inquiry. The implication is that the involvement of the City and major banks, not just in the arming of Iraq but across a range of potentially explosive arms deals concluded by the Thatcher governments of the 1980s, was so pervasive that revelations concerning Iraq could trigger off a whole series of disclosures that could seriously undermine confidence in the City. The inquiry's narrow remit was evident in those who did not give evidence to the Scott Inquiry but whose testimony could have been enlightening by virtue of the positions they held at the time—for example, Sir Peter Levene, Sir James (now Lord) Blythe, Sir John (now Lord) Cuckney,[80] and Sir Colin Chandler.[81] Other helpful witnesses could have included Stephan Kock, David Hastie, Gerald James, Chris Cowley, Peter Mitchell, and so on.

Would the Scott Inquiry be able to provide answers to all these questions? The British public did not seem to think so. A Gallup poll taken in March 1994 showed that 84 percent of those polled though government ministers were not telling the whole truth about the affair, while just 4 percent thought they were. Seventy-four percent had little or no confidence that the inquiry would reveal the whole truth.[82]

NOTES

1 Cited in a letter from Michael Heseltine, president of the Board of Trade, to Lord Justice Scott, 11.30.92.
2 Press release, 12.13.94, and the *Independent*, 12.28.95.
3 Opening statement of press conference, appended to press release, 3.31.93.
4 Letter from Lord Justice Scott to John Major, 7.14.93.
5 Press release, 2.4.93.
6 Letter from Sir Robin Butler to Lord Justice Scott, 3.17.93, and letter from Lord Justice Scott to Sir Robin Butler, 3.22.93.
7 Even prior to the Thatcher governments, British arms sales policy was being described as being "to sell arms to a client unless there is a good reason not to, rather than to sell only for positive reasons of foreign policy." Lawrence Freedman: *Arms Production in the United Kingdom: Problems and Prospects*, London, RIIA, 1978, p. 29.
8 Scott Inquiry—Day 81: Evidence of Lord Trefgarne, p. 23.
9 Alan Barrett, according to Glazebrook and "Mr. J" of MI6, told the Working Group that it needed, "to have very firm proof that equipment was going for military use before it was to be rejected." As put to Barrett by Presiley Baxendale. Barrett agreed that this had been the case. Scott Inquiry—Day 38: Evidence of Alan Barrett, p. 54.
10 Scott Inquiry—Day 82: Evidence of Lord Trefgarne, p. 9.
11 Scott Inquiry—Day 4: Evidence of Lt. Col. Glazebrook, p. 88.
12 Scott Inquiry—Day 37: Evidence of Alan Barrett, pp. 129–130. See also Scott's intervention, pp. 141–142. The umbrella-stand scenario was one first used by Ian Blackley, who argued: "The machine tools were of dual use capacity, and they could make shell cases or they could make umbrella stands." Scott Inquiry—Day 20: Evidence of Ian Blackley, p. 112.
13 Scott Inquiry—Day 38: Evidence of Alan Barrett, pp. 59–60.
14 Scott Inquiry—Day 25: Evidence of David Mellor, p. 49. This line of argument was contained in a memo from Tony Steadman of the DTI dated 13 January 1988.
15 Scott Inquiry—Day 14: Evidence of William Patey, p. 113.
16 Scott Inquiry—Day 21: Evidence of David Gore-Booth, p. 46.
17 Scott Inquiry—Day 22: Evidence of David Gore-Booth, p. 6.
18 Ibid., p. 146.
19 See chapter 7.
20 Scott Inquiry—Day 82: Evidence of Lord Trefgarne, pp. 39–40.
21 Scott Inquiry—Day 88: Evidence of Paul Henderson, p. 4.
22 Ibid., p. 18. Henderson told the inquiry: "I say he did not ask that question." p. 44.
23 Ibid., pp. 37–38.
24 *Economist*, 5.7.94, p. 29.
25 Scott Inquiry—Day 11: Evidence of Sir Stephen Egerton, pp. 138–139.
26 Scott Inquiry—Day 30: Evidence of William Waldegrave, p. 208.
27 Scott Inquiry—Day 19: Evidence of Sir David Miers, pp. 3, 19.
28 Scott Inquiry—Day 20: Evidence of Ian Blackley, p. 82.
29 Scott Inquiry—Day 31: Evidence of Simon Fuller, p. 4.
30 See the *Economist*, 5.7.94, p. 29.
31 Scott Inquiry—Day 17: Evidence of Mark Higson, pp. 105–106.
32 Scott Inquiry—Day 50: Evidence of Alan Clark, p. 24.
33 Scott Inquiry—Day 12: Evidence of Lt. Col. Glazebrook, pp. 4–7.
34 Ibid., p. 4.
35 Ibid., p. 74.

36 Ibid., p. 39.

37 Ibid., p. 42.

38 As paraphrased by Presiley Baxendale from Clark's statement. Scott Inquiry—Day 50: Evidence of Alan Clark, p. 25. He added: "I would never attach any significance to assurances from customers such as these, or indeed practically anyone. They are not worth the paper they are written on." Ibid., p. 31.

39 Ibid., pp. 84–85.

40 Scott Inquiry—Day 13: Evidence of Lt. Col. Glazebrook, p. 33.

41 Scott Inquiry—Day 19: Evidence of Sir David Miers, p. 14.

42 Scott Inquiry—Day 25: Evidence of David Mellor, p. 132. He went on: "One of the more interesting things I did do was to travel by land from Baghdad along the front line down to Basra and into Kuwait and saw for myself the flow of goods. What certainly was never suggested was that any of those were goods that had come from Britain." Ibid.

43 Summary record of the Interdepartmental Committee on Defence Sales to Iran and Iraq: 19 October 1988.

44 Scott Inquiry—Day 22: Evidence of David Gore-Booth, p. 28.

45 Scott Inquiry—Day 33: Evidence of Charles Haswell, p. 9.

46 Scott Inquiry—Day 30: Evidence of William Waldegrave, p. 212.

47 Scott Inquiry—Day 48: Evidence of Lady Thatcher, pp. 221–223.

48 Scott Inquiry—Day 11: Evidence of Sir Stephen Egerton, p. 108.

49 Scott Inquiry—Day 50: Evidence of Alan Clark, pp. 25, 27.

50 Scott Inquiry—Day 19: Evidence of Sir David Miers, pp. 6, 9.

51 Ibid., p. 26.

52 Scott Inquiry—Day 16: Evidence of Peter Vereker, p. 39.

53 Scott Inquiry—Day 33: Evidence of Charles Haswell, pp. 88–89; Day 31: Evidence of Simon Fuller, pp. 192–193.

54 Haswell was not seeking to deny that Jordan had ever acted as a conduit. At the Scott Inquiry he spoke of the "cosy arrangement" between Iraq and Jordan during the Iran-Iraq War whereby "we know that Jordan is assisting the Iraqi war effort. There are no secrets about that at all." Haswell's objection was based on whether Jordan continued to perform that role after August 1990. Scott Inquiry—Day 33: Evidence of Charles Haswell, p. 95.

55 Scott Inquiry—Day 33: Evidence of Charles Haswell, p. 115.

56 Ibid., pp. 81–82. Lord Justice Scott observed that the handwritten comment treated "the absence of Jordan as a matter of congratulation." p. 83.

57 Ibid., p. 128.

58 Ibid., p. 91.

59 In 1989 Sterling Armaments had sent £10,000 worth of submachine guns to Iraq with a Sudanese end-user certificate through Amsterdam and Jordan to Iraq. Dunk reportedly claimed at his trial that "he was competing in a trade in which the authorities turned a blind eye. The restrictions had been broken even by those who made them." *Guardian*, 11.28.85. See also the *Guardian*, 11.8.85.

60 Scott Inquiry—Day 18: Evidence of Sir David Miers, p. 184. The memo was dated 25 February 1983.

61 Ibid., pp. 187, 193.

62 Cited in Richard Norton-Taylor: *Truth Is a Difficult Concept: Inside the Scott Inquiry*, p. 194.

63 *Guardian*, 8.25.95. See also the *Times*, 8.12.95 and 8.17.95.

64 *Guardian*, 10.12.95.

65 Letter from Lord Justice Scott to John Major, 7.14.93.

66 *Guardian*, 9.9.95.

67 Christopher Muttukamaru, Briefing Note, 6.5.95.

68 Kevin Cahill: What Lord Justice Scott Hasn't Been Told, *Business Age*, Vol. 3 No. 34, 1993, p. 33.

69 Geoffrey Howe: Scott's Salami Tactics, *Times*, 3.1.94.

70 Scott Inquiry—Day 62: Evidence of Sir Robin Butler, pp. 177–179.

71 *Financial Times*, 6.2.95.

72 Richard Luce: This Is Not the Way to Find Out the Truth, *Sunday Telegraph*, 10.29.95. On the inquiry's procedures, he complained: "The thing that most shocked me as a witness was that Sir Richard Scott and Presiley Baxendale appeared to me to act as prosecuting advocates rather than independent seekers of the truth . . . Other witnesses felt equally perplexed and resentful."

73 Quoted in the *Independent*, 11.13.95.

74 Letter from Robin Cook to John Major, 5.12.95 and John Major to Robin Cook, 5.25.95.

75 Geoffrey Howe: A Judge's Long Contest with Reality, *Spectator*, 1.27.96, pp. 9–12. See the retort by Geoffrey Robinson, Paul Henderson's defense counsel at his trial in the *Sunday Times*, 2.4.96.

76 *Daily Telegraph*, 7.10.95.

77 Ibid.

78 The Scott Inquiry considers witnesses to be those who have given either oral or written evidence at the invitation of the inquiry team. This points to the fact that there were two categories of "evidence": (1) evidence—written statements in response to questionnaires sent out by the team (i.e., requested) and (2) information—written evidence/information sent to the inquiry team but unsolicited. The figure of 250 quoted here refers to the combined number of oral and written evidence testimonies—around two-thirds of this figure gave written evidence only. Telephone conversation with David Price, Scott Inquiry, 7.20.95.

79 In December 1995 John Major said that £750,790 had been spent in this way, while the Treasury solicitor's department had charged a further £306,320 for its advice to government departments. *Guardian*, 12.5.95.

80 Lords Blythe and Cuckney were both made life peers in the Queen's 1995 Birthday Honours list.

81 In a rare interview with Scott in the summer of 1993, Jimmy Burns of the *Financial Times* reported:
"The judge has not ruled out taking evidence from two former heads of the Ministry of Defence's defence export sales [*sic*] organisation—Sir James Blythe, now chief executive of Boots, and Sir Colin Chandler, chief executive of Vickers. He is yet to take a decision on Sir John Cuckney, who was chairman of International Military Services, the government-owned defence sales company, between 1974–85." *Financial Times*, 7.31.93.

82 *Economist*, 5.7.94, p. 30.

Why Did the West Arm Iraq?

A ll of this evidence suggests that during the 1980s, the U.S. and U.K. governments in particular conducted but sought to conceal a foreign policy considered too machiavellian to be openly defensible. Given its imperial past, Britain had a long-standing interest in Gulf stability.[1] None of the documents that emerged from the 1992 Matrix Churchill trial reveals much of the mindset of British government departments regarding British interests and the British role in the Middle East, although some evidence to the Scott Inquiry hints at it. However, during the 1961 Iraqi threat to Kuwait, a lengthy "top secret" report, *United Kingdom Interests in Kuwait*, was prepared. In its outline of the British stake in the region, its conception of British interests in the Middle East in 1961 is little different from NSD-26's conception of U.S. interests in 1989; both revolve around the maintenance of the pro-Western status quo, access to oil, and—in the 1961 case—profitability of the exploitation of that oil. Although Britain had yet to withdraw from the Gulf at this time, the central premise remains relevant:

> Our general political objective in Kuwait is the same as in other parts of the Persian Gulf, namely the maintenance of stability and the encouragement of good relations with neighbouring countries, in order to reduce the risk of Communist penetration through the exploitation of discontent or the jealousies of others.[2]

The largely covert nature of the policy can be explained by reference to the human rights situation in Iraq and fear of further worsening relations with Iran. After the invasion of Kuwait, worries that U.S. and British servicemen might be attacked with weapons made in Britain or whose purchase was facilitated by the United States were a further concern.[3]

Another good reason for keeping the policy quiet was that it further exposed the fragile fiction that the end-use certificate system is an effective way of regulating the international arms market, or at least that only unscrupulous

Third World states seek to manipulate it. Britain used Jordan and a range of other conduits to get equipment to Iraq, thus underwriting the fiction that British companies were exporting arms to Jordan, Saudi Arabia, and so on when these were clearly destined for the Iraqi war effort. The Scott Inquiry has confirmed governmental knowledge of Jordan's role as a conduit throughout this, although further investigation of the particular role of RO could be revealing. Nevertheless, even before, there was evidence from the government of its knowledge (it was, of course, an open secret in defense industry circles). For example, John Wyatt, a former IMS official, visited Kuwait at the end of the Gulf War, and recalled:

> We had clear cut evidence when I went in that the ammunition, rockets, mines, and all the rest of it had been supplied by Britain to Jordan which had subsequently got into Iraqi hands. I'm sure in 1988 there was definite knowledge of movement backwards and forwards between Jordan and Iraq and other places like that because I think at that stage there was a certain amount of support for Iraq against Iran. I know at that stage also that British companies, and IMS was certainly one of them, were doing extremely good Jordan business. Whether bits subsequently found their way to Iraq, they probably weren't too fussed.[4]

Although this explains why the policy was kept quiet, however, it does not explain the policy itself. In the case of Britain, this involves analyzing the shifting combination of economic and political-strategic interests tied up in sales that have been evident to differing extents elsewhere in the sale of British arms. Domestic economic and employment considerations were the ones most frequently used by ministers to defend their policy, specifically over the export of machine tools, after the collapse of the Matrix Churchill trial. For example, Michael Heseltine argued: "In interpreting policy guidelines, judgements had to be made about British contracts for British factories offering British jobs in circumstances where others in other nations were queuing up to fill the orders if we did not."[5] Following the seizure of the supergun, Geoffrey Howe had launched into a defense of British trade with Iraq on similar grounds, warning that "cutting off all trade with Iraq would serve only to create a satisfaction among our industrial competitors and the loss of jobs in Britain. That is not a sensible thing to allow, however much one may abhor the abuse of human rights."[6]

An associated consideration was the potential postwar market that existed in Iraq, both civilian and military. In *Guns, Lies and Spies*, Chris Cowley recalls a conversation in Baghdad with a Colonel Kadoori who had just returned from Britain, where he said he had been negotiating a large order for multiple rocket-launch systems. When Cowley asked Kadoori how he expected to get approval from the British government for such a deal, he replied: "No problem! The head of FMT wrote personally to Margaret Thatcher, and she passed it on to your Trade Ministry. The British know that, if they don't help us out a little, we won't place big orders with Vickers or British Aerospace at the Military Show."[7]

However, economic motivations alone cannot account completely for the British policy. British interests in the outcome of the Iran-Iraq War and interests in the future stability of the Gulf were similar to those of the United States. This was put to FCO officials by Stan Crowther, MP at the TISC hearings into the supergun affair:

> **Q:** . . . at that time [August 1988] British foreign policy was really in favour of neither side winning that war, was it not? . . .
> **A:** We were neutral in the conflict.
> **Q:** That was not exactly what I said . . . what was our foreign policy in this matter at the time? Was it not that we would have preferred to see neither side score a military victory in that war . . .
> **A:** An outright victory of a dominant kind by one party or the other would have had a destabilising effect on the region.
> **Q:** Exactly. Precisely; it would have destabilised the Middle East and we did not want to see that happen.[8]

It has been suggested by defense industry sources involved in the arming of Iraq that a common approach was directed from the British Embassy in Washington. All of those involved in the various aspects of Iraqgate (supergun, Astra, Matrix Churchill, etc.) explain the British government's interests in strategic rather than purely economic terms and in terms of Anglo-U.S. cooperation. At the January 1988 Machine Tools Technology Association meeting, Alan Clark told Paul Henderson that British policy toward equipping Iraq "was dependent on US policy towards Iraq." According to his solicitor, Henderson was "in no doubt that the information he and his colleagues were providing was shared with the CIA and available to the White House in formulating Western policy towards Saddam."

As already noted, there were other indications that, first, Iran must be prevented from winning the war and that the preferred outcome was that neither side should score an easy victory and dominate the upper Gulf, thereby potentially threatening the oil-rich lower Gulf states. Iran was considered the more likely of the belligerents to do this—hence the tilt toward Iraq, but also the continuation of some sales to Iran. At different times the United States facilitated the arming of both sides. British weapons, some categorized as nonlethal so that they could be said to be consistent with the Howe Guidelines, reached both sides; and a number of other European states, notably Italy and Spain, profited from arming both sides. In addition, the U.S. and U.K. governments turned a blind eye to diversions of arms to the belligerents, and in the case of the United States, even replaced weaponry of U.S. origin that was passed on to Iraq by its Middle Eastern allies.

Moreover, Western countries did not expect Iraq to invade Kuwait. Preoccupied with fears of Iranian expansionism, they assumed that any arms sold would be aimed only at the Iranians or the Kurds. Hence John Major's outline of the Foreign Office's reading of the developments that culminated in the invasion of Kuwait: "Prior to the invasion of Kuwait, the assessment made by the United Kingdom, and other countries . . . was that Iraq would use her military strength to bolster her position as a dominant power in the region, but that she would not risk world hostility by aggressive action."[9]

A similar note of surprise is sounded in the diaries of Alan Clark, one of the leading advocates of unrestricted trade with Iraq. On 7 August 1990, he recorded:

Yesterday I was in MOD all day. The Iraqis are starting to throw their weight around. I wouldn't have believed it possible, not on this scale. For nearly two years the FCO section of Cabinet minutes was a long moan about how the Iraqi Army was on its last legs, and the Iranians were going to break through. Now it turns out there are more Soviet tanks there than in Poland, Hungary and Czechoslovakia combined.[10]

Furthermore, arming Iraq with conventional arms and conventional arms-making technology also allowed the United States, Britain, and other Western countries a vantage point from which Iraqi efforts to develop nonconventional capabilities could be observed. Allowing British companies to construct components for certain of these both facilitated monitoring and allowed those technologies ultimately to be denied, as with the supergun.

Mark Higson, a desk officer for Iraq at the FCO from March 1989 to January 1990, told the Scott Inquiry that by 1989 the FCO was "actually aware of the strength of [the Iraqi] efforts to acquire equipment,"[11] which by this time included some evidence of its attempts to acquire nuclear and chemical/biological weapons. He reiterated his view that, after the 1988 cease-fire, the Iraqi market "was summed up as being the big prize."[12] This perception also explains why the tilt toward Iraq was rationalized as falling within the guidelines and therefore did not need to be announced as representing a shift in policy, even though that is what it clearly was. Higson explained that "obviously public perception of both regimes would have been that they were as vile as each other . . . but the potential for Britain in relation to trade was with Iraq . . . We were getting . . . letters over gassing of Kurds and political prisoners or hostages or whatever. It would have been unacceptable to have announced the fact that we were relaxing a policy in favour of Iraq" because of the likely parliamentary and public reaction.[13]

Hence, selling conventional arms and related technology had economic benefits, served strategic aims, and also allowed for the monitoring and frustration of Iraqi attempts to develop nonconventional weapons. However, the depth of involvement required to achieve these ends was so alien to the fiction of a principled stand enshrined in the Howe Guidelines that it had to be secret, and every effort had to be made to ensure that it stayed that way, despite the human cost involved. While the cover-up has so far meant that it has been without political cost, the arming of Iraq (and Iran) has not been without human cost. The collapse of Matrix Churchill, Astra Holdings, and the attendant unemployment; the attempt to imprison the three executives of Matrix Churchill; and the experiences of an entire cast with supporting roles—Ordtec and Paul Grecian, Polmadie and Frank Machon (whose offer to tell the Government what he knew was, remarkably, turned down), Ali Daghir, and so on—bear testimony to that. Many questions remain outstanding.

What is clear, however, is that the Western policy of arming and backing Iraq during the war with Iran, and of facilitating Iraq's massive rearmament program thereafter, indirectly led to the August 1990 Iraqi invasion of Kuwait and the ensuing 1991 Gulf War. James Baker called the idea that "somehow the United States was responsible for or contributed to Saddam Hussein's invasion of Kuwait . . . ludicrous."[14] However, as a subsequent report concluded: "It is unlikely that Saddam Hussein would have invaded Kuwait had he not calculated both that the regional balance of power stood in his favor and that local and outside powers would not react vigorously."[15]

This perception was a direct consequence of the approach to Iraq enshrined in NSD-26. Its logical outcome was the communication of ambiguous signals that Saddam chose to interpret as a "green light," which to Saddam may have borne some similarity to the type of signals emanating from Washington prior to his invasion of Iran in 1980. This situation had much in common with the British government's communication of similarly confused signals to the Argentinian military government just a decade before. Argentina then staged an invasion of the Falkland Islands, where British troops were attacked with British weapons.

Inevitably, the U.S. policy of intelligence sharing with Iraq must have contributed to this elevated and distorted sense of Iraqi self-importance, just as the U.S. use of Argentine military and police personnel in Central America in the early 1980s had elevated the Argentine military's sense of its importance to the United States. There is a further point of comparison with Argentina in 1982. The eight-year war with Iran had left Saddam with large debts, unfulfilled ambition, and a large and potentially restive military establishment, which could have moved against him as frustration mounted. Iraq began the Iran-Iraq War with $35 billion of reserves and ended it $80–100 billion in debt. Just as the Argentine generals turned to reclaiming Las Malvinas as a way of diverting attention from economic problems by generating a sense of national pride and national unity, so Saddam sought to unite Iraqis around the invasion of Kuwait.[16]

Steve Yetiv has also suggested that the invasion of Kuwait was directly related to the outcome of the Iran-Iraq War.[17] U.S. support for Iraq in that war made Saddam more confident when it came to making the preparations for the invasion of Kuwait. U.S. policy contributed to a situation whereby Iraq had "a considerably more developed military capability" than it had when it entered the war with Iran. Furthermore, the war (prolonged by Western arms deliveries) weakened Iran militarily. Again, this was largely a consequence of U.S. strategy.

This dramatic foreign policy failure also shared many of the characteristics of that other U.S. foreign policy debacle of the 1980s, Iran-Contra, which also arose out of the 1979 Iranian Revolution and its implications—albeit on the other side of the foreign policy coin. Like Iran-Contra, this policy was conceived and executed within the confines of the executive branch, and hence beyond the reach of any moderating congressional input. The administration viewed any such prospect as interference and sought to minimize it by retaining a high degree of secrecy. As Jentleson notes, such traits had also been central to the Bay of Pigs blunder almost thirty years before.[18]

Ultimately, while the United States and the West as a whole believed that they were using and manipulating Iraq for their own ends, in reality Iraq was exploiting these relationships to further its own agenda. As Jochen Hippler has observed:

> The strategy of using Iraq for non-Iraqi purposes meant looking the other way when Iraq was aggressive or repressive. In the end, Saddam Hussein managed to

use the Western powers (and the Soviet Union) for his own purposes. By accepting their political support during the war, and importing their weapons and military know-how, Iraq fought Iran to a draw and assumed a new degree of regional leadership. Saddam's policies were plainly Iraqi nationalist. What were supposed to be tools of Western influence have been employed now against Western interests.[19]

Furthermore, once Saddam had shown a willingness to deploy the firepower sold to him, steps had to be taken to neutralize some of that capability and ensure that the feat could not be repeated, leading to "the most dramatic, expensive, and violent product recall in history."[20] There are a number of examples of this dawning realization that the West had overstepped the mark in its willingness to sell Iraq virtually whatever it wanted. Lt. Col. Glazebrook told the Scott Inquiry that he was visited after the Iraqi invasion of Kuwait by an army officer who was looking to see what military equipment Britain had sold to Iraq, in order to find out what his forces might have to face in the field in the coming months. On being told that among the items purchased by Iraq was a modern Plessey radar-jamming system sold in 1987 over Glazebrook's objection, his response was: "Oh, bloody hell. We have nothing to touch that."[21]

However, nowhere was this clearer than in U.S. concerns about Iraqi artillery—artillery designed by Gerald Bull. In February 1991 General Norman Schwarzkopf told a press conference that this had been the greatest worry of military planners:

> The nightmare scenario for all of us would have been to go through, get hung up in this breach right here and then have the enemy artillery rain chemical weapons down on troops that were in a gaggle in the breach right there. That was the nightmare scenario. So one of the things that we felt we must have established is an absolute as much destruction as we could get of the artillery . . . that would be firing on that wire.[22]

As Bruce Jentleson concluded:

> It was one thing to feed the Iraqi population while it was at war with Iran, or to provide some industrial equipment, or even to share military intelligence and to bolster Iraqi defensive military capabilities. It was quite another to have loosened export controls on dual-use technology and equipment so that Iraq was able to develop its offensive military capabilities, and especially its nuclear, biological, and chemical weapons capabilities, far beyond the needs of its war with Iran—indeed,

to the point where it became the principal threat to the regional balance of power and to
US interests in the region.[23]

◆ Lessons

A number of foreign and arms sales policy lessons flow from the experience
of the West's flirtation with Iraq.

First, the experience reinforces the need for genuine legislative oversight
to guard against irresponsibility in arms sales policy. The Howe Guidelines
were so flexible as to be dishonest in conception and execution, a dishonesty
compounded by the government's approach to answering parliamentary
questions on the subject. Legislative oversight of arms sales was impossible
in the face of this. Just as with Iran-Contra, the executive manipulated and
deceived the legislature in the name of national security. In both the United
States and the United Kingdom, vested governmental interests have frustrated inquiries into Iraqgate. In the United States, Congressman Gonzalez
complained that the Bush administration stonewalled his investigation. In the
United Kingdom, the TISC investigation into the supergun was marked by an
inability to get the right witnesses to appear, and by the reluctance of witnesses who did appear to divulge the full extent of their knowledge. With
regard to the Scott Inquiry, accessing documents was a deliberately slow
process. The Matrix Churchill trial was to be conducted, like the earlier Ordtec trial, with the aid of PII certificates. If the government's PII application
had been successful, this would have denied a legitimate defense and, no
matter how established and misunderstood the PII system is claimed to be,
would have produced little more than a show trial. There could certainly
have been only one outcome had the attempt to claim PII succeeded. With
regard to Astra, documents had been shamelessly concealed for years, and in
their absence a subtle campaign of denigration was conducted against Gerald
James. No doubt these were the kind of considerations that led Shadow Cabinet Minister Michael Meacher, MP to conclude that

> since it is indubitable that most, if not all, of this illegal arms trading was known to
> the British security and intelligence services, one of two conclusions must follow.
> Either ministers were not told about their surveillance, in which case the security
> services are a law unto themselves, acting as a state within a state and beyond
> democratic control. Or, if ministers were informed, then, in collusion with the
> security services, they perpetrated a massive deception on Parliament and the pub-

lic throughout the 1980s, by pretending to uphold an international embargo whose systematic breach they were themselves orchestrating.[24]

Second, if the international community is serious about arms control, it needs to consider international controls and ways of reforming the system of end-user certification. It is an open secret in both defense industry and government circles that this does not work. Rather than regulate the trade, it serves merely to institutionalize the corruption that is endemic within it. Perhaps one way out, if the system is to be retained in principle, would be to restrict those approved to sign such certificates to clearly defined members of a government—such as ministers of defense, trade, or foreign affairs—and not officials, and to lodge copies, perhaps as a component of the U.N. Register of Conventional Arms initiative, at the United Nations. However, even this would not solve the problems in the Third World and parts of Europe, where the kind of cash associated with arms deals is regarded by politicians as a fundamental perk of the job, the financial rewards of which are otherwise relatively meager.

The lessons of Iraq are not encouraging for the U.N. Register of Conventional Arms initiative. On the basis of this account, calls for tougher controls in the aftermath of the Gulf War could be little more than a politically expedient measure that will not be allowed to develop into a genuine control regimen. With the passage of time, the political necessity that made it expedient will likely fade from memory. The arming of Iraq may have been a close thing. But through a combination of luck (the timing of the Iraqi invasion of Kuwait), the performance of the Iraqi forces (and their nondeployment of chemical weapons), and the power of the U.N. response, it was not catastrophic. As time passes, this fact may weaken the initial determination to be seen to be doing something.

The case of Iraq clearly shows how leading suppliers flouted their own regulations, guidelines, or public stances in order to gain financially from Iraq and/or exert influence over it. In these circumstances, the chances for the U.N. Register seem remote unless the conditions within national regulatory structures that allowed this to occur are tackled in a way that makes a repetition unlikely. As has been noted elsewhere:

> export controls are only as effective as the government of the day intends them to be. While the lessons of Iraq have been absorbed into the regulatory structure, they also have to be absorbed at the political level. After all, the purpose of such controls is to ensure that no goods with a military application can be exported

without the government's approval, not to prevent the export of such goods *per se.* Hence, the political will to enforce the controls has to exist for the controls to be effective.[25]

This would involve making arms sales decisions more open, and perhaps even require the involvement of a cross-party body in monitoring them. In the case of Britain, for example, it should not be beyond the bounds of possibility for a cross-party body of MPs to sit and consider recommendations relating to politically sensitive destinations. The concept of legislative oversight, albeit rather limited, of the intelligence services has recently been accepted in Britain via the formation of the Intelligence and Security Committee under the 1994 Intelligence Services Act. A similar body, which could distinguish between commercial confidentiality and spurious claims to confidentiality, could be useful here.

Where did the British and other governments think all these arms were going? On paper, states such as Singapore, Jordan, Kenya, and Morocco are among the most heavily armed in the world. On paper, Paraguay has a large modern air force. If there had been an interest in checking this trade with Iraq and Iran, many of these sales would not have gone through. It should be standard practice to check orders against likely requirements and capabilities, and then to err on the side of caution. For either political or commercial reasons, this was not always done. From both the United States and the United Kingdom, weapons went to destinations that could not possibly have had any use for them, thence to be passed on to Iraq and Iran. The United States, after issuing a telegram to a number of its Western embassies to alert allies to the dangers of certain dual-use technologies, went ahead and exported these to Iraq. In Belgium, anything was possible as long as the right people were paid. From Spain and Portugal, arms and ammunition were diverted to Iraq and Iran. The list is endless.

From this emerges a fourth lesson: the way in which the secrecy that attaches to foreign policy and the conduct of arms sales has proved a breeding ground for duplicity and illegality. As Robert Sheldon, MP has observed:

> . . . the problem with secrecy is that if too many matters are made secret, the currency of secrets is debased. Secrecy is used to avoid political embarrassment to Ministers far more frequently now than it used to be. It conceals matters which need to be kept out of public view. Certain matters must obviously be kept from the public view. However, so often a civil servant's brief is to ensure that by concealing matters the Minister's appearance at the Dispatch Box is more effective

than would otherwise have been the case . . . The danger is that a barrier may exist between important secrets and convenient secrets.[26]

The conclusion has to be that those caught up in the affair were to be sent to prison to protect more of the latter than the former.

Another issue this affair has highlighted is the inherent weakness in the regulatory structure in the United Kingdom. At present, within the MOD the minister in charge of defense procurement has to balance the responsibilities of arms sales with arms control or restraint. The arguments for control or restraint are rarely as compelling as those for sale and do not have the same vocal and influential constituencies behind them. In view of the trends that characterize the international arms market today, the arguments for restraint are never going to be as attractive as those for sale, and current and likely future developments will serve only to exacerbate the situation. Given this, the separation of ministerial responsibility for sale and regulation respectively would seem a sensible measure. During the inquiry, Scott outlined a scenario whereby "if you had two Ministers, one responsible for defence export sales and the other responsible for protection of security operational requirements, they would then have to meet and consider and decide what the recommendation from the Ministry would be."[27] However, officials from the MOD effectively went through this process at the level of the MOD Working Group, when Lt. Col. Glazebrook found the debate a somewhat uneven one in favor of sale.

Another lesson is that it would be naive to bestow on the intelligence services an image of omnipotence they do not deserve, although it would be just as naive to exaggerate their impotence. Iraq was always something of a special case, and its military-industrialization drive was something about which, in general terms, Western governments were only too well aware. Although monitoring, and even involvement in, the international arms trade had long been the task of domestic intelligence agencies through collection of SIGINT and exploitation of HUMINT, the actual tracking of certain types of covert procurement activity—particularly nuclear, chemical, and biological weapons and technology—remains highly problematic. It is now quite clear that Iraq had made much more progress in these directions than the West had supposed at the time.[28] This became even clearer after the defection of Hussein Kamel. For instance, it is now understood that Iraq undertook research into the deployment of cholera, typhoid, botulism, and anthrax. The problems these programs presented for intelligence agencies arose partly because of the nature of the technology and the mode of importation but partly

also because of the existence of a culture in the West that was itself a consequence of the "family of nations" logic of NSD-26. This logic dictated that
ties to Iraq had to be strengthened; hence the Iraqi market existed to be
satiated by Western companies as one way of fostering Iraqi dependence on
the West to such an extent as to preclude Iraq's breaking out of it. This
situation required a proclivity to sell even where suspicion about end-use
existed, and unless unimpeachable evidence could be produced to justify
doing otherwise. And even then, it might not be enough.

David Kay, talking about the policy—the Howe Guidelines—that allowed
the continued export of Matrix Churchill machine tools despite evidence of
their end destination, summed up the folly of this approach to Iraq this way:
"I think it was a policy decision that was wrong in formulation, wrong in
execution, and very very hazardous for the world. If Saddam had not attacked
Kuwait in August of 1990, but had waited two years later, we would have
been facing a situation the consequence of which . . . anyone would be very
foolish to predict the outcome of today."[29]

This view has been more than confirmed by Hussein Kamel's information
about Iraq's nuclear weapons program. He told his debriefers—representatives from the Pentagon, State Department, CIA, and NSC—that Iraq was
just three months away from testing an atomic bomb by the time the January
1991 Gulf War began. He is also reported to have said that, incredibly, Saddam planned to invade Kuwait for a second time in October 1994 and was
deterred only by the speed and scale of the U.S. response to Iraqi military
maneuvers.[30]

Futhermore, fresh information is still coming to light to show that the
scale of the Iraqi procurement operation was much broader than previously
thought, and that while Western intelligence agencies may have thought they
had the key elements covered, this was not necessarily always the case. For
example, as late as November 1995, it was revealed that a London-based
company operated by an Iraqi-born Briton had sent 500 SCUD missile guidance systems, worth around £6 million, to Baghdad between 1989 and 1991.
While most of the parts were flown directly to Baghdad from Heathrow Airport prior to the invasion of Kuwait, afterward they were diverted via Austria,
from where they were sent on to Iraq in crates marked "dental equipment,"
so as to beat the U.N. embargo on all except humanitarian goods. Although
five arrests were made in February 1995, Customs, mindful of its experience
elsewhere, did not press any charges.[31]

The Iraqgate affair has also revealed much of the modus operandi of the
intelligence services—so much so that it may well have weakened them for

the foreseeable future or, at the very least, may have forced them to rely more on SIGINT than HUMINT in certain areas. Now that the post–cold war intelligence agenda of Britain's allies, like the United States and France, for example, so clearly involves an emphasis on economic espionage, this may prove significant. This is the fault of the government for going ahead with an ill-advised prosecution. Didn't they realize that to Henderson and company the provision of intelligence was a quid pro quo that legitimized their otherwise illegal trade? The obvious weakness of this position from an intelligence point of view was that the government was constrained from acting on the damning intelligence provided by Henderson for fear of exposing him. Or, as Alan Clark put it: "There is an absurd paradox, that the intelligence was telling you what the machines were going to be used for, but the machines had to be provided in order to protect the source that was telling you the purpose for which they were going to be used."[32]

The wide-ranging PII certificate that Tristan Garel-Jones signed at the time of the Matrix Churchill trial argued in part:

> The disclosure of any sources or alleged sources of intelligence information, and any aspects of the means by which it was gathered . . . would cause unquantifiable damage to the functions of the security and intelligence services in relation to their role both in the United Kingdom and abroad. If this position is not maintained, there would be a real and serious danger that the supply of such information would be less readily forthcoming and could result in grave danger to those who have supplied or might in the future supply it.

This is indeed true, in that all British businesspeople abroad will now be suspected of being potential spies; and those who have been arrested in the past for spying in places like Saudi Arabia but maintained that they were just businesspeople unjustly held now look more suspect in the light of the Matrix Churchill case. By the same token, this too, is the government's fault. And it follows that businesspeople will be less willing to go along with the intelligence services in the future when their trade is wholly legitimate. Where their trade is otherwise illegal, however, the intelligence services will still be able to exert considerable leverage. However, the suggestion implicit in Garel-Jones's PII certificate, that revealing Henderson's identity would expose him, is perverse, given that he and his defense counsel considered it the thing most likely to save him from being convicted over the flexibility of the government's guidelines.

There is also clearly a need to distinguish between operational decisions on the use of intelligence information and times when a political decision needs to be made by, or at least cleared with, ministers. In the case of Matrix Churchill, as we have seen, a judgment had to be made about whether the protection of a source (either an individual providing information or the flow of information itself, although it generally seems to have meant the former) was so important as to take precedence over the achievement of the objective that the intelligence had been intended to facilitate. Clearly, this ceased to be a decision best made on operational grounds and became a policy decision that should instead have been made by ministers, although in this case the matter was not referred up to them. Similarly, decisions regarding PRB in the events leading up to the mysterious explosion at Kaulille appear, on the face of it, to have been taken without ministerial knowledge.

A further lesson is that in the post-COCOM, post-Iraq era, we need to alter our conception of what arms actually are, and what kind of equipment can be sold to what country, especially in areas of tension. This process should also take into account evidence of previous conduit or false end-user roles. Implicit in this change is the need to tighten export controls. In practice, however, the post-COCOM changes that have occurred have been to loosen export controls on a wide range of sensitive dual-use equipment, a charge led by the Clinton administration in the United States.[33] However, in the case of Britain, for example, it may be possible to reconcile trading interests and a loosening of controls with an enhanced intelligence role in tracking dual-use and suspect exports. With MI5 publicly angling for a new role in the post–cold war era, this would represent a worthy use of its resources and expertise. However, certain of the lessons of Iraq suggest that this could be like letting a cat look after a canary, and oversight to ensure that such a role is not manipulated for political ends would be a prerequisite.

Finally, one of the points raised here has been the close, almost symbiotic, relationship between government, senior military figures, and key national arms manufacturers, as well as the links between various major foreign arms companies. One illustration that post-Iraq all is well with these relationships, as the international arms trade rolls on, could be found at the Royal Naval and British Army Equipment Exhibition held in Aldershot in September 1995. There, on 8 September, the BAE diary for the event records BAE's lunch guests at the "top table" as including former MP and Astra consultant Gerald Howarth, who became a consultant to RO around the time of the EPREP agreement, alongside luminaries like Sir Colin Chandler, former head of DESO and now chief executive of Vickers plc, and Brigadier R. N. Lennox, director of Land Service Ammunition. Also being lunched during the week were various representatives of companies in or associated with the propellant cartel, like SNPE, Oerlikon, and Chartered Industries of Singapore.[34] This is the inheritance Andrew Undershaft foresaw in Shaw's *Major Barbara*.

N O T E S

1 On Britain's role in the shaping of the modern Middle East, see David Fromkin: *A Peace to End All Peace: Creating the Modern Middle East, 1914–1922*, London, Penguin, 1991.
2 Public Records Office: Cabinet Office Papers, C(61)140, 10.2.61, p. 3.
3 As *Time* noted: "If military ordnance bore fingerprints, British soldiers in the Gulf would have found evidence of their fellow countrymen's handiwork on some of the rockets and artillery shells that rained down as they advanced into Iraq and Kuwait." *Time*, 11.23.92, p. 46.
4 *Financial Times*, 11.14.92.
5 *Hansard*, 11.23.92, col. 644.
6 *Hansard*, 5.3.90, col. 1215.
7 Chris Cowley: *Guns, Lies and Spies*, p. 94. Flexible Manufacturing Technology (FMT) was a company Kadoori had been negotiating with while in Britain.
8 TISC: HC-86-viii, p. 287.
9 *Hansard*, 11.18.92, col. 215.
10 Alan Clark: *Diaries*, p. 321. The entries from 30 July to 5 August 1990 have been cut from the published version.
11 Scott Inquiry—Day 17: Evidence of Mark Higson, p. 8.
12 Ibid., p. 12.
13 Ibid., pp. 52–53.
14 *New York Times*, 11.3.90.
15 Initial report of the Washington Institute's Strategic Study Group: *Restoring the Balance: U.S. Strategy and the Gulf Crisis*, Washington, D.C., Washington Institute for Near East Policy, 1991, p. 13. Cited in B. W. Jentleson: *With Friends like These*, p. 19.
16 On the situation facing the Argentine generals, see, for example, David Pion-Berlin: The Fall of Military Rule in Argentina, 1976–1983, *Journal of InterAmerican Studies and World Affairs*, Vol. 27 No. 2 1985, pp. 55–75.
17 Steve A. Yetiv: The Outcomes of Operations Desert Shield and Desert Storm: Some Antecedent Causes, *Political Science Quarterly*, Vol. 107 No. 2 1992, pp. 195–214.
18 B. W. Jentleson: *With Friends like These*, p. 25.
19 Jochen Hippler: Iraq's Military Power: The German Connection, *Middle East Report*, Jan–Feb 1991, p. 31.
20 William E. Burrows and Robert Windrem: *Critical Mass: The Dangerous Race for Superweapons in a Fragmenting World*, London, Simon & Schuster, 1994, p. 25.
21 Scott Inquiry—Day 5: Evidence of Lt. Col. Glazebrook, p. 39.
22 Timewatch: *The Man Who Made the Supergun*.
23 B. W. Jentleson: *With Friends like These*, p. 195. My emphasis.
24 *New Statesman and Society*, 6.17.94, p. 24.
25 M. Phythian and W. Little: Administering Britain's Arms Trade, p. 266.
26 *Hansard*, 1.27.87, col. 250.
27 Scott Inquiry—Day 36: Evidence of Alan Barrett, p. 61.

28 See, for example, *Newsweek*: Plagues in the Making, 10.9.95, pp. 16–17.

29 Speaking in *Panorama*: UK Ltd: The Arming of Iraq, BBC1, 11.23.92. For David Kay's assessment of the sophistication of Iraqi deception techniques, see Denial and Deception Practices of WMD Proliferators: Iraq and Beyond, *Washington Quarterly*, Vol. 18 No. 1 Winter 1995, pp. 85–105.

30 *Observer*, 8.20.95.

31 Alan George: U.K. Companies Breached U.N. Iraqi Scud Embargo, *Flight International*, 11.8–14.95, p. 4.

32 Scott Inquiry—Day 50: Evidence of Alan Clark, p. 53.

33 On this see, for example, William D. Hartung: *And Weapons for All*, ch. 13.

34 *Guardian*, 9.6.95.

EPILOGUE: THE SCOTT REPORT

Finally, after more than three years in the making, the Scott Report—spanning five volumes and over two thousand pages—was published on 15 February 1996. That a government which felt obliged to initiate such a large-scale inquiry into allegations that, among other things, it deliberately sought to mislead Parliament should, upon publication of its report, seek to misrepresent its findings might be considered a supreme irony. Yet this is precisely what happened with the Scott Report.

The government spent the week during which it had the report prior to its publication putting together a detailed press pack rebuffing or minimizing the impact of Scott's charges against it. For example, it claimed that the report concluded there had been "no deliberate misleading of Parliament"[1] over the sale of arms and dual-use goods to Iraq. In reality, the report was critical of the way in which the government concealed information from Parliament, commenting: "The answers to PQs [parliamentary questions], in both Houses of Parliament, failed to inform Parliament of the current state of Government policy on non-lethal arms sales to Iraq. This failure was deliberate. . . ."[2] Similarly bold and unsubstantiated claims included those that the government "welcomes the clearing of its good name" (in reality, amongst a litany of criticisms, Scott found that ministers "failed to discharge the obligations imposed by the constitutional principle of Ministerial accountability")[3], William Waldegrave's assertion that "Sir Richard Scott clears me of lying to Parliament or intending to mislead anyone in letters I signed" (at his press conference to launch the report, Scott commented: "Some of the answers he gave and some of the letters he wrote were, in my opinion, misleading"), and President of the Board of Trade Ian Lang's claim that ministers "had a duty to sign PII certificates and [these] were applicable in criminal cases." (In his report, Scott says: "In my opinion, the view of the law on which the making of the PII class claims in the Matrix Churchill case was based was unsound. There was no clear prior judicial authority approving the making of PII class claims in criminal trials in order to keep from disclosure material documents which might be of assistance to the defence."⁴) Furthermore, the Cabinet Office claimed that there was "*no* change of policy in 1989"—i.e., that when the guidelines were changed and a new guideline iii) was being used, this did not amount to a change of policy, a view put forward during the inquiry, for example, by William Waldegrave. Scott concluded: "To describe this revised formulation as no more than an interpretation of the old is, in my opinion . . . so plainly inapposite as to be incapable of being sustained by serious argument."⁵ In sum, the report is critical of the way in which the government secretly changed its policy toward Iraq, kept this policy change from Parliament and the public, prepared the Matrix Churchill and other prosecutions, interfered in the Dunk prosecution, and deployed the PII certificate as a weapon in a criminal case.

Yet, crucially for the ministers at the center of the affair, when considering the culpability or otherwise of individual ministers, Scott takes refuge in a language awash with double negatives (e.g., "I do not accept that he was not personally at fault") and qualification. Indeed, some of the civil servants who appeared before the inquiry would themselves have been proud of it. It is the degree of latitude that this imprecise language has afforded those under closest scrutiny that has saved them from resigning. Scott himself has denied that this represented any softening of his position in response to public criticisms by the likes of Lord Howe, but differences in language between leaked drafts of sections of the report and the final version are plain for all to see.⁶ A related omission is the absence of any set of "Conclusions" at the end of the report (although there are "Recommendations") unambiguously outlining Scott's thoughts on the key issues discussed in detail in the body of the report.

While much attention has focused on the way in which Scott has opened up the workings of Whitehall and his criticisms of the government, with regard to the arms trade Scott has left a whole range of questions unanswered. It is now clear that the sale of arms to Iraq was not the subject of the inquiry but merely the context within which an inquiry into ministerial and Whitehall conduct was undertaken. This is not to say that Scott has not shed some light on a too-murky area of governmental activity. Yet, it seems clear that while Scott's procedures served him well in dealing with issues such as ministerial accountability, PII, and so on, they did not lend themselves equally well to an examination of the arms trade. In part, this is a reflection of the fact that the key element of the inquiry's terms of reference (drafted by the government and agreed by Scott after "minor amendments") was that it was required "to report on whether the relevant [government] Departments, Agencies, and responsible Ministers operated in accordance with the policies of Her Majesty's Government."[7] The natural corollary of this was that the inquiry

> was instituted to examine allegations regarding *the part played by Government officials and Ministers* in the decisions that led to the export of defence-related equipment to Iraq. I have, therefore, consistently declined to pursue allegations of illegal defence-related exports to Iraq unless there has been some reason, even if only tenuous, to suspect that some part in enabling the export to take place may have been played by Government officials or Ministers.[8]

Being given access to official documents with regard to PII certificates, and so on, clearly illuminated the processes by which these decisions were reached. But does access to export licensing documentation, shipping records, and the like necessarily allow for the arms trade to be similarly opened up? In the report, Scott says "Government involvement [in the arms trade] may be expected to be found in the export licensing process."[9] But in an era that witnessed the Iran-Contra scandal, how can this be guaranteed? If this were the case, Iran-Contra might never have been exposed.

Thorough investigation of a contemporary arms market where the system of end-use certification is almost routinely abused would have required an investigative reach beyond that of the Scott Inquiry. In reality, the inquiry's investigative efforts were limited, perhaps because of the belief that involvement could be divined from documents—that a paper trail would always exist. Hence, the report notes: "The investigative work of the Inquiry has been based almost entirely upon the collection and perusal of documents obtained from Government Departments."[10] Its further investigative efforts involved writing to private individuals to ask questions about their alleged involvements. Even here, lines of inquiry were not followed up as thoroughly as they could have been.

Hence, although the report confirms that British arms reached both Iraq and Iran via conduits, it does not consider the full range of conduits that were alleged to have been used. Scott traced British government knowledge of the use of Jordan as a conduit back to 1983, although Jordan's likely role was acknowledged even earlier. For example, after King Hussein appealed for Jordanian volunteers to fight alongside Iraqis in the Iran-Iraq War at the beginning of 1982, an FCO note warned: "If and when the Jordanian volunteers . . . actually assist Iraq's war effort, it will be very difficult indeed to escape any longer from the conclusion that Jordan ought to be treated as a co-belligerent with all that this entails for our arms supply policy."[11] Scott goes on to record a series of instances indicating government awareness of Jordan's conduit role, concluding that "the possibility that military exports to Jordan might be diverted to Iraq represented a continuing threat to the integrity of the Government's policy on restricting defence related exports to Iraq."[12] It did more than this; it blew a huge hole through it. In considering other diversionary routes, Scott shows evidence of, or British government knowledge of, the use of Egypt, Kuwait, Saudi Arabia, Austria, and Portugal as conduits, although the case against the United Arab Emirates remains, to his mind, not proven. Again, the inquiry's conclusions are based on points drawn from a range of internal memoranda, but as with Jordan, the detail in them falls short of allowing Scott to estimate the volume of equipment involved.

This investigative limitation is also apparent when the inquiry deals with allegations that RO ammunition reached Iraq via conduits ("As to whether actual diversion took place after export, I am not in a position to investigate this fully, nor do I consider it necessary for me to do so"[13]). It is even more apparent when the report comes to look into the propellant cartel and the alleged involvement of RO in it. The absence of an investigative arm meant that the inquiry had to rely on the MOD and Customs and Excise for information. Despite the Swedish customs investigation into the cartel, subsequent reports, and court cases, the MOD told Scott that it "had no knowledge or suspicion of a propellant cartel or a weapons cartel to which British companies belonged."[14] Notwithstanding the careful wording, the suggestion that the MOD was unaware of the activities of the cartel begs belief. Customs fared better; at least they were aware of it and had had contacts with Swedish customs officials over it. Scott's comments are inconclusive:

> The existence of international weapons/propellants cartels, and the alleged involvement in them of UK companies are, *per se*, matters which fall outside my terms of reference. If, on the other hand, there were evidence of British Government knowledge of, or acquiescence in, the activities of any cartels whose existence was intended to defeat the prohibitions and restrictions on exports from the UK to Iraq, it would have been incumbent on me to investigate. In fact there was no such evidence beyond mere assertion. It is also an issue in relation to which it would have been very difficult for me to obtain sufficiently cogent evidence to reach a concluded view without extensive investigation. Extensive investigation, even if the Inquiry were granted the necessary powers to conduct it, would have caused unnec-

essary delay to the publication of this Report. I have not, therefore, attempted to do so.[15]

The report's treatment of the supergun also leaves open a number of questions, although it undoubtedly represents an advance on the TISC's efforts in this area (the government's approach to which is severely criticized in the report). Here, Scott sought to corroborate Chris Cowley's account of Dr. Gerald Bull's search for the approval of the U.K., U.S., and Israeli governments before embarking on Project Babylon. While recognizing that ultimately "Dr Bull himself held the key to the puzzle" and that because of his death, "the question of [his] contacts, if any, with the British intelligence agencies could not be explored with him," Scott "examined relevant files held by British Government departments and intelligence agencies and . . . found no evidence that Dr Bull ever contacted the intelligence services or that Mr Wong was asked to act in the way described by Dr Bull."[16] Furthermore, the inquiry contacted Wong who, while agreeing he had been a close friend of Bull's, denied having any knowledge of Project Babylon or playing any role in facilitating its approval. On the basis of this investigative effort, and despite the wealth of circumstantial evidence supporting Bull's story put forward by Chris Cowley, the report—noting in passing that the TISC described Cowley as operating "at the heart of a web of deception"—concludes that "Dr Bull did not, as alleged, inform British intelligence about the long-range gun project."[17] Yet at the same time, the report notes:

> On 6 April 1988, SIS [MI6] were asked by another country's diplomats for information about Dr Bull in order "to establish whether rumours of unsavoury dealings are true." SIS made enquiries of a number of its posts worldwide. Having regard to their responses, it is clear that SIS were aware of the activities of Dr Bull and of SRC in the arms trade, including his involvement in the Canadian High Altitude Rocket Project (HARP). But none of the SIS posts mentioned a connection of any kind between Dr Bull and SIS or between Dr Bull and Iraq.[18]

All that this shows is that MI6 knew of Bull—clearly, although unstated in the report, about his dealings with South Africa and China. In April 1988, Bull was at the early stages of discussions with Iraq. No contracts had been signed and no discussions held with companies besides SRC.

The report also effectively dismisses Sir Hal Miller's claim that he spoke with a "third agency" over Walter Somers's involvement with Iraq, and seems to imply that his account of this contact is a function of his age:

Although Sir Hal undoubtedly believes that he was in contact with a third agency, it must be borne in mind that the first time that he had cause to recollect details of that contact was nearly two years later in April 1990. Memory fades over time and . . . I am not satisfied that Sir Hal's account of the "third agency" or the part played by "Mr Anderson" is correct.[19]

Yet an MI6 briefing note dated 6 October 1989 and cited by Scott indicates that intelligence knowledge of Walter Somers's involvement in the embryonic supergun project went back to June 1988—the month in which the contracts were signed. If MI6 had no knowledge of Bull's links with Iraq in April 1988, and if the accounts of Chris Cowley regarding Bull and of Sir Hal Miller are discounted—as they seem to be in the report—where did this come from? The obvious answer is Bill Weir, although acknowledging the probability of his involvement here itself lends credence to Miller's account, already rejected by Scott. But Weir was at best uncertain that he was the source, and an MI6 officer questioned ("Mr C2") denied that the information could have come from Weir, suggesting instead that it probably came from elsewhere within MI6, although Scott could not uncover any MI6 documentation with which to convince himself that this was the case. So where did this crucial early knowledge emanate from? Scott doesn't know: ". . . it would not be proper for me to reach a conclusion as to the source . . . which is not accepted by either of the two people directly involved . . . [it] must, therefore, remain an open unanswered question."[20] The report's coverage of the supergun affair ends inconclusively. Would this have been the case if it had sought documents from outside Whitehall? For example, could the documents seized by Belgian officials from SRC's Brussels offices following the murder of Bull have helped? Again, while able to apply a near-forensic analysis to Whitehall documents, the absence of an investigative arm that looks beyond Whitehall in any meaningful way served to limit the report's conclusions. In the event, Scott wraps up the long supergun section of his report by observing that

there is clear evidence that, some time before October 1989, Government officials had had information which raised the suspicion that Walter Somers' tubes were probably intended for use as artillery gun-barrels. There is no evidence that at that point officials suspected that they were for use in the kind of project which was eventually uncovered; but the evidence indicates suspicion that an Iraqi long-range artillery project with unusual features was in contemplation.[21]

Elsewhere in the report, a more detailed consideration of the relationship between government and arms trade, and of the mechanics of the arms trade with regard to Iraq and Iran, is hampered by the absence of any consideration of U.S. foreign policy toward Iraq and Iran, and the relationship between U.S. and U.K. foreign policy in this area. The presence of the United States and the implications of its position hang over a number of Foreign Office memoranda cited in the report, but they are not considered beyond this. Finally, there was no attempt by Scott to extend the inquiry into the financing of the arms trade with Iraq—to interview and take evidence from various businesspeople, bankers, insurance company executives, and others alleged to have been involved in it.[22]

Nevertheless, the very fact of the Scott Inquiry has turned the spotlight on the central role played by the British government in the international arms trade, especially since 1980. It may not have exposed the full extent of British, U.S., and Western involvement in the arming of Iraq—what William Safire called "the first global political scandal"[23]—but it has illuminated the way in which arms sales interests have shaped and influenced foreign policy, how other considerations have become secondary, and how central democratic concepts like accountability are undermined by this involvement and the secrecy it demands. The whole affair has also highlighted the way in which the de facto alliances that arms sales relationships produce lead to misperceptions and miscalculations. In the case of Iraq, these resulted in a war over Kuwait during which coalition forces faced weaponry and technology the West had sold to Iraq. The West not only armed Iraq. When Iraq used those arms to invade Kuwait, the West also provided the targets.

N O T E S

1 The following government positions are taken from the press pack made available to journalists along with the report on 15 February 1996. It contained ten separate briefings and ran to seventy-two pages.

2 The Right Honourable Sir Richard Scott, the Vice Chancellor: *Report of the Inquiry into the Export of Defence Equipment and Dual-Use Goods to Iraq and Related Prosecutions* [henceforth, Scott Report], London, HMSO, 1996, p. 495, para D4.42.

3 Scott Report, p. 507, para D4.63.

4 Ibid., p. 1530, para G18.94. Elsewhere in the Report, Scott comments: "The proposition that a Minister is ever under a legal duty to claim PII in order to protect documents from disclosure to the defence notwithstanding that in the Minister's view the public interest requires their disclosure to the defence is, in my opinion, based on a fundamental misconception of the principles of PII law." Ibid., p. 1507, para G18.54.

5 Ibid., p. 427, para D3.123.

6 On this see, for example, the *Independent*, 2.17.96. On the cases of William Waldegrave and

Sir Nicholas Lyell, the two ministers most under fire, and the language employed in the report, see Robert Preston: Escape After the Storm, *Financial Times*, 2.17/18.96.

7 Scott Report, p. 7, para A2.2.
8 Ibid., p. 12, para A3.7. My emphasis.
9 Ibid., p. 13, para A3.9.
10 Ibid., p. 19, para B1.2.
11 Ibid., p. 820, para E2.4.
12 Ibid., p. 850, para E2.62.
13 Ibid., p. 778, para D7.5.
14 Ibid., p. 781, para D7.11.
15 Ibid., p. 782–783, para D7.14.
16 Ibid., p. 948, paras F2.4 and F2.5.
17 Ibid., p. 950, para F2.10.
18 Ibid., p. 950, para F2.9.
19 Ibid., p. 970, para F2.37.
20 Ibid., p. 1029, para F3.55.
21 Ibid., pp. 1095–1096, para F4.80.
22 Ibid., p. 13, para A3.9.
23 *New York Times*, 11.12.92.

SELECTED BIBLIOGRAPHY

Books, Articles, and Official Reports

Adams, James. *Trading in Death*. London, Hutchinson, 1990.

———. *Bull's Eye: The Assassination and Life of Supergun Inventor Gerald Bull*. New York, Times Books, 1992.

Alani, Mustafa M. *Operation Vantage: British Military Intervention in Kuwait 1961*. Surbiton, LAAM, 1990.

Anthony, Ian, ed. *Arms Export Regulations*. Oxford, OUP/SIPRI, 1992.

Atkinson, Rick. *Crusade: The Untold Story of the Gulf War*. London, HarperCollins, 1994.

Ben-Menashe, Ari. *Profits of War: Inside the Secret U.S.-Israeli Arms Network*. New York, Sheridan Square Press, 1992.

Bennett, Alexander J. Arms Transfers as an Instrument of Soviet Policy in the Middle East. *Middle East Journal*, Vol. 39 No. 4, 1985.

Bermudez, Joseph S. Iraqi Missile Operations During "Desert Storm." *Jane's Soviet Intelligence Review*, March 1991.

Bill, James A., and Springborg, R. *Politics in the Middle East*, 4th ed. New York, HarperCollins, 1994.

British Petroleum. *BP Statistical Review of World Energy*. London, BP, June 1995.

Brzoska, Michael. Arming South Africa in the Shadow of the U.N. Arms Embargo. *Defense Analysis*, Vol. 7 No. 1, 1991.

Brzoska, Michael, and Ohlson, Thomas. *Arms Transfers to the Third World, 1971–85*. Oxford, OUP/SIPRI, 1987.

Bull, Gerald V., and Murphy, Charles H. *Paris Kanonen: The Paris Guns (Wilhelmgeschutze) and Project HARP: The Application of Major Calibre Guns to Atmospheric and Space Research*. Herford, Verlag E. S. Mittler & Sohn GmbH, 1988.

Bulloch, John, and Morris, Harvey. *Saddam's War: The Origins of the Kuwait Conflict and the International Response*. London, Faber and Faber, 1991.

Burrows, William E., and Windrem, Robert. *Critical Mass: The Dangerous Race for Superweapons in a Fragmenting World*. London, Simon & Schuster, 1994.

Cahill, Kevin. What Lord Justice Scott Hasn't Been Told. *Business Age*, Vol. 3 No. 34, July/August 1993.

Campaign Against Arms Trade. *Arming Saddam*. London, CAAT, 1991.

Campbell, Duncan. The Bribe Machine. *New Statesman*, 10.17.80.

Carus, W. Seth, and Bermudez, Joseph S. Iraq's Al-Husayn Missile Programme, Parts I & II. *Jane's Soviet Intelligence Review*, May & June 1990.

Chubin, Shahram, and Tripp, Charles. *Iran and Iraq at War*. London, I. B. Taurus, 1988.

Clark, Alan. *Diaries*. London, Weidenfeld & Nicolson, 1993.

Cordesman, Anthony. *The Iran-Iraq War and Western Security, 1984–87*. London, Jane's, 1987.

———. Arms to Iran: The Impact of U.S. and Other Arms Sales on the Iran-Iraq War. *American-Arab Affairs*, Spring 1987.

Cowley, Chris. *Guns, Lies and Spies*. London, Hamish Hamilton, 1992.

Darwish, Adel, and "Alexander, Gregory." *Unholy Babylon: The Secret History of Saddam's War*. London, Victor Gollancz, 1991.

Freedman, Lawrence. *Arms Production in the United Kingdom: Problems and Prospects*. London, RIIA, 1978.

Friedman, Alan. *Spider's Web: Bush, Saddam, Thatcher and the Decade of Deceit*. London, Faber & Faber, 1993.

Fromkin, David. *A Peace to End All Peace: Creating the Modern Middle East, 1914–1922*. London, Penguin, 1991.

Gause, F. Gregory. British and American Policies in the Persian Gulf, 1968–1973. *Review of International Studies*, Vol. 11 No. 4, 1985.

———. The Illogic of Dual Containment. *Foreign Affairs*, March/April 1994.

Gill, Stephen, and Law, David. *The Global Political Economy: Perspectives, Problems and Policies*. Hemel Hempstead, Harvester-Wheatsheaf, 1988.

Goddard, Donald, and Coleman, Lester K. *Trail of the Octopus: Behind the Lockerbie Disaster*. London, Bloomsbury, 1993.

Grant, Dale. *Wilderness of Mirrors: The Life of Gerald Bull*. Scarborough, Prentice-Hall Canada, 1991.

Halloran, Paul, and Hollingsworth, Mark. *Thatcher's Gold: The Life and Times of Mark Thatcher*. London, Simon & Schuster, 1995.

Hamdi, W., ed. *Kuwait-Iraq Boundary Dispute in British Archives*, Vols. 1 and 2. Quick Print, London, 1993.

Hartung, William D. *And Weapons for All*. New York, HarperCollins, 1994.

Henderson, Paul. *The Unlikely Spy: An Autobiography*. London, Bloomsbury, 1993.

Hippler, Jochen. Iraq's Military Power: The German Connection. *Middle East Report*, Jan–Feb 1991.

Hiro, Dilip. *The Longest War: The Iran-Iraq Military Conflict*. London, Paladin, 1990.

———. *Desert Shield to Desert Storm: The Second Gulf War*. London, HarperCollins, 1992.

House of Commons Trade and Industry Select Committee. *Exports to Iraq: Memoranda of Evidence, 17 July 1991*. London, HMSO, 1991.

————. *Exports to Iraq: Project Babylon and Long-Range Guns: Report.* (HC-86), London, HMSO, 1992.

House of Representatives Committee on Banking, Finance, and Urban Affairs. *The Banca Nazionale del Lavoro (BNL) Scandal and the Department of Argriculture's Commodity Credit Corporation (CCC) Program for Iraq, Parts I & II.* Washington, GPO, 1992.

Hoy, Claire, and Ostrovsky, Victor. *By Way of Deception: An Insider's Devastating Exposé of the Mossad.* London, Arrow, 1990.

International Institute for Strategic Studies. *The Military Balance.* London, IISS, annual.

Jentleson, Bruce W. *With Friends like These: Reagan, Bush, and Saddam 1982–1990.* New York, W. W. Norton, 1994.

Karsh, Efraim. *The Iran-Iraq War: A Military Analysis.* Adelphi Papers, London, IISS, 1987.

Kay, David. Denial and Deception Practices of WMD Proliferators: Iraq and Beyond. *Washington Quarterly*, Vol. 18 No. 1, 1995.

Klare, Michael T. Arms and the Shah: The Rise and Fall of the "Surrogate Strategy." *The Progressive*, Vol. 43 No. 8, 1979.

————. *American Arms Supermarket.* Austin, University of Texas, 1984.

Kolodziej, Edward, and Kanet, Roger, eds. *The Limits of Soviet Power in the Developing World.* Basingstoke, Macmillan, 1989.

Krapels, Edward N. The Commanding Heights—International Oil in a Changed World. *International Affairs*, Vol. 69 No. 1, 1993.

Krosney, Herbert. *Deadly Business: Legal Deals and Outlaw Weapons—The Arming of Iran and Iraq, 1975 to the Present.* New York, Four Walls Eight Windows, 1993.

Leigh, David. *Betrayed: The Real Story of the Matrix Churchill Trial.* London, Bloomsbury, 1993.

Lowther, William. *Arms and the Man: Dr Gerald Bull, Iraq and the Supergun.* London, Macmillan, 1991.

Mantius, Peter. *Shell Game: A True Story of Banking, Spies, Lies, Politics—and the Arming of Saddam Hussein.* New York, St. Martin's Press, 1995.

Matthews, Ken. *The Gulf Conflict and International Relations.* London, Routledge, 1993.

Meacher, Michael. Bomb Proof. *New Statesman and Society.* 10.14.94.

Norton-Taylor, Richard. *Truth Is a Difficult Concept: Inside the Scott Inquiry.* London, Fourth Estate, 1995.

Parsons, Anthony. Iran, Iraq and the West's Policy of Demonisation. *Middle East International*, 6.11.93.

Pearson, Frederic S. The Question of Control in British Defence Sales Policy. *International Affairs*, Vol. 59 No. 2, 1983.

Perlmutter, Amos, Handel, Michael, and Bar-Joseph, Uri. *Two Minutes over Baghdad.* London, Corgi, 1982.

Pion-Berlin, David. The Fall of Military Rule in Argentina, 1976–1983. *Journal of Inter-American Studies and World Affairs*, Vol. 27 No. 2, 1985.

Phythian, Mark, and Little, Walter. Parliament and Arms Sales: Lessons of the Matrix Churchill Affair. *Parliamentary Affairs*, Vol. 46 No. 3, 1993.

———. Administering Britain's Arms Trade. *Public Administration*, Vol. 71 No. 3, 1993.

Pilger, John. *Distant Voices*. London, Vintage, 1992.

Rimer, Colin P. F., and White, John. *Astra Holdings plc: Investigation Under Section 431 (2) (c) of the Companies Act 1985: Report*. London, DTI/HMSO, 1993.

Rubin, Barry. *Paved with Good Intentions: The American Experience and Iran*. New York, Penguin, 1981.

Sadowski, Yahya. Scuds Versus Butter: The Political Economy of Arms Control in the Arab World. *Middle East Report*, July–August 1992.

Sampson, Anthony. *The Arms Bazaar*, 2nd ed. Sevenoaks, Hodder & Stoughton, 1988.

Schultz, George P. *Turmoil and Triumph: My Years as Secretary of State*. New York, Scribner's, 1993.

Scott, Sir Richard. *Report of the Inquiry into the Export of Defence Equipment and Dual-Use Goods to Iraq and Related Prosecutions*. 5 vols., London, HMSO, 1996.

Sick, Gary. *October Surprise: America's Hostages in Iran and the Election of Ronald Reagan*. London, I. B. Taurus, 1991.

Sigler, John. Pax Americana in the Gulf: Old Reflexes and Assumptions Revisited. *International Journal*, Vol. XLIX, Spring 1994.

Simpson, John. *From the House of War*. London, Arrow, 1991.

SIPRI. *Armaments and Disarmament: SIPRI Yearbook*. Oxford, OUP/SIPRI, annual.

Smolansky, Oles M., and Smolansky, Bettie M. *The USSR and Iraq: The Soviet Quest for Influence*. Durham, N.C., Duke University Press, 1991.

Stockwell, John. *In Search of Enemies*. London, André Deutsch, 1978.

Swedish Peace and Arbitration Society. *International Connections of the Bofors Affair*. Stockholm, SPAS, 1987.

Sweeney, John. *Trading with the Enemy: Britain's Arming of Iraq*. London, Pan, 1993.

Teicher, Howard, and Radley, Gayle. *Twin Pillars to Desert Storm: America's Flawed Vision in the Middle East from Nixon to Bush*. New York, William Morrow, 1993.

Timmerman, Kenneth. Europe's Arms Pipeline to Iran, *The Nation*, 7.18–25.87.

———. *The Death Lobby: How the West Armed Iraq*. London, Fourth Estate, 1992.

Waas, Murray, and Ungar, Craig. In the Loop: Bush's Secret Mission. *The New Yorker*, 11.2.92.

Watt, Donald C. The Decision to Withdraw from the Gulf. *Political Quarterly*, Vol. 39 No. 3, 1968.

Westander, Henrik. *Classified: The Political Cover-Up of the Bofors Scandal*. Bombay, Sterling Newspapers, 1992.

Woodward, Bob. *Veil: The Secret Wars of the CIA, 1981–87*. London, Headline, 1988.

Yetiv, Steve A. The Outcomes of Operations Desert Shield and Desert Storm: Some Antecedent Causes. *Political Science Quarterly*, Vol. 107 No. 2, 1992.

Television Programs

Assignment, BBC2, 5.4.93. "Secrets of the Generals."

Channel 4 News, 1.28.94, 3.30.95.

Dispatches, Channel 4, 11.13.91. "The Swiss Connection."

Dispatches, Channel 4, 11.25.92. "The First Thatcherite."

Dispatches, Channel 4, 5.5.93. "Grecian Tragedy."

Horizon, BBC2, 8.23.92. "Hide and Seek in Iraq."

Newsnight, BBC2, 3.30.95.

Panorama, BBC1, 11.23.92. "U.K. Ltd: The Arming of Iraq."

Timewatch, BBC2, 2.12.92. "The Man Who Made the Supergun."

World in Action, ITV, 4.10.95. "Jonathan of Arabia."

Abraham, Trevor, 207; and Matrix Churchill trial, 231–32, 254n. 18
Adams, James, 87, 97
Adams, Steve, 96
Afghanistan, 20
Agriculture Department, 36–37, 53
Aitken, Jonathan, 5, 73, 128, 147, 168; and Kock, Stephan, 166; and Project LISI, 171–77, 179, 187n. 178, 187n. 180, 187n. 184, 187n. 196
Al Yamamah project, 29, 72, 73
Al Yamamah/Tornado agreement, 66
Algernon, Carl-Fredrik, 84
Allen, Peter, 207, 231–32, 254n. 18
Allivane International Group Ltd, 80–82
Al-Shiraa (Lebanon), 39
Anderson, John, 127, 150; and Astra, 152–53; and intelligence monitoring, 204–5; and Kock, Stephan, 164–65; and Project LISI, 171, 175–76, 178
Andreotti, Giulio, 36
Anglo-Iraqi Joint Trade Commission, 74
Arab-Israeli War, 5, 11
Ardbo, Martin, 84
Argentina, 22, 23
Ashwell, Paul, 120
Astra Holdings, xxv, 136–43, 147–48; arrests, 152–67; and Baghdad Exhibition, 148–49, 183n. 78; and BMARC, 128–30, 143–46, 180n. 9, 180–81n. 11, 181n. 14; collapse of, 149–51; development of, 125–28, 180n. 3–4; and EPREP agreement, 131–32, 181n. 15; group structure, 126 figure 5.1, 180n. 2; and intelligence monitoring, 199–200, 222n. 31; investigations into, 167–71; and MOD, 140–43; and PRB, 132–36, 181n. 24, 182n. 30; and Project LISI, 171–80, 187n. 179; and RO, 128–30, 180n. 13
Athel, Sheikh Fahad al-, 172
ATI (Advanced Technology Institute), 100
Australia, 210

Austria, 87–88, 93n. 110, 93n. 112
Avery, Graham, 144
Ayas, Said, 173
Aziz, Tariq, 53
Azzawi, Shabib, 38, 193, 198; and supergun, 100, 110, 114, 115, 122n. 14

Ba'ath Party, 11
BAE (British Aerospace) Hawk, 69–70, 76–78, 92n. 71
Baghdad International Military Exhibition, 79–80, 92n. 81, 148–49, 183n. 78
Baker, James, 32, 53, 291
Baker, Kenneth, 202
Baki, Misbah, 73
Baldrige, Malcolm, 38
Balsom, John, 208, 223n. 61, 229, 230, 233
Bandar, Prince, 172
Banks, Tony, 74
Barbados, 94–95
Barber, Roy, 151, 153
Barrett, Alan, 237; and Howe Guidelines, 62; and Scott Inquiry, 263–64, 284n. 9, 284n. 12
Barstow, A. G. S., 152
Barzani, Masoud, 78
Baxendale, Presiley, 277; and Howe Guidelines, 63, 65, 66; and Scott Inquiry, 264, 268, 275–76, 280, 284n. 9, 285n. 38, 286n. 72
Bayliss, Rex, 103–4, 204–5
Bazoft, Farzad, 79, 117; execution of, 243, 250
Belgium, 15, 117, 123n. 53; and PRB, 132–33; and propellant cartel, 141–43, 182n. 48, 182n. 52; and SRC, 95
Ben-Menashe, Ari, 118, 123n. 52, 124n. 60
Benedetti, Carlo, 133
Beston, Eric, 246, 255n. 59, 256n. 60; and Scott Inquiry, 267

Bevan, Nicholas, 110–11, 200, 222n. 33; and Howe Guidelines, 64–65; and intelligence monitoring, 192; and PRB, 140; and Project Babylon, 143, 183n. 58
Biggen, John, 70
Binek, Tony, 136, 182n. 33
Blackledge, Stuart, 202
Blackley, Ian: and BAe Hawk, 92n. 71; and Howe Guidelines, 63, 90n. 18; and intelligence monitoring, 190; and Scott Inquiry, 268–69, 284n. 12
Blythe, Sir James, 283, 286n. 81
BMARC (British Manufacture and Research Company), 128–30, 143–46, 147–48, 180n. 9, 180–81n. 11, 181n. 14
BNL, (Banca Nazionale del Lavoro) 45–48
Bonsor, Nicholas, 170–71, 186n. 172
Bosnia, 99
Bottomley, P. J., 113–14
Bourn, John, 129, 157, 180n. 7
Brazil: and Bull, Gerald, 99; and Iran-Iraq War, 21; Iraqi debt to, 51; and propellant cartel, 93n. 110
Brzezinski, Zbigniew, 32, 54n. 3
Bull, Gerald, xxv, 23–24, 37, 56n. 58, 89, 97, 121n. 10, 293; and Allivane, 81; and China, 97–98; death of, 117–19, 123n. 52, 124n. 60; and dual-use license applications, 43; and Gumbley, Christopher, 153–54; and HARP, 94–95; and intelligence monitoring, 193, 196–99, 211–12, 223n. 71; and Iran-Iraq War, 99–101; and Kock, Stephan, 159; and PRB, 133–35, 136, 137, 140; and propellant cartel, 84–85; and Scott Report, 307–8; and South Africa, 95–97; and supergun, 100–101, 106–7, 109–12, 114–16, 136, 141; and U.S., 121n. 11
Bull, Michel, 96, 97, 121n. 10, 196
Bull, Stephen, 212
Bush, George: and family of nations, 57n. 88; and Hussein, Saddam, xxvi, xxviin. 4; and Iran-Iraq War, 32; Iran Sanctions Act of 1990, 45, 57n. 72
Bush administration, 267, 294; and Baghdad Exhibition, 80; and CCC guarantees program, 37; and dual-use license applications, 42–45; and family of nations, xxiv, xxvi; Iran-Contra scheme, 48, 50; and Iran-Iraq War, 41; postwar relations with Iraq, 53
Business Age, 167
Butler, Sir Adam, 60
Butler, Sir Robin: and Howe Guidelines, 65, 90n. 22; and Scott Inquiry, 280
"Buy British Last" campaign, 18n. 36
Byers, Stephen, 178–79, 278
Byrne, Terry, Jr., 81

Cahill, Kevin, 167, 279
Campbell, Menzies, 222n. 33, 222n. 52, 224n. 80; and intelligence monitoring, 192; and Kock, Stephan, 166
Campbell-Savours, Dale, 179, 186n. 173
Canada: and Astra, 127; and HARP, 94–95; and SIGINT, 210
CARDE (Canadian Armament, Research and Development Establishment), 94
Cardinael, Guy, 136, 147
Cardoen, Carlos, 32, 55n. 31, 229
Carmoy, Hervé de, 133, 160; and Kock, Stephan, 165
Carrington, Lord, 15
Carter administration, 11; and Iran-Iraq War, 32, 54n. 3
Casey, Bill, 40
CCC guarantees program, 36–37
Chan, Jim, 118
Chandler, Sir Colin, 300; and Scott Inquiry, 283, 286n. 81
Channon, Paul, 74
Chemical Defence Establishment, 74
Chemical weapons, 29–31, 73–74, 91n. 60; against Israel, 118–19; against Kurds, 22, 49
Chemical weapons protection kits, 74, 91n. 57
Chevallier, Guy, 87
Chile, 26, 32, 55n. 31
Chile-Iraq Military Trade: Chilean Arms Firm to Turn Over Munitions Factory to Iraqi Government, 247–48
China, 21, 27; and Bull, Gerald, 97–98, 107, 122n. 11; and SRC, 97–98
CIA, 51, 54n. 15; and BNL, 46, 47, 48; and CCC guarantees program, 37; and Iran-Iraq War, 40
Claes, Willy, 117, 123n. 53
Clark, Alan, 38, 75, 91n. 63, 107, 218, 289, 290, 299; and EPREP, 131–32; and Howe Guidelines, 61–62, 63, 64, 89n. 7; and Matrix Churchill, 66, 228, 230, 232, 234, 237–39, 244–46, 248, 250, 254n. 27, 255n. 29; and Scott Inquiry, 265, 269, 271, 274, 285n. 38
Clarke, Kenneth, 231
Clinton administration, 223n. 66
COCOM (Co-Ordinating Committee for Multicultural Export Control), 97
Coeme, Guy, 123n. 53
Commerce Department, 53
Condor II ballistic missile program, 22, 23
Cook, Robin, 256n. 76, 281
Coolican, Mike, 231, 250–51
Cools, Andre, 117, 123n. 53
Cordesman, Anthony, 20, 56n. 37, 69

Cousins, Jim, 110, 178, 224n. 80; and intelligence monitoring, 216, 224n. 95; and Scott Inquiry, 267
Cowley, Chris, 23, 38, 68, 167, 231, 233; and BAE Hawk, 77; and *Guns, Lies and Spies*, 288–89; and intelligence monitoring, 191, 193, 195, 196–99, 203, 204, 213–17, 219, 220, 221n. 24, 221n. 25, 221n. 30, 223n. 72; and Jordan, 146; and Kock, Stephan, 159, 165; and Scott Inquiry, 267–68, 283; and Scott Report, 307–8; and supergun, 101–3, 107–8, 109–14, 120, 122n. 14, 123n. 52; and Wong, George, 98
Crowther, Stan, 158–59, 289
Cuba, 94–95
Cuckney, Sir John, 160, 227, 253n. 8; and PRB, 135, 181n. 28; and Scott Inquiry, 283, 286n. 81
Cunningham, Jack, 174
Curtis, Alan, 168–69
Cyprus, 146
Cywie, Georges, 123n. 53
Czechoslovakia, 27

Daghir, Ali, 203, 225n. 104, 291
Dalyell, Tam, 212
Davignon, Etienne, 133
Delanghe, Johan, 123n. 53
Der Spiegel, 31
DESO (Defence Export Services Organisation), 18n. 26
DRA (Defence Research Agency), 111
Draft Technical Proposal for a 600mm LRSB System, 113–14
Drogoul, Christopher, 46–48
DSO (Defence Sales Organisation), 13
Dual-use exports, xxiii–xxiv, 37–38; and intelligence monitoring, 203–4; and Matrix Churchill, 226–53; and supergun, 108–16; Dual-use license applications, 42–45
Dual-use machine tool industry, xxv
Dukakis, Michael, 48
Dunford, Campbell, 159–60, 185n. 139
Dunk, Reginald, 203, 276–78, 282, 285n. 59
Duronsoy, Jean, 133, 149
Durrani, Arif, 15

EASSP (European Association for the Study of Safety Problems in the Production and Use of Propellant Powders), 83, 92n. 93
ECGD (Export Credit Guarantee Department), 74
Egerton, Sir Stephen, 91n. 42; and Howe Guidelines, 60–61, 89n.4; and Scott Inquiry, 268, 274

Egypt, 21, 22, 27, 80; and Iran-Iraq War, 4, 35
Ekeus, Rolf, 111
El Salvador, 37
Ellis, Sir Ronald, 13
EPREP (Explosives, Propellants and Related End Products) agreement, 131–32, 181n. 15
Export of Goods (Control) (Amendment No. 6), 91n. 60

Fahd, King, 38, 147
Fahd, Prince Mohammed bin, 172, 173
Fairbanks, Richard, 35
Family of nations, xxiv, xxvi, 49, 57n. 88
FBI, 45–46
Financial Times, 155, 157, 164
Florio, Angelo, 48
Ford, Michael, 207, 208, 228; and Matrix Churchill trial, 233
Forouzandeth, Mohammed, 27
France, xxiv–xxv, 21, 24, 27, 28–29, 36; and Baghdad Exhibition, 80; and Iran-Iraq War, 4; and Iranian Revolution, 15, 16; Iraqi debt to, 51; and propellant cartel, 92n. 92; and Shah of Iran, 12–13
Freeman, Roger, 179
French, Stephen, 181n. 13
Friedman, Alan, 81
Frost, David, 281
Frost, Jack, 96
Fuisz, Richard, xxiii
Fuller, Simon, 269
Funk, Michael, 130

Garel-Jones, Tristan, 299; and Matrix Churchill trial, 231–32, 254n. 19
Gartmann, Werner, 108
Gates, Robert, 40
Georgetown University Center for Strategic and International Studies, 17n. 13
Germany: and Bull, Gerald, 99; and Paris Guns, 122n. 31; and SIGINT, 210, 223n. 67
Gilbert, John, 212, 224n. 80
Glaspie, April, 119
Glazebrook, Richard, 38, 54n. 8, 71–72, 297; and Howe Guidelines, 67; and Scott Inquiry, 263–64, 267–68, 270–72, 284n. 9
Glibert, Philippe, 136, 147, 212
Goldsworthy, Ian, 152
Gonzalez, Henry, 294; and BNL, 47–48; and Bush, George, 57n. 88; and export licenses, 43, 45, 57n. 70
Gore, Al, xxvi
Gore-Booth, Sir David, 276–78; and BAE Hawk, 76, 77–78; and Scott Inquiry, 273
Goulden, John, 64–65, 90n. 22

Great Britain: and Allivane, 80–82; and arms sales to Iraq, 68–78, 90n. 34, 91n. 42, 91n. 45; and BAE Hawk, 69–70, 76–78, 92n. 71; and chemical weapons, 74; and Condor II, 23; and dual-use license applications, 42–43; and Howe Guidelines, 59–68, 89n. 2, 89n. 4, 89n. 7; and Iran-Iraq War, 3–4; and Iranian Revolution, 14–16, 18n. 36; and Matrix Churchill, xxv, xxvi, 26, 226–53, 254n. 9; pre-1979 relations with Iran and Iraq, 8–10; and propellant cartel, 86–87; and Scott Inquiry, xxv, 257–83; and Shah of Iran, 12–13, 18n. 25; and supergun, 101–4, 105–6 table 4.1, 106–8, 117–21, 123n. 52; and trade with Iraq, 75 table 3.2; and training Iraqi and Iranian pilots, 77–78. *See also* United Kingdom

Grecian, Paul, 291; and intelligence monitoring, 201–3, 220, 222n. 37, 222n. 45
Greece, 80
Grenfell, Morgan, 74
Guardian, 173, 174
Guerin, James, 148
Guest, Martin, 153, 161
Gulf Co-operation Council, 90n. 34
Gulf War, 3; and long-range missiles, 22; oil politics, 5, 17n. 5
Gumbley, Christopher, 140–41, 169, 182n. 48, 184n. 80; and BMARC, 130, 181n. 11; and EPREP, 131–32; and intelligence monitoring, 195, 199–200, 220, 222n. 32; and Kock, Stephan, 157, 160–62, 166–67. *See also* James and Gumbley management team
Guns, Lies and Spies (Cowley), 288–89
Gutteridge, Mark, 47, 227–29; and intelligence monitoring, 206–9, 220; and Matrix Churchill, 233, 235

Habobi, Safa al-, 47, 227, 242, 248, 253n. 3, 256n. 60
Hampson, Keith, 158, 224n. 79
Hanabusa, Mosamichi, 17n. 5
Harding, Roger, 140, 143, 183n. 60, 217
HARP (High Altitude Research Project), 94–95, 98, 109
Hastie, David, 80, 92n. 81; and intelligence monitoring, 192; and Scott Inquiry, 283
Haswell, Charles, 273, 275, 276, 285n. 54
Helicopters, as dual-use goods, 37–38
Hellier, David, 165
Henderson, Paul, xxv, 227–31, 253n. 5, 253n. 7, 289, 299; and Allivane, 81–82; and intelligence monitoring, 192, 199, 201, 204, 206–9, 218, 220; and Kock, Stephan, 165; and Matrix Churchill, 231–33, 235–36, 245, 254n. 18; and Scott Inquiry, 265–67

Hersh, Seymour, 34
Heseltine, Michael, 170, 288; and Matrix Churchill trial, 231; and Project LISI, 171, 173–74, 176, 177–78, 187n. 177; and Scott Inquiry, 281
Higson, Mark, 202, 245, 290–91; and Howe Guidelines, 62; and Scott Inquiry, 269
Hippler, Jochen, 292–93
Hiro, Dilip, 14
Hobbs, Brian, 74
Hogg, Douglas, 212, 275
Holdness, Mr., 141, 182n. 48, 200
Hollingsworth, Larry, 153
House Committee on Banking, Finance, and Urban Affairs, 45
Howard, Michael, 202
Howarth, Gerald, 128, 300; and intelligence monitoring, 214–15, 224n. 86
Howe, Sir Geoffrey, 62, 236, 288, 304; and Scott Inquiry, 279–80, 281
Howe Guidelines, 35–36, 59–68, 77, 89n. 2, 89n. 4, 89n. 7, 294, 298
Hoyle, Doug, 143, 216, 224n. 80, 224n. 95
Hungary, 27
Hurd, Douglas, 70, 202, 252
Hussein, King, 38, 157, 268, 272–73, 274, 278
Hussein, Saddam, 218; and Austria, 87–88; and Bull, Gerald, 118–19; and Bush, George, xxvi, xxviin. 4; and Iran-Iraq War, 19–21, 54n. 1; and Kuwait, 291–93, 298; military industrialization drive, 28, 43, 54n. 15, 54n. 16; and supergun, 109, 110; and U.S., 32–36, 50–51, 52, 56n. 37, 56n. 40; and War of the Cities, 22

Idilby, Dr., 169
Implications of a Ceasefire for Defence Sales to Iran and Iraq, 236
Ingham, Graham, 193
Intelligence, and Scott Inquiry, 165–67
Intelligence monitoring, 189–220
Iran, 23–24; arms suppliers, 25–26 table 2.1, 54n. 11, 88–89; and Bull, Gerald, 99–101; dependence on U.S. and U.K., 13 table 1.6; pilots, British training of, 77–78; pre-1979 Western relations with, 8–11; and Project LISI, 171–80; and propellant cartel, 82–88, 92n. 92, 92n. 93; and Rushdie, Salman, 243. *See also* Shah of Iran
Iran-Contra scandal, 21, 39, 48, 50, 292; arms-for-hostages deal, 36
Iran-Iraq War, 3–4; arms suppliers, 20–32, 25–26 table 2.1, 33–36, 54n. 11; and Bull, Gerald, 99–101, 121n. 10, 121n. 11; and chemical weapons, 73–74; and dual-use im-

ports, xxiii-xxiv; geopolitics of, 19–58; and Howe Guidelines, 59–68
Iran Sanctions Act of 1990, 45, 57n. 72
Iranian National Oil Company, 69
Iranian Revolution, impact of, 14–16, 18n. 30
Iraq: and Allivane, 80–82; arms procurement operation, 24–27, 54n. 10, 117, 118; arms suppliers, 11 table 1.5, 23–36, 54n. 11, 55n. 21, 68–78, 90n. 34, 91n. 42, 91n. 45; and Astra, 136–43; Baghdad International Exhibition, 79–80, 92n. 81; and ccc guarantees program, 36–37; and chemical weapons, 22, 29–31, 49, 73–74, 91n. 60; and intelligence monitoring, 189–220; invasion of Kuwait, 287, 288, 291–93, 298, 301n. 3; and Iranian Revolution, 14–16, 18n. 36; and Israel, 118–19; long-range missiles, 22–23; nuclear weapons program, xxviin. 4; oil politics, 17n. 9; pilots, British training of, 77–78; and PRB, 136–43, 182n. 34, 182n. 39; pre-1979 Western relations with, 8–11; and propellant cartel, 82–88, 92n. 93; and src, 99–101, 114 table 4.2; trade with Great Britain, 75 table 3.2; and U.S. export licenses, 44 table 2.3; and U.S. military and intelligence assistance, 37–42; and U.S. postwar relations, 48–53, 58n. 95. See also Iran-Iraq War
Iraq Machine Tools for Various Facilities, 240
Iraq: The Procurement of Machinery for Armaments Production, 235
Iraqi-Kuwaiti border dispute, 11, 17n. 17
Iraqi Long Range Projectile, 235
Isles, Donald, 130; and BMARC, 146; and Project LISI, 175–76, 188n. 204
Israel, 21; and Bull, Gerald, 118–19, 123n. 52, 124n. 64; and Iran-Iraq War, 4, 20, 33, 34, 56n. 37; and Iranian Revolution, 15. See also Arab-Israeli War
Italy, 13, 24, 27, 31–32, 36; and Baghdad Exhibition, 80; and BNL, 46; Iraqi debt to, 51; and propellant cartel, 85

James, David, 220; and intelligence monitoring, 204–6, 223n. 55, 223n. 57
James, Gerald, 78–79, 125, 148, 184n. 80, 294; and Allivane, 81; and Astra investigations, 167–71, 186n. 163, 186n. 166, 186n. 172; and BMARC, 129–30, 180n. 9, 181n. 11, 181n. 13; and EPREP, 131–32; and intelligence monitoring, 194, 195, 199–200, 213, 214–15, 219, 220, 222n. 32, 224n. 86; and Kock, Stephan, 154–55, 157, 160–63, 165, 166–67, 184n. 100, 185n. 139; and PRB, 135–36, 136–37, 139–40, 181n. 28, 182n. 48; and Project LISI, 171–72, 175–76, 178, 180, 186n. 173, 187n. 196; and Saudi Arabia, 147; and Scott Inquiry, 267–68, 283. See also James and Gumbley management team
James and Gumbley management team: and BMARC, 143–46; and collapse of Astra, 149–54, 184n. 84, 184n. 89; and development of Astra, 125–28
Jamine, Monique, 198
Japan: Iraqi debt to, 51; oil politics, 17n. 5
Jentleson, Bruce, 36, 39, 293–94
Joiret, Marie-Hélène, 123n. 53
"Jonathan of Arabia," 173
Jordan, xxvi, 146, 288; arms channeling to Iraq, 31, 288; and Iran-Iraq War, 19, 35; and Iranian Revolution, 14; and propellant cartel, 87–88; and Scott Inquiry, 267–76; and supergun, 136, 137, 140–43, 183n. 52
Jourdain, Jean Louis, 136–37, 147

Kadoori, Colonel, 288–89
Kamel, Hussein, 26, 28, 278, 298; and Bull, Gerald, 99; and supergun, 100, 110
Kamel, Saddam, 278
Kay, David, 228, 298
Keel, Alton, 39
Keen, Bob, 167–68
Kent Today, 177
Kerrison, Bryan, 107
Kershaw, Sir Anthony, 128
Khalid, Prince, 172
Khalilzad, Zalmay, 50
Kharg Island, 19
Khashoggi, Adnan, 73
Khomeini, the Ayatollah, 19–21; and U.S., 32; and War of the Cities, 22
Khuzestan Province, 19
Kissinger, Henry, 10
Klare, Michael, 13–14
Kock, Stephan, 125, 128, 130, 150–51, 169; and Astra arrests, 152, 154–67, 184n. 99–100, 185n. 114, 185n. 116, 185n. 139, 186n. 154; and BMARC, 144; and intelligence monitoring, 194; and PRB, 136; and Project LISI, 175; and Scott Inquiry, 283
Kossioris, C., 116
Kurds, chemical weapons against, 22, 49
Kuwait, xxvi, 39; and BMARC, 148; and Iran-Iraq War, 20, 35; Iraqi invasion of, xxv, 5, 16, 287, 288, 291–93, 298, 301n. 3. See also Iraqi-Kuwaiti border dispute

Landry, Peter, 181n. 13
Lang, Ian, 169–70, 303
Langevin, David, xxiii
Lasarge, Bernard, 193
Lavi, Hushang, 15
Lefebvre, Jacques, 123–24n. 53

Lennox, R. N., 300
Lenz, Randolph, xxiii
l'Estoile, Hugues de, 80
Levene, Sir Peter, 130, 169, 181n. 13; and
EPREP, 131; and PRB, 133; and Scott Inquiry,
283
Libya, 28
License, export, 42–45, 52–53, 89n. 2; and
Scott Inquiry, 262–65
Lilley, Peter, 202
Long-range missiles, and War of the Cities,
22–23
Los Angeles Times, 33
Lowther, William, 96
Luce, Sir Richard, 8, 18n. 30, 60, 68, 90n. 34;
and Scott Inquiry, 281, 286n. 72
Lundberg, Mats, and propellant cartel, 86–87
Lyell, Sir Nicholas, 281

MacGregor, John, 213
Machon, Frank, 80–81, 82, 291
Macmillan, Harold, 129
Major, John, 172, 177, 187n. 177, 290; and Al-
livane, 82; and intelligence monitoring, 209,
210; and Matrix Churchill, 255n. 29; and
Scott Inquiry, 257, 278, 281, 286n. 79
Malaysia, "Buy British Last" campaign, 18n.
36
Mange, Etienne, 123n. 53
Marz, Garston, 108
Mason, Bryan, 202
Mathot, Guy, 123n. 53
Matrix Churchill, xxv, xxvi, 26, 51, 52, 254n.
9, 254n. 18, 254n. 20, 255n. 29, 255n. 58,
255n. 59; and BNL, 46–47; and the docu-
ments, 235–50; and dual-use exports,
226–53; and export license, 53; and intelli-
gence monitoring, 206–9, 223n. 59; trial,
66, 231–35
Mayhew, Sir Patrick, 217
McCann, Anthony, 153
McFarlane, Robert, 32
McGill University, 94
McNamara, Kevin, 211
McNaught, Bill, 130, 144, 145, 146
Meacher, Michael, 166, 170, 294–95
Meadway, John, 212
Mellor, David, 69; and Howe Guidelines,
66–67; and Scott Inquiry, 273, 285n. 42
Meshed, Yahia al-, 118
MI6, and Astra, 140–43
Middle East oil, politics of, 4–8
Miers, Sir David, 277; and Howe Guidelines,
66; and Scott Inquiry, 268, 272–73, 274
Miller, Sir Hal, 104, 161, 233; and Astra ar-
rest, 153; and intelligence monitoring,

204–6, 213, 217, 220, 223n. 55; and Scott
Report, 307–8; and supergun, 119–20
Miller, William, and Project LISI, 175–76
Ministry of Industry and Military Industrial-
ization, 26
Mishari, Prince, 147
Mitchell, Peter, 120, 203, 231; and intelli-
gence monitoring, 205, 213, 217; and Scott
Inquiry, 283
Moberly, Sir John, 60
MOD (Ministry of Defence), and Astra, 140–43
Monckton, Walter, 156
Monkbridge, Major, 199, 200, 222n. 33
Morrice, Tom, 127
Morrison, Peter, 107
Moses, Alan, and Matrix Churchill trial, 232,
254n. 20
Mossad, and Bull, Gerald, 117–18, 123n. 52
Mossadegh, Mohammed, 9
Mubarak, President, 38
Murphy, Richard, 39; and Iran-Iraq War, 32,
35–36
Muttukumaru, Christopher, 179; and Scott
Inquiry, 278

NATO, 15
Nayif, Abderrazak, 15
Needham, Richard, 211
Nettlefold, Julian, 175
New Scientist, 74, 91n. 57
New Statesman, 14
New York Times, 34
New Zealand, 210, 223n. 66
Nidal, Abu, 32
Nixon, Richard, 9–10, 41
Nobari, Ali Reza, 15
North, Oliver, 32, 86
North Korea, 21
Noseworthy, John, 266
Nott, John, 16
NSD-26 (National Security Directive 26), 51,
52, 53, 70

Oil importation, reliance on, 9 table 1.4, 17n.
11; imports from Iraq, 37; main consumers
of, 7 figure 1.1, 7 table 1.2; Middle Eastern,
politics of, 4–8, 17n. 5; principal producers
and exporters of, 6 table 1.1, 17n. 9; reserves, distribution of proven, 8 figure 1.2,
8 table 1.3
Operation Desert Storm, 168 figure 5.2; and
dual-use imports, xxiii–xxiv
Operation Staunch, 3, 21, 34–35, 41, 88
Ordtec, 201–3
Ostrovsky, Victor, 123n. 52

Pakistan, 11
Palacio, Luis, 96
Palme, Olaf, 85
Pappas, Alec, 96
Paraguay, 88–89
Paris Guns, 109, 122n. 31
Parkinson, Cecil, 15
Parsons, Anthony, 90n. 16
Patey, William, 264–65
Patten, John, 244
Pattie, Geoffrey, 74, 76
Pedde, Giacomo, 48
Pentagon, 32, 95
Pergau Dam scandal, 155, 184n. 104, 187n. 176, 282; and Thatcher, Mark, 134
Perot, Ross, xxvi, xxviin. 4
Pike, John, 149, 183n. 79, 219
Pinaud, M., 139
PLO, 11
Poland, 27
Portugal, 31; and propellant cartel, 84–85
Powell, Charles, 82
PRB (Poudreries Réunies de Belgique), 96, 125, 136–43, 182n. 34, 182n. 39; contracts, 138 table 5.1, 182n. 40; purchase of, 132–36, 181n. 24, 182n. 30
Primrose, Bob, 140–41, 143, 182n. 48, 200, 217; and BMARC, 145
Project Babylon, 100–101; and HARP, 94–95; and Jordan, 140–43; purpose of, 108–16. See also Supergun
Project LISI, 171–80, 186n. 173, 187n. 184, 187n. 196, 187nn. 177–80, 188n. 204, 188n. 222
Propellant cartel, 82–88, 92n. 92, 92n. 97, 93n. 100, 93n. 110; and Belgium, 141–43, 182n. 48, 182n. 52; members, 83 table 3.3
Puelinckx, Alfons, 123n. 53

Qassim, Abdul Karim, 11
Quinlan, Michael, 232

RARDE (Royal Armament Research and Development Establishment), 111
Reagan, Ronald, xxviin. 4, 40
Reagan administration, 3, 20, 37; and dual-use license applications, 42–45; and intelligence monitoring, 223n. 66; and Iran-Contra, 39, 48, 50; and Iran-Iraq War, 32–33, 35, 36, 41
Reagan-Bush campaign, 15
Renton, Jane, 225n. 109; and BMARC, 144
Renton, Tim, 68, 90n. 36; and Howe Guidelines, 63
Revolutionary Guards Corps, 19
Ricks, Roy, 127–28, 227, 253n. 5

Ridley, Nicholas, 120, 189; and intelligence monitoring, 204; and Matrix Churchill, 250–52; and Project Babylon, 143, 183n. 60
Rifkind, Malcolm, 178; and Matrix Churchill trial, 231
RO (Royal Ordnance), 128–30, 180n. 13
Robertson, Geoffrey: and Matrix Churchill trial, 232, 234; and Scott Inquiry, 267
Robertson, Patrick, 176
Robison, Robin, 209, 222n. 33, 222n. 52; and Kock, Stephan, 159
Rogers, Allan, 166, 167
Romania, 27
Rushdie, Salman, 243
Russell, Alexander, 212–13

Saadi, Amir, 100
Sadowski, Yahya, 4
Safire, William, 309
Said, Wafic, 73, 169, 172; and PRB, 136
Sainsbury, Tim, 200; and Scott Inquiry, 275
Satanic Verses, The (Rushdie), 243
Saudi Arabia, xxvi, 10, 24, 36, 50; and Al Yamamah/Tornado agreement, 66; and Astra, 147; and Britain's Iraq policy, 72; and Condor II, 22; and Hussein, Saddam, 28; and Iran-Iraq War, 4, 19–20, 35, 39
Schlesinger, Alexander, 276–77
Schmidt, Maurice, 80
Schmitz, Karl Erik, 85–86, 93n. 104
Schultz, George, 38, 50
Schwarzkopf, Norman, 293
Scotland, 86–87
Scott, Sir Richard, 178, 190, 258, 261, 303–9; and Howe Guidelines, 63–64, 65, 90n. 18, 90n. 24
Scott Inquiry, xxv, 3, 18n. 30, 28, 38, 55n. 32, 257–62; and access to documents, 279; assessment, 282–83, 286n. 81; and conduits, 267–76; cost, 281–82, 286n. 78, 286n. 79; criticisms of, 279–81; delays in publication, 278–79; and export licensing procedure, 262–65; and Howe Guidelines, 60–68, 89n. 4, 89n. 7, 90n.18, 90n.22, 90n. 24, 90n. 34, 90–91n. 36, 91n. 42; and intelligence, 165–67; and misleading Parliament, 265; and Vereker "gap," 275; witnesses, 259–61 table 8.1
Scott Report, 303–9, 309n. 4
Sellens, John, 147, 184n. 80; and Astra arrest, 153; and BMARC, 144; and PRB, 142
SGB (Société Générale de Belgique), 133
Shah of Iran, 9–10, 12–14, 17n. 21, 17n. 22; fall of, 32
Shaker, Bin, 272
Sheffield Forgemasters, 101–8, 120

Sheldon, Robert, 296–97
Sherrington, Simon, 190, 248, 256n. 64
Shoob, Marvin, 48
Shore, Peter, 167
Shqaqi, Fathi, 118
Shrimpton, John, 169
Sick, Gary, 15, 19
SIGINT, 209–11, 223n. 63, 223n. 69
Simpson, John, 40
Singapore: and BMARC, 146; and Iran-Iraq War, 21; and Project LISI, 171–80, 188n. 222; and propellant cartel, 84
Slack, Tony, 110, 113–14, 115, 116
Smedley, Judge, 232
Smith, Ian, 157
Smith, Llew, 179
Soghanalian, Sarkis, 23–24, 37
South Africa: and Bull, Gerald, 95–97, 121n. 11; and propellant cartel, 85
South America, 32
Soviet bloc countries, 35
Soviet Union, 21, 24, 27–28, 70; and Baghdad Exhibition, 80; and Iran-Iraq War, 4, 20; pre-1979 relations with Iran and Iraq, 9–11
Spain, 24, 31; and Bull, Gerald, 99; and propellant cartel, 84–85
Speckman, Jeanine, 203, 225n. 104
Spitaels, Guy, 124n. 53
SRC (Space Research Corporation), 95, 99–101; and China, 97–98; and dual-use license applications, 43; gun projects for Iraq, 114 table 4.2; and intelligence monitoring, 196–99
Stanley, Martin, 251
Steadman, Tony, 246–47, 249, 256n. 60
Steel, Sir David, 59, 166; and Project LISI, 174
Sterling Guns Affair, 276–78, 285n. 59
Stockholm International Peace Research Institute (SIPRI), 24
Suez, 5
Sultan, Prince, 172
Sunday Mirror, 177
Sunday Times, 72–73
Supergun, 37, 101–4, 105–6 table 4.1, 106–8, 122n. 14; contract, 136–40; and dual-use, 108–16, 123n. 48; and Great Britain, 117–21, 123n. 52; seizure of, 119–20. *See also* Project Babylon
Sweden, 82–87, 92n. 93, 92n. 95
Switzerland, 31, 42
Syria, 28

Taylor, Lord, 202, 277
TECO (Technical Corporation for Special Projects), 53
Teicher, Gayle, 19

Teicher, Howard, 19–20, 33; and Thatcher, Mark, 72–73; and Weinberger, Caspar, 41
Thailand, and PRB, 132
Thatcher, Margaret, 15–16, 70–71, 289; and Allivane, 81; and BAE Hawk, 77, 78; and DESO, 18n. 26; and EPREP, 131–32; and Howe Guidelines, 62; and intelligence monitoring, 213, 215; and Kock, Stephan, 157, 162–63, 167; and Matrix Churchill, 237, 251–52; and Scott Inquiry, 273
Thatcher, Mark, 72–73, 91n. 51, 124n. 60, 258; and Pergau Dam scandal, 134
Three Guys, case of the, 117, 123–24n. 53
Timmerman, Kenneth, 29
TISC (Trade and Industry Select Committee), 212–17
Treaty of Friendship and Cooperation, 11
Trefgarne, Lord: and Howe Guidelines, 62; and Matrix Churchill, 230, 237–39, 244–49, 255n. 58, 255n. 59; and Scott Inquiry, 262–63, 265–67
Turkey, 11
Turp, Robert, 109, 193

U.K.-U.S.A. Agreement, 210
U.N. Special Commission, 116
Ungar, Craig, 33, 36
United Arab Emirates, 148
United Kingdom, 24, 35–36, 47, 55n. 32, 128–29; Iranian dependence on, 13 table 1.6. *See also* Great Britain
United Kingdom Interests in Kuwait, 287
United Kingdom–Iraq Joint Commission, 70
United States, 88, 89; and BNL, 45–48; and Britain's Iraq policy, 73–74; and Bull, Gerald, 95, 121n. 11; and chemical weapons, 74; and dual-use license applications, 42–45; export licenses to Iraq, 42–45, 44 table 2.3; and Hussein, Saddam, 32–36, 56n. 37, 56n. 40, 119; and Iran-Iraq War, 3–4, 19–20; Iranian dependence on, 13 table 1.6; and Iranian Revolution, 14–16; and Iraq, postwar relations, 48–53, 58n. 95; military and intelligence assistance to Iraq, 37–42; oil imports, 6; oil politics, 17n. 5; pre-1979 relations with Iran and Iraq, 9–11; and Shah of Iran, 12–13. *See also under specific administrations*
Unlikely Spy, The (Henderson), 267
Unterweger, Peter, 88
Unwin, Richard, 128, 157, 163
Unwin, Sir Brian, 217
U.S.-Iraq Business Forum, 49, 57n. 87

Vandenbroucke, Frank, 123n. 53
Vereker, Peter, 190

Vereker "gap," 275
Véronique Ancia, 124n. 53
Vietnam, 21
Vietnam War, 9–10

Waas, Murray, 33, 35
Wadi, Anees, 227, 253n. 4
Wagstaffe, Colin, and BMARC, 130
Waldegrave, William, 55n. 32, 117, 223n. 74;
and BAE Hawk, 76; and Howe Guidelines,
64, 65–66, 90n. 22, 90n. 24; and Matrix
Churchill, 230, 237–41, 244–46, 248–50,
255n. 51, 255n. 58, 255n. 59; and Scott Re-
port, 303–4
Walker, Sandy, and PRB, 135
Wall Street Journal, 86
Wallyn, Luc, 123n. 53
Walter Somers, 101–8, 119–20, 122n. 24,
124n. 66; and intelligence monitoring,
204–6
Walters, Ed, 128, 151, 180n. 5
War of the Cities, 22–23
Warren, Kenneth, 160, 168, 214; and intelli-
gence monitoring, 216, 219, 224n. 95

Wedel, Paul von, 229
Weinberger, Caspar, 32, 41
Weir, Bill, 104, 112; and intelligence monitor-
ing, 222n. 52; and Scott Report, 308
West Germany, 13; and chemical weapons,
29–31, 91n. 60; and Condor II, 22; and
dual-use license applications, 42; Iraqi debt
to, 51
Whitehead, Sir Edgar, 155, 156
Whitney, Raymond, 74
Wilkinson, Steven, 201
Wilson, Brian, 178
Wong, George, 97, 98, 117, 196, 216–17; and
Scott Report, 307
World in Action, 173, 174, 176
Wright, Philip, 107–8
Wyatt, John, 288
Wykeham, Sir Peter, 79

Yetiv, Steve, 292
Young, Rob, 230, 266
Yugoslavia, 27; and Bull, Gerald, 99; Iraqi
debt to, 51; and propellant cartel, 85–86,
93n. 110